WHERE ARE THE LESSON FILES?

P9-BZU-940

Purchasing this Classroom in a Book gives you access to the lesson files that you'll need to complete the exercises in the book, as well as other content to help you learn more about Adobe software and use it with greater efficiency and ease. The diagram below represents the contents of the lesson files directory, which should help you locate the files you need. Please see the Getting Started section for full download instructions.

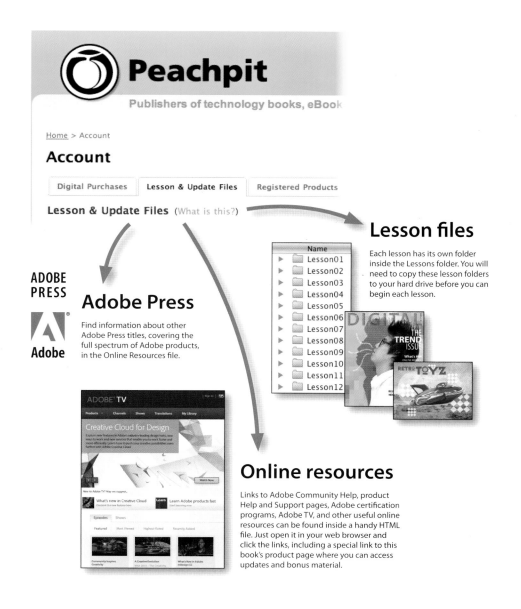

Peachpit
Publishers of technology books, eBook

Home > Account

Account

Digital Purchases | **Lesson & Update Files** | Registered Products

Lesson & Update Files (What is this?)

Adobe Press

Find information about other Adobe Press titles, covering the full spectrum of Adobe products, in the Online Resources file.

Lesson files

Each lesson has its own folder inside the Lessons folder. You will need to copy these lesson folders to your hard drive before you can begin each lesson.

Name
▶ Lesson01
▶ Lesson02
▶ Lesson03
▶ Lesson04
▶ Lesson05
▶ Lesson06
▶ Lesson07
▶ Lesson08
▶ Lesson09
▶ Lesson10
▶ Lesson11
▶ Lesson12

Online resources

Links to Adobe Community Help, product Help and Support pages, Adobe certification programs, Adobe TV, and other useful online resources can be found inside a handy HTML file. Just open it in your web browser and click the links, including a special link to this book's product page where you can access updates and bonus material.

CONTENTS

GETTING STARTED

Adobe® Dreamweaver® CC is the industry-leading web authoring program. Whether you create websites for a living or plan to create one for your own business, Dreamweaver offers all the tools you need to get professional-quality results.

About Classroom in a Book

Adobe Dreamweaver CC Classroom in a Book® is part of the official training series for graphics and publishing software developed with the support of Adobe product experts.

The lessons are designed so that you can learn at your own pace. If you're new to Dreamweaver, you'll learn the fundamentals of putting the program to work. If you are an experienced user, you'll find that *Classroom in a Book* teaches many advanced features, including tips and techniques for using the latest version of Dreamweaver.

Although each lesson includes step-by-step instructions for creating a specific project, you'll have room for exploration and experimentation. You can follow the book from start to finish, or complete only those lessons that correspond to your interests and needs. Each lesson concludes with a review section containing questions and answers on the subjects you've covered.

TinyURLs

In several points in the book, we reference external information available on the Internet. The uniform resource locators (URLs) for this information are often long and unwieldy, so we have provided custom TinyURLs in their place for your convenience. Unfortunately, the TinyURLs sometimes expire over time and no longer function. If you find that a TinyURL doesn't work, look up the actual URL provided in the Appendix.

Prerequisites

Before using *Adobe Dreamweaver CC Classroom in a Book*, you should have a working knowledge of your computer and its operating system. Be sure you know how to use the mouse, standard menus, and commands, and also how to open, save, and close files. If you need to review these techniques, see the printed or online documentation included with your Windows or Mac operating system.

Installing the program

Before you perform any exercises in this book, verify that your computer system meets the hardware requirements for Dreamweaver CC, that it's correctly configured, and that all required software is installed.

Adobe Dreamweaver CC software must be purchased separately; it is not included with the lesson files that accompany this book. For system requirements, go to www.adobe.com/products/dreamweaver/tech-specs.html.

Downloading the Classroom in a Book files

In order to work through the projects in this book, you will need to download the lesson files from peachpit.com. You can download the files for individual lessons, or download them all at one time.

To access the Classroom in a Book files:

● **Note:** Do not copy one lesson folder into any other lesson folder. The files and folders for each lesson cannot be used interchangeably.

1 On a Mac or PC, go to www.peachpit.com/redeem and enter the code found at the back of your book.

2 If you do not have a Peachpit.com account, you will be prompted to create one.

3 The downloadable files will be listed under the Lesson & Update Files tab on your Account page.

4 Click the lesson file links to download them to your computer.

5 Rename the Lessons folder as **DW-CC**.

This folder will be used as the local site root folder.

6 If you want to complete one or more lessons individually, proceed to the "Jumpstart" section for more instructions.

Recommended lesson order

The training in this book is designed to take you from A to Z in basic to intermediate website design, development, and production. Each new lesson builds on previous exercises, using the files and assets to create an entire website. We recommend that you download all lesson files at once and then perform each lesson in sequential order to achieve a successful result and the most complete understanding of all aspects of web design.

The ideal training scenario will start in Lesson 1 and proceed through the entire book to Lesson 15 (Lesson 15 is online and can be found on your Account page at www.peachpit.com). Since each lesson builds essential files and content for the next, once you start this scenario you shouldn't skip any lessons, or even individual exercises. While ideal, this method may not be a practicable scenario for every user. So, if desired, individual lessons can be accomplished using the jumpstart method described in the next section.

Jumpstart

For users who don't have the time or inclination to perform each lesson in the book in sequence, or who are having difficulty with a particular lesson, a jumpstart method is included to facilitate the performance of individual lessons in or out of sequence. Once you start using the jumpstart method, you will have to use this method for all subsequent lessons. For example, if you want to jumpstart Lesson 6, you will have to jumpstart Lesson 7, too. In many instances, essential files needed for subsequent exercises were built in earlier lessons and exercises and may not be present in a jumpstart environment.

Each lesson folder includes all the files and assets needed to complete the exercises contained within that lesson. Each folder contains finished files, staged files, and customized Template and Library files, but not always a complete set of files that may have been used or completed in other lessons. You may think these folders contain seemingly duplicative materials. But these duplicate files and assets, in most cases, cannot be used interchangeably in other lessons and exercises. Doing so will probably cause you to fail to achieve the goal of the exercise.

The jumpstart method for completing individual lessons treats each folder as a stand-alone website. To jumpstart a lesson, copy the lesson folder to your hard drive and create a new site for that lesson using the Site Setup dialog box. Do not define sites using subfolders of existing sites. Keep your jumpstart sites and assets in their original folders to avoid conflicts. One suggestion is to organize the lesson folders, as well as your own site folders, in a single *web* or *sites* master folder near the root of your hard drive. But avoid using the Dreamweaver application folder or any folders that contain a web server, like Apache, ColdFusion, or Internet Information Services (IIS).

Feel free to use the jumpstart method for all lessons, if you prefer.

To set up a jumpstart site, do the following:

1 Choose Site > New Site.

   The Site Setup dialog box appears.

2 In the Site Name field, enter the name of the lesson, such as **lesson06**.

3 Click the Browse (□) icon next to the Local Site Folder field. Navigate to the desired lesson folder among the files you downloaded from your Account page on Peachpit.com and click Select/Choose.

4 Click the arrow (▶) next to the Advanced Settings category to reveal the tabs listed there. Select the Local Info category.

5 Click the Browse icon next to the Default Images Folder field. When the dialog box opens, navigate to the Images folder contained within the lesson folder and click Select/Choose.

6 In the Site Setup dialog box, click Save.

7 The name of the currently active website will appear in the Files panel's site pop-up menu. If necessary, press F8 to display the Files panel, and select the desired website you wish to work on from the Show menu.

These steps will have to be repeated for each lesson you wish to jumpstart. For a more complete description of how to set up a site in Dreamweaver, see Lesson 4, "Creating a Page Layout." Remember, if you use the jumpstart method for all lessons, you may not end up with a complete set of site files in any individual folder when you are finished.

Setting up the workspace

Dreamweaver includes two main workspaces to accommodate various computer configurations and individual workflows. For this book the Expanded workspace is recommended.

1 In Dreamweaver CC, locate the Application bar. It appears along the top of the program.

2 If the Expanded workspace is not displayed by default, you can select it from the Workspace pop-up menu on the right side of the screen.

3 If the default Expanded workspace has been modified—where certain toolbars and panels are not visible (as they appear in the figures in the book)—you can restore the factory setting by selecting Reset 'Expanded' from the Workspace pop-up menu.

These Workspace Layout options can also be accessed from the Windows menu.

Most of the figures in this book show the Expanded workspace. When you finish the lessons in this book, experiment with both workspaces to find the one that you prefer, or build your own configuration and save the layout under a custom name.

For a more complete description of the Dreamweaver workspaces, see Lesson 1, "Customizing Your Workspace."

Windows vs. OS X instructions

In most cases, Dreamweaver performs identically in both Windows and OS X. Minor differences exist between the two versions, mostly due to platform-specific issues out of the control of the program. Most of these are simply differences in keyboard shortcuts, how dialog boxes are displayed, and how buttons are named. Screen shots may alternate between platforms throughout the book. Where specific commands differ, they are noted within the text. Windows commands are listed first, followed by the OS X equivalent, such as Ctrl-C/Cmd-C. Common abbreviations are used for all commands whenever possible, as follows:

WINDOWS	OS X
Control = Ctrl	Command = Cmd
Alternate = Alt	Option = Opt

Finding Dreamweaver information

For complete, up-to-date information about Dreamweaver panels, tools, and other application features, choose Help > Dreamweaver Help. Help files are cached locally so you can access them even when you are not connected to the Internet. You can also download a PDF version of the Dreamweaver Help files from the Adobe Help application.

For additional information resources, such as tips, techniques, and the latest product information, visit http://helpx.adobe.com/dreamweaver.html.

Checking for updates

Adobe periodically provides software updates. To check for updates in the program, go to the Help menu and select Updates. For book updates and bonus material, visit your Account page on Peachpit.com.

Additional resources

Adobe Dreamweaver CC Classroom in a Book is not meant to replace documentation that comes with the program or to be a comprehensive reference for every feature. Only the commands and options used in the lessons are explained in this book. For comprehensive information about program features and tutorials, please refer to these resources:

Adobe Dreamweaver CC Help and Support: http://helpx.adobe.com/ dreamweaver.html is where you can find and browse Help and Support content on adobe.com.

Adobe Creative Cloud Learning: For inspiration, key techniques, cross-product workflows, and updates on new features go to the Creative Cloud Learn page https://helpx.adobe.com/creative-cloud/tutorials.html. Available only to Creative Cloud subscribers.

Adobe Forums: forums.adobe.com lets you tap into peer-to-peer discussions, questions, and answers on Adobe products.

Adobe TV: tv.adobe.com is an online video resource for expert instruction and inspiration about Adobe products, including a How To channel to get you started with your product.

Adobe Design Center: www.adobe.com/designcenter offers thoughtful articles on design and design issues, a gallery showcasing the work of top-notch designers, tutorials, and more.

Adobe Developer Connection: www.adobe.com/devnet is your source for technical articles, code samples, and how-to videos that cover Adobe developer products and technologies.

Resources for educators: www.adobe.com/education and http://edex.adobe.com offer a treasure trove of information for instructors who teach classes on Adobe software. Find solutions for education at all levels, including free curricula that use an integrated approach to teaching Adobe software and can be used to prepare for the Adobe Certified Associate exams.

Also check out these useful links:

Adobe Marketplace & Exchange: www.adobe.com/cfusion/exchange is a central resource for finding tools, services, extensions, code samples, and more to supplement and extend your Adobe products.

Adobe Dreamweaver CC product home page: www.adobe.com/products/ dreamweaver

Adobe Labs: labs.adobe.com gives you access to early builds of cutting-edge technology, as well as forums where you can interact both with the Adobe development teams building that technology and with other like-minded members of the community.

Adobe certification

The Adobe training and certification programs are designed to help Adobe customers improve and promote their product-proficiency skills. There are four levels of certification:

- Adobe Certified Associate (ACA)
- Adobe Certified Expert (ACE)
- Adobe Certified Instructor (ACI)
- Adobe Authorized Training Center (AATC)

The Adobe Certified Associate (ACA) credential certifies that individuals have the entry-level skills to plan, design, build, and maintain effective communications using different forms of digital media.

The Adobe Certified Expert program is a way for expert users to upgrade their credentials. You can use Adobe certification as a catalyst for getting a raise, finding a job, or promoting your expertise.

If you are an ACE-level instructor, the Adobe Certified Instructor program takes your skills to the next level and gives you access to a wide range of Adobe resources.

Adobe Authorized Training Centers offer instructor-led courses and training on Adobe products, employing only Adobe Certified Instructors. A directory of AATCs is available at partners.adobe.com.

For information on the Adobe Certified programs, visit www.adobe.com/support/certification/index.html.

1 CUSTOMIZING YOUR WORKSPACE

Lesson Overview

In this lesson, you'll familiarize yourself with the Dreamweaver Creative Cloud (CC) program interface and learn how to do the following:

- Switch document views
- Work with panels
- Select a workspace layout
- Adjust toolbars
- Personalize preferences
- Create custom keyboard shortcuts
- Use the Property inspector

 This lesson will take about 30 minutes to complete. Download the project files for this lesson from the Lesson & Update Files tab on your Account page at www.peachpit.com and store them on your computer in a convenient location, as described in the "Getting Started" section of this book. Your Accounts page is also where you'll find any updates to the lessons or to the lesson files. Look on the Lesson & Update Files tab to access the most current content.

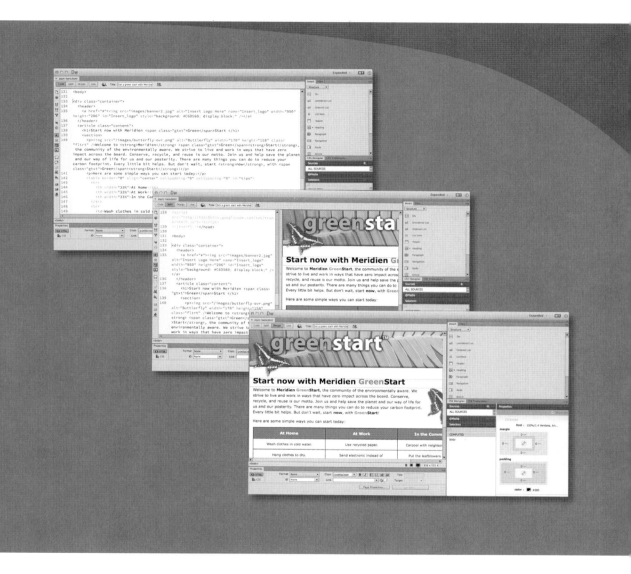

Dreamweaver offers a customizable and easy-to-use WYSIWYG HTML editor that doesn't compromise on power and flexibility. You'd probably need a dozen programs to perform all the tasks that Dreamweaver can do—and none of them would be as fun to use.

Touring the workspace

Dreamweaver is the industry-leading Hypertext Markup Language (HTML) editor, with good reasons for its popularity. The program offers an incredible array of design and code-editing tools. Dreamweaver offers something for everyone.

Coders love the variety of enhancements built into the Code view environment, and developers enjoy the program's support for a variety of programming languages. Designers marvel at seeing their text and graphics appear in an accurate What You See Is What You Get (WYSIWYG) depiction as they work, saving hours of time previewing pages in browsers. Novices certainly appreciate the program's simple-to-use and power-packed interface. No matter what type of user you are, if you use Dreamweaver you don't have to compromise.

A Menu bar	**E** Application bar	**I** Assets panel	**M** Code view
B Document tab	**F** Workspace menu	**J** Behaviors panel	**N** Design view
C Document toolbar	**G** Files panel	**K** CSS Designer	**O** Tag selectors
D Standard toolbar	**H** Insert panel	**L** Coding toolbar	**P** Property inspector

The Dreamweaver interface features a vast array of user-configurable panels and toolbars. Take a moment to familiarize yourself with the names of these components.

You'd think a program with this much to offer would be dense, slow, and unwieldy, but you'd be wrong. Dreamweaver provides much of its power via dockable panels and toolbars you can display or hide and arrange in innumerable combinations to create your ideal workspace. In most cases, if you don't see a desired tool or panel you'll find it in the Window menu.

This lesson introduces you to the Dreamweaver interface and gets you in touch with some of the power hiding under the hood. If you want to follow along on the tour, choose File > Open. In the Lesson01 folder, choose **start-here.html**. Click Open.

Switching and splitting views

Dreamweaver offers dedicated environments for coders and designers as well as a composite option that blends both together.

Design view

Design view focuses the Dreamweaver workspace on its WYSIWYG editor, which provides a close, but not perfect, depiction of the webpage as it would appear in a browser. To activate Design view, click the Design view button in the Document toolbar. Most HTML elements and cascading style sheet (CSS) formatting will be rendered properly within Design view, with a major exception for dynamic content and interactivity, such as link behaviors, video, audio, jQuery widgets, some form elements, and others.

Design view

Code view

Code view focuses the Dreamweaver workspace exclusively on the HTML code and a variety of code-editing productivity tools. To access Code view, click the Code view button in the Document toolbar.

Code view

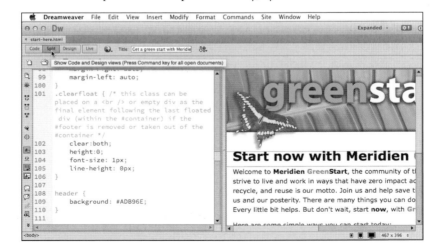

Split view

Split view provides a composite workspace that gives you access to both the design and the code simultaneously. Changes made in either window update in the other instantly. To access Split view, click the Split view button in the Document toolbar. Dreamweaver splits the workspace vertically, by default.

Split view

You can also split the screen horizontally by disabling the option Split Vertically in the View menu.

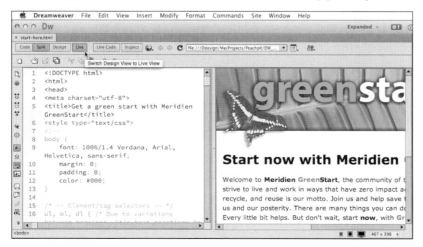

Split view horizontally

Live view

To speed up the process of developing modern websites, Dreamweaver also includes a fourth display mode called Live view, which provides a browser-like preview of most dynamic effects and interactivity. Live view can be accessed at any time by clicking the Live button at the top of the document window whenever an HTML file is open. When Live view is activated, most HTML will function as it would in an actual browser, allowing you to preview and test most applications. While Live view is active, the content displayed in the Design view window is not editable. You can still make changes in the Code view window and to the cascading style sheets. To see any changes, you'll have to refresh the Design view window using the Refresh (C) icon that appears at the top of the document window or by pressing F5.

Live view horizontally

Live Code

Live Code

Live Code is an HTML code troubleshooting display mode available whenever Live view is activated. To access Live Code, activate Live view, and then click the Live Code button at the top of the document window. While active, Live Code displays the HTML code as it would appear in a live browser on the Internet. The Code window will render changes to the elements, attributes, and styling interactively.

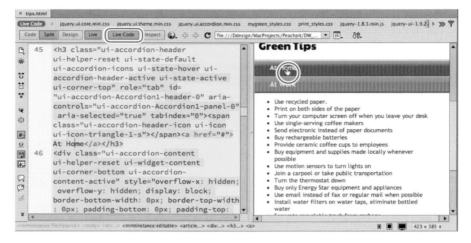

Inspect mode

Inspect mode

Inspect mode is a CSS troubleshooting display mode available whenever Live view is activated. It is integrated with the CSS Designer and allows you to identify CSS styles applied to content within the page by moving the mouse cursor over elements within the webpage. The Design view window highlights the targeted element and displays the pertinent CSS rules applied or inherited by it. Inspect mode can be accessed at any time by clicking the Live button whenever an HTML file is open and then clicking the Inspect button at the top of the document window.

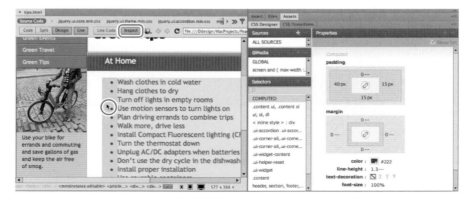

Working with panels

Although you can access most commands from the menus, Dreamweaver scatters much of its power in user-selectable panels and toolbars. You can display, hide, arrange, and dock panels at will around the screen. You can even move them to a second or third video display if you desire.

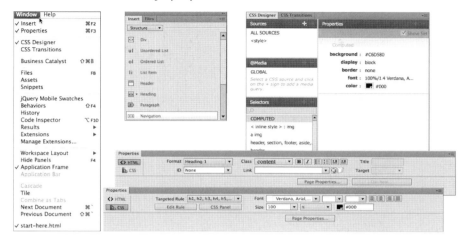

Standard panel grouping

The Window menu lists all the available panels. If you do not see a specific panel on the screen, choose it from the Window menu. A check mark appears in the menu to indicate that the panel is open. Occasionally, one panel may lie behind another on the screen and be difficult to locate. In such situations, simply choose the desired panel in the Window menu and the panel will rise to the top of the stack.

Minimizing

To create room for other panels or to access obscured areas of the workspace, you can minimize or expand individual panels in place. To minimize a panel, double-click the tab containing the panel name. To expand the panel, click the tab again.

Minimizing a panel by double-clicking the tab

You can also minimize one panel within a stack of panels individually by double-clicking its tab. To open the panel, click once on the tab.

Minimizing one panel in a stack using its tab

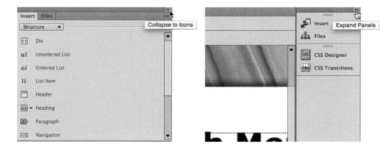

To recover more screen real estate, you can minimize panel groups or stacks down to icons by double-clicking the title bar. You can also minimize the panels to icons by clicking the double arrow (▶▶) icon in the panel title bar. When panels are minimized to icons, you access any of the individual panels by clicking its icon or button. The selected panel will appear on the left or right of your layout wherever room permits.

Collapsing panel to icons

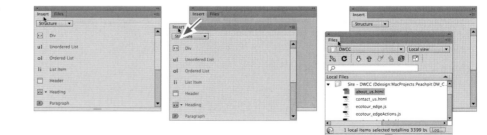

Floating

A panel grouped with other panels can be floated separately. To float a panel, drag it from the group by its tab.

Pulling a panel out by its tab

Dragging

You can reorder a panel tab by dragging it to the desired position within the group.

Dragging a tab to change its position

To reposition panels, groups, and stacks in the workspace, simply drag them by the title bar.

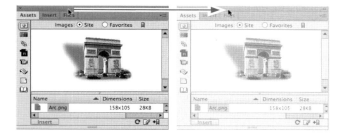

Dragging a whole panel group or stack to a new position

Grouping, stacking, and docking

You can create custom groups by dragging one panel into another. When you've moved the panel to the correct position, Dreamweaver highlights the area, called the drop zone, in blue (as shown in the following figure). Release the mouse button to create the new group.

Creating new groups

In some cases, you may want to keep both panels visible simultaneously. To stack panels, drag the desired tab to the top or bottom of another panel. When you see the blue drop zone appear, release the mouse button.

Creating panel stacks

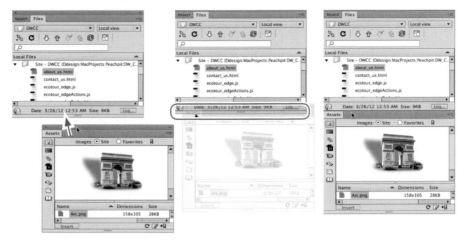

Floating panels can be docked to the right, left, or bottom of the Dreamweaver workspace. To dock a panel, group, or stack, drag its title bar to the edge on which you wish to dock. When you see the blue drop zone appear, release the mouse button.

Docking panels

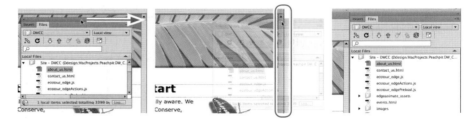

Selecting a workspace layout

A quick way to customize the program environment is to use one of the prebuilt workspaces in Dreamweaver. These workspaces have been optimized by experts to put the tools you need at your fingertips.

Dreamweaver CC includes two prebuilt workspaces: Expanded and Compact. To access these workspaces, choose them from the Workspace menu located in the Application bar.

Workspace menu

Users with smaller displays or who work on laptops may use the Compact workspace because it optimizes the panels and windows to provide an effective workspace in the smaller area.

Compact workspace

The Expanded workspace takes advantage of the available real estate on larger computer displays. It opens the panels and provides larger windows to give you the most space to let your creativity take flight.

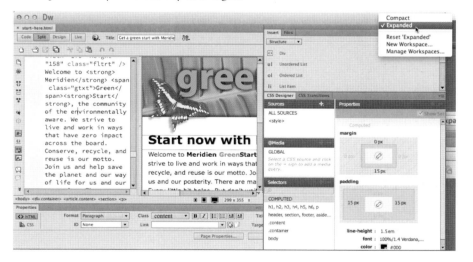

Expanded workspace

Adjusting toolbars

Some program features are so handy you may want them available all the time in toolbar form. Two of the toolbars—Document and Standard—appear horizontally at the top of the document window. The Coding toolbar, however, appears vertically, but only in the Code view window. You will explore the capabilities of these toolbars in later exercises. Display the desired toolbar by choosing it from the View menu.

Document

Document (Live view)

Standard

Coding

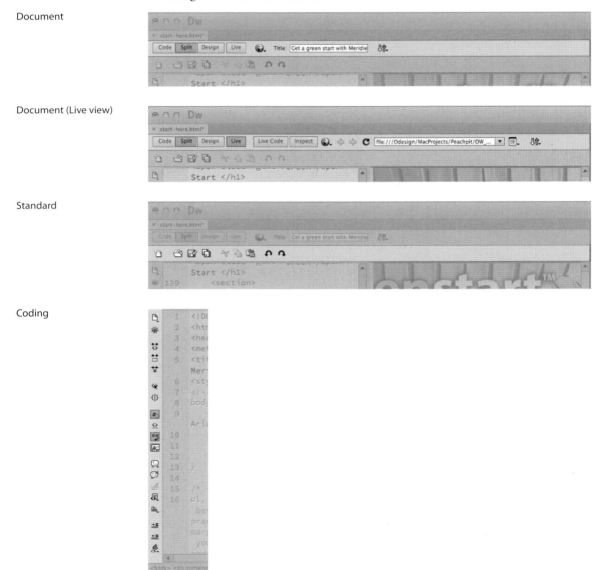

Personalizing preferences

As you continue to work with Dreamweaver, you will devise your own optimal workspace of panels and toolbars for each activity. You can store these configurations in a custom workspace of your own naming.

To save a custom workspace, create your desired configuration, choose New Workspace from the Workspace menu, and then give it a custom name.

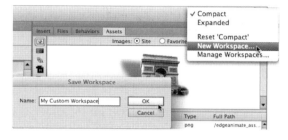

Saving a custom workspace

Creating custom keyboard shortcuts

Another power feature of Dreamweaver is the capability of creating your own keyboard shortcuts as well as editing existing ones. Keyboard shortcuts are loaded and preserved independent of custom workspaces.

Is there a command you can't live without that doesn't have a keyboard shortcut? Create it yourself. Try this:

1 Choose Edit > Keyboard Shortcuts (Windows) or Dreamweaver > Keyboard Shortcuts (Mac).

2 Click the Duplicate Set (🔲) button to create a new set of shortcuts.

3 Enter a name in the Name Of Duplicate Set field. Click OK.

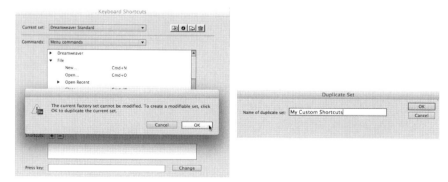

4   Choose Menu Commands from the Commands pop-up menu.

5   In the Commands window, select Save All from the list of File commands.

Note that the Save All command does not have an existing shortcut, although you will use this command frequently in Dreamweaver.

6   Insert the cursor in the Press Key field. Press Ctrl-Alt-S/Cmd-Option-S.

Note the error message indicating that the keyboard combination you chose is already assigned to a command. Although we could reassign the combination, let's choose a different one.

7   Press Ctrl-Alt-Shift-S/Cmd-Ctrl-S.

This combination is not currently being used, so let's assign it to the Save All command.

8   Click the Change button.

The new shortcut is now assigned to the Save All command.

9   Click OK to save the change.

You have created your own keyboard shortcut—one you will use in upcoming lessons.

Using the Property inspector

One tool vital to your workflow is the Property inspector. This panel typically appears at the bottom of the workspace. The Property inspector is context driven and adapts to the type of element you select.

Using the HTML tab

Insert the cursor into any text content on your page, and the Property inspector provides a means to quickly assign some basic HTML codes and formatting. When the HTML button is selected, you can apply heading or paragraph tags, as well as bold, italics, bullets, numbers, and indenting, among other formatting and attributes.

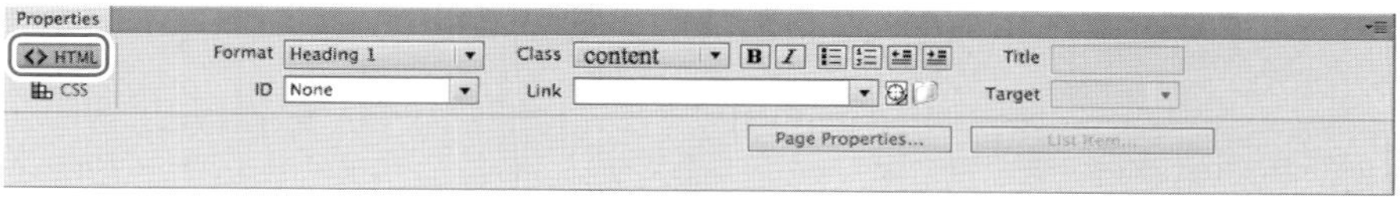

HTML Property inspector

Using the CSS tab

Click the CSS button to quickly access commands to assign or edit CSS formatting.

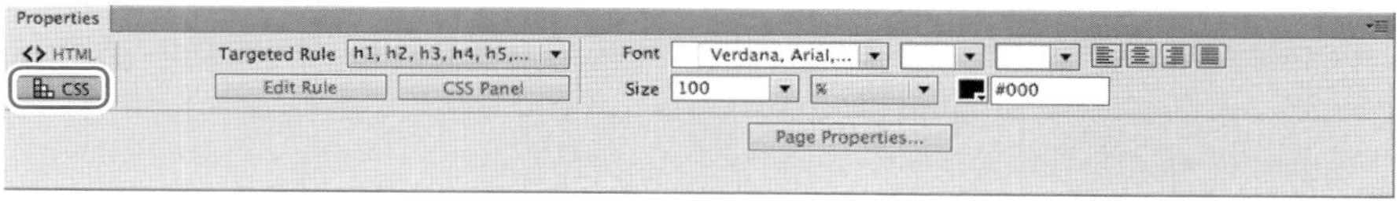

CSS Property inspector

Image properties

Select an image in a webpage to access the image-based attributes and formatting control of the Property inspector.

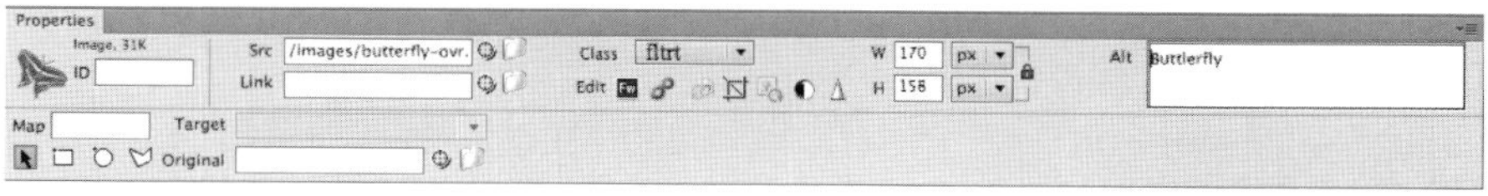

Image Property inspector

Table properties

To access table properties, insert your cursor in a table and then click the table tag selector at the bottom of the document window.

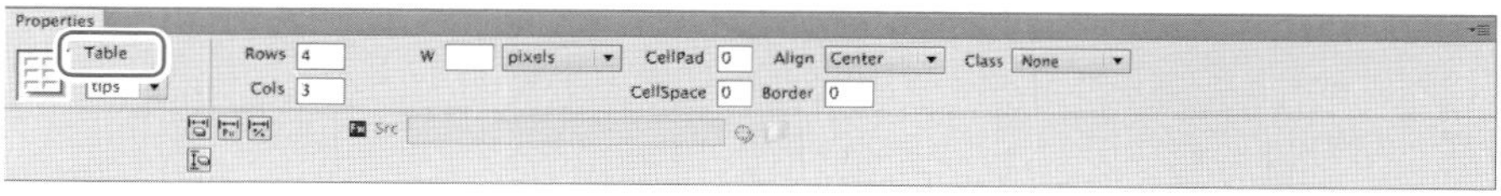

Table Property inspector

Using the CSS Designer

The CSS Designer is new in Dreamweaver Creative Cloud. It offers a new method of creating, editing, and troubleshooting CSS styling in a more visual manner.

The panel consists of four panes: Sources, @Media, Selectors, and Properties. The Sources pane allows you to create, attach, define, and remove internal and external style sheets. The @Media pane is used to define media queries to support various types of media and devices. The Selectors pane is used to create and edit the CSS rules that format the components and content of your page. Once a selector, or rule, is created you define the formatting you wish to apply in the Properties pane.

In addition to allowing you to create and edit CSS styling, the CSS Designer can also be used to identify styles already defined and applied, and troubleshoot issues or conflicts with these styles. To do this, simply insert the cursor into any element. The panes within the CSS Designer will then display all the pertinent style sheets, media queries, rules, and properties applied to or inherited by the selected element.

The CSS Designer features two basic modes. By default, the Properties pane will display all available CSS properties in a list, organized in five categories: Layout, Text, Borders, Background, and Other. You can scroll down the list and apply styling, as desired. You can also select the option Show Set at the upper-right edge of the window, and the Properties panel will then filter the list down to only the properties actually applied. In either mode, you can add, edit, or remove style sheets, media queries, rules, and/or properties.

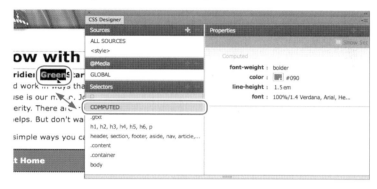

The Selectors pane also features a COMPUTED option that displays the aggregated list of styles applied to the selected element. The COMPUTED option will appear at any time you select an element or component on the page. When creating any type of styling, the code created by Dreamweaver will comply with industry standards and best practices. Dreamweaver will even apply vendor prefixes automatically to certain types of advanced styling as needed.

In addition to the CSS Designer, you may also create and edit CSS styling manually within Code view while taking advantage of many productivity enhancements like code hinting and auto completion.

Explore, experiment, learn

The Dreamweaver interface has been carefully crafted over many years to make the job of webpage design and development fast and easy. Feel free to explore and experiment with various menus, panels, and options to create the ideal workspace to produce the most productive environment for your own purposes. You'll find the program endlessly adaptable with power to spare for any task. Enjoy.

Review questions

1 Where can you access the command to display or hide any panel?

2 Where can you find the Code, Design, Split, and Live view buttons?

3 What can be saved in a workspace?

4 Do workspaces also load keyboard shortcuts?

5 What happens in the Property inspector when you insert the cursor into various elements on the webpage?

Review answers

1 All panels are listed in the Window menu.

2 These buttons are components of the Document toolbar.

3 Workspaces can save the configuration of the document window, the open panels, and the panels' size and position on the screen.

4 No, keyboard shortcuts are loaded and preserved independently of a workspace.

5 The Property inspector adapts to the selected element, displaying pertinent information and formatting commands.

2 HTML BASICS

Lesson Overview

In this lesson, you'll familiarize yourself with HTML and learn how to:

- Write HTML code by hand
- Understand HTML syntax
- Insert code elements
- Format text
- Add HTML structure
- Create HTML with Dreamweaver

 This lesson will take about 60 minutes to complete. There are no support files for this lesson.

HTML is the backbone of the web, the skeleton of your webpage. Like the bones in your body, it is the structure and substance of the Internet, although it is usually unseen except by the web designer. Without it, the web would not exist. Dreamweaver has many features that help you access, create, and edit HTML code quickly and effectively.

What is HTML?

"What other programs can open a Dreamweaver file?"

This question was asked by an actual student in a Dreamweaver class; although it might seem obvious to an experienced developer, the question illustrates a basic problem in teaching and learning web design. Most people confuse the program with the technology. They assume that the extension .htm or .html belongs to Dreamweaver or Adobe. Designers are accustomed to working with files ending with .ai, .psd, .indd, and so on; it's just a function of their jobs. These extensions are proprietary file formats created by programs that have specific capabilities and limitations. The goal in most cases is to create a final printed piece. The program in which the file was created provides the power to interpret the code that produces the printed page. Designers have learned over time that opening these file formats in a different program may produce unacceptable results or even damage the file.

On the other hand, the goal of the web designer is to create a webpage for display in a browser. The power and/or functionality of the originating program has little bearing on the resulting browser display. The display is all contingent on the HTML code and how the browser interprets it. Although a program may write good or bad code, the browser does all the hard work.

The web is based on the Hypertext Markup Language (HTML). The language and the file format don't belong to any individual program or company. In fact, it is a nonproprietary, plain-text language that can be edited in any text editor, in any operating system, on any computer. Dreamweaver is, in part, an HTML editor, although it is also much more than this. But to maximize the potential of Dreamweaver, you first need to have a good understanding of what HTML is and what it can (and can't) do. This lesson is intended as a concise primer for HTML and its capabilities and as a foundation for understanding Dreamweaver.

Where did HTML begin?

HTML and the first browser were invented in the early 1990s by Tim Berners-Lee, a scientist working at the CERN (Conseil Européen pour la Recherche Nucléaire, which is French for European Council for Nuclear Research) particle physics laboratory in Geneva, Switzerland. He intended the technology as a means for sharing technical papers and information via the fledgling Internet. He shared his HTML and browser inventions openly as an attempt to get the scientific community at large and others to adopt it and engage in the development themselves. He did not copyright or try to sell his work, which started a trend for web openness and camaraderie that continues to this day.

The language that Berners-Lee created over 20 years ago was a much simpler construct of what we use now, but HTML is still surprisingly easy to learn and master. At the time of this writing HTML is at version 4.01, officially adopted in 1999. It consists of around 90 *tags*, such as html, head, body, h1, p, and so on. The tag is written between angle brackets (<>), as in <p>, <h1>, and `<table>`. These tags are used to enclose, or *mark up*, text and graphics to enable a browser to display them in a particular way. HTML code is considered properly *balanced* when the markup features both an opening (<...>) and a closing (</...>) tag, such as <h1>...</h1>. When two matching tags appear this way, they are known as an *element* and entail any contents contained within the two tags, as well.

Some elements are used to create page structures, others to structure and format text, and yet others to enable interactivity and programmability. Even though Dreamweaver obviates the need for writing most of the code manually, the ability to read and interpret HTML code is still a recommended skill for any burgeoning web designer. And, sometimes it's the only way to find an error in your webpage.

Here you see the basic structure of a webpage:

Basic HTML Code Structure

You may be surprised to learn that "Welcome to my first webpage" is the only text from this code that displays in the web browser. The rest of the code creates the page structure and text formatting. Like an iceberg, most of the content of the actual webpage remains out of sight.

● **Note:** If you are dead set against learning how to read and write good HTML, you should check out Adobe Muse. This program allows you to create professional-looking webpages and complete websites using point-and-click techniques in a graphical user interface similar to Adobe InDesign, while never exposing you to the code running behind the scenes.

Properly structured, or balanced, HTML markup consists of an opening and a closing tag. Tags are enclosed within angle brackets (<>). You create a closing tag by repeating the original tag and typing a slash (/) after the opening bracket. Empty tags, like the horizontal rule, can be written in an abbreviated fashion, as shown.

Writing your own HTML code

● **Note:** Feel free to use any text editor for these exercises. But, be sure to save your files as plain text.

● **Note:** TextEdit may default to saving the file as rich text (.rtf); in this case you need to choose Format > Format As Plain Text before you can save the file as .html.

● **Note:** Some text editors may try to change the .html extension or prompt you to confirm the choice.

The idea of writing code may sound difficult or at least tedious, but creating a webpage is actually much easier than you think. In the next few exercises, you will learn how HTML works by creating a basic webpage and adding and formatting some simple text content:

1 Launch Notepad (Windows) or TextEdit (Mac).

2 Enter the following code in the empty document window:

```
<html>
<body>
Welcome to my first webpage
</body>
</html>
```

3 Save the file to the desktop as **firstpage.html**.

4 Launch Chrome, Firefox, Internet Explorer, Safari, or another installed web browser.

5 Choose File > Open. In some browsers you may need to press Ctrl-O or Cmd-O to access the dialog box. Navigate to the desktop and select **firstpage.html**, and then click OK/Open.

Congratulations, you just created your first webpage. As you can see, it doesn't take much code to create a serviceable webpage.

Text editor   Browser

Understanding HTML syntax

Next you'll add content to your new webpage to learn some important aspects of HTML code syntax:

1 Switch back to the text editor, but don't close the browser.

2 Insert your cursor at the end of the text "Welcome to my first webpage" and press Enter/Return to insert a paragraph return.

3 Type **Making webpages is fun**. Press the spacebar five times to insert five spaces, and then finish by typing **and easy!** on the same line.

4 Save the file.

5 Switch to the browser.

Although you saved the changes, you'll notice that the new text doesn't appear in the browser. That's because you never see a webpage live on the Internet. It must be first downloaded to your computer and saved, or *cached*, on the hard drive. The browser is actually displaying the page it downloaded originally. To see the latest version of the webpage, you'll have to reload it, which is important to remember. People frequently miss changes in a website because they are looking at the cached versions of a page instead of the most current versions. (If your website will be updated frequently, you can insert a piece of JavaScript code that will reload a page automatically each time a browser window accesses it.)

6 Refresh the window to load the updated page.

▶ **Tip:** In most browsers you can press Ctrl-R/Cmd-R to refresh the page view. In Internet Explorer, press F5.

As you can see, the browser is displaying the new text, but it's ignoring the paragraph return between the two lines as well as the extra spaces. In fact, you could add hundreds of paragraph returns between the lines and dozens of spaces between each word and the browser display would be no different. The browser is programmed to ignore extra white space and honor only HTML code elements. By inserting a tag here and there, you can easily create the desired text display.

Inserting HTML code

In this exercise you will insert HTML tags to produce the correct text display:

1 Switch back to the text editor.

2 Add the tags to the text as follows:

```
<p>Making webpages is fun and easy!</p>
```

To add extra spacing, or other special characters within a line of text, HTML provides code elements called *entities*. Entities are entered into the code differently than tags. For example, the method for inserting a nonbreaking space is by typing the entity .

3 Replace the five spaces in the text with five nonbreaking spaces:

```
<p>Making webpages is fun     
and easy!</p>
```

4 Save the file. Switch to the browser and reload or refresh the page display.

The browser is now showing the paragraph return and desired spacing.

When you add tags and entities, the browser can display the desired paragraph structure and spacing.

```
<html>
<body>
Welcome to my first webpage
<p>Making webpages is fun      andd
easy!</p>
</body>
</html>
```

Welcome to my first webpage

Making webpages is fun   and easy!

Although line breaks, spacing, and even indentation is ignored by the browser, web designers and coders frequently use such white space to make the code easier to read and edit. But don't go crazy. Although white space doesn't affect the display of a page in a browser, it can contribute to the overall time a webpage takes to download and render. White space and extraneous code contributes to what web developers call the overall *weight* of a page. When a page has too much weight, it downloads, renders, and operates in a suboptimum manner. Later in the book, we'll talk about how you can minimize this weight to make your pages load quicker and operate at more acceptable speeds.

Formatting text with HTML

Tags often serve multiple purposes. Besides creating paragraph structure and creating white space as demonstrated earlier, they can impart basic text formatting, as well as identify the relative importance of the page content. For example, HTML provides six heading tags (<h1> to <h6>) to set headings off from normal paragraphs. The tags not only format the heading text differently than paragraph text, they also impart additional meaning. Heading tags are automatically formatted in bold and often at a larger relative size. The number of the heading (1–6) also plays a role: Using the <h1> tag identifies the heading as being the highest in importance by default. In this exercise, you will add a heading tag to the first line:

1 Switch back to the text editor.

2 Add the highlighted tags to the text as follows:

```
<h1>Welcome to my first webpage</h1>
```

3 Save the file. Switch to the browser and reload or refresh the page display.

Note how the text display changed. It is now larger and formatted in boldface.

Web designers use heading tags to identify the importance of specific content to help improve their site rankings on Google, Yahoo, and other search engines.

```
<html>
<body>
<h1>Welcome to my first webpage</h1>
<p>Making webpages is fun      and
easy!</p>
</body>
</html>
```

Welcome to my first webpage

Making webpages is fun   and easy!

Applying inline formatting

So far, all the tags you have used work as paragraph or stand-alone elements. These are referred to as *block* elements. You can also apply formatting and structure to content that's contained within the flow of another tag, or *inline*. A typical use of inline code would be to apply bold or italic styling to a word or a portion of a paragraph. In this exercise, you will apply inline formatting:

1   Switch back to the text editor.

2   Add the highlighted tags to the text as follows:

```
<p>Making webpages is fun$#160;$#160;$#160;$#160;$#160;
<strong><em>and easy!</em></strong></p>
```

3   Save the file. Switch to the browser and reload or refresh the page display.

Strong and emphasis (em) are used in place of the tags bold <b> and italic <i> because they provide enhanced semantic meaning for visitors with disabilities or visual impairment, but the result is basically identical.

Most formatting, both inline and otherwise, is properly applied using cascading style sheets (CSS). The <strong> and <em> tags are among the few still acceptable ways to apply inline formatting using specific HTML code elements. Technically speaking, these elements are intended to add semantic meaning to text content, but the effect is still the same—the text still appears by default as bold and italic in most applications.

However, in the near future this may change. The last decade has featured an industry-supported move to separate the content from its presentation, or formatting. Although most browsers and HTML readers currently apply default formatting based on specific tags, this may not always be the case. See Lesson 3, "CSS Basics," for a full explanation of the strategy and application of CSS in standards-based web design.

Adding structure

Most webpages feature at least three fundamental elements: a root (typically <html>), <head>, and <body>. These elements create the essential underlying structure of the webpage. The root element contains all the code and content and is used to declare to the browser, and any browser applications, what types of code elements to expect within the page. The <head> element holds code that performs vital background tasks, including styling, external links, and other information. The <body> element holds all the visible content, such as text, tables, images, movies, and so on.

The sample page you created doesn't have a `<head>` element. A webpage can exist without this section, but adding any advanced functionality to this page without one would be difficult. In this exercise, you will add `<head>` and `<title>` elements to your webpage:

1   Switch back to the text editor.

2   Add the highlighted tags and content to the text as follows:

```
<html>
<head>
<title>HTML Basics for Fun and Profit</title>
</head>
<body>
```

3   Save the file. Switch to the browser and reload or refresh the page display.

Did you notice what changed? It may not be obvious at first. Look at the title bar or window tab of the browser. The words "HTML Basics for Fun and Profit" now magically appear above your webpage. By adding the `<title>` element, you have created this display. But, it's not just a cool trick, it's good for your business, too.

The content of the `<title>` tag will appear in the browser title bar when the page is refreshed.

Google, Yahoo, and the other search engines catalog the `<title>` element of each page and use it, among other criteria, to index and rank webpages. The content of the title is one of the items typically displayed within the results of a search. A well-titled page could be ranked higher than one with a bad title or one with none at all. Keep your titles short but meaningful. For example, the title "ABC Home Page" doesn't really convey any useful information. A better title might be "Welcome to the Home Page of ABC Corporation." Check out other websites (especially peers or competitors) to see how they title their pages. It's also important to know that the title will be used when visitors bookmark your pages in their browser.

Writing HTML in Dreamweaver

So, the inevitable question is "If I can write HTML in any text editor, why do I need to use Dreamweaver?" Although a complete answer awaits you in the lessons that follow, the question begs for a quick demonstration. In this exercise, you will re-create the same webpage using Dreamweaver:

1   Launch Dreamweaver CC.

2   Choose File > New.

3   In the New Document window, select Blank Page from the first column.

4   Select HTML from the Page Type section.

5   Select <none> from the Layout section.

6   Choose HTML5 from the DocType pop-up menu.

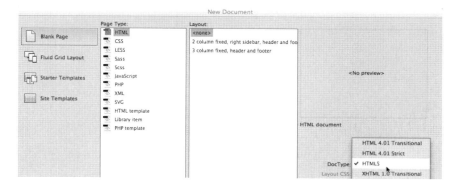

Dreamweaver allows you to create different types of web-compatible files. You will learn more about this dialog box later in subsequent lessons.

7   Click Create.

> A new document window opens in Dreamweaver. The window may default to one of three displays: Code view, Design view, or Split view.

8   If it's not already selected, click the Split view button.

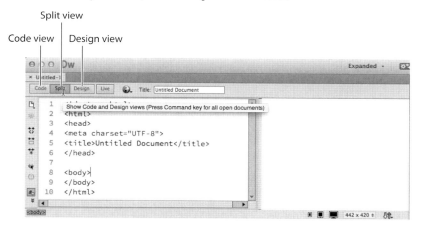

The advantages of using Dreamweaver to create HTML are evident from the very beginning: much of the page structure is created already.

Notice that the Code window has provided a huge head start over using a text editor. The basic structure of the page is already in place, including the root, head, body, and even title tags, among others. The only thing Dreamweaver makes you do is add the content itself.

9   Insert the cursor after the opening <body> tag and type **Welcome to my second page** following the tag.

Dreamweaver makes it a simple matter to format the first line as a heading 1.

10 Move the cursor to the beginning of the text "Welcome to my second page." Type **<h** to open the code hinting feature.

Note how Dreamweaver automatically provides a list of compatible code elements.

When activated, code hinting provides a drop-down list of applicable HTML, CSS, and JavaScript elements, as well as some other languages.

11 Double-click h1 from the list to insert it in the code. Type > to close the tag.

12 Move the cursor to the end of the text. Type </ at the end of the sentence.

Note how Dreamweaver closes the <h1> element automatically. But many coders add the tags as they write.

13 Press Enter/Return to insert a line break. Type **<p** and press Enter/Return to insert the element. Type > to close the tag.

14 Type **Making webpages in Dreamweaver is even more fun!** and then type </ to close the <p> element.

Tired of hand-coding yet? Dreamweaver offers multiple ways for formatting your content.

15 Select the word *more*. In the Property inspector, click the **B** and then the **I** buttons to apply the `<strong>` and `<em>` tags to the text.

These tags produce bold and italic formatting on the selected text.

Something missing?

When you reached for the B and I buttons in step 15, were they missing? When you make changes in Code view, the Property inspector occasionally needs to be refreshed before you can access the formatting commands featured there. Simply click the Refresh button to make the formatting commands reappear.

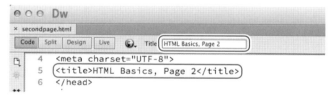

Only two more tasks remain before your new page is complete. Note that Dreamweaver created the `<title>` element and inserted the text *Untitled Document* within it. You could select the text within the code window and enter a new title, or you could change it using another built-in feature.

16 Locate the Title field at the top of the document window and select the *Untitled Document* text.

17 Type **HTML Basics, Page 2** in the Title field.

18 Press Enter/Return to complete the title.

The Title field enables you to change the content of the `<title>` element without having to work in the HTML code.

Note that the new title text appears in the code, replacing the original content. It's time to save the file and preview it in the browser.

19 Choose File > Save. Navigate to the desktop. Name the file **secondpage** and click Save.

Dreamweaver adds the proper extension (html) automatically.

20 Choose File > Preview in Browser.

The completed page appears in the browser window.

Using Dreamweaver, you completed the task in a fraction of time it took you to do it manually.

You have just completed two webpages—one by hand and the other using Dreamweaver. In both cases, you can see how HTML played a central role in the whole process. To learn more about this technology, go to the website of the W3 Consortium at www.w3schools.com, or check out any of the books in the following sidebar.

Recommended books on HTML 4

HTML and CSS: Visual QuickStart Guide, 8th Edition, Elizabeth Castro and Bruce Hyslop (Peachpit Press, 2013), ISBN: 0321928830

HTML and XHTML Pocket Reference, 4th Edition, Jennifer Niederst Robbins, (O'Reilly, 2009), ISBN: 978-0-596-80586-9

Head First HTML with CSS & XHTML, Elizabeth and Eric Freeman, (O'Reilly, 2005), ISBN: 978-0-596-10197-8

Frequently used HTML 4 codes

HTML code elements serve specific purposes. Tags can create structures, apply formatting, identify logical content, or generate interactivity. Tags that create stand-alone structures are called block elements; the ones that perform their work within the body of another tag are called inline elements.

HTML tags

The following table shows some of the most frequently used HTML tags. To get the most out of Dreamweaver and your webpages, it helps to understand the nature of these elements and how they are used. Remember, some tags can serve multiple purposes.

Table 2.1 Frequently used HTML tags

TAG	DESCRIPTION	STRUCTURAL	BLOCK	INLINE
`<!--...-->`	Designates an HTML comment. Allows you to add notes within the HTML code that are not displayed in the browser in the viewable page.	✓		
`<a>`	Anchor. Creates a hyperlink.			✓
`<blockquote>`	Quotation. Creates a stand-alone, indented paragraph.		✓	
`<body>`	Designates the document body. Contains the visible portions of the webpage content.	✓		
` `	Break. Inserts a line break without creating a new paragraph.	✓	✓	
`<div>`	Division. Used to divide page content into discernible groupings. Used extensively to simulate columnar layouts.	✓	✓	
`<em>`	Emphasis. Adds semantic emphasis. Displays as italic by default in most browsers and readers.			✓
`<form>`	Designates an HTML form.	✓		
`<h1> to <h6>`	Headings. Creates bold headings. Implies semantic value.		✓	
`<head>`	Designates the document head. Contains code that performs background functions, such as meta tags, scripts, styling, links, and other information.	✓		
`<hr />`	Horizontal rule. Empty element that generates a horizontal line.	✓	✓	
`<html>`	Root element of most webpages. Contains an entire webpage, except in certain cases where server-based code must load before the opening `<html>` tag.	✓		
`<iframe>`	Inline frame. A structural element that can contain another document.	✓		✓
`<img />`	Image.	✓		✓
`<input />`	Input element for a form such as a text field.	✓		✓
`<li>`	List item.		✓	
`<link />`	Designates the relationship between a document and an external resource.	✓		
`<meta />`	Metadata.	✓		
`<ol>`	Ordered list. Defines a numbered list. List items display in a numbered sequence.	✓	✓	
`<p>`	Paragraph. Creates a stand-alone paragraph.		✓	
`<script>`	Script. Contains scripting elements or points to an external script.	✓		
`<span>`	Designates a document section. Provides a means to apply special formatting or emphasis to a portion of an element.			✓
`<strong>`	Adds semantic emphasis. Displays as bold by default in most browsers and readers.			✓
`<style>`	Calls CSS style rules.	✓		
`<table>`	Designates an HTML table.	✓	✓	
`<td>`	Table data. Designates a table cell.	✓		
`<textarea>`	Multi-line text input element for a form.	✓	✓	
`<th>`	Table header.	✓		
`<title>`	Title.	✓		
`<tr>`	Table row.	✓		
`<ul>`	Unordered list. Defines a bulleted list. List items display with bullets.	✓	✓	

HTML character entities

Entities exist for every letter and character. If a symbol doesn't appear on a keyboard, you can insert it by typing the name or numeric value listed in the following table:

Table 2.2 HTML character entries

CHARACTER	DESCRIPTION	NAME	NUMBER
©	Copyright	&copy;	&#169;
®	Registered trademark	&reg;	&#174;
™	Trademark		&#153;
•	Bullet		&#149;
–	En dash		&#150;
—	Em dash		&#151;
	Nonbreaking space		

One note: Some entities, such as the copyright symbol, can be created using either a name or a number, but named entities may not work in all browsers or applications. So, either stick to entity numbers, or test the specific named entities you want to use.

Introducing HTML5

The current version of HTML has been around for over 10 years and, like many technologies, it has not kept pace with the advances that have occurred on the web, such as in smart phones and other mobile devices. The World Wide Web Consortium (W3C), the standards organization responsible for maintaining and updating HTML and other web standards, has been working diligently on updating the language. It released the first working draft of HTML5 (written as one word) in January 2008, with regular updates since then and the latest published as recently as December 2012. Although adoption of the new standard wasn't envisioned until 2020 at the earliest, W3C accelerated the plan and now wants to finalize HTML5 as soon as 2014. So, what does all this mean for current or up-and-coming web designers? Not much, yet.

Why? Adoption of the new language is not a mandatory process. The entire community works together cooperatively to develop and implement the new technology. As a result there's no final deadline and no Internet police enforcing HTML5's adoption or proper use. Today, the current crop of web browsers are working to incorporate the new features outlined in the HTML5 specifications, but the support is not complete and varies from browser to browser. In some cases, the browser manufacturers even disagree on how certain features should be implemented. Until the specifications are finalized, HTML5 sits in a state of limbo that may continue for some time.

Some designers and developers are taking a "wait and see" approach, maintaining good web design practices and implementing HTML5 features when they are safe and make sense to do so. Others have the attitude that "it's all good" and are starting to rely heavily on HTML5 tools and techniques. These designers and developers feel that early adopters will attract users interested in the latest and greatest, and older non-HTML5-compliant browsers will be abandoned more quickly. In any case, backward-compatibility to HTML 4.01 is a primary goal of the W3C and will be certain well into the future. So, no matter what category you fall into, don't worry; there's no threat that older webpages and sites will suddenly explode or disappear.

In this book, we focus more on the "wait and see" approach. Our lessons and exercises use the HTML5 features and techniques that have widespread support and utility, and stick to tried-and-true techniques elsewhere. Additionally, we also explore some of the newer, experimental features of HTML5 but leave their adoption on your own sites up to you.

What's new in HTML5

Every new version of HTML has made changes both to the number and purpose of the elements that make up the language. HTML 4.01 consisted of approximately 90 elements. Some of these elements have been removed altogether, and new ones have been adopted or proposed.

Changes to the list usually revolve around supporting new technologies or different types of content models and removing features that were bad ideas or ones infrequently used. Some changes simply reflect customs or techniques popularized within the developer community over time. Other changes have been made to simplify the way code is created to make it easier to write and faster to disseminate.

HTML5 tags

The table on the next page shows some of the important new tags in HTML5. At the moment, it consists of well over 100 tags. Almost 30 old tags have been removed, which means HTML5 features nearly 50 new elements. In this book's exercises, we use many of these new HTML5 elements as appropriate and explain their intended role on the web. Take a few moments to familiarize yourself with these tags and their descriptions.

Semantic web design

Many of the changes to HTML have been implemented to support the concept of *semantic web design*. This movement has important ramifications for the future of HTML, its usability, and the interoperability of websites on the Internet. At the moment, each webpage stands alone on the web. The content may link to other pages and sites, but there's really no way to combine or collect the information available on multiple pages or multiple sites in a coherent manner. Search engines do their best to index the content that appears on every site, but much of it is lost due to the nature and structure of old HTML code.

HTML was initially designed as a presentation language. In other words, it was intended to display technical documents in a browser in a readable and predictable manner. If you look carefully at the original specifications of HTML, it basically looks like a list of items you would put in a college research paper: headings, paragraphs, quoted material, tables, numbered and bulleted lists, and so on.

The Internet before HTML looked more like MS DOS or the OS X Terminal applications—no formatting, no graphics, and no color. The element list in the first version of HTML basically identified how the content would be displayed. These tags did not convey any intrinsic meaning or significance. For example, using a heading tag displayed a particular line of text in bold, but it didn't tell you what relationship the heading had with the following text or to the story as a whole. Is it a title, or merely a subheading?

HTML5 has added a significant number of new tags to help add meaning to markup. Tags such as <header>, <footer>, <article>, and <section> allow you for the first time to identify specific content without having to resort to additional attributes. The end result is simpler code and less of it. But most of all, the addition of semantic meaning to your code allows you and other developers to connect the content from one page to another in new and exciting ways—many of which haven't even been invented yet. It's truly a work in progress.

Table 2.3 Important new HTML5 tags

TAG	DESCRIPTION	STRUCTURAL	BLOCK	INLINE
`<article>`	Designates independent, self-contained content, which can be distributed independently from the rest of the site.	✓	✓	
`<aside>`	Designates sidebar content related to the surrounding content.	✓	✓	
`<audio>`	Designates multimedia content, sounds, music, or other audio streams.	✓		✓
`<canvas>`	Designates graphics content created using a script.	✓		
`<figure>`	Designates a section of stand-alone content containing an image or video.	✓	✓	
`<figcaption>`	Designates a caption for a `<figure>` element.	✓		✓
`<footer>`	Designates a footer of a document or section.	✓	✓	
`<header>`	Designates the introduction of a document or section.	✓	✓	
`<hgroup>`	Designates a set of <h1> to <h6> elements when a heading has multiple levels.	✓		
`<nav>`	Designates a section of navigation.	✓	✓	
`<section>`	Designates a section in a document, such as chapters, headers, footers, or any other sections of the document.	✓	✓	
`<source>`	Designates resource file for media elements, a child element of video or audio elements. Multiple sources can be defined for browsers that do not support the default resource.	✓		✓
`<track>`	Designates text tracks used in media players.	✓		
`<video>`	Designates video content, such as a movie clip or other video streams.	✓		

New techniques and technology

HTML5 has also revisited the basic nature of the language to take back some of the functions that previously required third-party plug-in applications and external programming. If you are new to web design, this transition will be painless, because you have nothing to relearn or bad habits to break. If you already have experience building webpages and applications, this book guides you safely through some of these waters and introduces the new technologies and techniques in a logical and straightforward way. But best of all, semantic web design doesn't mean you have to trash all your old sites and rebuild everything from scratch. Valid HTML 4 code will remain valid for the foreseeable future. HTML5 was intended to make your task easier, by allowing you to do more, with less work. So let's get started!

To learn more about HTML5, check out http://tinyurl.com/html5-info-1

To see the complete list of HTML5 elements, see http://tinyurl.com/html5-Elements

To learn more about W3C, see www.w3.org

Review questions

1 What programs can open HTML files?

2 What does a markup language do?

3 HTML is comprised of how many code elements?

4 What are the three main parts of most webpages?

5 What's the difference between a block and inline element?

6 Is HTML5 the current version of HTML?

Review answers

1 HTML is a plain-text language that can be opened and edited in any text editor and viewed in any web browser.

2 It places tags contained within brackets < > around plain-text content to pass information concerning structure and formatting from one application to another.

3 Fewer than 100 code elements are defined in the HTML 4 specifications; HTML5 contains over 100.

4 Most webpages are composed of three sections: a root, head, and body.

5 A block element creates a stand-alone element. An inline element can exist within another element.

6 No. The current version is HTML 4.01. A draft version of HTML5 has been published, but it is not slated to be completed until 2014. Full adoption may take several years after it is finalized.

3   CSS BASICS

Lesson Overview

In this lesson, you'll familiarize yourself with CSS and learn

- CSS (cascading style sheets) terms and terminology

- The difference between HTML and CSS formatting

- How the cascade, inheritance, descendant, and specificity theories affect how browsers apply CSS formatting

- How CSS can format objects

- New features and capabilities of CSS3

This lesson will take about 2 hours to complete. If you have not already done so, download the project files for this lesson from the Lesson & Update Files tab on your Account page at www.peachpit.com, and store them on your computer in a convenient location, as described in the Getting Started section of this book. Your Accounts page is also where you'll find any updates to the lessons or to the lesson files. Look on the Lesson & Update Files tab to access the most current content. If you are starting from scratch in this lesson, use the method described in the "Jumpstart" section of "Getting Started."

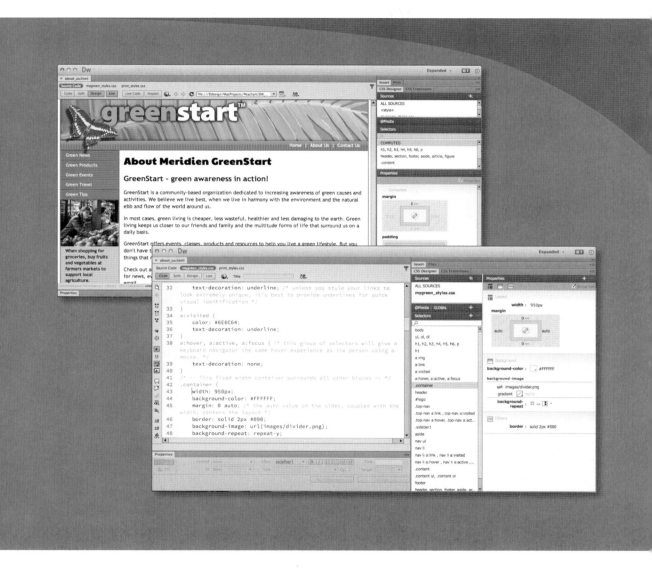

Cascading style sheets control the look and feel of a webpage. The language and syntax is complex, powerful, and endlessly adaptable; it takes time and dedication to learn and years to master. A modern web designer can't live without them.

● **Note:** If you have not already downloaded the project files for this lesson to your computer from your Account page, make sure to do so now. See "Getting Started" at the beginning of the book.

What is CSS?

HTML was never intended to be a design medium. Other than bold and italic, version 1 lacked a standardized way to load fonts or format text. Formatting commands were added along the way up to version 3 of HTML to address these limitations, but these changes still weren't enough. Designers resorted to various tricks to produce the desired results. For example, they used HTML tables to simulate multicolumn and complex layouts for text and graphics, and they used images when they wanted to display typefaces other than Times or Helvetica.

Using the expanded table mode in Dreamweaver (top), you can see how this webpage relies on tables and images to produce the final design (bottom).

HTML-based formatting was so misguided a concept that it was deprecated from the language less than a year after it was formally adopted, in favor of cascading style sheets (CSS). CSS avoids all the problems of HTML formatting, while saving time and money, too. Using CSS lets you strip the HTML code down to its essential content and structure and then apply the formatting separately, so you can more easily tailor the webpage to specific applications.

HTML vs. CSS formatting

When comparing HTML-based formatting to CSS-based formatting, it's easy to see how CSS produces vast efficiencies in time and effort. In the following exercise, you'll explore the power and efficacy of CSS by editing two webpages, one formatted by HTML, the other by CSS.

● **Note:** If you are completing this lesson separately from the rest of the lessons in book, see the detailed "Jumpstart" instructions in the "Getting Started" section at the beginning of the book. Then, follow the steps in this exercise.

1 Launch Dreamweaver, if it is not currently running.

2 Choose File > Open.

3 Navigate to the Lesson03 folder and open **HTML_formatting.html**.

4 Click the Split view button. If necessary, choose View > Split Vertically to split the Code view and Design view windows vertically, side by side.

Each element of the content is formatted individually using the deprecated `<font>` tag. Note the attribute `color="blue"` in each `<h1>` and `<p>` element.

5 Replace the word `blue` with **green** in each line in which it appears. Click in the Design view window to update the display.

The text displays in green now. As you can see, formatting using the obsolete `<font>` tag is not only slow, but prone to error, too. Make a mistake, like typing **greeen** or **geen** and the browser will ignore the color formatting altogether.

6 Open **CSS_formatting.html** from the Lesson03 folder.

7 If it's not currently selected, click the Split view button.

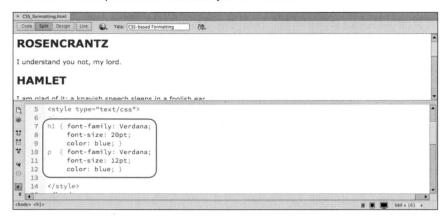

The content of the file is identical to the previous document, except that it's formatted by CSS. The code that formats the HTML elements appears in the <head> section of this file. Note that the code contains only two color: blue; attributes.

8 Select the word blue in the code h1 { color: blue; } and type **green** to replace it. Click in the Design view window to update the display.

In Design view, all the heading elements display in green. The paragraph elements remain blue.

9 Select the word blue in the code p { color: blue; } and type **green** to replace it. Click in the Design view window to update the display.

In Design view, the paragraph elements have changed to green.

In this exercise, CSS accomplished the color change with two simple edits, whereas the HTML <font> tag required you to edit *every* line. Are you beginning to understand why the W3C deprecated the <font> tag and developed cascading style sheets? This exercise highlights just a small sampling of CSS formatting power and productivity enhancements that can't be matched by HTML alone.

HTML defaults

Each of the nearly 100 HTML 4 tags comes right out of the box with one or more default formats, characteristics, or behaviors. So even if you do nothing, the text will already be formatted in a certain way. One of the essential tasks in mastering CSS is learning and understanding these defaults. Let's take a look.

1   Open **HTML_defaults.html** from the Lesson03 folder. If necessary, select Design view to preview the contents of the file.

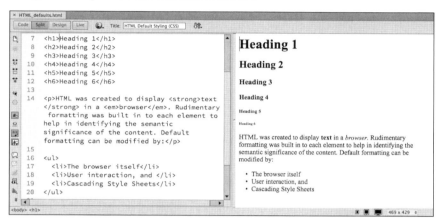

The file contains the full range of HTML headings and text elements. Each element exhibits basic styling for traits such as size, font, and spacing, among others.

2   If necessary, click the Split view button. In the Code view window, locate the <head> section, and try to identify any code that may be formatting the HTML elements.

A quick look will tell you that there is no obvious styling information in the file, but the text still displays different kinds of formatting. So where does it come from? And what are the settings?

The answer is: It depends. HTML 4 elements draw characteristics from multiple sources. The first place to look is the W3C, the web standards organization that establishes Internet specifications and protocols. The default style sheet at www.w3.org/TR/CSS21/sample.html defines the standard formatting and behaviors of all HTML 4 elements. This is the style sheet on which all browser vendors base their default rendering of HTML elements.

HTML5 defaults?

Over the last decade, there has been a consistent movement on the web to separate "content" and "styling." At the time of this writing, the concept of "default" formatting in HTML is officially dead. Technically speaking, there are no default styling standards for HTML5 elements. If you look for a default style sheet for HTML5 on w3.org, you won't find one. But for the time being, browser manufacturers are still honoring and applying HTML 4 default styling to HTML5-based webpages. Confused? Join the club. What this means is that, in the future, HTML elements may not display any formatting at all by default, but at least for the moment your HTML5 webpages will still display the same default styling used for HTML 4, even if you forget to apply CSS formatting.

To save time and give you a bit of a head start, the following table pulls together some of the most common defaults:

Table 3.1 Common HTML defaults

ITEM	DESCRIPTION
Background	In most browsers, the page background color is white. The background of <div>, <table>, <td>, <th>, and most other tags is transparent.
Headings	Headings <h1> through <h6> are bold and align to the left. The six heading tags apply differing font size attributes (<h1> is the largest; and <h6> is the smallest).
Body text	Outside of a table cell, text aligns to the left and starts at the top of the page.
Table cell text	Text within table cells <td> aligns horizontally to the left and vertically to the center.
Table header	Text within header cells <th> aligns horizontally and vertically to the center.
Fonts	Text color is black. Default typeface and font is specified and supplied by the browser (or by browser preferences specified by the manufacturer, which can be overridden by the user).
Margins	Spacing external to the element border/boundary. Many HTML elements feature some form of margin spacing.
Padding	Spacing between the box border and the content. According to the default style sheet, no element features default padding.

The next task is to identify the browser (and its version) that is displaying the HTML. That's because browsers frequently differ in the way they interpret, or *render*, HTML elements and CSS formatting. Unfortunately, even different versions of the same browser can produce wide variations from identical code.

The best practice is to build and test your webpages to make sure that they work properly in the browsers employed by the majority of web users—especially the browsers preferred by your own visitors. In January 2013, the W3C published the following statistics identifying the most popular browsers:

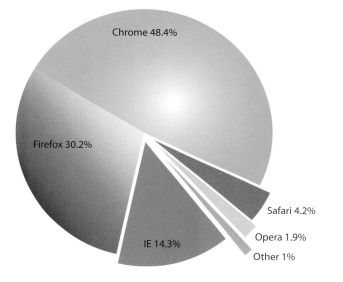

Knowing which browsers are the most popular among the general public is nice, but before building and testing your pages, identifying the browsers that visitors in your target audience use is crucial.

Be aware, however, that multiple versions of each browser are still in use, which is important to know because older browser versions are less likely to support the latest HTML and CSS features and effects. To make matters more complicated, although these statistics are valid for the Internet overall, the statistics for your own site may vary wildly.

CSS box model

The browser normally reads the HTML code, interprets its structure and formatting, and then displays the webpage. CSS does its work by stepping between HTML and the browser, redefining how each element should be rendered. It imposes an imaginary box around each element and then enables you to format almost every aspect of how that box and its contents are displayed.

The box model is a programmatic construct imposed by CSS that enables you to format, or redefine, the default settings of any HTML element.

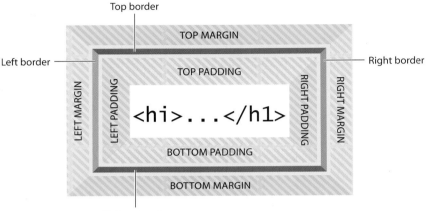

CSS permits you to specify fonts, line spacing, colors, borders, background shading and graphics, margins, and padding, among other things. In most instances these boxes are invisible, and although CSS gives you the ability to format them, it does not require you to do so.

1   Launch Dreamweaver, if necessary. Open **boxmodel.html** from the Lesson03 folder.

2   Click the Split view button to divide the workspace between the Code view and Design view windows.

```
19  <body>
20  <h1>This is a sample heading</h1>
21  <p> This  sample paragraph demonstrates
    the power of the CSS box model. This
    paragraph displays text in<strong>bold</
    strong> and <em>italic.</em> CSS can
    control how  browsers renders each HTML
    element. </p>
22  <p>Remember, with great power comes great
    responsibility.</p>
23  </body>
24  </html>
```

This is a sample heading

This sample paragraph demonstrates the power of the CSS box model. This paragraph displays text in **bold** and *italic.* CSS can control how browsers renders each HTML element.

Remember, with great power comes great responsibility.

Content vs. presentation

A basic tenet in web standards today is the separation of the *content* (text, images, lists, and so on) from its *presentation* (formatting). Here is identical HTML content, side by side. The CSS formatting has been removed entirely from the file on the left. Although the text on the left is not wholly unformatted, it's easy to see the power of CSS to transform HTML code.

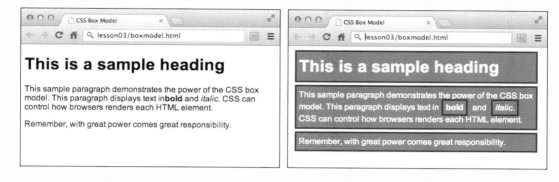

The file's sample HTML code contains a heading and two paragraphs with sample text that is formatted to illustrate some of the properties of the CSS box model. The text displays visible borders, background colors, margins, and padding.

The working specifications found at www.w3.org/TR/css3-box describe how the box model is supposed to render documents in various media.

Multiples, classes, and IDs, oh my!

By taking advantage of the cascade, inheritance, descendant, and specificity theories, you can target formatting to almost any element anywhere on a webpage. But CSS offers a few more ways to optimize and customize the formatting even further.

Applying formatting to multiple elements

To speed things up, CSS allows you to apply formatting to multiple elements at once by listing each in the selector, separated by commas. For example, the formatting in these rules:

```
h1 { font-family: Verdana; color: blue; }
h2 { font-family: Verdana; color: blue; }
h3 { font-family: Verdana; color: blue; }
```

can also be expressed like this:

```
h1, h2, h3 { font-family: Verdana; color: blue; }
```

which saves three lines of unnecessary code.

Creating class attributes

Frequently, you will want to create unique formatting to apply to objects, paragraphs, phrases, words, or even individual characters appearing within a webpage. To accomplish this, CSS allows you to make your own custom attributes, called *class* and *ID*.

● **Note:** Dreamweaver will warn you when you enter a name that's inappropriate.

Class attributes may be applied to any number of elements on a page, whereas ID attributes may appear only once. If you are a print designer, think of classes as similar to a combination of Adobe InDesign's paragraph, character, table, and object styles. Class and ID names can be a single word, an abbreviation, any combination of letters and numbers, or almost anything, but they may not start with a number or contain spaces. Although not strictly prohibited, avoid using HTML tag or attribute names for class and ID names.

To declare a CSS class selector, insert a period before the name within the style sheet, like this:

```
.intro
.copyright
```

Then, apply the CSS class to an entire HTML element as an attribute, like this:

```
<p class="intro">Type intro text here.</p>
```

or to individual characters or words inline, like this:

```
Here is <span class="copyright">some text</span> formatted
differently.
```

Creating ID attributes

HTML designates ID as a unique attribute. Therefore, a specific ID should not be assigned to more than one element per page. In the past, many web designers used ID attributes to point at specific components within the page, such as the header, the footer, or articles. With the advent of HTML5 elements—header, footer, aside, article, and so on—the use of ID and class attributes for this purpose is less necessary than it was. But IDs can still be used to identify specific text elements, images, and tables to assist you in building powerful hypertext navigation within your page and site. You will learn more about using IDs this way in Lesson 9, "Working with Navigation."

To declare an ID attribute in a style sheet, insert a number sign, or hash mark, before the name, like this:

```
#contact_info
#disclaimer
```

You apply the CSS ID to an entire HTML element as an attribute, like this:

```
<div id="contact_info"></div>
<div id="disclaimer"></div>
```

Formatting text

You can apply CSS formatting in three ways: *inline*, *embedded* (in an internal style sheet), or *linked* (via an external style sheet). A CSS formatting instruction is called a *rule*. A rule consists of two parts—a *selector* and one or more *declarations*. The selector identifies what element, or combination of elements, is to be formatted; the declaration, or declarations, contains the formatting specifications. CSS rules can redefine any existing HTML element, as well as define "class" and "ID" attributes.

A rule can also combine selectors to target multiple elements at once or to target specific instances within a page where elements appear in unique ways, such as when one element is nested within another.

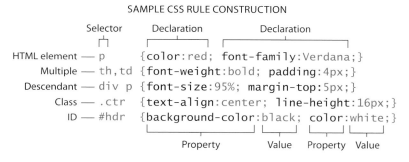

These sample rules demonstrate some typical constructions used in selectors and declarations. The way the selector is written determines how the styling is applied and how the rules interact with one another.

Applying a CSS rule is not a simple matter of selecting some text and applying a paragraph or character style, as in Adobe InDesign or Adobe Illustrator. CSS rules can affect single words, paragraphs of text, or combinations of text and objects. A single rule can affect an entire webpage. A rule can be specified to begin and end abruptly, or to format content continuously until changed by a subsequent rule.

There are many factors that come into play in how a CSS rule performs its job. To help you better understand how it all works, the exercises in the following sections illustrate four main CSS concepts, which we'll refer to as theories: cascade, inheritance, descendant, and specificity.

CSS rule syntax: write or wrong

CSS is powerful adjunct to HTML. It has the power to style and format any HTML element, but the language is sensitive to even the smallest typo or syntax error. Miss a period, comma, or semicolon and you may as well have left the code out of your page entirely.

For example, take the following simple rule:

```
p { padding: 1px;
    margin: 10px; }
```

that applies both padding and margins to the paragraph <p>(paragraph) element.

This rule can also be written properly without spacing as:

```
p{padding:1px;margin:10px;}
```

The spaces and line breaks used in the first example are unnecessary, merely accommodations for the humans who may write and read the code. The browsers and other devices processing the code do not need them. But, the same cannot be said of the various punctuation marks sprinkled throughout the CSS.

Use parentheses ( ) or brackets [ ] instead of braces { }, and the rule (and perhaps your entire style sheet) is useless. The same goes for the use of colons ":" and semicolons ";" in the code.

Can you catch all the errors in the following sample rules?

```
p { padding; 1px: margin; 10px: }
p { padding: 1px; margin: 10px; ]
p { padding 1px, margin 10px, }
```

Similar problems can arise in the construction of compound selectors, too. For example, putting a space in the wrong place can change the meaning of a selector entirely.

This `article.content { color: #F00 }` rule formats the `<article>` element and all its children in this code structure:

```
<article class="content"><p>...</p></article>
```

While `article .content { color: #F00 }`, with a space after the `article` element, would ignore the previous HTML structure altogether and format only the <p> element in the following code:

```
<article><p class="content">...</p></article>
```

As you can see, a tiny error can have dramatic repercussions. A good web designer keeps their eyes constantly searching for any little error, misplaced space or punctuation mark to keep their CSS and HTML functioning properly.

Cascade theory

The cascade theory describes how the order and placement of rules in the style sheet or on the page affects the application of styling. In other words, if two rules conflict, which one wins out? Let's take a look at how cascade influences CSS formatting.

1 Open **cascade.html** from the Lesson03 folder.

The file contains HTML headings and text formatted by the default HTML styling.

2 Click the Split view button, if necessary, and observe the `<head>` section in the Code view window for any CSS rules.

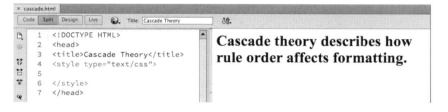

Note that the code contains a `<style>` section but no CSS rules.

3 Insert the cursor between the beginning `<style>` and end `</style>` tags.

4 Type `h1 { color:blue; }` and click in the Design view window to refresh the display.

The h1 heading now displays in blue. The rest of the text continues with the default formatting. Congratulations, you wrote your first CSS rule.

● **Note:** CSS does not require line breaks between rules, but breaks do make the code easier to read

● **Note:** Each declaration must end with a semicolon (;). The rule will not function at all without it and may break subsequent rules if it is missing.

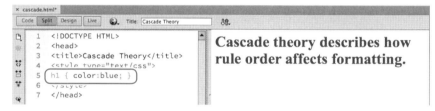

5 In Code view, insert the cursor at the end of the new CSS rule. Press Return/Enter to create a new line.

6 Type `h1 { color:red; }` and click in the Design view window to refresh the display.

The h1 heading now displays in red. The styling of the new rule superseded the formatting applied by the first. Realize that the two rules are identical except that they apply different colors: red or blue. Both rules want to format the same elements, but only one will be honored.

Obviously, the second rule won. Why? Because the second rule is the last one declared, which makes it the closest one to the actual content. In CSS, a style applied by one rule may be overridden by commands declared subsequently.

7 Select the h1 { color: blue; } rule.

8 Choose Edit > Cut.

9 Insert the cursor at the end of the h1 { color: red; } rule.

10 Choose Edit > Paste.

You have switched the order of the rules.

11 Click in the Design view window to refresh the preview display.

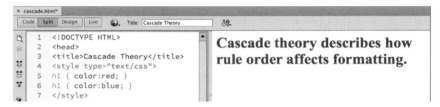

The headings now display in blue.

Both *proximity* and the *order* in which rules appear within the markup are powerful factors in how CSS is applied. When you try to determine which CSS rule will be honored and which formatting will be applied, browsers typically use the following order of hierarchy, with number 3 being the most powerful.

1 Browser defaults.

2 External or embedded (in the <head> section) style sheets. If both are present, the one declared last supersedes the earlier entry in conflicts.

3 Inline styles (within the HTML element itself).

Inheritance theory

The inheritance theory describes how one rule can be affected by one or more previously declared rules. Inheritance can affect rules of the same name as well as rules that format parent elements or elements that nest one inside another. Let's take a look at how inheritance influences CSS formatting.

1   Open **inheritance.html** from the Lesson03 folder. In Split view, observe the HTML code.

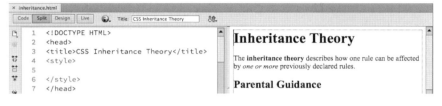

The webpage contains multiple headings and paragraph elements, as well as internal bold and italic all in HTML defaults. The page contains no CSS rules.

2   Insert the cursor between the beginning `<style>` and end `</style>` tags.

3   Type `h1 { font-family: Arial; }` and click in the Design view window to refresh the display.

The `h1` element appears in Arial. The other content remains formatted by default styling.

4   In the Code view, insert the cursor at the end of the `h1` rule. Press Enter/Return to create a new line.

5   Type `h1 { color: blue; }` and refresh the Design view display.

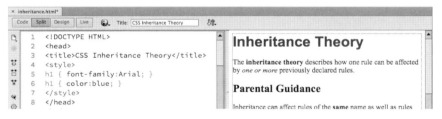

Now, there are two CSS rules that format the `<h1>` element. Can you tell, by looking at the Design view window, which of the rules is formatting the `<h1>` text? If you said *both* of them, you're the winner.

At first glance, you may think that there are two separate rules for `<h1>`. (And, technically, that's true.) But if you look closer, you'll see that the second rule doesn't contradict the first. It's not *resetting* the `color` attribute as you did in the previous exercise; it's declaring a new, additional attribute. In other words, since both rules do something different, both will be honored, or *inherited*, by the <h1> element. All <h1> elements will be formatted as blue and Arial.

Far from being a mistake or an unintended consequence, the ability to build rich and elaborate formatting using multiple rules is one of the most powerful and complex aspects of cascading style sheets.

6   Insert the cursor after the last h1 rule. Insert a new line in the code.

7   Type h2 { font-family: Arial; color: blue; } and click in the Design view window to refresh the display.

The h2 element appears in Arial and blue. Rules often contain multiple declarations.

8   After the h2 rule, enter the following code:

```
h3 { font-family: Arial; color: blue; }
p { font-family: Arial; color: blue; }
```

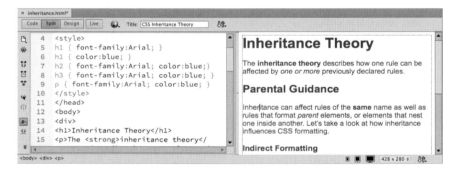

9   Refresh the Design view window display.

All the elements now display the same formatting—including the bold and italic text—but five rules were needed to format the entire page. Although CSS styling is far more efficient than the obsolete HTML-based method, inheritance can help you optimize your styling chores. For example, all the rules include the statement {color: blue; font-family: Arial; }. Avoid redundant code like this whenever possible. It adds to the size of the each webpage as well as to the download and processing time. By using inheritance, sometimes you can create the same effect with a single rule. One way is to apply styling to a parent element instead of to the elements themselves.

10 Create a new line in the <style> section and type the following code:

```
div { font-family: Arial; color: blue; }
```

This rule applies the style to the element that contains much of the content. If inheritance works as described, you should be able to delete some of the CSS rules.

11 Select and delete the rule: h2 { font-family: Arial; color: blue; }. Refresh the Design view window display.

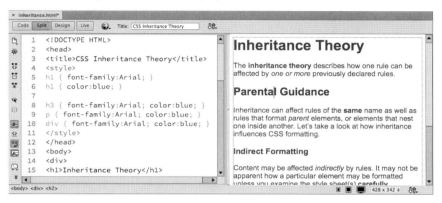

The h2 element remains formatted as blue Arial. The rule formatting the <div> element can even replace the two rules formatting the h1.

12 Select and delete both h1 rules. Refresh the Design view display.

The styling has not changed. The h1 and h2 elements are both contained within a <div> element and inherit the formatting correctly. But the page also includes some content outside the <div>. Can you guess what's going to happen if you delete the rules formatting the h3 and p elements?

13 Select and delete the h3 and p rules. Refresh the Design view display.

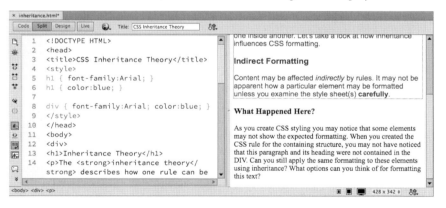

The content contained in the <div> remains formatted. The text outside the <div> has returned to the default formatting. This is the way inheritance works. You could simply recreate the rules that format all h3 and p elements, but there's an alternative. Can you figure out a way to still use inheritance to format all the content on the page the same way? Look carefully at the entire structure of the webpage.

If you thought about using the <body> element, you win again. The <body> element contains all the visible content on the webpage and therefore is the parent of all of them.

14 Change the rule selector from div to **body** and refresh the Design view display.

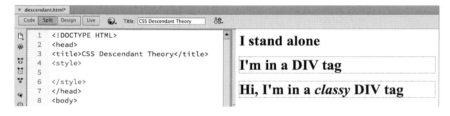

All the text displays in blue Arial. One rule is now formatting all the content at once: body { color: blue; font-family: Arial; }.

Descendant theory

The descendant theory describes how formatting can target a particular element based on its position relative to other elements. By constructing a selector using multiple elements, in addition to ID and class attributes, you can target the formatting to specific instances of text as it appears within your webpage. Let's take a look at how descendant selectors influence CSS formatting.

1 Open **descendant.html** from the Lesson03 folder. In Split view, observe the structure of the HTML content.

The page contains three h1 elements. The elements appear in three different ways: alone, within a <div>, and within a <div> that features an applied class attribute. You will learn how to create descendant CSS rules that will target styling to each element.

2 In Code view, insert the cursor within the <style> </style> element.

3   Type the following code: `h1 { font-family: Verdana; color: blue; }` and refresh the Design view display.

All three `h1` elements display in blue Verdana. Although two of the headings appear in separate, stand-alone `<div>` elements, they still respond to the CSS styling applied by the `h1` rule. In other words, a rule formatting `h1` elements formats all such elements on the page no matter where they appear. But, by using descendant selectors you can target CSS styling to specific relationships by using that very HTML structure.

4   Create a new line after the new `h1` rule and type the following code:

```
div h1 { font-family: Impact; color: red; }
```

Inserting the `h1` immediately after the `<div>` element in the selector tells the browser to format `h1` elements that are children, or *descendants*, of `<div>` elements. Remember, *child* elements are elements contained or nested within another element.

5   Refresh the Design view display.

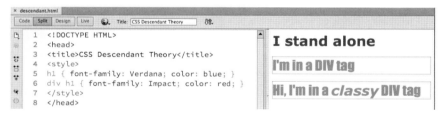

Both headings that appear within `<div>` elements display now in red Impact. By adding the text **div** to the selector, you are telling the browser to display all `h1` elements contained within `div` elements in red Impact. The first rule is still being inherited, but wherever the two rules conflict the descendant rule wins, overriding and applying its formatting instead.

So far, you've learned that you can create a CSS rule that formats specific HTML elements and rules that can target specific HTML structures or relationships. In some instances, you may want to apply unique formatting to an element that is formatted by an existing rule. In such cases, you could use CSS classes or ID attributes to differentiate the element. In our example, the last `h1` is assigned a class attribute of `product`; by adding the attribute value to the selector name, you can target the CSS styling to the specific element.

6   Create a new line after the `div h1` rule. Type the following code:

`div.product h1 { font-family: "Times New Roman"; color: green; }`

and refresh the Design view display.

The last heading appears in green Times New Roman. By adding the text `div.product` to the selector, you are telling the browser to display all `h1` elements contained within `div` elements that have a class attribute of `"product"` in green Times New Roman. In CSS syntax, the period "." refers to a *class* attribute, the hash "#" mark means *ID*. Again, what's important to understand here is that the other two CSS rules are still being inherited. It's just that the descendant selector based on the class attribute is more powerful. It overrides any conflicting commands and applies its formatting instead. Why? We'll explain that later.

Understanding descendant selectors

CSS formatting can be very confusing for designers coming from the print world. These designers are accustomed to applying styles directly to text and objects one at a time. In some cases, styles can be based on one another, but this relationship is intentional. On the other hand, CSS formatting of one element can overlap or influence another unintentionally.

Thinking of it as if the elements are formatting themselves may be helpful. Formatting is not intrinsic to the element, but to the entire page and the way the code is structured. You don't apply the formatting to the element per se, as much as the elements adopt styling from their position within the code. The following exercise is designed to help you understand this concept.

● **Note:** The best way to select HTML elements is to use the tag selectors appearing at the bottom of the document window.

1   In the Code view window, select the entire first `<h1>` element, including the opening and closing tags.

2   Choose Edit > Copy.

3   Insert the cursor after the closing tag of the code `<h1>I'm in a DIV tag</h1>`.

4 Choose Edit > Paste. Click in the Design view window to refresh the display.

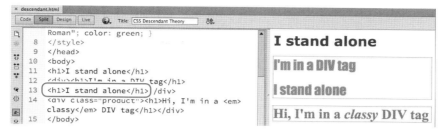

The new `<h1>` element appears, formatted as red Impact, exactly like the other `<h1>` element within the same `<div>`. What happened to blue Verdana? The CSS automatically differentiates stand-alone h1 elements from those that appear within a `<div>`. In other words, you don't have to apply a special format or change an existing one. Just move the element into the proper structure or location within the code, and it formats itself. Cool. Let's try it again.

5 In the Code view window, insert the cursor after the closing tag of `<h1>Hi, I'm in a <em>classy</em> DIV tag</h1>`.

6 Choose Edit > Paste. Click in the Design view window to refresh the display.

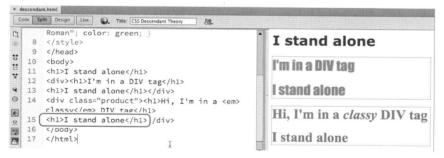

The `<h1>` element appears, formatted as green Times New Roman. Once again the pasted text matches the formatting applied to the other h1 element within the `<div>`, its original styling ignored altogether. But this behavior also works in reverse. You can copy the text inside the div elements and paste it elsewhere; it will automatically adopt the styling appropriate for that structure or location.

7 Select the code `<h1>Hi, I'm in a <em>classy</em> DIV tag</h1>` and copy it.

8   Paste the code two times, once after the first h1 element and then into the second <div>. Refresh the Design view display.

The h1 elements automatically adopt the formatting appropriate for their position within the page structure. The ability to separate the content from its presentation is an important concept in modern web design. It allows you great freedom in moving content from page to page and structure to structure without worrying about the effects of residual or latent formatting. Since the formatting doesn't reside with the element itself, it's free to adapt instantly to its new surroundings.

Specificity theory

Specificity describes how browsers determine what formatting to apply when two or more rules conflict. Some refer to this as *weight*—giving certain rules more priority based on order (cascade), proximity, inheritance, and descendant relationships. Such conflicts are the bane of most web designers' existence and can waste hours of time in troubleshooting errors in CSS formatting. Let's take a look at how specificity affects the weight of some sample rules.

1   Open **specificity.html** from the Lesson03 folder. In Split view, observe the CSS code and the structure of the HTML content. Then, note the appearance of the text in the Design view window.

The <head> section of the file has three CSS rules. All of them potentially could format the <h1> element on the page. But, at the moment, none of the rules is actually formatting the text.

Do you see the slash and asterisk (/*) at the beginning of the CSS markup? This notation is used to create a comment within CSS code and effectively disables the rules that follow. The commented code ends with a similar notation reversing the order of the slash and the asterisk (*/). In Dreamweaver, commented code usually appears dimmed.

Also, note that the opening tag of the <h1> element features an attribute: @style. This inline CSS style markup has been disabled by appending the @ symbol to the beginning of the word. You can re-enable all the CSS styling by merely deleting the /* and */ notations, along with the @ symbol within the attribute.

But before you do this, can you determine—based on the syntax and order of the rules—what formatting will apply to the sample text? For example, will the text appear in Times New Roman, Impact, or Verdana? Will it be blue, red, green, or orange? Let's see.

2 Select the notation /* at the beginning of the CSS code and delete it.

3 Select the notation */ at the end of the CSS code and delete it.

4 Select the @ symbol in the <h1> attribute and delete it.

5 Click in the Design view window to refresh the display. Save the file as **myspecificity.html**.

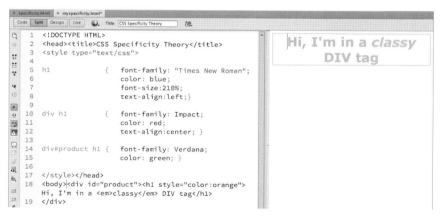

Did you say the text was going to be formatted by all the rules? If you did, then you won, and you go to the head of the class. In fact, each rule contributes some aspect of the final formatting. Where two or more rules conflict, specificity spells out which rule or portion of a rule wins.

For example, inline styles usually trump formatting applied by other means, but the inline style attribute supplies only the final color to this text. The `div#product` rule is the next most specific and supplies the final font-family. The `div` `h1` rule then supplies the text alignment, and the `h1` rule supplies the font-size. As this file demonstrates, CSS rules often don't work alone. They may style more than one HTML element at a time and may overlap or inherit styling from one another.

Each of the theories described here has a role to play in how CSS styling is applied through your webpage and across your site. When the style sheet is loaded, the browser will use the following hierarchy—with number 4 being the most specific—to determine how the styles are applied, especially when rules conflict:

1 Cascade

2 Inheritance

3 Descendant structure

4 Specificity

Of course, knowing this hierarchy doesn't help much when you are faced with a CSS conflict on a page with dozens or perhaps hundreds of rules. In such cases, Dreamweaver comes to the rescue with a fantastic feature named Code Navigator.

Code Navigator

Code Navigator is a Dreamweaver editing tool that allows you to instantly inspect an HTML element and assess its CSS-based formatting. When activated, it displays all the embedded and externally linked CSS rules that have some role in formatting an element, and it lists them in the order of their cascade application and specificity. Code Navigator works in both Code view and Design view.

1 If necessary, open **myspecificity.html** as modified in the previous exercise. In Split view, observe the CSS code and the structure of the HTML content.

Although this file is simple in nature, it features three CSS rules that may format the <h1> element. In an actual webpage, the possibility of styling conflicts grows with each new rule added. But with Code Navigator, sussing out such problems becomes child's play.

2 In Design view, insert the cursor in the heading text.

The Code Navigator (✳) icon provides instant access to Code Navigator.

3 Click the Code Navigator icon or press Ctrl-Alt-N/Cmd-Option-N.

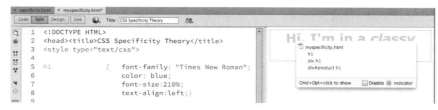

● **Note:** You can also access Code Navigator by right-clicking the element and choosing it from the context menu or by choosing View > Code Navigator.

A small window displays a list of three CSS rules that apply to this heading. If you position the cursor over each rule, Dreamweaver displays any properties formatted and their values. Unfortunately, it doesn't show styling applied via inline styles, so you'll have to calculate the effect of inline styles in your head. Otherwise, the sequence of rules in the list indicates both their cascade order and their specificity. When rules conflict, rules farther down in the list override rules that are higher up. Remember, elements may inherit styling from one or more rules, and default styling—that is not overridden—may still play a role in the final presentation. Code Navigator doesn't display what, if any, default styling characteristics may be in effect.

● **Note:** Code Navigator doesn't display inline CSS rules. Since most CSS styling is not applied this way, it's not much of a limitation, but you should still be aware of this blind spot as you work with your pages.

The `div.product h1` rule appears at the bottom of the Code Navigator window, indicating that its specifications are the most powerful ones styling this element. But many factors can influence which of the rules may win. Sometimes it's simply the order (cascade) in which rules are declared in the style sheet that determines which one is actually applied. As you saw earlier, changing the order of rules can often affect how the rules work. There's a simple exercise you can perform to determine whether a rule is winning because of cascade or specificity.

4 In the Code view window, select the entire `div#product h1` rule and choose Edit > Cut.

5 Insert the cursor in front of the `h1` rule.

6 Choose Edit > Paste. Press Enter/Return, if necessary, to insert a line break.

7 Click in the Design view window to refresh the display.

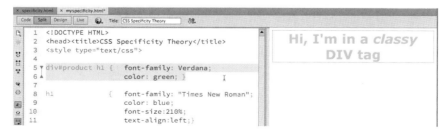

The styling did not change.

8 In Code view, insert the cursor into the text of the <h1> element. Activate Code Navigator.

Although the rule was moved to the top of the style sheet, the display of rules did not change, because the div#product h1 rule has a higher specificity than the other two rules. In this instance, it would win no matter where it was placed in the code, but its specificity can easily be changed by modifying the selector.

9 In Code view, select and delete the #product ID notation in the selector.

10 Click in the Design view window to refresh the display.

Did you notice how the styling changed?

11 Insert the cursor in the heading and activate Code Navigator.

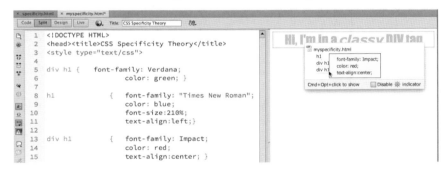

By removing the ID notation from its selector, the rule now has equal value to the other div h1 rule, but since this rule is the last one declared in the code, it now takes precedence by virtue of its cascade position. Is it starting to make more sense? Don't worry—it will over time. Until that time, just remember that the rule appearing last in Code Navigator has the most influence on any particular element.

CSS Designer

Code Navigator was introduced in Dreamweaver CS4 and has been an invaluable aid for troubleshooting CSS formatting. But a new tool may supersede it in the hearts of the Dreamweaver faithful. The CSS Designer provides all the features of Code Navigator with a couple of additional benefits.

Like Code Navigator, CSS Designer displays all the rules that pertain to any selected element and allows you to see all the properties affected, but with several key advantages. With Code Navigator you still have to access and assess the effect of all the individual rules to determine the actual final effect. Since some elements can be affected by a dozen or more rules, this can be a daunting task for even a veteran web coder. CSS Designer eliminates this pressure altogether by providing a separate Properties panel that computes the final CSS display for you. It also shows you the effect of *inline* styling, which Code Navigator ignores altogether.

If this feature wasn't enough all by itself, CSS Designer also allows you to access CSS rules individually to edit existing properties or add new ones much more efficiently than before. It's a great addition to the program.

1   Open **specificity.html**. Save the file as **myspecificity2.html**.

2   If necessary, switch to Split view.

3   In the `<style>` section, delete the /* and */ markup to remove the commenting from the CSS code. Delete the @ symbol from the inline style attribute. Save the file.

By removing the comment markup, the CSS styling becomes active again.

4   If necessary, choose Window > CSS Designer.

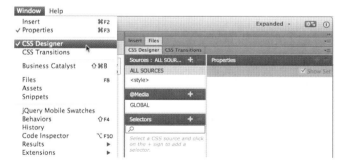

The CSS Designer appears. It displays four panes: Sources, @Media, Selectors, and Properties. At the moment, the windows are mostly blank.

5   Insert the cursor in the word "Hi".

The Selectors pane of the CSS Designer displays a list of the rules and properties applied to or inherited by the h1 element.

6   In the CSS Selectors pane, click the h1 rule.

The Properties pane of CSS Designer displays a list of all the properties that you can style for this element. This can be confusing as well as inefficient. For one thing, it'll be difficult to identify the properties actually assigned. Luckily, you can limit the display to only the ones applied.

● **Note:** The Show Set option may be selected by default.

7   At the top of the Properties pane, click the Show Set option to enable it.

When enabled, the Properties pane shows only the items that have been set in a CSS rule and that affect the selected element.

● **Note:**
The COMPUTED option will show styling results only when the cursor is inserted in a styled element on the page. Otherwise it will be blank.

8   Select each rule that appears in the CSS Selectors pane and observe the properties set by each one. To see the expected result of all the rules combined, select the COMPUTED option.

The COMPUTED option analyzes all the CSS rules and generates a list of properties that should be displayed by any browser or HTML reader. By displaying a list of pertinent CSS rules and then computing how the CSS should render, the CSS Designer does the Code Navigator one step better. But, it doesn't stop there. Whereas Code Navigator allows you to select a rule to edit it in Code view, the CSS Designer lets you edit the CSS properties right inside the panel itself. And, best of all, it can even compute inline styles, too.

9 Select COMPUTED from the CSS Selectors pane. In the Properties pane, change the `color:` property from `orange` to `purple`. Press Return/Enter to complete the change.

The text displays in purple. What you may not have noticed is that the change was actually entered directly in the rule that contributed the styling. In this case, the color was applied by the inline style.

10 In Code view, observe the inline style property.

As you can see, the color was changed within the inline code. The CSS Designer is like an amalgam of the Code Navigator and the old CSS Styles panel. In upcoming exercises, you'll get the chance to experience all aspects of the CSS Designer as you learn more about cascading style sheets.

Formatting objects

You may think that CSS styling of text is perplexing and difficult to understand. But, in fact, the last concept you'll explore in this lesson is even more complex and prone to display inconsistencies and error: object formatting. Consider object formatting as specifications directed at modifying an element's size, background, borders, margins, padding, and positioning. Since CSS can redefine any HTML element, object formatting basically can be applied to any tag, although it's most commonly directed at the `<div>` element and other containers.

CSS can control all of these default constraints and lets you size, style, and position elements almost any way you want them.

Size is one of the most basic specifications for an HTML element. CSS can control both the width and the height of an element with varying degrees of success. All specifications can be expressed in *absolute* terms (pixels, inches, points, centimeters, and so on) or in *relative* terms (percentages, ems, or exs).

Width

Setting the width of an HTML element is simple. Let's take a look at an example.

1   Open **width.html** from the Lesson03 folder. Save the file as **mywidth.html**.

2   View the page in Split view, and observe the CSS code and HTML structure.

    By default, block elements occupy 100 percent of the width of the browser window.

Fixed Widths

The file contains four `<div>` elements that have some basic CSS formatting applied but no `width` or `height` specifications. Each has a custom class assigned to it so you can format them individually. As block elements they currently occupy 100 percent of the width of the browser window, by default. CSS allows you to control the width by applying absolute (fixed) or relative measurements.

1   If necessary, open **mywidth.html.** In the Code view, insert the cursor in the `<style>` section after the existing `div` rule.

2   Type `.box2 { width: 200px; }` and press Return/Enter to create a new line. Save the file.

3   If necessary, refresh the Design view display.

    Box 2 now occupies only 200 pixels in width; the other boxes are unchanged. By using pixels you have set the width of Box 2 by an absolute, or *fixed*, measurement, which means the box will maintain its width regardless of changes to the browser window or screen orientation.

4   Select the dividing line between Code and Design view and drag it to the left and right and observe how the `<div>` elements react.

Boxes 1, 3, and 4 adapt automatically to the change in screen size displaying at the full width automatically. Box 2 remains 200 pixels in width no matter what size the screen assumes. Fixed widths are very popular all over the Internet, but in some cases, you'll want elements to change or adapt as the screen size does. CSS provides three methods for setting widths using *relative* measurements: em, ex, and percentage (%).

Relative widths

Relative measurements set by percentage (%) are the easiest to define and understand. The width is set in relation to the size of the screen: 100% is the entire width of the screen, 50% is half, and so on. If the screen or browser window changes, so does the width of the element. Percentage-based designs are popular because they can adapt instantly to different displays and devices. But they are also problematic because changing the width of a page layout dramatically can also play havoc with your content. In response to these problems, new properties of `min-width` and `max-width` were created to limit the amount of change permissible.

1   If necessary, open **mywidth.html**. Insert the cursor after the `.box2` rule and type the following code: `.box3 { width:50%; }`

2   Press Return/Enter to create a new line and save the file. Refresh the Design view display.

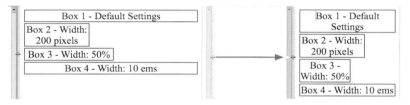

Box 3 displays at 50 percent of the width of the screen. It will adapt automatically to any changes to the screen size.

3   Select the dividing line between Code and Design view and drag it to the left and right and observe how the `<div>` elements react.

Box 2 remains at a fixed width. Box 3 scales larger and smaller, continuing to occupy 50 percent of the screen width no matter what size it becomes, even to the point that the text wraps within the element several times. Note how when the `<div>` shrinks to the size of the largest word it will finally stop scaling. Many designers forego the use of percentage-based settings for this reason. Although they like that `<div>` scales to fit the browser window, they'd prefer it to stop scaling when it affects the content detrimentally. This is the reason for which the property `min-width` was created.

4   Insert the cursor after the `width:50%;` notation and type `min-width: 175px;` and save the file.

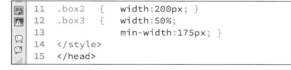

```
11   .box2    {    width:200px; }
12   .box3    {    width:50%;
13                 min-width:175px; }
14   </style>
15   </head>
```

By setting `min-width` it prevents the element from scaling smaller than 175 pixels. Note how the `min-width` specification uses units in "pixels." When combining the `width` setting with `min-width` or `max-width`, using differing measurement units is recommended.

5   Refresh the Design view display, drag the dividing line between Code and Design view left and right, and observe how the `<div>` elements react.

Box 3 displays at 50 percent of the screen width until you scale it smaller than 175 pixels. When the screen becomes narrower than 175 pixels, Box 3 stops scaling and remains at a fixed width of 175 pixels. You can also add the property `max-width` to limit scaling at the upper end.

● **Note:** You can type CSS declarations on one line or insert line breaks between properties. The styling works the same either way.

6   Insert the cursor after the `min-width` property, type `max-width:500px;` and save the file.

```
11   .box2   {   width:200px; }
12   .box3   {   width:50%;
13               min-width:175px;
14               max-width:500px; }
15   </style>
```

7   Refresh the Design view display and drag the dividing line between Code and Design view left and right.

Box 3 displays at 50 percent of the screen between the widths of 175 pixels and 500 pixels where it stops scaling at the specified dimension.

It's all relative, or not

Ems and exs are kind of a hybrid cross between fixed and relative systems. The em is a measurement that is more familiar to print designers. It's based on the size of the typeface and font being used. In other words, use a large font and the em gets bigger; use a small font and the em gets smaller. It even changes based on whether the font is a condensed or expanded face. This type of measurement is typically used to build text-based components, like navigation menus, where you want the structure to adapt to user actions that may increase or decrease the font size on a site.

1   If necessary, open **mywidth.html**. Insert the cursor after the `.box3` rule and type the following code: `.box4 { width:10em; }`

```
11   .box2   {   width:200px; }
12   .box3   {   width:50%;
13               min-width:175px;
14               max-width:500px; }
15   .box4   {   width:10em; }
16   </style>
17   </head>
```

2 Press Return/Enter to create a new line and save the file. Refresh the Design view display.

Box 4 displays at the width of 10 ems. Although ems are considered a relative measure, they work differently from widths set in percentages.

3 Drag the dividing line between Code and Design view left and right and observe how the `<div>` elements react.

Box 4 displays like it's set with a fixed measurement: The box doesn't change size as you make the screen bigger and smaller. That's because the "relative" nature of the measure isn't based on screen size but on the "font" size.

4 In the body rule, change the `font-size: 200%;` property to `font-size: 300%;` and refresh the Design view display.

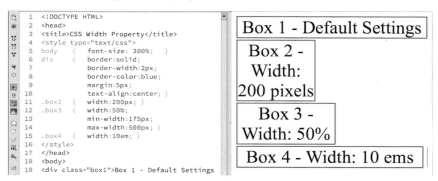

Widths specified in ems allow your page elements to adapt to user requests for increases or decreases in font size.

The text scales larger. In Box 2 and Box 3 the text has to wrap to fit within each `<div>`. Note how Box 4 scales larger to accommodate the larger text. By using em measurements you can build containers that scale automatically to adapt to user requests for larger font sizes via browser controls.

But there's one small caveat when you use ems. The measurement is based on the base font size of the nearest parent element, which means it can change any time the font-size changes within the element's HTML structure. The size of the em can also be influenced by inheritance.

5 In the div rule, add the following notation: `font-size:20px;`

6 Save the file and refresh the Display view.

The text in all the `<div>` elements displays at 20 pixels, but only Box 4 changes width to reflect the size of 10 ems based on 20 pixels. If you want to ensure a certain width, set the `font-size` directly on the element. This is suggested even if the element contains no text at all.

7　In the `.box4` rule, add the `font-size:40px;` notation.

```
10          text-align:center;
11          font-size:20px; }
12 .box2  { width:200px; }
13 .box3  { width:50%;
14          min-width:175px;
15          max-width:500px; }
16 .box4  { width:10em; font-size:40px; }
17 </style>
18 </head>
```

```
                    Box 1 - Default Settings
Box 2 - Width: 200
       pixels
    Box 3 - Width: 50%

Box 4 - Width: 10 ems
```

Box 4 enlarges to adapt to the new larger font specification. If the specification uses a fixed unit, the width should not react to other changes in other elements.

Height

Height settings are not specified as frequently as width. That's mainly because the height of an element or component is determined by its content, plus any margins and padding that may be assigned. In some cases, setting a fixed height could result in undesirable effects, truncating or clipping text or pictures. Most designs actually allow the height of an element to fluctuate freely to the size and type of content it contains. At times you may want to set the height of an element directly; in that case you can use either fixed or relative measurements.

Fixed height

Ideally, you should be able to specify the height of all elements the same way you do the width. Unfortunately, the reality is not so simple. Past browser support for the `height` property was not consistent or reliable. Today, modern browsers shouldn't present many surprises if you're working in absolute measurements, like pixels, points, inches, and so on. Relative measurements in ems or exs probably won't disappoint either. But measurements in percentages require a small workaround, or hack, to make most browsers honor them.

1　Open **height.html** from the Lesson03 folder. Save the file as **myheight.html**. Display the file in Split view, and observe the CSS and HTML code.

```
4  <style type="text/css">
5  <!--
6  body  { font-size:200% }
7  div   { border:solid;
8          border-width:2px;
9          border-color:blue;
10         margin:5px;
11         text-align:center; }
12 -->
13 </style>
```

```
      Box 1 - Default Settings
      Box 2 - Height: 100 pixels
      Box 3 - Height: 5 ems
      Box 4 - Height: 50%
```

The file contains four `<div>` elements that have a width specification but no height. Heights set in fixed units are the most predictable.

2 In Code view, insert the cursor after the `div` rule in the `<style>` section.

3 Create a new line, if necessary, and type `.box2 { height:150px; }`

4 Save the file and refresh the Display view.

Box 2 displays at a fixed height of 150px. The other `<div>` elements display at a height determined by the amount and the size of content they contain. The height of these elements is not affected by the size of the browser window.

5 Drag the bottom edge of the program or document window up and down to adjust the vertical size, and then right and left to observe how the `<div>` elements react.

None of the elements react to the changing size of the window. You'll get a similar response using em measurements.

6 Insert the cursor after the `.box2` rule. Create a new line if necessary and type

`.box3 { height:5em; }`

7 Save the file and refresh the Display view.

Box 3 displays at a fixed height of 5 ems, based on the default font size. Remember ems, like measurements in pixels, don't react to changes in the screen size.

8 Drag the bottom edge of the program or document window up and down to adjust the vertical size and right and left to observe how the `<div>` elements react.

Like Box 2, Box 3 maintains its height of 5 ems regardless of changes to the screen. But ems do react to changes in the font size.

9 In the `body` rule, change the `font-size: 200%;` property to `font-size: 300%;` save the file and refresh the Design view display.

Box 3 expands in height to reflect the change of the base-font size. As with width, heights set in ems will also change any time the font-size changes within the element's structure.

Relative or not, here we come

So far, so good. The height property seems to be pretty straightforward and works as expected in the first three elements. But Box 4 is the one that's going to cause all the trouble. Let's set it to a height of 50% and see what happens.

1 If necessary, open **mywidth.html.** In the body rule, change the font-size: 300%; property to font-size: 100%; and then save the file. Refresh the Design view display.

The boxes resize to accommodate the new base font size.

2 Insert the cursor after the .box3 rule. Create a new line, if necessary, and type .box4 { height:50%; }

3 Save the file and refresh the Display view.

Nothing changes. You probably expected it to be taking up half the height of the screen, right? But, as you can see in the Design view window, it's no taller than Box 1. What's the problem?

Most browsers, and even the Dreamweaver Design view window, ignore heights set in percentages. The reasons for this have to do with how browsers calculate the size of the page window. Basically, browsers calculate width but don't calculate height. This behavior doesn't affect fixed measurements or measurements set in ems or exs, but it does mess up percentages. To make Dreamweaver and most browsers honor percentage-based heights, you can use a simple CSS hack.

4 Insert the cursor at the beginning of the CSS <style> section.

5 Type html, body { height: 100%; } and save the file.

Adding the height property to the root and body elements of your webpage gives the browser the information it needs to calculate any heights set in percentages. But to see the results, you'll have to use Live view or preview the page in an actual browser.

6 Click the Live view button to enable Live view.

```
1   <!DOCTYPE HTML>
2   <head>
3   <title>CSS Height Property</title>
4   <style type="text/css">
5   <!--
6   html, body { height: 100% }
7   body    {   font-size:100% }
8   div     {   border:solid;
9               border-width:2px;
10              border-color:blue;
11              margin:5px;
12              text-align:center; }
13  .box2   {   height:150px; }
14  .box3   {   height:5em; }
15  .box4   {   height:50%; }
16  -->
17  </style>
18  </head>
19  <body>
20  <div class="box1">Box 1 - Default
    Settings</div>
21  <div class="box2">Box 2 - Height:
    100 pixels</div>
22  <div class="box3">Box 3 - Height: 5
    ems</div>
23  <div class="box4">Box 4 - Height:
    50%</div>
24  </body>
25  </html>
```

Box 1 - Default Settings

Box 2 - Height: 100 pixels

Box 3 - Height: 5 ems

Box 4 - Height: 50%

● **Note:** In most applications, height won't be strictly observed by any element. By default, it is intended to be a fluid specification that allows an element to automatically adapt to the space requirements of its content.

Box 4 now occupies 50 percent of the height of the Design view window.

Although browser support is much better today, it's vital to test all your design settings in all the popular browsers to ensure that the pages display properly.

Margins and padding

Margins create spacing outside an element—between one element and another; padding adds spacing between the content of an element and its border, whether or not it's visible. The effective use of such spacing is vital in the overall design of your webpage.

1 Open **margins_padding.html** from the Lesson03 folder.

2 Save the file as **mymargins_padding.html**.

3 Display the file in Split view, and observe the CSS and HTML code.

Sample Generic Div Element
Sample Generic Div Element
Sample Generic Div Element

Heading 1

Heading 2

Heading 3

Heading 4

Heading 5

Heading 6

Paragraph text and headings come with default margin specifications already applied by default. The spacing between elements can be controled using CSS styling. Borders were applied to all HTML elements on this page so you could see graphically the effects margin and padding settings have on each type of element.

- HTML lists can be constructed using three elements
- The tag <ol> designates an ordered list, using automatically numbered entries.
- The tag <ul> designates an unordered list, using automatically bulleted entries.
- The tag <li> designates individual items within the list.

The file contains several `<div>` elements stacked one on top of the other, sample text headings, paragraph, and even list elements. All the elements display the default HTML formatting for margins and padding. Borders have been applied to all the elements to make the spacing effects easier to see.

Adding margins

To add spacing between the `<div>` elements, you can add a margin specification.

1 Insert the cursor in the CSS section of the code. Type `div { margin: 30px; }`

2 Click to refresh the Design view window.

```
1   <!DOCTYPE HTML>
2   <head>
3   <title>CSS Margins and Padding</title>
4   <style type="text/css">
5   <!--
6   * { border: 2px solid #06C; }
7   div    { margin: 30px; }
8   -->
9   </style>
10  <link href="lesson03_styles.css" rel=
```

Sample Generic Div Element

Sample Generic Div Element

Sample Generic Div Element

Heading 1

The `<div>` elements are now spaced 30 pixels apart.

By using the `margin: 30px` notation, you added 30 pixels to all four sides, but don't expect to see 60 pixels between the elements. Spacing doesn't always add up. When two adjacent elements both have margins, the settings don't combine; instead, browsers use only the larger of any two settings. Dreamweaver can give you a visual display of the new setting.

3 In Design view, click the edge of one of the `<div>` elements to select it.

Design view highlights the element and displays a hashed pattern to show the margin specifications.

Adding padding

Padding is used to put spacing between an element's content and its border.

1 In the `div` rule, insert the cursor after `margin: 30px;`

2 Type `padding: 30px;` and save the file.

3 Refresh the Design view window.

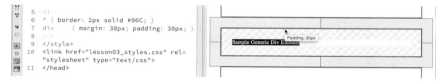

You can see 30 pixels of padding appear within each `<div>` element.

Since padding is applied within the element boundaries, it will combine with margin settings to affect the overall spacing that appears between elements. Padding can also affect the specified width of an element and must be factored into the design of your page components.

Unlike the `<div>` element, text elements, such as `<p>`, `<h1>` through `<h6>`, `<ol>`, and `<ul>`, already have margin settings applied to them, as you can see from the sample text within the page. Many designers abhor these default specifications, especially because they vary among browsers. Instead, they start off most projects by purposely removing these settings in a technique that's called *normalization*. In other words, they declare a list of common elements and reset their default specifications to more desirable, consistent settings, as you'll do now.

4 In the CSS section, create a new line after the `div` rule.

5 Type `p, h1, h2, h3, h4, h5, h6, li { margin: 0px }` and save the file.

The comma means "and" in CSS syntax, meaning you want to format all the tags listed.

6 Refresh the Design view window.

```
1  <!DOCTYPE HTML>
2  <head>
3  <title>CSS Margins and Padding</title>
4  <style type="text/css">
5  <!--
6  * { border: 2px solid #06C; }
7  div     { margin: 30px; padding: 30px; }
8  p, h1, h2, h3, h4, h5, h6, li { margin: 0px }
9  -->
10 </style>
11 <link href="lesson03_styles.css" rel=
```

Heading 1
Heading 2
Heading 3
Heading 4
Heading 5
Heading 6

Paragraph text and headings come with default margin specifications already applied by default. The spacing between elements can be controled using CSS styling. Borders were applied to all HTML elements on this page so you could see graphically the effects margin and padding settings have on each type of element.

The text elements now display without the default spacing. Using zero margins may be a bit extreme for your own tastes, but you get the picture. As you become more comfortable with CSS and webpage design, you can develop your own default specifications and implement them in this way.

Positioning

By default, all elements start at the top of the browser screen and appear consecutively one after the other from left to right, top to bottom. Block elements generate their own line or paragraph breaks; inline elements appear at the point of insertion.

CSS can break all these default constraints and let you place elements almost anywhere you want them to be. As with other object formatting, positioning can be specified in *relative* terms (such as left, right, center, and so on) or by *absolute* coordinates measured in pixels, inches, centimeters, or other standard measurement systems. Using CSS, you can even layer one element above or below another to create amazing graphical effects. By using positioning commands carefully, you can create a variety of page layouts, including popular multicolumn designs.

1 Open **positioning.html** from the Lesson03 folder. Save the file as **mypositioning.html**. Display the file in Split view, and observe the CSS and HTML code.

```
1  <!DOCTYPE HTML>
2  <head>
3  <title>CSS Element Positioning
   </title>
4  <style type="text/css">
5  <!--
6  div {
7      width: auto;
8      float: none;
9      height: 70px;
10     text-align: center;
11     border: 1px solid #06C;
12     margin: 5px;
13     vertical-align: middle;
14     padding-top: 50px;
15 }
16 .box2 { float:       }
17
```

Box 1 - Default Settings

Box 2 - Float: Left

Box 3 - Float: Right

The file contains three <div> elements; they are stacked one on top of the other and occupy the full width of the Design view window, in the default manner of all block elements. Using CSS, you can control the placement of these elements and even place them side-by-side. But first, you'll have to reduce the width of the elements so that more than one item can fit on the same line.

2 In the div rule, change the width:auto; property to width:30%; and save the file.

3 Refresh the Design view display.

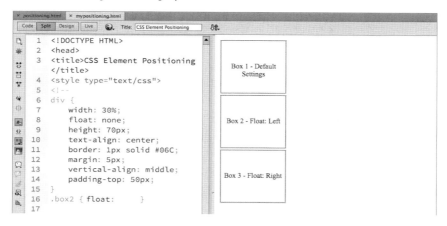

The <div> elements resize but remain stacked. Remember, block elements always stack no matter how small they may be. Several methods can change this behavior, but the *float* method is by far the most popular.

4 In the div rule, change the float:none; property to float:left; and save the file.

5 Refresh the Design view display.

Tip: If your boxes do not appear side by side, open the Design view window wider to provide more space.

All three <div> elements now display in a single row, side by side. Using class attributes, you can control each <div> individually.

6   In the div rule, change the property float:left; to float:none;

7   In the .box2 rule, change the property float:none; to float:left;

8   In the .box3 rule, change the property float:none; to float:right;

9   Save the file. Refresh the Design view window.

The page now contains a mix of default and float specifications. Box 1 displays on a line of its own in the default manner. Box 2 appears on the next line, aligned to the left side of the screen as specified. Box 3 appears on the right side of the screen, but on the same line as Box 2.

In subsequent lessons, you will learn how to combine different float attributes with various width, height, margin, and padding settings to create sophisticated layouts for your website designs.

Unfortunately, as powerful as CSS positioning seems to be, it is the one aspect of CSS that is most prone to misinterpretation by the various browsers in use today. Commands and formatting that work fine in one browser can be translated differently or totally ignored—with tragic results—in another. In fact, specifications that work fine on one page of your website can fail on another page containing a different mix of code elements.

Borders and backgrounds

Each element can feature four individually formatted borders (top, bottom, left, and right). These are handy for creating boxed elements, but you can also place them at the top or bottom (or both) of paragraphs in place of <hr/> (horizontal rule) elements to separate text areas.

1   Open **borders.html** from the Lesson03 folder. Display the file in Split view, and observe the CSS and HTML code.

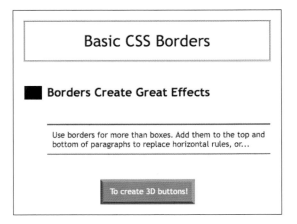

The file contains four examples of text elements formatted with varying border specifications. As you can see, borders can be used for creating boxes and other effects. Here you see them used as graphical accents to paragraphs and even to simulate a three-dimensional button effect.

Note that there is no extraneous markup within the actual content; all the effects are generated by CSS code alone. That means you can quickly adjust, turn on and off effects, and you can move the content easily without having to worry about graphical elements cluttering up the code.

By default, all element backgrounds are transparent, but CSS enables you to format them with colors, images, or both. If both are used, the image will appear above, or in front of, the color. This behavior allows you to use an image with a transparent background to create layered graphical effects. If the image fills the visible space or is set to repeat, it may obscure the color entirely.

2   Open **backgrounds.html** from the Lesson03 folder. Display the file in Split view, and observe the CSS and HTML code.

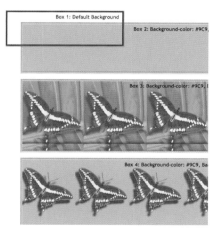

The file contains several examples of CSS background effects. Borders have been added to the `<div>` elements to make the effects easier to see.

Box 1 displays the default HTML transparent background. Box 2 depicts a background with a solid color. Box 3 shows a background image that repeats in both directions along the x-axis and y-axis. It also features a background color, but it's completely obscured by the repeating image. Box 4 also shows a background image, but its transparency and drop-shadow effect allow you to see the background color around the edges of the image.

Be sure to fully test any background treatments. In some applications, CSS background specifications are not fully supported or are supported inconsistently.

CSS3 overview and support

The Internet doesn't stand still for long. Technologies and standards are evolving and changing constantly. The members of the W3C have been working diligently to adapt the web to the latest realities, including powerful mobile devices, large flat-panel displays, and HD video—all of which seem to get better and cheaper every day. This is the urgency currently driving the development of HTML5 and CSS3.

Although these standards have not been officially adopted, browser vendors are racing to implement many of the features and techniques. The current plan by W3C is to formally adopt HTML5 and CSS3 sometime in 2014. In the meantime, if you feel adventuresome and would like to live on the edge, Dreamweaver won't leave you in the lurch. While adoption in the industry is continuing, Dreamweaver hasn't waited either. The latest version provides many new features based on these evolving standards, including ample support for the current mix of HTML5 elements and CSS3 formatting. As new features and capabilities are developed, you can count on Adobe to add them to the program as quickly as possible.

As you work through the upcoming lessons, you will be introduced to many of these new and exciting techniques and actually implement many of the more stable HTML5 and CSS3 features within your own sample pages.

CSS3 features and effects

There are over two dozen new features in CSS3. Many are ready now and have been implemented in all the modern browsers; others are still experimental and are supported less fully. Among the new features, you will find

- Rounded corners and border effects
- Box and text shadows
- Transparency and translucency
- Gradient fills
- Multicolumn text elements

All these features and more can be implemented via Dreamweaver today. The program will even assist you in building vendor-specific markup when necessary. To give you a quick tour of some of the coolest features and effects brewing, we've provided a sample file of CSS3 styling.

1 Open **css3_demo.html** from the Lesson03 folder. Display the file in Split view, and observe the CSS and HTML code.

Many of the new effects can't be previewed directly in Design view, so you'll need to use Live view or preview the page in an actual browser.

2 Click the Live view button to preview all the CSS3 effects.

The file contains a hodgepodge of features and effects that may surprise and even delight you—but don't get too excited. Although many of these features are already supported in Dreamweaver and will work fine in modern browsers, a lot of the older hardware and software out there can turn your dream site into a nightmare. And, there's at least one additional twist.

Some of the new CSS3 features have not been standardized, and certain browsers may not recognize the default markup generated by Dreamweaver. In these instances, you may have to include specific vendor commands to make them work properly. These commands are preceded by a vendor prefix, such as –ie, –moz, and –webkit. If you look carefully in the code of the demo file, you'll be able to find examples of these within the CSS markup.

```
65    -moz-column-count: 2;
66    -webkit-column-count: 2;
67    -moz-column-gap: 20px;
68    -webkit-column-gap: 20px;
```

Additional CSS support

CSS formatting and application is so complex and powerful that this short lesson can't cover all aspects of the subject. For a full examination of CSS, check out the following books:

- *Bulletproof Web Design: Improving Flexibility and Protecting Against Worst-Case Scenarios with HTML5 and CSS3 (3rd edition),* Dan Cederholm (New Riders Press, 2012) ISBN: 978-0-321-80835-6

- *CSS: The Missing Manual,* David Sawyer McFarland (O'Reilly Media, 2009) ISBN: 978-0-596-80244-8

- *Stylin' with CSS: A Designer's Guide (3rd edition),* Charles Wyke-Smith (New Riders Press, 2012) ISBN: 978-0-321-85847-4

- *The Art & Science of CSS,* Jonathan Snook, Steve Smith, Jina Bolton, Cameron Adams, and David Johnson (SitePoint, 2007) ISBN: 978-0-975-84197-6

Review questions

1 Should you still use HTML-based formatting?

2 What does CSS impose on each HTML element?

3 True or false? If you do nothing, HTML elements will feature no formatting or structure.

4 What four "theories" affect the application of CSS formatting?

5 What is the difference between block and inline elements?

6 True or false? CSS3 features are all experimental, and you should not use them at all.

Review answers

1 No. HTML-based formatting was deprecated in 1997 when HTML 4 was adopted. Industry best practices recommends using CSS-based formatting instead.

2 CSS imposes an imaginary box on each element and can then apply borders, background colors and images, margins, padding, and other types of formatting.

3 False. Even if you do nothing, many HTML elements feature built-in formatting.

4 The four theories that affect CSS formatting are cascade, inheritance, descendant, and specificity.

5 Block elements create stand-alone structures; inline elements appear at the insertion point.

6 False. Many CSS3 features are already supported by modern browsers and can be used today.

4 CREATING A PAGE LAYOUT

Lesson Overview

In this lesson, you'll learn the following:

- The basics of webpage design
- How to create design thumbnails and wireframes
- How to insert and format new components into a predefined CSS layout
- How to use the CSS Designer to identify applied CSS formatting
- How to check for browser compatibility

 This lesson will take about 1 hour and 30 minutes to complete. If you have not already done so, download the project files for this lesson from the Lesson & Update Files tab on your Account page at www.peachpit.com, and store them on your computer in a convenient location, as described in the Getting Started section of this book. Your Accounts page is also where you'll find any updates to the lessons or to the lesson files. Look on the Lesson & Update Files tab to access the most current content. If you are starting from scratch in this lesson, use the method described in the "Jumpstart" section of "Getting Started."

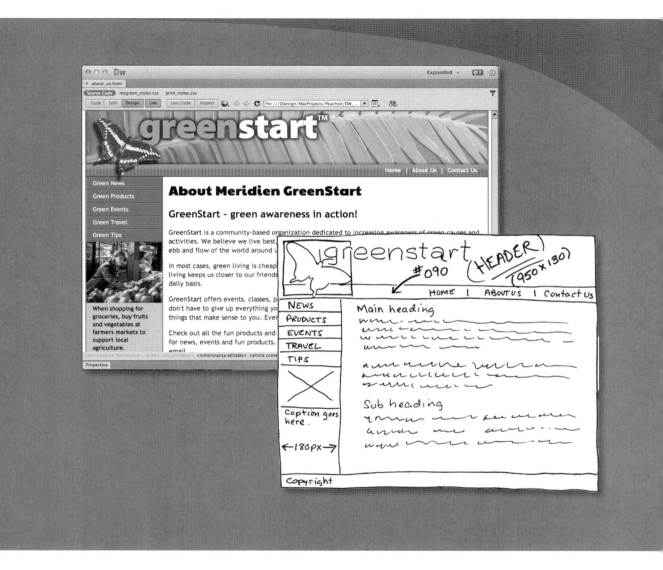

Whether you use thumbnails and wireframes or just
a vivid imagination, Dreamweaver can quickly turn
design concepts into complete, standards-based
CSS layouts.

Note: If you have not already downloaded the project files for this lesson to your computer from your Account page, make sure to do so now. See "Getting Started" at the beginning of the book.

Web design basics

Before you begin any web design project for yourself or for a client, you need to answer three important questions:

* What is the purpose of the website?

* Who is the audience?

* How do they get here?

What is the purpose of the website?

Will the website sell or support a product or service? Is your site for entertainment or games? Will you provide information or news? Will you need a shopping cart or database? Do you need to accept credit card payments or electronic transfers? Knowing the purpose of the website tells you what type of content you'll be developing and working with and what types of technologies you'll need to incorporate.

Who is the customer?

Is the audience adults, children, seniors, professionals, hobbyists, men, women, everyone? Knowing *who* your market will be is vital to the overall design and functionality of your site. A site intended for children probably needs more animation, interactivity, and bright engaging colors. Adults will want serious content and in-depth analysis. Seniors may need larger type and other accessibility enhancements.

A good first step is to check out the competition. Is there an existing website performing the same service or selling the same product? Are they successful? You don't have to mimic others just because they're doing the same thing. Look at Google and Yahoo. They perform the same basic service, but their site designs couldn't be more different from one another.

How do they get here?

This sounds like an odd question when speaking of the Internet. But, just as with a brick-and-mortar business, your online customers can come to you in a variety of ways. For example, are they accessing your site on a desktop computer, laptop, tablet, or cell phone? Are they using high-speed Internet, wireless, or dial-up service? What browser do they most like to use, and what is the size and resolution of the display? These answers will tell you a lot about what kind of experience your customers will expect. Dial-up and cell phone users may not want to see a lot of graphics or video, whereas users with large flat-panel displays and high-speed connections may demand as much bang and sizzle as you can send at them.

So, where do you get this information? Some you'll have to get through painstaking research and demographic analysis. Some you'll get from educated guesses based on your own tastes and understanding of your market. But a lot of it is actually available on the Internet itself. W3Schools, for one, keeps track of tons of statistics regarding access and usage, all updated regularly:

- **w3schools.com/browsers/browsers_stats.asp**: Provides more information about browser statistics.

- **w3schools.com/browsers/browsers_os.asp**: Gives the breakdown on operating systems. In 2011, they started to track the usage of mobile devices on the Internet.

- **w3schools.com/browsers/browsers_display.asp**: Lets you find out the latest information on the resolutions, or size, of screens using the Internet.

If you are redesigning an existing site, your web hosting service itself may provide valuable statistics on historical traffic patterns and even the visitors themselves. If you host your own site, you can incorporate third-party tools, such as Google Analytics and Adobe Omniture, into your code to do the tracking for you for free or for a small fee.

As of the beginning of 2013, Windows (80 to 90 percent) still dominates the Internet, with most users favoring Google Chrome (48 percent), followed by Firefox (30 percent), and then various versions of Internet Explorer (13 percent) a distant third. The vast majority of browsers (90 percent) are set to a resolution *higher* than 1024 pixels by 768 pixels. If it weren't for the rapid growth in usage of tablets and smartphones for accessing the Internet, these statistics would be great news for most web designers and developers. But, designing a website that can look good and work effectively for both flat-panel displays and cell phones is a tall order.

Responsive web design

Each day, more people are using cell phones and other mobile devices to access the Internet. Some people may use them to access the Internet more frequently than they use desktop computers. This presents a nagging problem to web designers. For one thing, cell phone screens are a fraction of the size of even the smallest flat-panel display. How do you cram a two- or three-column page design into a meager 200 to 300 pixels? Another problem is that most device manufacturers have decided to follow Apple's decision to drop support for Flash-based content on their mobile devices.

Until recently, web design usually required that you target an optimum size (height and width in pixels) for a webpage and then build the entire site on these specifications. Today, that scenario is becoming a rare occurrence. Now, you are presented with the decision to either build a site that can adapt to displays of multiple different dimensions or build two or more separate websites to support desktop *and* mobile users at the same time.

Your own decision will be based in part on the content you want to provide and on the capabilities of the devices accessing your pages. Building an attractive website that supports video, audio, and other dynamic content is hard enough without throwing in a panoply of different display sizes and device capabilities. The term *responsive web design* was coined by a Boston-based web developer name Ethan Mercotte in a book by the same name (2011), which describes the notion of designing pages that can adapt to multiple screen dimensions automatically. As you work through the following lessons, you will learn many techniques for responsive web design. By the time you get to Lesson 14, "Designing for Mobile Devices," you'll be fully prepared to tackle this weighty subject.

Many of the concepts of print design are not applicable to the web, because you are not in control of the user's experience. A page carefully designed for a typical flat panel is basically useless on a cell phone.

Scenario

For the purposes of this book you will be working to develop a website for Meridien GreenStart, a fictitious community-based organization dedicated to green investment and action. This website will offer a variety of products and services and require a broad range of webpage types, including dynamic pages using server-based technologies like PHP.

Your customers come from a broad demographic including all ages and education levels. They are people who are concerned about environmental conditions and who are dedicated to conservation, recycling, and the reuse of natural and human resources.

Your marketing research indicates that most of your customers use desktop computers or laptops, connecting via high-speed Internet services, but that you can expect 10 to 20 percent of your visitors via cell phone and other mobile devices. To simplify the process of learning Dreamweaver, we will focus on creating a fixed-width site design. In Lesson 14, "Designing for Mobile Devices," you will learn how to adapt your fixed-width design to work with smartphones and tablet devices.

Working with thumbnails and wireframes

The next step, after you have nailed down the answers to the three questions about your website purpose, customer demographic, and access model, is to determine how many pages you'll need, what those pages will do, and finally, what they will look like.

Creating thumbnails

Many web designers start by drawing thumbnails with pencil and paper. Think of thumbnails as a graphical shopping list of the pages you'll need to create for the website. Thumbnails can also help you work out the basic website navigation structure. Draw lines between the thumbnails showing how your navigation will connect them.

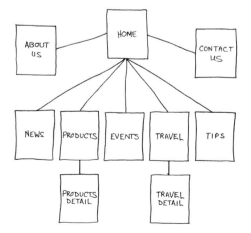

Thumbnails list the pages that need to be built and how they are connected to each other.

Most sites are divided into levels. Typically, the first level includes all the pages in your main navigation menu, the ones a visitor can reach directly from the home page. The second level includes pages you can reach only through specific actions or from specific locations, say from a shopping cart or product detail page.

Creating a page design

Once you've figured out what your site needs in terms of pages, products, and services, you can then turn to what those pages will look like. Make a list of components you want on each page, such as headers and footers, navigation, and areas for the main content and the sidebars (if any). Put aside any items that won't be needed on every page. What other factors do you need to consider?

Identifying the essential components for each page helps in creating an effective page design and structure that will meet your needs.

1. Header (includes banner and logo)
2. Footer (copyright info)
3. Horizontal navigation (for internal reference, i.e., Home, About Us, Contact Us)
4. Vertical navigation (links to products and services)
5. Main content (one-column with chance of two or more)

Do you have a company logo, business identity, graphic imagery, or color scheme you want to accent? Do you have publications, brochures, or current advertising campaigns you want to emulate? It helps to gather them all in one place so you can see everything all at once on a desk or conference table. If you're lucky, a theme will rise organically from this collage.

Once you've created your checklist of the components that you'll need on each page, sketch out several rough layouts that work for these components. Most designers settle on one basic page design that is a compromise between flexibility and sizzle. Some site designs may naturally lean toward using more than one basic layout. But resist the urge to design each page separately. Minimizing the number of page designs may sound like a major limitation, but it's key to producing a professional-looking site. It's the reason why some professionals, like doctors and airline pilots, wear uniforms. Using a consistent page design, or template, conveys a sense of professionalism and confidence to your visitor.

Wireframes allow you to experiment with page designs quickly and easily without wasting time with code.

While you figure out what your pages will look like, you'll have to address the size and placement of the basic components. Where you put a component can drastically affect its impact and usefulness. In print, designers know that the upper-left corner of a layout is considered one of the "power positions," a place where you want to locate important aspects of a design, such as a logo or title. This is because in western culture we read from left to right, top to bottom. The second power position is the lower-right corner because this is the last thing your eyes will see when you're finished reading.

Unfortunately, in web design this theory doesn't work so well because of one simple reason: You can never be certain how the user is seeing your design. Are they on a 20-inch flat panel or a 2-inch cell phone?

In most instances, the only thing you can be certain of is that the user can see the upper-left corner of any page. Do you want to waste this position by slapping the company logo here? Or, make the site more useful by slipping in a navigation menu? This is one of the key predicaments of the web designer. Do you go for design sizzle, workable utility, or something in between?

Creating wireframes

After you pick the winning design, wireframing is a fast way to work out the structure of each page in the site. A wireframe is like a thumbnail, but bigger, that sketches out each page and fills in more details about the components, such as actual link names and main headings. This step helps to catch or anticipate problems before you smack into them when working in the code.

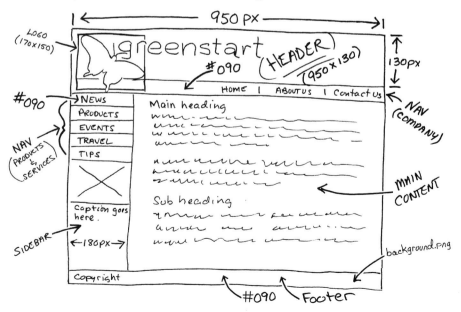

The wireframe for the final design should identify the components and feature markup for content, color, and dimensions.

► **Tip:** For years, designers have started the design process in Fireworks, where they can create a fully functional mockup that can then be exported to a CSS-based HTML layout and then edited in Dreamweaver.

Once the basic concepts are worked out, many designers take an extra step and create a full-size mockup or "proof of concept" using a program like Adobe Fireworks, Photoshop, or even Illustrator. It's a handy thing to do because you'll find that some clients just aren't comfortable giving an approval based only on pencil sketches. The advantage here is that all these programs allow you to export the results to full-size images (JPEG, GIF, or PNG) that can be viewed in a browser. Such mockups are as good as seeing the real thing but may take only a fraction of the time to produce.

In some cases, creating a mockup in Photoshop, Fireworks, or Illustrator can save hours of tedious coding to receive a needed approval.

Jumpstart method

The method we recommend for learning how to use Dreamweaver and to build the website pages and components described in the book is to work consecutively through each of the lessons until you have successfully completed all the exercises. For readers who can follow this model, you will use the site defined in the previous exercise for all lessons in the book.

For readers who cannot work through each lesson in order, or those who need to focus on a specific lesson topic, a Jumpstart method was developed to allow you to start a lesson out of sequence by defining the site on the folder provided for that lesson. Within that folder, components and partially completed files have been staged to permit this type of workflow. This method was described in detail in the "Getting Started" section of the book.

The Jumpstart requires you to define a site, using the steps defined earlier, targeting the desired lesson folder itself as the site root folder. In this case, you would target the Lesson04 folder provided in the online assets and then name the site appropriately, such as *Lesson04*.

Defining a Dreamweaver site

From this point forward, the lessons in this book will function within a Dreamweaver site. You will create webpages from scratch and use existing files and resources that are stored on your hard drive, which combined make up what's called your *local* site. When you are ready to upload your site to the Internet (see Lesson 13, "Publishing to the Web"), you publish your completed files to a web host server, which then becomes your *remote* site. The folder structures and files of the local and remote sites are usually mirrors of each other.

First, let's set up your local site:

1   Launch Adobe Dreamweaver CC if necessary.

2   Open the Site menu.

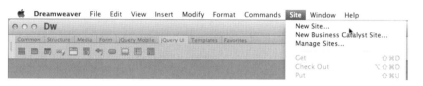

The Site menu provides options for creating and managing standard Dreamweaver sites, or to create a Business Catalyst site. Business Catalyst is an online, hosted application that allows you to build and manage rich, dynamic web-based businesses. To learn more about the capabilities of Business Catalyst, check out www.BusinessCatalyst.com.

3   Choose New Site.

To create a standard website in Dreamweaver CC, you need only name it and select the local site folder. Site names typically relate to a specific project or client and will appear in the Files panel. This name is intended for your own purposes, so there are no limitations to the name you can choose. Use a name that clearly describes the purpose of the website.

4   In the Site Name field, type **DW-CC**.

5   Next to the Local Site Folder field, click the folder (📁) icon. When the Choose Root Folder dialog box opens, navigate to the DW-CC folder containing the lesson files you downloaded from the *Adobe Dreamweaver CC Classroom in a Book* online resources.

You could click Save at this time and begin working on your new website, but we'll add one more piece of handy information.

6   Click the arrow (▶) next to the Advanced Settings category to reveal the categories listed there. Select Local Info.

Although it's not required, a good policy for site management is to store different file types in separate folders. For example, many websites provide

Note: If you are completing this lesson separately from the rest of the lessons in book, see the detailed "Jumpstart" instructions in the "Getting Started" section at the beginning of the book. Then, follow the steps in this exercise.

Note: If you have not already downloaded the project files for this lesson to your computer from your Account page, make sure to do so now. See "Getting Started" at the beginning of the book.

Note: If you are following the Jumpstart method name the site Lesson04. For each subsequent lesson you will create a new site and use the lesson number for the site name.

individual folders for images, PDFs, video, and so on. Dreamweaver assists in this endeavor by including an option for a Default Images folder. Later, as you insert images from other places on your computer, Dreamweaver will use this setting to automatically move the images into the site structure.

● **Note:** In the Jumpstart method you would target the images folder appearing in the lesson folder itself.

7   Next to the Default Images Folder field, click the folder (📁) icon. When the dialog box opens, navigate to the DW-CC > images folder containing the files you downloaded from the *Adobe Dreamweaver CC Classroom in a Book* online resources.

You've entered all the information required to begin your new site. In subsequent lessons, you'll add more information to enable you to upload files to your remote site and test dynamic webpages.

8   In the Site Setup dialog box, click Save.

The site name DW-CC now appears in the site list pop-up menu in the Files panel.

Setting up a site is a crucial first step in beginning any project in Dreamweaver. Knowing where the site root folder is located helps Dreamweaver determine link pathways and enables many site-wide options, such as orphaned-file checking and Find and Replace.

Using the Welcome screen

The Dreamweaver Welcome screen provides quick access to recent pages, easy creation of a range of page types, and a direct connection to several key Help topics. The Welcome screen appears when you first start the program or when no other documents are open. Let's use the Welcome screen to explore ways you can create and open documents.

1   In the Create New column of the Welcome screen, click HTML to create a new, blank HTML page instantly.

2 Choose File > Close.

The Welcome screen reappears.

3 In the Open A Recent Item section of the Welcome screen, click the Open button.

This feature allows you to browse for files to open in Dreamweaver.

4 Click Cancel.

The Welcome screen shows you a list of up to nine of your recently opened files; however, your installation may not display any used files at this point. Choosing a file from this list is a quick alternative to choosing File > Open when you want to edit an existing page.

You may use the Welcome screen at any time while working in this book. When you've completed the lessons, you may prefer not to use the Welcome screen, or even to see it. If so, you can disable it by selecting the Don't Show Again option. To re-enable the Welcome screen, access the General category of the Dreamweaver Preferences panel.

Previewing your completed file

To understand the layout you will work on in this lesson, preview the completed page in Dreamweaver.

● **Note:** If you are using the Jumpstart method, you will already be in the Lesson04 folder.

1 In Dreamweaver, press F8 to open the Files panel, and select DW-CC or the Jumpstart name from the site list.

2 In the Files panel, expand the Lesson04 folder.

3 Double-click **layout_finished.html** to open it.

Note: If for some reason you can't or don't want to use an HTML5-based layout, see the sidebar "Alternate HTML 4 workflow" later in this lesson.

This page represents the completed layout you will create in this lesson. It is based on the wireframe drawings made earlier in this lesson and uses one of the new Dreamweaver HTML5 CSS layouts. Take a few moments to familiarize yourself with the design and components on the page. Can you determine what makes this layout different from existing HTML 4–based designs? You will learn the differences as you work through this lesson.

4   Choose File > Close.

Modifying an existing CSS layout

The predefined CSS layouts provided by Dreamweaver are always a good starting point. They are easy to modify and adapt to most projects. Using a Dreamweaver CSS layout, you will create a proof-of-concept page to match the final wireframe design. This page will then be used to create the main project template in subsequent lessons. Let's find the layout that best matches the wireframe.

1   Choose File > New.

2   In the New Document dialog box, select Blank Page > HTML.

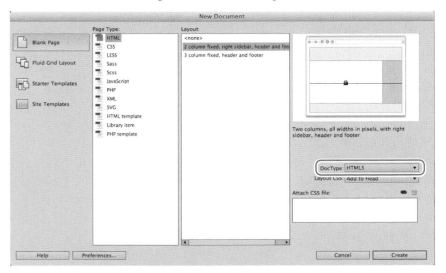

At the time of this writing, Dreamweaver CC offers two HTML5-based CSS layouts. The exact number and features of these layouts may change over time through automatic updates via Creative Cloud. The changes to this list may occur without notice or fanfare, so keep your eyes peeled for new options in this dialog box.

The featured HTML5 layouts use some of the new semantic content elements and will help you get some experience with this evolving standard. Unless you need to support an installed base of older browsers (like IE5 and 6), there's little to worry about using the newer layouts. Let's choose one of the HTML5 layouts that best fits the needs of the new site.

Note: If for some reason you can't or don't want to use an HTML5-based layout, see the sidebar "Alternate HTML 4 workflow" later in this lesson.

The layout "HTML: 2 column fixed, right sidebar, header and footer" has the most in common with the target design. The only difference is that the sidebar element is aligned to the right of the layout instead of to the left. You will align this element to the left later in this lesson.

3 Select **HTML: 2 column fixed, right sidebar, header and footer** from the layout list. Click Open/Create.

4 Switch to Design view, if necessary.

5 Insert the cursor anywhere in the page content. Observe the names and order of the tag selectors at the bottom of the document window.

The display order of elements in the tag selector directly correlates to the page's code structure. Elements appearing to the left are parents, or containers, of all elements to the right. The element farthest to the left is the highest in the page structure. As you can see, the <body> element is highest and <div.container> is second.

As you click around the page sections, you will be able to determine the HTML structure without having to delve into the Code view window at all. In many ways, the tag selector interface makes the job of identifying the HTML skeleton much easier, especially in complex page designs.

Semantics is all in the name

In HTML5 you will see several new *semantic* elements you may not be familiar with yet, such as <section>, <article>, <aside>, and <nav>. In the past, you would have seen <div> elements identified and differentiated with class or id attributes, such as <div class="header"> or <div id="nav">, to make it possible to apply CSS styling. HTML5 has simplified this construction down to <header> and <nav>. By using elements that are named for specific tasks or types of content, you can streamline code construction while achieving other benefits as well. For example, as search engines, such as Google and Yahoo, are optimized for HTML5, they will be able to locate and identify specific types of content on each page more quickly, making your site more useful and easier to browse.

The page consists of four main content elements, three subsections, and a single element that wraps around all the others. All but one of these are new HTML5 elements, including <header>, <footer>, <nav>, <aside>, <article>, and <section>. The only <div> elements in this layout are being used to hold the sidebar content and to hold everything together. Using these new elements means that you can apply complex CSS styling while reducing the complexity of the code overall. You can still use class and id attributes, but the new semantic elements reduce the need for this technique.

To understand exactly how much this design depends on CSS, sometimes shutting off CSS styling is a good idea.

6   Choose View > Style Rendering > Display Styles to disable CSS styling in Design view.

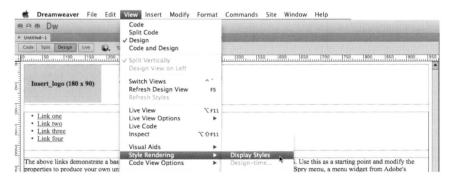

Style display is typically on by default (showing a check mark in the menu). By clicking this option in the menu, you'll toggle CSS styling off temporarily.

7 Note the identity and order of each page component.

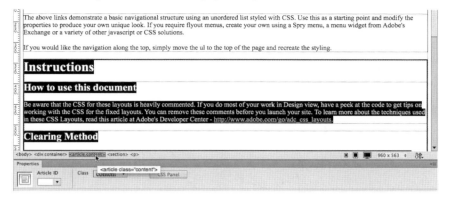

Without CSS, the HTML skeleton is exposed for all to see. It's instructive to know what the page will look like if somehow the cascading style sheet is disabled or not supported by a particular browser. Now it's easier to identify the page components and their structure. Although it is not strictly required, items that display higher on the page, like <header>, usually are inserted before other elements that appear lower, like <footer>.

Another important aspect you should notice is the navigation menu. Without the CSS styling, the navigation menu reverted back to a simple bulleted, or unordered, list with hyperlinks. Not too long ago this menu would have been built with tables, images, and complex rollover animation. If the images failed to load, the menu usually became a jumbled, unusable mess. The hyperlinks continued to work, but without the images there were no words to tell users what they were clicking. But navigation built on text-based lists, on the other hand, will always be usable, even without styling.

8 Choose View > Style Rendering > Display Styles to turn on CSS styling again.

Getting into the habit of saving files before you modify any settings or add content is always a good idea. Dreamweaver doesn't offer a backup or recovered-file feature; if it crashes before you save, all your work in any open, unsaved file will be lost. Save your files on a regular basis to prevent the loss of data and important changes to your files.

Alternate HTML 4 workflow

HTML5 is coming on strong all over the Internet and for most applications the suggested workflow will work perfectly well. But HTML5 is not the current web standard and some pages or components may not display properly on certain older browsers and devices. If you'd rather work with code and structures that are more tried and true, feel free to substitute HTML 4–based components for the HTML5 elements.

However, if you create this layout you'll have to adapt the steps within all the following lessons and exercises to the new components and structures. For example, HTML5 uses the new semantic elements, such as the following:

```
<header>...</header>
<footer>...</footer>
<section>...</section>
<article>...</article>
<nav>...</nav>
```

For an HTML 4–compatible layout, you would substitute a generic <div> element and use a class attribute that identifies the component this way:

```
<div class="header">...</div>
<div class="footer">...</div>
<div class="section">...</div>
<div class="article">...</div>
<div class="nav">...</div>
```

You'll also have to adapt the CSS styling for the new HTML 4 elements by modifying or rebuilding the HTML5-based selector names (header, footer, nav, and so on).

That way, the CSS rule header {color:#090} becomes .header { color:#090 } instead.

With all the caveats out of the way, the ugly truth is that even when you use standard HTML 4 code and components, older browsers and certain devices will still fail to render some of them properly. Some web designers believe that the longer we persist in using the older code, the longer the older software and devices will hang around making our lives difficult and delaying the inevitable adoption of HTML5. These designers say we should abandon the older standards and force users to upgrade as soon as possible.

The final decision is yours or your company's to make. In most cases, the problems you experience with HTML5 will be minor flaws—a font that's too big or too small—not a complete meltdown.

For more information about the differences between HTML 4 and HTML5, check out the following links:

* http://tinyurl.com/html-differences
* http://tinyurl.com/html-differences-1
* http://tinyurl.com/html-differences-2

9 Choose File > Save. In the Save As dialog box, navigate to the site root folder, if necessary. Name the file **mylayout.html** and click Save.

● **Note:** Dreamweaver may try to save this file back to the Lesson04 folder; if this is not the site root folder, click the Site Root button to navigate to the proper location.

Dreamweaver normally saves HTML files to the default folder specified in the site definition, but double-check the destination to make sure your files end up in the right place. All HTML pages created for the final site will be saved in the site root folder.

Adding a background image to the header

CSS styles are the current standard for all web styling and layout. In the following exercises, you'll apply background colors and a background image to a page section, adjust element alignment and the page width, and modify several text properties. All these changes are accomplished using Dreamweaver's CSS Designer panel (new with Dreamweaver CC).

If you start at the top of the page and work down, the first step would be to insert the graphical banner that appears in the final design. You could insert the banner directly into the header, but adding it as a background image has the advantage of leaving that element open for other content. It will also allow the design to be more adaptable to other devices, like cell phones and other mobile devices.

1 If necessary, switch to Design view. Select the image placeholder **Insert_logo (180x90)** in the header. Press Delete.

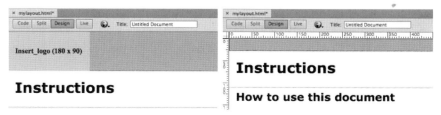

When you delete the image placeholder, the empty header will collapse to a fraction of its former size because it has no CSS height specification. You can identify all the formatting assigned to the layout components by using the new CSS Designer.

2 If necessary, choose Window > CSS Designer to display the panel.

To maximize the effectiveness of the CSS Designer you can use one of the predefined workspaces.

3 From the Workspace menu, choose Expanded.

The Dreamweaver workspace changes to display the CSS Designer in a two-column layout. This design will give you extra room to work with the CSS styling. If you want to increase the width of the CSS Designer, you can drag the edge of the document window to the left.

From the tag selector display, you can see that the element contained the image placeholder. Examine the CSS Designer panel. Can you identify any CSS rules that may format the header element?

4 In the CSS Designer panel, select the header rule in the Selectors pane. Examine the CSS properties applied to the element.

The Properties pane of the CSS Designer displays any existing specifications. For `header` it shows only a background color assigned to it. The panel also allows you to create new specifications. It works in two basic modes. If you are familiar with CSS syntax, you can create specifications by typing them directly. Otherwise, you can display a complete list of available CSS properties in the panel and define them as you go. You will experiment with both methods in this lesson.

First, you will add a background image to the `header` element and then adjust its size. To see a complete list of CSS properties, make sure the Show Set option is not enabled.

5 If necessary, deselect the Show Set option in the Properties pane.

When Show Set is deselected, the Properties pane displays the list of available CSS specifications. The list is organized into five categories: Layout, Text, Border, Background, and Others. To focus the display on a particular category, you can use the navigation icons at the top of the Properties pane.

6 Click the Background ( ) category icon. In the background-image section, click the text *Enter file path* beside the URL property. Click the Browse button next to the URL field.

7 In the Select Image Source dialog box, navigate to the default images folder and select **banner.jpg** and note the dimensions of the image in the preview.

The image is 950 by 130 pixels.

8 Click OK/Open to select the background image.

Background images repeat both vertically and horizontally by default. This isn't a problem at the moment, but to ensure that this behavior doesn't cause any undesirable effects in the future, you'll need to change the repeat specification.

● **Note:** You may need to modify your folder display to see the pixel dimensions of the image. In Windows, hover the cursor over the image to display its size. On the Mac, select column view within the dialog box.

9 In the background-repeat options, click the no-repeat icon.

The background image appears in the `<header>` element. The element is wide enough but not tall enough to display the entire background image. Since background images aren't truly inserted into an element, they have no effect (positive or negative) on the size of it. To ensure that the `<header>` is large enough to display the entire image, you need to add a height specification to the `header` rule.

10 If necessary, select the `header` rule in the Selectors pane. In the Properties pane, click the Layout (⛶) icon.

The Properties pane provides a list of CSS layout specifications you can set.

11 In the Layout category Height field, choose px from the measurement pop-up list. Enter **130** and press Enter/Return.

The height of the `<header>` element immediately adjusts, displaying the full banner image. Note that the image is slightly narrower than the container. You'll adjust the width of the layout later. You don't want to set the width on the `<header>` element itself. You learned in Lesson 3, "CSS Basics," that the width of block elements, like `<header>`, defaults to the entire width of their parent element. Let's add some finishing touches to the element.

You may have noticed that the `<header>` element already contained a background color that doesn't really match your site color scheme. Let's apply one that does.

12 In the Properties pane, click the Background category icon. Replace the existing background-color specification with **#090** and press Enter/Return to complete the change.

A bit of the background color is peeking out from the right edge of the banner, but once you adjust the width of the layout you won't see this color at all unless the background image fails to load. Adding background colors like this is a common precaution since certain devices or browsers may not load images and/or background graphics by default.

13 Choose File > Save.

Inserting new components

The wireframe design shows two new elements that don't exist in the current layout. The first contains the butterfly image, the second the horizontal navigation bar. Did you notice that the butterfly actually overlaps both the header and the horizontal navigation bar? There are several ways to achieve this effect. In this case, an absolutely positioned (AP) div will work nicely.

Note: To better understand how this technique works, try this step in Split view.

1 Insert the cursor into the header, if necessary. Select the `<header>` tag selector. Press the Left Arrow key once.

This procedure inserts the cursor in the HTML code before the opening `<header>` tag. If you had pressed the Right Arrow key, the cursor would move outside the closing `</header>` tag instead. Remember this technique—you'll use it frequently in Dreamweaver when you want to insert the cursor in a specific location before or after a code element without resorting to Code view. Always remember that your webpage is actually created by elements defined by HTML code and CSS. Knowing how to create, edit, and insert elements in the proper way will result in clean and error-free code.

AP-divs used to be a popular feature in previous versions of Dreamweaver, but the built-in workflow was deprecated in the latest version. This change is primarily in response to the industry-wide move away from fixed width and absolutely positioned components and toward flexible or fluid designs. But, for this application in the current site an AP-div is still a valid option. Later, we'll explore ways to deal with this element for mobile devices.

Note: AP-divs were used extensively in the past to create highly structured, fixed-layout web designs. This technique has declined dramatically in recent years as the need to support cell phones and other mobile devices has increased. For certain applications, AP-divs are still handy.

2 Choose Insert > Div.

The Insert Div dialog box appears. The AP-div will be the only one on this page. The positioning and formatting will be unique to it. Let's use an ID to name the element.

3 Enter **apDiv1** in the ID field.

The Insert Div dialog box allows you to create the CSS rule immediately to format the AP-div.

4 Click the New CSS Rule button.

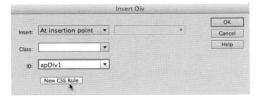

The New CSS rule dialog box appears. The ID apDiv1 appears automatically in the Selector Name field. ID-based selectors have the highest specificity, so the formatting you create in this dialog box will not affect any other elements.

5 Click OK to create the CSS rule.

The CSS Rule Definition dialog box for #apDiv1 appears. This dialog box allows you to quickly create the CSS specifications you will need for the AP-div.

6 Select the Box category. Enter **170** in the Width field. Choose px as the unit of measurement. Enter **158** in the Height field.

These settings set the width and height of the div that will hold the butterfly logo image.

7 Deselect the Same For All option for Margin.

8 Enter **15 px** in the Top and Left margin fields.

These settings help to position the AP-div in the proper location from the top and left of the layout. But the most important of all the settings are in the Positioning category.

9 Select the Positioning category. Choose Absolute from the Position pop-up menu.

By selecting Absolute you are effectively removing the element from the regular document flow. An absolutely positioned element can be placed almost anywhere within its parent structure regardless of other elements on the page.

Once the div has been positioned absolutely, you then have to decide whether it will appear above or below other elements. The property that controls this attribute is *z-index*. Normally, all elements in a layout appear at the same level; they all have a z-index of zero (0). But the AP-div needs to float above the other elements. By giving the AP-div a z-index greater than zero, you will ensure that it appears higher than the other elements.

10 Enter **1** in the z-index field. Click OK to complete the rule definition.

The CSS Rule Definition dialog box closes, displaying the Insert Div dialog box again.

11 Click OK to insert the AP-div.

The AP-div appears in the layout displaying the placeholder text *Content for id "apDiv1" Goes Here*, which is selected and ready to be replaced.

12 Press Delete to remove the placeholder text.

13 Choose Insert > Image > Image. Navigate to the default images folder and select **butterfly-ovr.png**.

14 Click OK/Open.

The butterfly logo appears in the AP-div. Thanks to the absolute positioning and z-index, the butterfly appears above the banner and other layout elements.

Best web practices call for the use of alternate text to describe images for accessibility purposes. You can enter this attribute directly in the Property inspector.

15 In the Property inspector enter **GreenStart Logo** in the Alternate text field. Save the file.

The `<div#apDiv1>` is complete. Now, let's add another new component that will hold the horizontal navigation shown in the site design specs. The vertical navigation menu will hold links to the organization's products and services. The horizontal navigation will be used to link back to the organization's home page, mission statement, and contact information.

Inserting a navigation component

In HTML 4, you probably would have inserted the links into another `<div>` element and used a `class` or `id` attribute to differentiate it from the other `<div>` elements in the file. Instead, HTML5 provides a new element geared specifically toward such components: `<nav>`.

1 Insert the cursor into the header. Click the `<header>` tag selector. Press the Right Arrow key.

The cursor now appears after the ending `</header>` tag.

2 Choose Insert > Structure > Navigation.

The Insert Navigation dialog box appears.

3 Enter **top-nav** in the Class field. Click New CSS Rule.

The New CSS Rule dialog box appears.

4 Click OK to create the `top-nav` class.

The "CSS Rule Definition for *.top-nav*" dialog box appears.

5 In the Type category, enter **90** in the Font-size field and choose the percentage sign (%) from the pop-up. Enter **#FFC** in the Color field. Choose bold from the Font-weight pop-up.

6 Type **#090** in the background-color field.

7 In the Block category, choose Right from the Text-align pop-up.

8 In the Box category, deselect the Same For All check box for Padding. Enter **5 px** in the Top padding fields. Enter **20 px** in the Right padding fields. Enter **5 px** in the Bottom padding fields.

9 In the Border category, deselect the Same For All check boxes for Style, Width, and Color. Enter the following values only in the corresponding Bottom border fields: **solid, 2 px, #060**

▶ **Tip:** To enter separate values in the Bottom field, remember to deselect the Same For All check boxes in each section first.

10 Click OK in the CSS Rule Definition dialog box. Click OK in the Insert Navigation dialog box

A <nav> element appears displaying the placeholder text *Content for class "top-nav" Goes Here*. The new element and placeholder text is already formatted based on the specifications you created in the CSS `.top-nav` rule.

● **Note:** The <nav> element is new in HTML5. If you need to use HTML 4 code and structures, see the sidebar "Alternate HTML 4 workflow" earlier in this lesson.

11 Type **Home | About Us | Contact Us** to replace the placeholder text. In the Property inspector, choose Paragraph from the Format pop-up menu.

You will convert this text to actual hyperlinks in Lesson 9, "Working with Navigation." For now, let's create a new CSS rule to format this element.

12 Press Ctrl-S/Cmd-S to save the file.

As you can see, adding new components to the CSS layouts is fairly easy, which is what makes them a good starting point for a new project. In the following exercises, you will explore other ways you can customize the predefined layout.

Changing element alignment

The proposed design calls for the sidebar to appear on the left side of the page, but this layout puts it on the right. However, adjusting the layout is a lot easier than you may think. The first step is to determine what existing CSS rule is responsible for the current alignment.

1 If necessary, choose Window > CSS Designer to display the panel.

   The CSS Designer provides the capability to format HTML components by creating and editing CSS rules. But you can also use it to inspect existing styling. If you click a selector in the list, the Properties pane displays formatting contained in the rule.

2 In Design view, insert the cursor anywhere in the right sidebar.

3 Examine the Selectors pane of the CSS Designer.

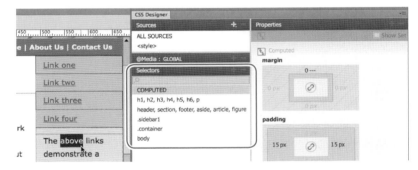

   The Selectors pane displays a list of all the CSS rules that have an effect, even minimally, on the targeted element, with the rule at the top of the list having the strongest influence. The list also features the option COMPUTED. Selecting this option displays the aggregated formatting from all rules in the list.

4 In the Selectors pane, select the body rule. In the Properties pane, select the Show Set option.

   The Show Set option limits the Properties pane display only to properties set by the selected rule.

5 Click each rule in the list until you find the one controlling the float property.

The .sidebar1 rule applies the float:right property.

6 Select the .sidebar1 rule, and change the float property from right to left.

The sidebar moves to the left side of the layout.

7 Save the file.

With each modification the layout is getting closer to the site design.

Modifying the page width and background color

Before you convert this file into the project template, let's tighten up the formatting and the placeholder content. For example, the page width has to be modified to match the banner image. But first, you'll have to identify the CSS rule that controls the page width.

1 If necessary, choose View > Rulers > Show or press Alt-Ctrl-R/Option-Cmd-R to display the rulers in the Design window.

You can use the rulers to measure the width and height of HTML elements or images. The orientation of the rulers defaults to the upper-left corner of the Design window. To give you more flexibility, you can set this zero point anywhere in the Design window.

2   Position the cursor over the axis point of the horizontal and vertical rulers. Drag the crosshairs to the upper-left corner of the header element in the current layout. Note the width of the layout.

Using the ruler, you can see that the layout is between 960 and 970 pixels wide.

● **Note:** When you select each tag selector, observe how the CSS Designer display updates to show you any applied styling.

3   Insert the cursor into any content area of the layout.

Observe the tag selector display to locate any elements that may control the width of the entire page; it would have to be an element that contains all the other elements. The only elements that fit this criterion are <body> and <div.container>.

4   Click each of the tag selectors displayed at the bottom of the document window. Examine the Properties pane display in the CSS Designer for each element. If necessary, select the Show Set option to truncate the display to applied properties only.

Can you identify the rule that controls the width of the entire page? The .container rule seems to match the description; it contains the width: 960px declaration. By now you should be getting good at CSS forensics using the tag selector interface and the CSS Designer.

You can edit rules individually as you did in previous exercises, or you can use the display within the COMPUTED option.

5   Click the <div.container> tag selector. In the Properties pane, select the COMPUTED option. Change width to **950 px** and press Enter/Return to complete the specification.

The <div.container> element now matches the width of the banner image, but you may have experienced an unintended consequence when you changed the overall width. In our example, the main content area shifted down below the sidebar. To understand what happened, you'll have to do a quick investigation.

6 In the Sources pane of the CSS Designer panel, select `<style>`.

This displays all the CSS rules defined in the current page. At the moment, all rules are embedded in the `<head>` section.

7 Click the `.content` rule and check its properties. Note its width: 780 pixels.

8 Click the `.sidebar1` rule and check its width: 180 pixels.

Combined, the two `<div>` elements total 960 pixels, the same as the original width of the layout. The elements are too wide to sit side by side in the main container and thereby prompted the unexpected shift. This type of error is common in web design and is easily fixed by adjusting the width of either of the two child elements.

9 In the CSS Designer panel, click the `.content` rule. In the Properties section of the panel, change the width to **770 px**.

The `<div.content>` element returns to its intended position. This was a good reminder that the size, placement, and specifications of page elements have important interactions that can affect the final design and display of your elements and of the entire page.

The current background color of the page detracts from the overall design. Let's remove it.

10 In the CSS Designer, select the body rule. In the Background category, change the background-color to **#FFF** and press Enter/Return.

Note how the absence of the background color gives the impression that the page's content area drifts off into the wide expanse. You could give `<div.container>` a different background color, or you could simply add a border to give the content elements a definitive edge. Let's add a thin border to the element.

11 In the CSS Designer, select the `.container` rule. If necessary, select Show Set in the Properties pane.

12 Click the Add CSS Property (![+]) icon.

An empty field appears in the Properties pane.

13 Type **border** and press Enter/Return to create the new property.

An empty value field appears.

▶ **Tip:** You can select the desired property from the hint list any time while you are typing. Use your mouse and double-click or arrow down the list and press Enter/Return.

► Tip: In many cases, you can enter values manually as shown or select them from options displayed within the Properties pane.

14 Type **solid 2px #090** and press Enter/Return to create the new value.

A dark green border appears around `<div.container>`.

15 Save the file.

Modifying existing content and formatting

As you can see, the CSS layout comes equipped with a vertical navigation menu. The generic hyperlinks are simply placeholders waiting for your final content. Let's change the placeholder text in the menu to match the pages outlined in the thumbnails created earlier and modify the colors to match the site color scheme.

1 Select the placeholder text *Link one* in the first menu button. Type **Green News**. Change *Link two* to read **Green Products**. Change *Link three* to read **Green Events**. Change *Link four* to read **Green Travel**.

One of the advantages of using bulleted lists as navigational menus is that inserting new links is easy.

2 With the cursor still at the end of the words *Green Travel*, press Enter/Return. Type **Green Tips**.

The new text appears in what looks like a button structure, but the background color doesn't match and the text doesn't align with other menu items. You could probably figure out what's wrong in Design view, but in this case, the problem may be identified faster in Code view.

3 Click the `<li>` tag selector for the new link item, and select Code view. Observe the menu items and compare the first four with the last one. Can you see the difference?

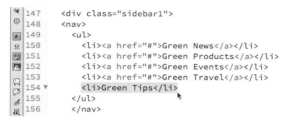

```
147   <div class="sidebar1">
148   <nav>
149     <ul>
150       <li><a href="#">Green News</a></li>
151       <li><a href="#">Green Products</a></li>
152       <li><a href="#">Green Events</a></li>
153       <li><a href="#">Green Travel</a></li>
154 ▼     <li>Green Tips</li>
155     </ul>
156   </nav>
```

The difference is obvious in Code view. The last item is tagged with the `<li>` element like the others—as part of the bulleted list—but it doesn't feature the markup `<a href="#">` used in the other items to create the hyperlink placeholder. For *Green Tips* to look like the other menu items, you have to add a hyperlink, or at least a similar placeholder.

4 Select the text *Green Tips*. In the Link field of the HTML Property inspector, type **#** and press Enter/Return.

The code in all the items is identical now.

5 Switch to Design view.

All the menu items are identically formatted now. You'll learn more about how to format text with CSS to create a dynamic HTML menu in Lesson 5, "Working with Cascading Style Sheets."

The current menu color doesn't match the site color scheme. To change the color, let's use the CSS Designer to find the CSS rule that controls this formatting.

6 Insert the cursor into any of the menu items. If necessary, select the COMPUTED option in the Properties pane of the CSS Designer. If necessary, select the Show Set option.

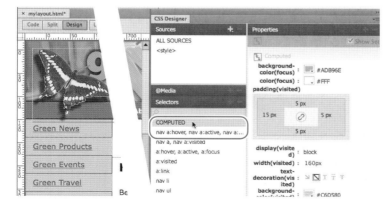

The Properties pane displays properties assigned to the navigation menu. By using the COMPUTED option, you are seeing the aggregated styling of all the applicable rules in one place, making it a simple matter to make the desired changes.

But be careful, in some cases, the styling shown may not affect the element directly, but via inheritance. If you change a specification within the COMPUTED option, the change affects the applicable rule. Be aware that such modifications may produce undesirable results, changing other elements on the page. Keep your eyes peeled for any unintended consequences.

Before you make any changes, it's important to understand how some of the rules are being applied to the page elements. If you look closely at the COMPUTED option in the Properties pane, you'll notice that more than one background color is applied to the element. How can that be?

The reason you see two background colors is because the item is a hyperlink that actually changes formatting in response to user interaction. When the user moves his mouse over the menu item, the background color changes. It can also change when the user visits a link. Although in this case, the menu shows the same color for visited or unvisited links. In Lesson 5, "Working with Cascading Style Sheets," you will explore how these different effects are applied. For now, let's just change the default state of the link.

7   In the Properties pane, change `background-color (visited)` to **#090** and press Enter/Return.

The background-color of the menu items now matches the horizontal <nav> element. But the black text is difficult to read against the green background color. As you see in the horizontal menu, a lighter color would be more appropriate. Let's change the text color for the link, too.

If you examine the COMPUTED properties for the <li>, you will notice four different "color" properties set for it. Confused? Each of the properties is being applied to and, in some cases, inherited by the text in the menu item. However, before you change the color of any of these properties you should examine the individual rules to identify the correct one.

In this instance, the rules that are most important are #1 and #2 in the list. They both apply to the link text in the vertical menu. For now you only need to change the default color of the links themselves.

8 Select the nav a, nav a:visited rule. Examine the properties assigned to it.

The rule has no color specification. The link text color is being inherited from another rule. Let's set a new color specification.

9 Click Add CSS Property (■).

A new property field appears.

10 Type color and press Enter/Return.

A new color property appears with an empty value.

11 Click the *undefined* label and enter **#FFC** and press Enter/Return.

The link text does not change color as expected. Unfortunately, Dreamweaver missed a problem in the style sheet. The hyperlink display in Design view is currently honoring the formatting in the `a:link` rule, which applies default formatting to hyperlinks on the page. But the CSS Designer shows the `nav a, nav a:visited` rule, which turns off the text decoration, higher in the list. Confused?

The selectors `a` and `a:link` are supposed to be equivalent; they both format the default state of hyperlinks. Yet, in a battle between `a` and `a:link`, `a:link` will always win. So, then why is the `nav a, nav a:visited` rule listed higher than `a:link`? Because the rule combines two selectors: `nav a` and `nav a:visited`. Although the property `a:visited` is equal in specificity to `a:link`, combining two selectors gives the rule a higher rating than a rule with just one (even though part of the rule actually has lower specificity). Whatever the reason, the links are still formatted incorrectly. Luckily, there's an easy fix.

● **Note:** The CSS notation a:link is one of four pseudo-selectors used to format various default hyperlink behaviors. You will learn more about these pseudo-selectors in Lesson 5, "Working with Cascading Style Sheets."

12 In the CSS Designer, select `<style>` in the Sources panel. In the Selectors pane, click the `nav a, nav a:visited` rule. If you click the selector a second time, the name becomes editable.

13 Change `nav a` to `nav a:link` and press Enter/Return to complete the selector.

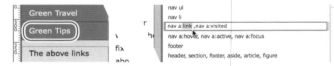

The link text in the vertical menu now displays in the desired color, and the underline disappears.

14 Save the file.

Inserting an image placeholder

The sidebar will feature photos, captions, and short blurbs on environmental topics. Let's insert a placeholder image and caption below the vertical menu. Dreamweaver no longer provides a built-in feature for creating image placeholders, but you can create one using the Quick Tag Editor or by inserting the code directly into the Code view window. Use the following steps to create the image placeholder.

1　Insert the cursor into the text directly below the vertical menu. Click the `<p>` tag selector.

The placeholder image should not be inserted within the `<p>` element. If it were, it would inherit any margins, padding, and other formatting applied to the paragraph, which could cause it to disrupt the layout.

2　Press the Left Arrow key.

▶ **Tip:** Use Split view whenever you're unsure where the cursor is inserted.

As you have seen in earlier exercises, the cursor moves to the left of the opening `<p>` tag in the code but stays within the `<aside>` element.

3　Press Ctrl-T/Cmd-T to open the Quick Tag Editor.

The Quick Tag Editor appears with the text cursor inserted within tag brackets.

4　Type `img` and press the spacebar.

5　Type `id="Sidebar" src="" width="180" height="150" alt="Alternate text goes here"` and press Return/Enter to complete the image placeholder.

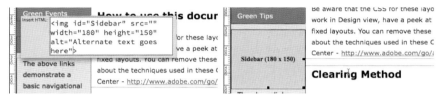

An image placeholder appears in `<div.sidebar1>` below the vertical menu. When you use this layout to create pages for your actual site, you will replace the placeholder image with an actual image, and update the attributes of this element, as necessary.

6　Select all the text below the image placeholder. Type **Insert caption here**.

The caption placeholder replaces the text.

7　Press Ctrl-S/Cmd-S to save.

Inserting placeholder text

Let's simplify the layout by replacing the existing headings and text in the main content area.

1　Double-click to select the heading *Instructions*. Type **Insert main heading here** to replace the text.

2　Select the heading *How to use this document*. Type **Insert subheading here** to replace the text.

3 Select the placeholder text in that same `<section>` element.
Type **Insert content here** to replace it.

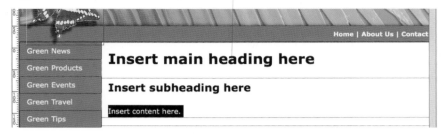

4 Insert the cursor in the next section. Click the `<section>` tag selector. Press Delete. Select and delete the remaining two `<section>` elements and their contents.

5 Press Ctrl-S/Cmd-S to save.

Modifying the footer

Let's reformat the footer and insert the copyright information.

1 In the Sources pane of the CSS Designer panel, select `<style>`. In the Selectors pane, select the `footer` rule.

2 Change the background-color to #**090**

3 Click the Add CSS Property (✚)icon. Type **font-size** and press Enter/Return.

4 Click the value field to edit it. Choose **%** from the pop-up menu. Type **90** in the value field, and press Enter/Return.

5 Click the Add CSS Property icon. Type `color` and press Enter/Return.

6 Click the value field to edit it. Type **#FFC** in the value field and press Enter/Return.

7 Select the placeholder text in the footer. Type **Copyright 2013 Meridien GreenStart. All rights reserved.**

8 Delete the `<address>` element at the bottom of the footer.

9 Press Ctrl-S/Cmd-S to save.

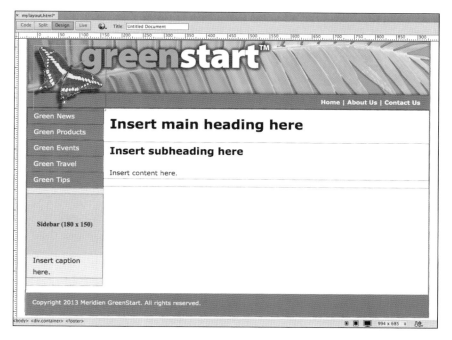

The basic page layout is complete.

Validating webpages

The CSS layouts included with Dreamweaver have been thoroughly tested to work flawlessly in all modern browsers. However, during the lesson you made major modifications to the original layout. These changes could have ramifications in the quality of the code. Before you use this page as your project template, you should check to make sure the code is correctly structured and meets web standards.

1 If necessary, open **mylayout.html** in Dreamweaver.

2 Choose File > Validation > Validate Current Document (W3C).

A W3C Validator Notification dialog box appears, indicating that your file will be uploaded to an online validator service provided by the W3C. Before clicking OK, you will need to have a live Internet connection.

3 Click OK to upload the file for validation.

File/URL	Line	Description
mylayout.html	161	Bad value for attribute src on element img: Must be non-empty. [HTML5]

Current document validation complete [1 Errors, 0 Warnings, 0 Hidden]

After a few moments you receive a report indicating any errors in your layout. The only error you should see is the empty `src` attribute for the image placeholder.

Congratulations. You created a workable basic page layout for your project template and learned how to insert additional components, image placeholders, text, and headings; adjust CSS formatting; and check for browser compatibility. In the upcoming lessons, you will continue to work on this file to complete the site template, tweak the CSS formatting, and set up the template structure.

Review questions

1 What three questions should you ask before starting any web design project?

2 What is the purpose of using thumbnails and wireframes?

3 What is the advantage of inserting the banner as a background image?

4 How can you insert the cursor before or after an element without using Code view?

5 How does the CSS Designer assist in designing your website layout?

6 What advantages does using HTML5-based markup provide?

Review answers

1 What is the purpose of the website? Who is the customer? How did they get here? These questions, and their answers, are essential in helping you develop the design, content, and strategy of your site.

2 Thumbnails and wireframes are quick techniques for roughing out the design and structure of your site without having to waste lots of time coding sample pages.

3 By inserting the banner or other large graphics as a background image, you leave the container free for other content.

4 Select an element using its tag selector, and press the Left Arrow or Right Arrow key to move the cursor before or after the selected element.

5 The CSS Designer serves as a CSS detective. It allows you to investigate what CSS rules are formatting a selected element and how they are applied.

6 HTML5 has introduced new semantic elements that help to streamline code creation and styling. These elements also allow search engines, like Google and Yahoo, to index your pages more quickly and effectively.

5 WORKING WITH CASCADING STYLE SHEETS

Lesson Overview

In this lesson, you'll work with cascading style sheets (CSS) in Dreamweaver CC and do the following:

- Manage CSS rules using the CSS Designer
- Learn about the theory and strategy of CSS rule design
- Create new CSS rules
- Create and apply custom CSS classes
- Create descendant selectors
- Create styles for page layout elements
- Move CSS rules to an external style sheet
- Create style sheets for print applications

This lesson will take about 2 hours to complete. If you have not already done so, download the project files for this lesson from the Lesson & Update Files tab on your Account page at www.peachpit.com, and store them on your computer in a convenient location, as described in the Getting Started section of this book. Your Accounts page is also where you'll find any updates to the lessons or to the lesson files. Look on the Lesson & Update Files tab to access the most current content. If you are starting from scratch in this lesson, use the method described in the "Jumpstart" section of "Getting Started."

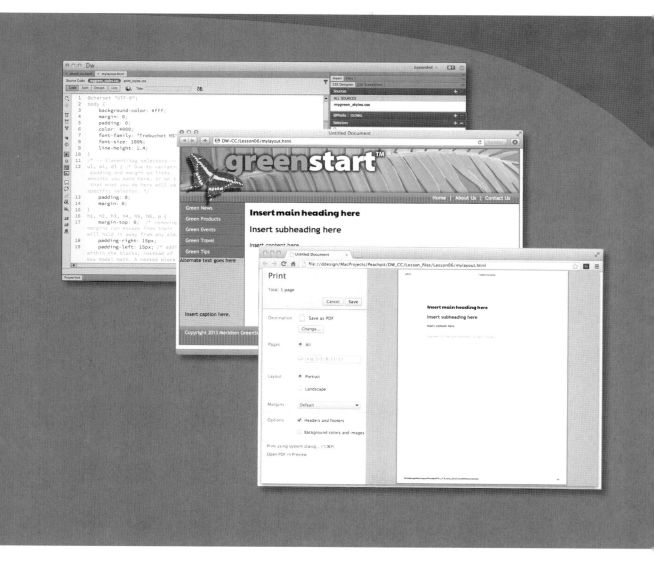

Today, pages designed in compliance with web standards separate the content from the formatting. Stored in a cascading style sheet (CSS), the formatting can be quickly changed and substituted for specific applications and devices.

Note: If you have not already downloaded the project files for this lesson to your computer from your Account page, make sure to do so now. See "Getting Started" at the beginning of the book.

Note: If you are completing this lesson separately from the rest of the lessons in book, see the detailed "Jumpstart" instructions in the "Getting Started" section at the beginning of the book. Then, follow the steps in this exercise.

Previewing the completed file

To see the finished page you'll create in this lesson, you can open it in Dreamweaver.

1   Launch Dreamweaver. Choose File > Open or press Ctrl-O/Cmd-O.

2   Navigate to the Lesson05 folder. Select **layout_finished.html** and click OK/Open.

The page loads in the Dreamweaver window. Note the layout, various colors, and other formats applied to the text and page elements—all created by cascading style sheets (CSS).

3   Switch to Design view if necessary.

You can use Live view to see what the finished page will look like in a browser.

4   Click the Live view button.

Notice the difference in the page display between Design and Live views. In Live view you can test and preview all graphical effects, video, audio, and most interactivity.

Design view   Live view

5   Position the mouse over the items in the vertical and horizontal menus to test the hyperlink interactivity.

The menu displays different background and text colors as the mouse moves over and off the link.

6   Close **layout_finished.html**.

Working with the CSS Designer

In Lesson 4, "Creating a Page Layout," you used one of the CSS layouts provided by Dreamweaver to start building your project site template page. These layouts come equipped with an underlying structure and a set of predefined CSS rules that establish the basic design and formatting of the page components and content.

In the upcoming exercises in this lesson, you'll modify these rules and add new ones to complete the basic site template design. But before you proceed it's vital to your role as a designer to understand the existing structure and formatting before you can effectively complete your tasks. Take a few minutes to examine the rules and understand what role they perform in the current document.

1   Open **mylayout.html** created in Lesson 4 from the site root folder, if necessary.

2   If the CSS Designer panel isn't visible, choose Window > CSS Designer to display it. If necessary, choose Window > Workspace > Expanded.

● **Note:** If you are starting from scratch in this exercise, see the "Jumpstart" instructions in the "Getting Started" section at the beginning of the book.

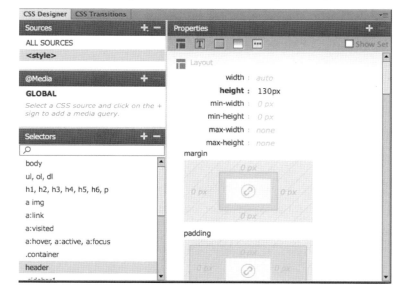

The CSS Designer has several panes that display different aspects of the CSS structure and styling. If you have a second display or plenty of screen space, the Expanded workspace provides more room for the CSS Designer to do its work. In the Sources pane, you'll see the `<style>` tag, indicating that the style sheet is embedded in the `<head>` section of the document.

▶ **Tip:** If you don't see line numbers along the side of your Code view window, choose View > Code View Options > Line Numbers to turn on this feature.

● **Note:** The CSS markup is contained within an HTML `<!-- -->` comment entry. That's because CSS is not technically valid HTML markup and may not be supported in some applications or devices. Using the comment structure allows such applications to ignore the CSS altogether.

3 Switch to Code view and locate the `<head>` section (starting at line 3). Locate the `<style type="text/css">` element (line 6) and examine the subsequent code entries.

All the CSS rules displayed in the list are contained within the `<style>` element.

4 Note the names and order of the selectors within the CSS code.

5 In the Selectors pane in CSS Designer, expand the panel and examine the list of rules. If necessary, you may need to select the `<style>` reference in the Sources pane to display the full list of rules.

The list shows the same selector names in the same order you saw in Code view. There is a one-to-one relationship between the CSS code and the CSS Designer. When you create new rules or edit existing ones, Dreamweaver makes all the changes in the code for you, saving you time and reducing the possibility of code-entry errors. The CSS Designer is just one of the many productivity enhancements you'll use and master in this book.

You have 20 rules at this time—18 that came with the CSS layout, and 2 you made yourself in the previous lesson. The order of your rules may vary from that shown in the figure, but you can easily reorder the list in the CSS Designer.

In the last lesson, you created `<div#apDiv1>` and inserted it into the layout. The `#apDiv1` rule applies to the `<div>` holding the butterfly logo, which appears in the code between `<div.container>` and `<header>`. But as you can see in the CSS Designer, the rule reference appears near the bottom of all the rules. In this instance, moving this rule within the style sheet will not affect how it formats the element, but if you need to edit it later it will be easier to find.

● **Note:** The names and order of styles in your panel may vary from those pictured.

● **Note:** Before you move any other rules, you should first understand what function each one performs and how they relate to one another.

6   Select the `#apDiv1` rule and drag it directly underneath the `.container` rule.

Selectors + −	Selectors + −	Selectors + −
body	body	body
ul, ol, dl	ul, ol, dl	ul, ol, dl
h1, h2, h3, h4, h5, h6, p	h1, h2, h3, h4, h5, h6, p	h1, h2, h3, h4, h5, h6, p
a img	a img	a img
a:link	a:link	a:link
a:visited	a:visited	a:visited
a:hover, a:active, a:focus	a:hover, a:active, a:focus	a:hover, a:active, a:focus
.container	.container	.container
header	header	#apDiv1
.sidebar1	.sidebar1	header #apDiv1 defined under GLOBAL
.content	.content	.sidebar1
.content ul, .content ol	.content ul, .content ol	.content
nav ul	nav ul	.content ul, .content ol
nav li	nav li	nav ul
nav a:link ,nav a:visited	nav a:link ,nav a:visited	nav li
nav a:hover, nav a:active, nav a:focus	nav a:hover, nav a:active, nav a:focus	nav a:link ,nav a:visited
footer	footer	nav a:hover, nav a:active, nav a:focus
header, section, footer, aside, article, figure	header, section, footer, aside, article, figure	footer
#apDiv1	#apDiv1	header, section, footer, aside, article, figure
.top-nav #apDiv1 defined under GLOBAL	.top-nav	.top-nav

Dreamweaver has moved the rule within the list but that's not all. It has also rewritten the code in the embedded style sheet, moving the rule to its new position. Arranging related rules together can save time later when you need to format specific elements or components. But be on the lookout for unintended consequences. Moving rules in the list can upset the established cascade or inheritance relationships you have already created. Review Lesson 3, "CSS Basics," if you need a refresher on these theories.

7   In the CSS Designer, select the body rule. Observe the properties and values that appear in the Properties pane of the panel.

Most of these settings came with the layout, although you changed the background color in the last lesson. Note that the margins and padding are set to zero.

8 Select the ul, ol, dl rule and observe the values that appear.

As in the body rule, this rule sets all margin and padding values to zero. Do you know why? An experienced web designer could select each rule in turn and probably figure out the reasons for each of the formats and settings. But you don't need to resort to hiring a consultant when Dreamweaver provides much of the information you need already.

9 Right-click the ul, ol, dl rule and choose Go To Code from the context menu.

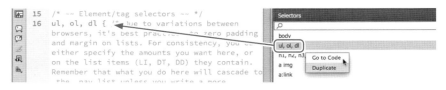

If you are in Design view, Dreamweaver will display the document in Split view and then focus on the section of code that contains the ul, ol, dl rule. In Code view, it will jump to the appropriate lines that contain the rule. Observe the text between the opening /* and closing */ notation. This is the way you add comments to cascading style sheets. Like HTML comments, this text usually provides behind-the-scenes information that will not be displayed within the browser or affect any elements. Comments are a good way to leave handy reminders within the body of the webpage or to leave notes to yourself or others explaining why you wrote the code in a particular fashion. You'll notice that some of the comments are used to introduce a set of rules, and others are embedded in the rules themselves.

10 Scroll down through the style sheet and study the comments, paying close attention to the embedded ones.

The more you understand what these predefined rules are doing, the better results you can achieve for your final site. Here's what you'll find: the body, header, .container, .sidebar1, .content, and footer rules define the basic structural elements of the page. The rules a:img, a:link, a:visited, a:hover, a:active, and a:focus set up the appearance and performance of the default hyperlink behavior; nav ul, nav li, nav a, nav a:visited, nav a:hover, nav a:active, and nav a:focus define the look and behavior of the vertical menu. The remaining rules are intended to reset default formatting or add some desired styling as outlined in the embedded comments.

For the most part, there's nothing unacceptable or fatal in the current order of the rules, but keeping related rules together will pay productivity dividends later when the style sheet gets more complicated. This type of organization will help you find specific rules quickly and remind you what you have already styled within your page.

11 Using the Selectors pane in the CSS Designer, reorder the rules in the list, as necessary, so they match the order shown in the following figure.

● **Note:** When moving rules using the CSS Designer, the position of comments that are not embedded may not be preserved.

```
Selectors
🔍
body
ul, ol, dl
h1, h2, h3, h4, h5, h6, p
a img
a:link
a:visited
a:hover, a:active, a:focus
.container
#apDiv1
header
.top-nav
.sidebar1
nav ul
nav li
nav a:link ,nav a:visited
nav a:hover, nav a:active, nav a:focus
.content
.content ul, .content ol
footer
header, section, footer, aside, article, figure
```

Now that you are more aware of the CSS rules and rule order, remember that taking special care with rule order when you create new styles is a good practice from this point forward.

12 Save **mylayout.html**.

Working with type

Most of the content of your site will be represented in text. Text is displayed in the web browser using digitized typefaces. Based on designs developed and used for centuries on the printing press, these typefaces can evoke all sorts of feelings in your visitors, ranging from security to elegance to sheer fun and to humor.

Some designers may use multiple typefaces for different purposes throughout the site. Others select a single base typeface that may match their normal corporate themes or culture. CSS gives you tremendous control over page appearance and the formatting of text. In the last few years, there have been many innovations in the way typefaces are used on the web. The following exercises describe and experiment with these methods.

First, let's see what basic settings are applied to this layout.

1 If necessary, open **mylayout.html** and switch to Design view.

2 In the CSS Designer, click `<style>` in the Sources pane.

By selecting the `<style>` source, the Selectors pane displays all the CSS rules contained in the embedded style sheet.

▶ **Tip:** Depending on the size of the window, you may not see the entire attribute for font. Just hover the cursor over the font value to see the whole reference.

3   Select the body rule. In the Properties pane, select Show Set, if necessary.

Show Set limits the window display to only properties that have been styled.

4   Observe the entry displayed for the font property.

This setting was written in a sort of CSS shorthand that may be hard to understand. The Font field displays the following attribute: 100%/1.4 Verdana, Arial, Helvetica, sans-serif. The attribute is actually composed of three different properties: font-size, line-height, and font-family. Many CSS properties can be combined like this to economize the code.

The first entry—100%—refers to the font size and sets it to the default size set in the browser itself. You can use specific measurements if you prefer, such as 18pt, 18px, or .25in. But, you can run into trouble with this method when the webpage is displayed on various devices, like cell phones and tablets. Fixed sizes also don't take into account the resolution of the device or user preferences. Some users like smaller fonts; some need larger sizes.

By using 100%, the rule is setting a threshold for the body rule based on the device or software being used. Then, by using percentages (%) for other rules you will create a relationship with this base setting that will automatically adjust the type size when the user adjusts the browser default. In other words, if you set the headings to be 200% of the size of the body, the heading will always be twice the size of the body text regardless of the device or user interaction.

The second entry—1.4—refers to the line height, called *leading* by graphic designers, which is the spacing between lines of type in the same paragraph. Written together—100%/1.4—is the same as saying: *font-size/line height*. Written this way, it means 1.4 times the height of the font or 140%. Most designers prefer a line height between 1.2 and 1.6 for most applications, depending on the font used. These ratios provide good legibility without wasting too much vertical space.

Line height set at 100%	**Line height set at 120%**	**Line height set at 140%**
Rum essi berum ut fuga. Nem harum quodite mporrum quis idunt quidit, quaes acest ent quam non pratene paritatibust quias apisti debitat hicium explis dignim denihic ieturis sequod minullaccus quis num quibeatemos am, tem volum ipsundu ciatempe dolorem voluptatur, ut explitatur rem fuga. Et eum quam, sit et il moditia pos eumquaspiet eicia nobitatet fuga. Bus exerovit,	Rum essi berum ut fuga. Nem harum quodite mporrum quis idunt quidit, quaes acest ent quam non pratene paritatibust quias apisti debitat hicium explis dignim denihic ieturis sequod minullaccus quis num quibeatemos am, tem volum ipsundu ciatempe dolorem voluptatur, ut explitatur rem fuga. Et eum quam, sit et il moditia pos	Rum essi berum ut fuga. Nem harum quodite mporrum quis idunt quidit, quaes acest ent quam non pratene paritatibust quias apisti debitat hicium explis dignim denihic ieturis sequod minullaccus quis num quibeatemos am, tem volum ipsundu ciatempe dolorem voluptatur, ut explitatur rem

The third entry—Verdana, Arial, Helvetica, sans-serif—refers to the setting font-family. But it calls *three* typefaces and a design category, *sans-serif*. Why? Can't Dreamweaver make up its mind?

The answer is a simple but ingenious solution to a problem that has nagged the web from the very beginning. Until recently, the fonts you see in your browser are not actually part of the webpage or the server; they are supplied by the computer *browsing* the site. Although most computers have many fonts in common, they don't all have the same fonts. So if you choose a specific font and it isn't installed on the visitor's computer, your carefully designed and formatted webpage could immediately and tragically appear in Courier or some other equally undesirable typeface.

Normal browser display   Same page in Courier

For most people, the solution has been to specify fonts in groups, or *stacks*; the browser is given a second, third, and perhaps fourth (or more) choice to default to before it picks for itself (egads!). Some call this technique *degrading gracefully*. Dreamweaver Creative Cloud offers nine predefined font groups. If you don't see a combination you like, you can click the Manage Fonts option at the bottom of the Set Font-family pop-up menu and create your own.

Baskerville, Palatino Linotype, Palatino, Century Schoolbook L, Times New Roman, serif
Cambria, Hoefler Text, Liberation Serif, Times, Times New Roman, serif
Consolas, Andale Mono, Lucida Console, Lucida Sans Typewriter, Monaco, Courier New, monospace
Constantia, Lucida Bright, DejaVu Serif, Georgia, serif
Gill Sans, Gill Sans MT, Myriad Pro, DejaVu Sans Condensed, Helvetica, Arial, sans-serif
Gotham, Helvetica Neue, Helvetica, Arial, sans-serif
Impact, Haettenschweiler, Franklin Gothic Bold, Arial Black, sans-serif
Lucida Grande, Lucida Sans Unicode, Lucida Sans, DejaVu Sans, Verdana, sans-serif
Segoe, Segoe UI, DejaVu Sans, Trebuchet MS, Verdana, sans-serif

Manage Fonts...

Before you start building your own group, remember this: Go ahead and pick *your* favorite font, but then try to figure out what fonts are installed on your visitors' computers and add them to the list, too. For example, you may prefer the font Hoefelter Allgemeine Bold Condensed, but the majority of web users are unlikely to have it installed on their computers. By all means, select Hoefelter as your first choice, just don't forget to slip in some of the more tried-and-true or *web-safe* fonts, such as Arial, Helvetica, Tahoma, Times New Roman, Trebuchet MS, Verdana, and finally, a design category like serif or sans serif.

In the last few years a new trend has been gaining momentum to use fonts that are actually hosted on the site or by a third-party service. The reason for the popularity is obvious, your design choices are no longer limited to the dozen or so fonts from which everyone can choose. You can choose among thousands of designs and develop a unique look and personality that was nearly impossible in the past. But this option also comes with a cost.

Web-hosted fonts offer a vast variety of design options.

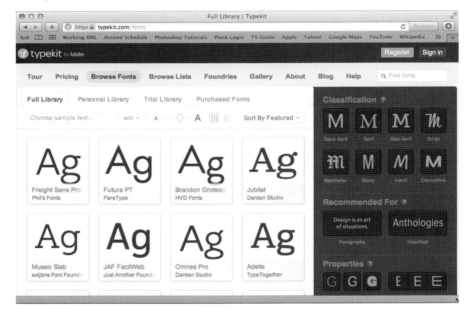

Licensing restrictions prohibit many fonts within web-hosted applications altogether. Some free fonts have file formats that are not compatible with certain cell phones and mobile devices. You can buy fonts designed for web hosting or pay for third-party font hosting services. Multiple sources, such as Google and Font Squirrel, even have free fonts. Luckily, Dreamweaver CC has a new service called Adobe Edge Web Fonts built right into the program. We will explore this option later in this lesson.

Typeface vs. font: Know the difference?

People throw the terms *typeface* and *font* around all the time as if they were interchangeable. They are not. Do you know the difference? Typeface refers to the design of an entire family of letterforms. Font refers to one specific design. In other words, a typeface is usually comprised of multiple fonts. Typically, a typeface will feature four basic designs: regular, italic, bold, and bold-italic. When you choose a font in a CSS specification, you usually choose the regular format, or font, by default.

When a CSS specification calls for italic or bold, the browser will normally load the italic or bold versions of the typeface automatically. However, you should be aware that many browsers can actually generate italic or bold effects when these fonts are not present or available. Purists resent this capability and go out of their way to define rules for italic and bold variations with specific calls to italic and bold versions of the typefaces they want to use.

Setting the font-family

The first choice for most web designers is selecting the basic typeface to display their content. In this exercise, you will learn how to apply a global site typeface by editing a single rule.

1 If necessary, open **mylayout.html**, and switch to Design view.

2 In the CSS Designer, click `<style>` in the Sources pane.

3 In the Properties pane of CSS Designer, click to deselect the Show Set option.

   The Properties pane now displays all CSS specifications set for the body rule. Note how the font setting we reviewed earlier is divvied up to its individual properties. You can edit the setting either way, but you may find this method to be easier and more accurate.

4 At the top of the Properties pane, click the Text category icon.

The window display focuses on CSS Properties for text.

5   Locate the font-family property and click the "Verdana, Arial, Helvetica, sans-serif" value.

A window appears showing the nine predefined Dreamweaver font stacks. You can select one of these or create your own.

6   At the bottom of the font stack window, click Manage Fonts.

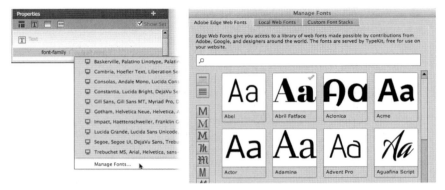

The Manage Fonts dialog box is divided into three tabs: Adobe Edge Web Fonts, Local Web Fonts, and Custom Font Stacks. The first two tabs provide access to a new technique for using custom fonts on the web; you'll experiment with web fonts in the next exercise. For the site's base font, let's create a custom font stack.

7   Click the Custom Font Stacks tab.

This tab displays the nine predefined font stacks and a list of available fonts on your computer. Creating your own font stack is easy.

8   In the Available Fonts, locate the Trebuchet MS font. To find it quickly, type the name in the search field at the bottom of the list.

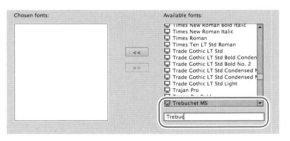

9 When you locate Trebuchet MS, select it and click the << button to add it to the Chosen Fonts list.

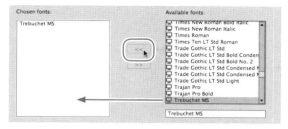

10 Repeat steps 8 and 9 to add Verdana, Arial, Helvetica, and sans-serif to the Chosen Fonts list.

The fonts added to the stack are used by the browser in the order selected, with Trebuchet MS having the highest preference. If Trebuchet MS is not active on the user's computer, it will default to the next font in the list: Verdana. If none of the named fonts are available, the browser will automatically select a font in the sans-serif category. You can even add names for fonts that are not installed on your own computer by just typing them into the Available Fonts search field. Just be sure to type the name correctly or the browser will ignore the named font.

All the fonts selected in step 10 typically are installed on every computer using the Windows or the Mac operating systems, so it's unlikely that all of them will be missing. Using fonts other than the ones named is OK, but there's no guarantee that any of them will be present on the user's computer when they visit your site. If you do this, just remember to add several of the common web-safe fonts to the end of your stack.

Your new custom stack appears at the bottom of the Font List. You can rearrange the items in the list by clicking the up (▲) or down (▼) icons.

11 Select the new stack, and move it to the top of the list. Click Done.

The Manage Fonts dialog box closes, but the font-family specification has not changed.

12 Click "Verdana, Arial, Helvetica, sans-serif" again and select your custom font stack.

Your font stack appears as the value for the font-family property. The text in the layout is now displayed in the Trebuchet MS font.

You have successfully changed the basic font of the entire webpage by editing one rule. All the text on the page now displays in Trebuchet MS. If Trebuchet MS is *not* available on a visitor's computer, the page will default to Verdana, then to Arial, then to Helvetica, and then to a sans-serif font on the user's computer.

Introducing Adobe Edge Web Fonts

The latest trend around the Internet is the rising use of custom typefaces. For years we've been stuck with the familiar but faded presence of the same web-safe fonts gracing most of our websites: Arial, Tahoma, Times New Roman, Trebuchet MS, Verdana, and others. To use another less common typeface was to chance fate and flirtation with font substitution, or to render the custom typeface out as a graphic (and all that entails).

If the concept of web fonts is new to you, you're not alone. At the time of this writing "web fonts" had only been in existence a little over five years and only starting to gain widespread popularity for the last two.

The basic concept is relatively simple: The desired font is copied to your website or linked to from a common web server and the browser loads the font as needed. Simple, right? Using this method selecting a web-safe font would no longer be a concern. A longtime major design restraint would simply vanish. But, life and web design is not as simple as all that.

There are still a few hurdles for using fonts this way. First, many fonts have licenses that prohibit you from distributing them in self-running apps or hosting them on your website, where they could easily be accessed and purloined by your visitors. So, don't upload the contents of your local fonts folder to your website. The font owner (you're only renting them) could sue you and shut your site down. Second, some font formats are incompatible with certain devices and browsers, meaning that they might not work or could even crash the browser itself. Third, font files can contain viruses; loading fonts you obtained from a vendor or third-party service could expose users' computers to a host of unknown issues. Some IT managers may lock down their company browsers, restricting them from loading web-based fonts altogether.

However, all these limitations and others are not slowing down the use of web fonts. And, by using Dreamweaver CC, two main hurdles have already been dealt with. The Edge Web Fonts service gives you access to a vast library of high-quality free or open-source fonts built right into the program. But Edge Web Fonts is not the only source for web-based fonts. Adobe also provides a paid service named Typekit, which offers a much larger type library and many more design options.

Here are some handy links for more information on web fonts:

- Adobe Edge Web Fonts: http://html.adobe.com/edge/webfonts/
- Adobe Typekit: https://typekit.com/

Here are some other font services:

- Extensis WebINK: www.webink.com/
- Google Web Fonts: www.google.com/fonts/
- Font Squirrel: www.fontsquirrel.com/
- MyFonts.com: www.myfonts.com/search/is_webfont:true/fonts/

Using Edge Web Fonts

There's no need to be intimidated about using web fonts. Everything you need to implement this technology is built right into Dreamweaver CC. In this exercise, you will see how easy it is to use web fonts on your own site.

1 Open **mylayout.html**, if necessary. Switch to Design view and display the CSS Designer.

2 Insert the cursor in the *Insert main heading here* text. Examine the Selectors pane of the CSS Designer.

The COMPUTED option is selected, displaying the current formatting of the text in the Properties pane. The main heading is currently formatted in Trebuchet MS. Let's select a web font more in line with the design of the GreenStart logo and the mission of the organization.

The first step is to decide where to put the declaration. To make sure the new font is applied only to the heading in the main content, use a rule targeting only the `<h1>` element. There isn't one in the current file, so we'll create one.

3 In the Sources pane, click the `<style>` reference. Select the `h1, h2, h3, h4, h5, h6, p` rule in the Selectors pane.

These steps are setting up the CSS Designer to insert the new rule in the embedded style sheet directly after the `h1, h2, h3, h4, h5, h6, p` rule.

4 At the top of the Selectors pane, click the Add Selector (⊞) icon.

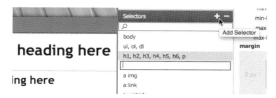

A new selector field appears.

5   Type **h1** in the new field.

heading here

ing here

The hinting window will focus on HTML tags that begin with *h*. You may type the entire tag name or simply select it using the mouse or by pressing the Down Arrow key and then Enter/Return. The selector is complete and targets only `<h1>` elements.

6   Press Enter/Return to complete the selector.

In the Selectors pane, the completed h1 selector appears below the h1, h2, h3, h4, h5, h6, p rule. If the rule appears in a different location, drag it to the proper position in the list.

7   In the Properties pane, select the Text (T) category icon. Click the default font reference next to the font-family property.

The Font list pop-up window appears.

8   Choose Manage Fonts.

The Manage Fonts dialog box gives you two options for using web fonts. You can buy or find free web-compatible fonts that are licensed for this purpose and host them yourself or use the Adobe Edge Web Fonts service to access hundreds of fonts in multiple design categories right inside the program. For the main heading, let's use Edge Web Fonts.

The tab for Adobe Edge Web Fonts displays samples of all the fonts available from the service. You can filter the list to show specific designs or categories of fonts.

9   In the Manage Fonts dialog box, select the option "List of fonts recommended for Headings."

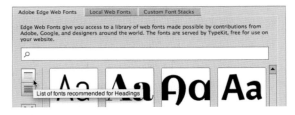

The window shows a list of fonts that are typically used for headings and titles. Since the logo is a sans-serif design, let's filter the list further.

10 Select the "List of Sans fonts" option.

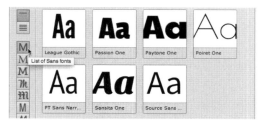

The list now shows only sans-serif, heading fonts.

11 Select the Paytone-one font, and click Done.

Paytone-one has been added to your font list.

12 In the Properties pane, click the default font reference next to the font-family property. Select Paytone-one from the Font list.

Paytone-one appears in the font-family property for the h1 rule. The heading display has changed, but it doesn't look like the preview of Paytone-one in the dialog box. What gives?

Because Edge Web Fonts are hosted on the Internet, you won't be able to see them until you display the page in an actual browser or, in this case, the next best thing: Live view.

13 Save the file. Switch to Live view.

The page renders again, this time with the Paytone-one font styling the main heading.

As you can see, using Edge Web Fonts on your website is really easy. But don't be fooled into thinking they're any less problematic than old-fashioned font stacks. In fact, if you want to use Edge Web Fonts, the best practice would be to include them in a custom font stack of their own.

Building font stacks with web fonts

If you're lucky, your web fonts will display every time for every user. But luck can run out, and it's better to be safe than sorry. In the last two exercises, you created a custom font stack and formatted the main heading with a font from Edge Web Fonts. In this exercise, you'll combine those two techniques by building a custom stack anchored on a web font.

1 Open **mylayout.html**, and switch to Design view, if necessary.

2 In the CSS Designer, select the h1 rule. In the Properties pane, click the Text category ([**T**]) icon. Click the value specification for font-family.

   The Font list pop-up menu appears.

3 Choose Manage Fonts.

4 In the Manage Fonts dialog box, click the Custom Font Stacks tab.

5 Click the plus ([**+**]) icon to create a new font stack.

6 In the Available Fonts list, locate the Paytone-one font. Click the << button to move it to the Chosen Fonts list.

► **Tip:** If you do not have one or more of the fonts, you can type the names manually to add them to the list.

7 Repeat step 6 and add Trebuchet MS, Verdana, Arial, Helvetica, and sans-serif to the Chosen Fonts list. Click Done.

Feel free to add more web or web-safe fonts to your list as desired.

8 In the Properties pane, select the new font stack for the font-family value.

The display doesn't change, but the new font stack, based on the Edge Web Font, will ensure that your headings will be formatted in all contingencies.

9 Save the file.

Now you've learned how to specify the look of your text content. Next, you'll learn how to control the size of the text.

Specifying font size

Font size can convey the relative importance of the content on the page. Headings are typically larger than the text they introduce. This page is divided into two areas: the main content and the sidebar. In this exercise, you will increase the size of the main heading and reduce the size of the sidebar text under the vertical menu, to give the main content more emphasis.

1   Open **mylayout.html** and switch to Design view, if necessary.

2   In the Selectors pane, select the h1 rule. In the Properties pane, click the Text category (**T**) icon.

3   Enter **220%** in the Font-size property and press Enter/Return to complete the specification.

The main heading increases in size. Now let's reduce the size of the text in the sidebar section. The first step is to identify whether any of existing rules are already formatting the section.

4   Insert the cursor in the caption text placeholder under the vertical menu. Observe the tag selectors at the bottom of the document window. Can you identify the HTML structure containing the caption element?

The caption is a <p> element. It is contained in an <aside> element nested in <div.sidebar1>. From the display in the Properties pane, you can see that formatting is being inherited, but that no rule is styling these elements directly. To reduce the text size, you could create a new rule to format any of the named elements. But before you choose which element you want to format, let's examine any potential conflicts that may arise.

Creating a rule for the <p> element would target paragraphs within the sidebar but ignore any other elements you wish to insert there. You could apply the format to <div.sidebar1> itself. Such specifications would certainly affect both headings and paragraphs, but it would also apply to every element in the sidebar, including the vertical menu.

In this instance, the best option would be to create a new rule targeting the <aside> element. Such a rule would style all contents contained therein but ignore the vertical menu altogether.

▶ **Tip:** By using a compound selector, you are targeting only <aside> elements that appear in <div. sidebar1>, which will prevent any unwanted inheritance issue if an <aside> element exists elsewhere in the page.

5   In the Sources pane, select <style>. In the Selectors pane, select .sidebar1. Click the Add Selector (➕) icon.

A new selector field appears below the .sidebar1 rule.

6   Create the following selector: aside

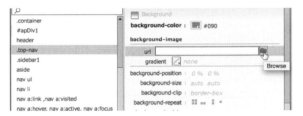

7   In the Properties pane, select the Text category, enter **90%** for the font-size property, and press Enter/Return to complete the setting.

The text in the <aside> element now displays at 90 percent of its original size.

8   Save the file.

Working with background graphics

Many designers resort to images to add graphical flair when code-based techniques can be problematic. But large images can consume too much Internet bandwidth and make pages slow to load and respond. In some cases, a strategically designed small image can be used to create interesting shapes and effects. In this exercise, you will learn how to create a three-dimensional effect with the aid of a tiny image and the CSS background property.

1   Select Design view, if necessary.

2   In the CSS Designer, select the .top-nav rule.

3   In the Properties pane, click the Background (▢) category icon. In the background-image section, click to edit the URL value. Click the Browse icon.

4   Navigate to the default site images folder and select **background.png**. Observe the image dimensions and thumbnail preview.

(The images folder view showing files: background.png, banner.jpg, butterfly-ovr.png, divider.png; Name background.png, Kind Portable Network..., Size 50 KB, Created 2/22/12 3:35 PM, Modified 2/22/12 3:35 PM, Dimensions 8 × 75; URL: images/background.png)

The image is 8 pixels by 75 pixels and approximately 50 kilobytes in size. Notice the lighter shade of green at the top of the graphic. Since the page is 950–pixels wide, you know that normally this graphic could never fill the horizontal menu, unless it were copied and pasted hundreds of times. But you don't need to resort to such antics if you know how to use the background-image property.

5   Click OK/Open to load the image.

By default, background images repeat automatically—both vertically and horizontally. The entire horizontal menu is filled seamlessly, but you can't see the final effect in Design view. To get the true impression created by this graphic, you may have to preview the page in Live view.

6   Select Live view.

The background graphic and chosen settings give the menu a three-dimensional appearance and an interesting textural effect. Some graphics, like this one, are not designed to repeat in both directions. This graphic was intended to create a rounded 3D effect for the top edge of a page element, so you shouldn't let it repeat vertically at all. CSS allows you to control the repeat function and limit it to either the vertical or horizontal axis.

▶ **Tip:** In Windows, you may need to right-click the image file to obtain the dimensions.

▶ **Tip:** When a graphic provides a textural effect along with shading, like background.png, it must be tall enough or wide enough to fill the entire element as necessary. Note that this graphic is much taller than the element it was inserted into.

7   Click the Repeat-x () icon.

The graphic will repeat only horizontally now; it automatically aligns to the top of the `<nav>` element by default. Let's add the same background to the `<footer>` element, too.

8   Insert the cursor in the `<footer>` element. In the Selectors pane, select the `footer` rule.

9   In the background-image URL field, browse, and select **background.png**. Click the Repeat-x () icon.

You may need to refresh the display to see that the background image fills the `<footer>` element, too.

10   Choose File > Save.

Working with classes, IDs, and descendant selectors

You've created and edited several CSS rules now that format various elements on the page. Some of the rules format individual elements like `<h1>` or `<p>`, while others format whole containers, like `<aside>` and `<footer>`. But formatting this way is like trying to do surgery with a sledgehammer. It can get messy.

As you learned in Lesson 3, you can target styling not only to specific elements, but also to elements as they appear in specific HTML structures. This is done by combining two or more tags together to create descendant selectors. Add custom classes and IDs to the mix and you can really fine-tune your styling. First, you'll learn how to work with custom classes and IDs.

Creating custom classes

CSS class attributes allow you to apply custom formatting to a specific element or to a portion of a specific element. Let's create a class that will allow you to apply the logo color to text in the file.

1 In the CSS Designer, click the `<style>` reference in the Sources pane.

In most instances, a `class` attribute has a higher specificity than the default styling applied to any given element and will override it, so the attribute's location in the style sheet shouldn't matter. Let's insert the new class at the end.

2 In the Selectors pane, select the last rule in the list. Click the Add Selector (⊞) icon.

A new selector field appears at the end of the list.

3 In the new selector field, type . (period).

A list of existing classes appears in the hinting window. You could select one of these classes using the mouse, or by arrowing down to it and pressing Enter/Return. The class we want to create doesn't exist yet, so you'll have to type it entirely yourself.

4 Type **green** in the Selector name field. Press Enter/Return to complete the selector.

The `.green` rule is added to the style sheet. The name of a class or ID can be almost anything you want. Dreamweaver will warn you when you create a name that is not allowed.

5 Create the following property: `color: #090`

Dreamweaver makes it easy to apply classes. Let's apply the class to an entire element.

6 Insert the cursor anywhere in the `<h1>` element in `<article.content>`. Make sure the cursor is flashing in the element and that no text is selected.

If any text is selected, Dreamweaver will apply the class to the selection using the `<span>` tag.

7 In the Property inspector, choose **green** from the Class menu.

Note: You may need to refresh the page display to see the updated tag selector.

All the text in the <h1> element is now formatted in the color #090 (green). At the bottom of the document window, <h1.green> now displays in the tag selector.

8 Switch to Code view. Examine the opening tag of the <h1> element.

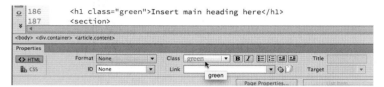

The rule is applied as an attribute to the tag as <h1 class="green">. When the cursor is inserted in an existing element, Dreamweaver assumes you want to apply the class to the entire element.

Now, let's remove the CSS class from the element.

▶ **Tip:** In some cases, you may have to click the appropriate tag selector before selecting the class from the Property inspector.

9 Insert the cursor anywhere in the formatted <h1> element in Code view.

Even while you are in Code view, the tag selector displays <h1.green> and green appears in the Class menu of the Property inspector.

10 Choose None from the Class menu of the Property inspector.

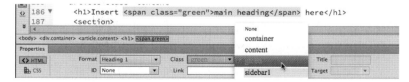

The class attribute is removed from the code. The tag selector now displays a plain <h1> tag. But oddly, although you applied None, the Class menu displays content instead. Don't worry. Nothing is actually applied to the <h1> element; the Class menu is simply indicating the class attribute assigned to the parent element containing the <h1>. Whenever you're confused, simply look at the tag selector. It always shows you whether a class or ID is assigned to a specific element.

Now let's apply a class to only a portion of the text.

▶ **Tip:** Class attributes can be applied and removed in either Design or Code view.

11 In the <h1> element, select the words *main heading*. Choose green from the Class menu in the Property inspector.

The class is applied to the selected text using the notation `<span class="green">`. The `<span>` tag is a generic container, similar to a `<div>`. The only difference is that `<span>` is an inline element and `<div>` is a block element. Otherwise it has no default formatting of its own and is usually employed to apply custom inline styling like this.

Now we will remove the class.

12 Switch to Design view. Insert the cursor anywhere in the formatted text. Choose None from the Class menu.

The text returns to the original formatting. When the cursor is inserted in a class-formatted element, Dreamweaver assumes you want to remove the formatting from the entire range of text.

13 Save the file.

Working with custom IDs

The CSS ID attribute is given the highest specific weight in CSS styling because it is used to identify *unique* content on a webpage and therefore should trump all other styling. The AP-div containing the butterfly logo is a good example of a unique element. The `<div#apDiv1>` is being used to position the butterfly logo at a carefully chosen location on the page, and you can be certain you'll have only one such `<div>` on each page.

Because of its unique nature, Dreamweaver provides some built-in features that affect only the ID-based formatting. Let's experiment with IDs by modifying the rule to reflect its use in the layout.

1 Select `<div#apDiv1>` in **mylayout.html**.

You can click the butterfly to select it and then click the `<div#apDiv1>` tag selector at the bottom of the document window.

The first thing that's different is that the Property inspector displays specifications, like width, height, and z-index, applied to `<div#apDiv1>` that it doesn't do for other `<div>` elements. There's also a special trick Dreamweaver will do for IDs that it doesn't do for any other type of selector. Note the ID field in the Property inspector.

2 In the Property inspector, change the ID to **butterfly**. Press Enter/Return to complete the editing process. Observe the selector list in the CSS Designer.

Notice that the rule name has also changed and now says: #butterfly. This relationship works for all ID references regardless of the type of element when you edit the name in the Property inspector. But it doesn't work in reverse. If you change the name of the ID in the CSS Designer, Dreamweaver doesn't update the element in the layout.

3 In the CSS Designer, change the selector name #butterfly to #logo

When you change the selector in the CSS Designer, the ID applied to the AP-div does not change. What's more, the rule no longer formats <div#butterfly>. The layout reflects the default behavior of an unformatted <div> element— without height, width, and other key properties applied—and it expands to the full width of <div.container> pushing the <header> element down below the height of the butterfly image.

To restore the layout to its intended appearance, you have to assign the newly renamed #logo rule to <div#butterfly>. This is also supported in a Dreamweaver feature.

4 In the Property inspector, open the Div ID pop-up menu.

Note that the menu has two apparent options: butterfly and logo.

5 Choose logo from the Div ID pop-up menu.

Reformatted, <div#logo> resumes its previous size and positioning.

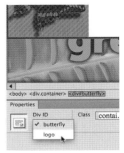

6 Save the file.

Use once and forget

Classes can be used as many times as you want, but an ID is supposed to be used only once per page. Although you could conceivably manually type the same ID multiple times yourself, Dreamweaver won't offer any help in your attempt at such rule breaking. You can demonstrate this functionality with a simple test.

1   Examine the CSS Designer and note the available class and ID selectors.

    Five classes and one ID selector are defined in the panel.

2   Select the butterfly logo. Click the `<div#logo>` tag selector.

3   Open the ID field pop-up menu and examine the available IDs.

    The only ID available is `logo`. What happened to `apDiv1` and `butterfly`? The original name `apDiv1` no longer appears in the style sheet and therefore won't appear in the pop-up menu. Additionally, as each ID stored in the style sheet is used in your layout, Dreamweaver interactively removes it from the menu to prevent you from accidentally using it a second time.

    Don't take this behavior to mean that there's a law saying `id` and `class` attributes must appear in the style sheet before you can use them within a page. Many designers create these attributes first and then define them later, or use them to differentiate specific page structures, or to create hyperlink destinations. Some `class` and `id` attributes may never appear in the style sheets or pop-up menus. The Dreamweaver menus are intended to make assigning existing classes and IDs easier, not to limit your creativity.

4   In the Class field menu, choose **green**.

    The tag selector now displays `<div#logo.green>`. As you can see, assigning both an `id` and a `class` attribute to an element at the same time is possible, which may come in handy in certain situations. For example, IDs are normally used to identify unique elements within a layout. Styling applied by an ID selector could format only a single element. On the other hand, a class attribute can apply to multiple elements, allowing you to format them in a similar manner.

5 In the Class field menu, choose None.

The tag selector reverts back to `<div#logo>`. To ensure you understand how ID selectors work differently from classes, let's try one more experiment. Let's try to assign the `logo` ID to another element in the layout.

6 Insert the cursor in the horizontal `<nav>` menu. Click the `<nav>` tag selector.

● **Note:** On a Mac, you may not be able to open the ID field at all if no IDs are available.

7 In the Property inspector, open the ID menu, and examine the available IDs.

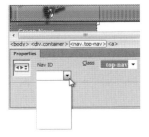

No IDs are visible in the menu; `logo` is already assigned to the butterfly.

8 Open the Class field menu. Examine the available class attributes.

Note that all class attributes are available. The Dreamweaver interface allows you to apply class attributes to multiple elements and prevents you from applying ID attributes more than once.

9 Close the Class menu without making a selection.

10 Save the file.

You now know some of the differences between classes and IDs, as well as how to create, edit, and assign them to elements on your page. Next, you'll learn how to combine these attributes using CSS to create descendant selectors to assign interactive behaviors to hyperlinks.

Creating an interactive menu

For the most part, CSS is used to apply static styling and effects to your HTML content. In the following exercises, you'll learn how to combine tags, classes, and IDs to produce interactive behaviors on normal hyperlinks.

1   If necessary, open **mylayout.html** in Design view. Click the Live view button.

Live view simulates the environment of an actual web browser. Video, audio, animation, and most JavaScript behaviors will perform as they would on the Internet.

2   Position the cursor over the vertical navigation menu in the sidebar. Observe the behavior and appearance of the menu items.

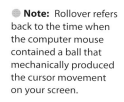

As the mouse moves over each button, the cursor icon changes to the hand pointer, indicating that the menu items are formatted as hyperlinks. The buttons also change color momentarily as the mouse passes, or rolls, over each, producing a dynamic graphical experience. These *rollover* effects are all enabled by the default HTML hyperlink behaviors and can be formatted by CSS.

3   Position the mouse cursor over the items in the horizontal navigation menu in `<nav>`. Observe the behavior and appearance of the menu items, if any.

The pointer and background color do not change. The items are not formatted as hyperlinks.

4   Click the Live view button to return to the normal Design view display.

5   Select the word *Home* in `<nav.top-nav>`. Do not select the spaces on either side of the word or the vertical bars, or pipes, that separate the words.

6   Type # in the Link field of the Property inspector. Press Enter/Return.

Adding a hash mark (#) in the Link field creates a hyperlink placeholder. This will allow you to create and test the necessary formatting, but at the moment it has also created a major conflict in the layout.

Note: Rollover refers back to the time when the computer mouse contained a ball that mechanically produced the cursor movement on your screen.

Note: Dreamweaver prevents you from making changes to your content in the Design view window while Live view is enabled. If desired, you can change both the content and styling using either the Code view window or the CSS Designer, at any time.

Troubleshooting CSS conflicts

For some reason the Home link has assumed the same styling as the ones in the vertical menu. Unintentional styling is a frequent problem with cascading style sheets, often caused by a selector that isn't specific enough. Then, formatting can bleed to other elements sharing similar tags or structures.

To track down the problem, the first step is to find out what rules are formatting both menus and then to adjust the specificity of the appropriate rules. Since the Home item is still selected, let's start with it. The CSS Designer is displaying the rules that apply to the link placeholder.

1 Observe and note the rules that appear in the Selectors pane.

2 Insert the cursor in a link in the vertical menu. Observe and note the rules that appear in the Selectors pane.

Rules affecting horizontal menu   Rules affecting vertical menu

Both menus are being formatted by the nav a:link, nav a:visited and nav a:hover, nav a:active, nav a:focus rules. Basically, these rules combine two tags <nav> and <a> to create several descendant selectors that target and style the vertical menu and different states of the hyperlink element. Because both menus share nearly the same structure, the rules are formatting the horizontal menu, too.

The trick to preventing CSS rules from formatting the wrong elements is to make the selectors as specific as possible. Let's look more closely at the two menus to see how we can limit the formatting to the correct elements.

3 Switch to Code view. Compare the structure of the two menus.

```
169 ▼   <nav class="top-nav"> <a href="#">Home</a> | About Us | Contact Us</nav>
170      <div class="sidebar1">
171       <nav>
172        <ul>
173          <li><a href="#">Green News</a></li>
174          <li><a href="#">Green Products</a></li>
175          <li><a href="#">Green Events</a></li>
176          <li><a href="#">Green Travel</a></li>
177          <li><a href="#">Green Tips</a></li>
178        </ul>
179       </nav>
```

As you can see, the horizontal and vertical menus share certain elements but they're also vastly different in several ways. For one thing, the horizontal menu has a class of `.top-nav` assigned to it, while the vertical menu contains `<ul>` and `<li>` elements and is contained in a `<div>` with a class of `.sidebar1`. With this information, an advanced user could devise several solutions to the issue in a few moments. But, what's a beginner to do?

Creating descendant selectors

The existing selectors are incorrectly formatting the link in the horizontal menu like the ones in the vertical menus. The solution to the problem is to create selectors that target one menu or the other but not both. Luckily, Dreamweaver can provide the answer.

1   Switch to Design view. Insert the cursor in the *Green News* link. Select the `<a>` tag selector.

2   In the CSS Designer, select the `<style>` reference in the Sources pane.

    The full list of embedded rules appears in the Selectors pane.

3   Click the Add Selector icon.

    A new rule appears in thelist: `.container .sidebar1 nav ul li a` selector.

    Dreamweaver has automatically created a very specific selector, containing four tags and two classes. If you swapped the a tag in each of the rules that currently format the vertical menu with this selector, the CSS conflict would be fixed. But such a drastic solution isn't needed. In reality, we only have to change the rules just enough so that they no longer format the horizontal menu, which we can do by simply adding any of the additional tags or classes shown above. Since the vertical menu may at some point appear outside `<div.container>` or `<div.sidebar1>`, the best solution is to use either the `<ul>` or `<li>` tags.

    Since we don't need this new selector, let's discard it.

4   Press the Esc key to cancel the creation of the new selector.

5   Change the selector: `nav a:link, nav a:visited` to `nav li a:link, nav li a:visited`

    The Home link is no longer formatted like the vertical menu. It's moved back to its original position and displays the formatting of a typical hyperlink.

6 Change the `nav a:hover`, `nav a:active`, `nav a:focus` selector to `nav li a:hover`, `nav li a:active`, `nav li a:focus`

7 Add hyperlink placeholders to the *About Us* and *Contact Us* items.

Be sure to select both words in each item before applying the placeholder. If you don't, each word will be treated as two separate links instead of as one.

Correct   Incorrect

Creating dynamic hyperlink effects with CSS

Now that you've successfully resolved the CSS conflict, you can learn how to recreate the dynamic hyperlink behavior you saw in the vertical menu. To make the horizontal menu look more like the vertical one, you'll first have to remove the underscore and change the text color. Let's start with the underscore.

1 Insert the cursor in the *Home* link. Select the tag selector for <a>.

2 In the Sources pane, select the `<style>` reference. In the Selectors pane, select the `.top-nav` rule. Click the Add Selector icon.

A new `.container .top-nav a` selector appears. The name `.top-nav a` is specific enough to format only links in the horizontal menu so you can delete `.container` from the name.

3 Delete `.container`. Press Esc, if necessary, to close the hinting window.

The selector created so far will target the default state of the hyperlink.

When a user clicks a link within a site, it usually changes color, indicating that the user visited that destination earlier. This is the normal, or default, behavior of hyperlinks. However, in the vertical and horizontal menus, we don't want the links to change their appearance after you click them. To prevent this behavior, you could make two rules that format the link and visited states, or simply create a compound selector that formats both states of the link at once. Let's modify the selector name `.top-nav a` while it is still open and editable.

4 Press Ctrl-A/Cmd-A to select the entire selector name. Press Ctrl-C/Cmd-C to copy the selector.

Hyperlink pseudo-classes

The <a> element (hyperlink) provides five *states,* or distinct behaviors that can be modified by CSS using what are called *pseudo-classes*. A pseudo-class is a CSS feature that can add special effects or functionality to certain selectors, such as the <a> anchor tag:

- The a:link pseudo-class creates the default display and behavior of the hyperlink, and in many cases is interchangeable with the a selector in CSS rules. However, as you experienced earlier, a:link is *more* specific and may override specifications assigned to a less-specific selector if both are used in the style sheet.

- The a:visited pseudo-class formats the link after it has been visited by the browser. This resets to default styling whenever the browser cache, or history, is deleted.

- The a:hover pseudo-class formats the link when the cursor passes over it.

- The a:active pseudo-class formats the link when the mouse clicks it.

- The a:focus pseudo-class formats the link when accessed via keyboard as opposed to mouse interaction.

When used, the pseudo-classes must be declared in the order as listed above to be effective. Remember, whether declared in the style sheet or not, each state has a set of default formats and behaviors.

5 Press the Right Arrow key to move the cursor to the end of the selector text. Type :link to add it at the end of the selector name.

The new .top-nav a:link selector is more specific and will be able to override any potential inheritance from the default a:link rule appearing elsewhere in the style sheet, as happened with the vertical menu earlier.

> **Tip:** As you type the selector name, notice how Dreamweaver offers you code hinting for the element. Feel free to select the correct pseudo class from the menu, which will help to speed up the task and prevent typing errors.

6 With the cursor at the end of the selector, type a comma (,) and press Ctrl-V/ Cmd-V to paste the selector from the clipboard.

7 Type :visited at the end of the pasted selector.

The selector now appears as .top-nav a:link, .top-nav a:visited in the Selectors pane. The comma works like the word *and*, allowing you to include two or more selectors in one name. By combining these two selectors into one rule, you are formatting the default properties of both hyperlink states at once.

8 In the Text category, enter **#FFC** in the Color field.

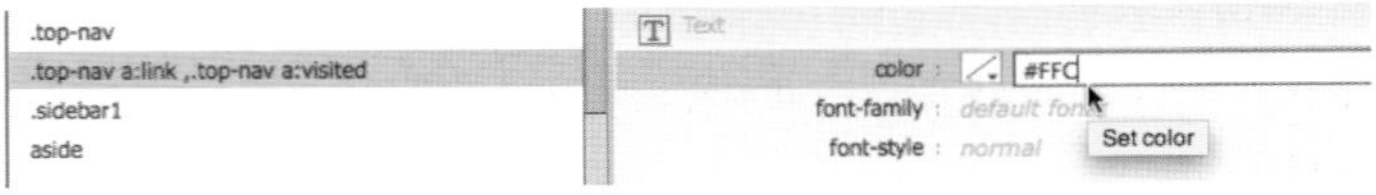

The hyperlink text color now matches the vertical menu. Now let's remove the underline from the hyperlinks.

9 For text-decoration, select the icon for none.

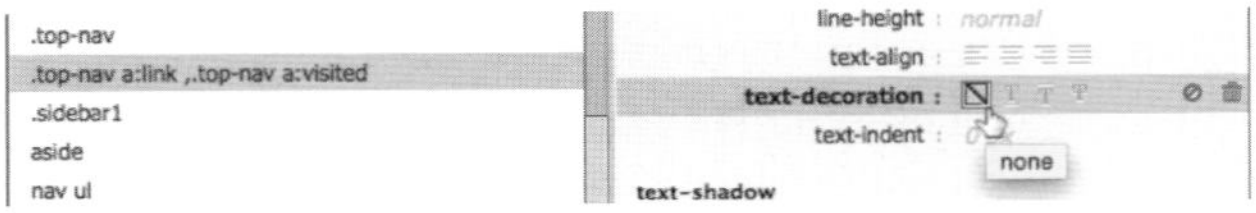

Let's test the hyperlink properties of the items in the horizontal menu.

10 Click the Live view button. Position the cursor over the hyperlink placeholders in the horizontal menu.

The mouse icon changes to the hand pointer, indicating that the text is formatted as a hyperlink. But these hyperlinks have none of the flair of the vertical menu with its changing background color. As explained, that interactive behavior is controlled by the pseudo-class `a:hover`. Let's use this selector to create a similar behavior.

11 Click the Live view button to return to the normal document display. Save the file.

Creating hyperlink rollover effect

In this exercise, you will modify the default hyperlink behavior and add interactivity.

1 Insert the cursor in the *About Us* link. In the Selectors pane, select the `.top-nav a:link, .top-nav a:visited` rule. Click the Add Selector icon.

A new selector field appears below the rule. The previous selector is still on the clipboard.

2 Press Ctrl-V/Cmd-V to paste `.top-nav a` into the selector field. Enter `:hover` at the end of the name (with no space between `a:hover`).

To make sure no undesirable formatting occurs, add the `a:active` pseudo-class to the hover state.

3 Type **,** (comma) and press Ctrl-V/Cmd-V to paste the selector again. Enter `:active` to the end of the selector name. Type a comma (,) and press Ctrl-V/Cmd-V to paste the selector again. Enter `:focus` to the end of the selector name.

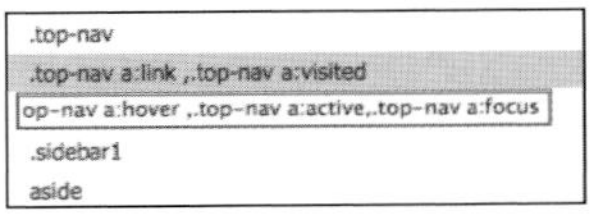

The new `.top-nav a:hover, .top-nav a:active, .top-nav a:focus` rule appears in the CSS Designer.

4   In the Properties pane, deselect the Show Set option. In the Text category's Color field, enter **#FFF**

5   In the Background category, set background-color to **#060**

This color is darker than the one used in the vertical menu, but more in keeping with the site theme. We'll update the vertical menu to match later.

6   Activate Live view and test the hyperlink behavior in the horizontal menu.

The background behind the hyperlink text changes to dark green as the mouse passes over it. This is a good start, but you may notice that the color doesn't extend to the top or bottom edges of the `<nav>` or even to the pipes dividing one link from another. You can create a more interesting effect by adding a little padding to the element.

7   Deactivate Live view. In the CSS Designer, select the `.top-nav a:hover, .top-nav a:active, .top-nav a:focus` rule.

8   In the Layout category, enter **5px** in the Top Padding field. If necessary, click the Link (🔗) icon in the center of the Padding diagram to modify all four settings at once.

9   Activate Live view, and test the hyperlink behavior in the horizontal menu.

The background color of each link now extends five pixels all around the hyperlink. Unfortunately, there's an unintended consequence: Not only does the padding cause the background to extend five pixels out from the text on either side of the link, but it also causes the other text to shift five pixels from its default position whenever the `a:hover` state is activated. Luckily, the solution to this problem is quite simple.

Have you already figured out what you need to do?

10 In the CSS Designer Properties pane, select the padding property for the `.top-nav a:hover, .top-nav a:active, .top-nav a:focus` rule. Click the Remove CSS Property (🗑) icon beside the padding diagram.

● **Note:** The `a:hover` state inherits much of its formatting from a or `a:link`. In most cases, you only need to declare values for formatting that will change when this state is activated.

▶ **Tip:** Do you know why you added space to padding and not to margins? Adding space to the margins won't work because margins would add the space outside the background color.

11 In the CSS Designer, select the `top-nav a:link`, `.top-nav a:visited` rule. In the Layout category, enter **5px** in the Padding field. If necessary, click the Link (🔗) icon in the center of the Padding diagram.

12 Activate Live view, and test the hyperlink behavior in the horizontal menu.

When the mouse moves over the links, the background color extends five pixels around the link without shifting. Do you understand why you added the padding to the default hyperlink? By adding padding to the default state, the `hover` state automatically inherits the extra padding and allows the background color to work as desired, without shifting the text.

13 Save the file.

Congratulations. You've created your own version of the interactive navigation menu in the horizontal `<nav>` element. But you may have noticed that the pre-defined background color selection for the `a:hover` state in the vertical menu doesn't match the color of the horizontal menu. To be consistent, the colors used in the site should adhere to the overall site theme.

Modifying existing hyperlink behavior

As you gain more experience in web design and working with CSS, identifying design inconsistencies and knowing how to correct them becomes easier. Since you know that the hover state is responsible for creating the interactive link behavior, it should be a simple matter to change the background color in the vertical menu. The first step is to assess what rules pertain specifically to the vertical menu itself.

1 If necessary, activate Live view, and compare the rollover effects between the horizontal and vertical menus.

The background color is darker in the horizontal menu. Although you probably already know what rule is responsible for this color, let's confirm your suspicions.

2 Click one of the vertical menu items. Observe the names and the order of rules in the Selectors pane.

The `nav li a:hover`, `nav li a:active`, `nav li a:focus` rule appears first.

3 In the Background category, change background-color to **#060**

4 Test the behavior of the vertical menu in Live view.

The background color of the vertical menu now matches the horizontal menu and the site color scheme.

5 Save the file.

Adding visual appeal to menus

Another popular CSS trick that can give menus a bit more visual interest is to vary the border colors. By applying different colors to each border, you can give the buttons a 3D appearance. As you've learned in the previous exercises, you first need to locate the rules formatting the elements.

1   If necessary, open **mylayout.html** in Design view. Insert the cursor in one of the vertical menu items, and examine the tag selector display.

The menu buttons are built using `<nav>`, `<ul>`, `<li>`, and `<a>` elements. You know that the `<ul>` element creates the entire list—not the individual items or buttons—and that you can eliminate it as a suspect. The `<li>` element creates the list items.

2   In the CSS Designer, select the `nav li` rule. Observe the attributes displayed in the Properties pane.

The `nav li` rule formats the basic structure of the menu button. The Properties panel shows the specifications for a 1 pixel dark gray border on all four sides.

To create a 3D visual effect, you'll need to enter different colors for each border. We'll use a lighter color for the top and left and a darker color for the right and bottom.

3   Enter **#0C0** for the border-color.

All four borders display the lighter color.

4   Enter **#060** in border-right color and border-bottom color.

Green News	Green News
Green Products	Green Products
Green Events	Green Events
Green Travel	Green Travel
Green Tips	Green Tips

Before   After

The 3D effect is complete. By adding lighter colors to the top and left and darker colors to the right and bottom, you have created a subtle but effective effect. However, this styling has one unfortunate effect. If you look closely, you'll notice that the menus are protruding from the sidebar.

Adding borders to a fixed-width element adds to its overall dimensions. As you experienced in Lesson 4, a change in an element's width can break your layout. The borders haven't broken the menus or the sidebar at this moment, but there may be future ramifications if you don't deal with the issue now. The possible remedies include removing the borders, increasing the width of the sidebar, or decreasing the width of the menu. In this case, the best solution with the fewest side effects is to reduce the width of the menu. Don't forget to deduct one pixel for the left and right borders.

5 Insert the cursor in the vertical menu. In the Selectors pane, select the COMPUTED value option.

The COMPUTED option displays the aggregated properties of all rules affecting the menu. The best part about this feature is that it allows you to edit the values, too.

◆ **Warning:**
The COMPUTED properties display can show settings from multiple rules at once. Be careful, changes made here can have unintended effects in the page or elsewhere in the site.

6 Change width to **158px**

The appropriate rule is automatically updated. The vertical menu no longer protrudes from the sidebar.

7 Save the file.

The master layout is getting close to completion. Another tweak to the design and you'll be ready to finalize the site template.

Creating faux columns

Although multicolumn designs are very popular on the web, HTML and CSS have no built-in commands to produce true column structures in a webpage. Instead, columnar designs—like the one used in the Dreamweaver CSS layouts—are simulated by using several types of HTML elements and various formatting techniques, usually combining margins and the float attribute. HTML5 and CSS3 can display text in multiple columns, but for the time being, the page layouts themselves will still depend on the older techniques.

Unfortunately, these methods have their limitations and downsides. For example, one of the problems you'll find with this layout is getting both columns to display at the same height. Either the sidebar or the main content section will appear to be shorter. This might not be a problem if the sidebar didn't have a background color, but since it does there will be a visible gap at the bottom as content is added to the main section.

There are methods, using JavaScript, and other coding tricks, to force columns to display at equal height, but these are not fully supported by all browsers and could cause your page to break unexpectedly. Many designers sidestep the issue altogether simply by refusing to use background colors. Then no one will notice any discrepancy.

Insert caption here.

Copyright 2013 Meridien GreenStart. All rights reserved.

Using only CSS formatting, getting all the columns to appear to be the same length in multicolumn designs is difficult.

Instead, in this exercise you'll learn how to create the effect of a full-height sidebar column by using a background graphic combined with the CSS repeat function. This technique works well with fixed-width website designs, like this one.

1. Using the CSS Designer, can you determine which rule applies the background color to the sidebar?

   This should be an easy one. The `.sidebar1` rule applies a background color to the sidebar. You're going to replace the background color with a background image. But you have to choose to which element in the layout to assign this image. Since the background color assigned to `<div.sidebar1>` was failing to extend to the bottom of the document, using that element is not the solution.

   The best candidate for the faux column is `<div.container>` because it holds both the sidebar as well as the main content elements. First, since we no longer need it, let's remove the background color from the sidebar.

2. In the Selectors pane, select `.sidebar1`. In the Properties pane, select the Show Set option. Click the Remove CSS Property (🗑) icon for background-color.

   Now you need to add the background-image to the `.container` rule.

3   Select the `.container` rule. In the Properties pane, deselect the Show Set option. In the Background category, edit the URL value for background-image. Browse to the default site images folder and select **divider.png**.

A graphic 182 pixels wide fills `<div.container>` from top to bottom and repeats from left to right across the entire `<div>`. The graphic should repeat only vertically, not horizontally.

4   In the Background-repeat property, click the Repeat-y (▮) icon.

The graphic appears behind the sidebar filling the element along the left edge, from top to bottom. Since the other structural elements are contained entirely within `<div.container>`, the background appears behind them and is visible only where appropriate.

Background images align to the top and left by default.

5   Save the file.

The column effect looks perfect, and the best thing about it is that it will fill the sidebar no matter how long the page becomes.

Final adjustments

We need to make a couple more tweaks to the sidebar. First, let's remove the extra space that appears between the menu and the image placeholder. As always, you'll need to identify the rule or rules creating this gap. You may be able to tick off the various culprits in your head by now. The obvious candidates would include the vertical menu, the image placeholder itself, the `<aside>` element containing it, or a combination of all three. Let's start with the vertical menu and work down, if necessary.

1   Insert the cursor in the *Green Tips* text in the vertical menu.

If you study the COMPUTED properties display in the CSS Designer, you see the styling for the `<a>` element by default. It's unlikely that any properties assigned to the hyperlink are causing the gap; otherwise you'd be seeing gaps between each of the menu items, too. The problem lies further up the structure.

2   Select the `<li>` tag selector.

None of the settings for this element are targeting any spacing property.

3 Select the `<ul>` tag selector.

Styling applied to `<a>`	Styling applied to `<li>`	Styling applied to `<ul>`
Properties _Computed_ **background-color(focus)** : ▇ #060 **color(focus)** : ▢ #FFF **padding(visited)** 5 px 15 px ⬭ 5 px 5 px	**Properties** _Computed_ **border-bottom** : 1px solid #666 **list-style** : none **color** : ▇ #000 **font-family** : "Trebuchet MS", Verdana, Arial, H **font-size** : 100% **line-height** : 1.4 ---	**Properties** _Computed_ **list-style** : none **border-top** : 1px solid #666 **margin** 0 px 0 px ⬭ 0 px 15 px

The `<ul>` element is formatted with 15 pixels of bottom margin. It looks like we found our culprit.

4 In the Properties pane, delete the bottom-margin setting.

The gap between the menu and the image placeholder disappears. For our last change, let's make the text in the vertical menu match the size of the text in the horizontal menu.

5 Select the `nav ul` rule. In the Text category, enter **90%** in the font-size field. Press Enter/Return to complete the change.

6 Save the file.

Moving rules to an external style sheet

When prototyping a webpage design, keeping the CSS embedded in the layout is more practical. Doing so makes the process of testing and uploading files quick and simple. But an internal style sheet can style only one page at a time. An external style sheet can be linked to any number of pages and, for most web applications, is the normal and preferred workflow. Before this page is put into production as a template, moving the rules from the `<head>` section of the document to an external CSS style sheet is a good idea. Dreamweaver provides the means to handle that task quickly and easily.

1 If necessary, open **mylyout.html** in Design view. In the CSS Designer, click the Add CSS Source (➕) icon.

2 Choose Create A New CSS File from the pop-up menu.

The Create A New CSS File dialog box appears.

3 Type **mygreen_styles** in the File/URL field. Click OK.

Dreamweaver creates a new file in the site root and adds the .css extension to the filename automatically. You can now move any of the embedded rules to the new CSS file.

4 In the Sources pane, select the `<style>` reference. Select the first rule, body. Hold Shift and select the last rule in the list.

5 Release the Shift key and drag the selected rules to **mygreen_styles.css** in the Sources pane.

If the `<style>` reference remains selected, the Selectors pane becomes empty. The empty `<style>` reference is no longer needed and can be removed.

6 In the Sources pane, select the `<style>` reference and then click the Remove CSS Source (⊟) icon.

The `<style>` reference is deleted.

▶ **Tip:** Once you move the CSS to an external file, remember to use the Save All command moving forward. Pressing Ctrl-S/ Cmd-S saves only the top document in the Dreamweaver interface. Other files that are open and referenced that have been changed are not saved automatically.

7 Choose File > Save All. Or, press Ctrl-Alt-Shift-S/ Cmd-Ctrl-S to access the keyboard shortcut for the Save All command you created in Lesson 1, "Customizing Your Workspace."

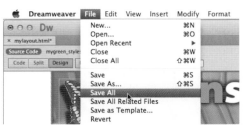

Congratulations, you've completed the basic layout for your new website. Before we convert the file into a Dreamweaver template, you'll perform one last CSS chore.

Creating style sheets for other media

Current best practices call for the separation of presentation (CSS) from content (the HTML tags, text, and other page elements). The reason is simple: By separating the formatting, which may only be relevant for one type of medium, one HTML document can be formatted instantly for multiple purposes. This is done by attaching more than one style sheet to a page. By creating and attaching style sheets optimized for other media, the specific browsing application can select the appropriate style sheet (and formatting) for its own needs. For example, the style sheet created and applied in the previous exercises was designed for a typical desktop computer display. In this exercise, you'll convert a screen-media CSS file to one optimized for printing devices.

Today, designers frequently include a Print link on pages heavy with text or for sales receipts, so that users can send the information to a printer more effectively. "Print" style sheets often adjust colors to work better for laser and inkjet printers, hide unneeded page elements, or adjust page sizes and layouts to be more suitable for printing.

When the print queue is activated, the printing application checks for a print-media style sheet. If one is present, the relevant CSS rules are taken into account. If not, the printer defers to the rules in the existing "screen" or "all-media" style sheets or to the CSS defaults for print output supported by the browser.

Creating a print-media style sheet

Although you can develop a print style sheet from scratch, converting an existing screen-media style sheet is usually much faster. The first step is to save the existing external style sheet under a new name.

1 In the Files panel, double-click **mygreen_styles.css** to open it.

2 Choose File > Save As.

3 When the Save As dialog box opens, type **print_styles.css** in the File Name/ Save As field. Make sure the site root folder is targeted. Click Save.

4 If necessary, open **mylayout.html** from the site root folder. In the CSS Designer, click the Add CSS Source icon in the Sources pane.

5 In the pop-up menu, choose Attach Existing CSS File.

   The Attach Existing CSS File dialog box appears.

6 For the Add As value, select Link.

7 Click to view the Conditional Usage option. From the Conditions section, choose Media: Print.

◆ **Warning:**
In this situation, Dreamweaver sometimes tries to save the wrong file when you select Save As.

8 Click Browse.

The Select Style Sheet File dialog box appears.

9 Select **print_styles.css** from the site root folder. Click OK.

A new entry—**print_styles.css**—has been added to the Sources pane. At the moment, both style sheets are identical. You will modify the print style sheet in the next exercise.

10 Close **print_styles.css** and **mygreen_styles.css**.

11 Save **mylayout.html**.

Hiding unwanted page components

A print media style sheet is called only in a printing workflow. But that doesn't mean that all devices or workflows will use it or be compatible with it. Print style sheets inherit styling from all other style sheets so there is no need to keep duplicative styles. In the same sense, rules that style onscreen elements you want to hide or reformat for print must appear in the print style sheet. In this exercise, you will learn how to create CSS rules for print output. First, let's see how web pages are processed by printers. Dreamweaver has no print feature, so you'll have to first display the page in a browser.

1 If necessary, open **mylayout.html**.

2 Choose File > Preview in Browser. Select your default browser.

The page is loaded into your browser.

3 Choose File > Print.

The print dialog box appears, but you may not actually have to print the page. Some browsers will provide a thumbnail preview in the print dialog box. Some dialog boxes will have a Preview button that opens a full-size page preview. In some browsers you must have a printer installed to see a preview image. If the dialog box doesn't offer a preview image, it may allow you to print or export to Adobe PDF. Or, you may just have to commit the layout to paper.

Regardless of how you see it, the preview shows a dramatically transformed page, even without changing a single CSS rule. Background images are dropped completely, as are most colors and text styling. The various content elements are now stacked in order, one atop the next. You can probably see a few candidates for modification already.

For example, the most important interactive items for a webpage are meaningless in print, including all navigation elements in both the horizontal and vertical menus. Using the print-media style sheet, you can hide unwanted portions of a page, and turn off colors to prevent a lot of wasted ink, toner, and paper. Let's start with the horizontal and vertical menus. The horizontal menu is styled by the `.top-nav` rule.

4 In the Sources pane, select the **print_styles.css** reference.

Be sure to select the CSS source before editing any rules to ensure that your edits are applied to the proper source file.

5 In the Selectors pane, select `.top-nav`.

6 In the Properties pane Layout category, set display to **none**.

Don't expect to see a change in the document window. Dreamweaver's interface supports only the screen media type and media queries. We'll preview the changes in the browser print preview at the end.

The vertical menu and the rest of the content of `<div.sidebar1>` are also not needed for printing. Let's turn them off, too.

7 In the Selectors pane, select `.sidebar1`.

8 In the Layout category, set display to `none`.

The butterfly logo was the only graphic visible in the preview, but it isn't needed for print output.

9 In the Selectors pane, select `#logo`. Set display to `none`

10 Select `.container` and apply or change the following specifications:

```
width: 100%
margin-left: 1in
margin-right: 1in
border-style: none
```

You must choose the **none** option for items you want to turn off. Print applications will inherit styling from other linked style sheets, in many cases. If you simply delete a rule or specification from the print-based sheet, elements may still be formatted by the main screen-media style sheet.

11 Select `.content` and apply or change the following specifications.

```
width: 100%
float: none
```

12 Save all files. Choose File > Preview in Browser and select your preferred browser.

13 Select Print Preview or print the page.

You've successfully removed all the unnecessary content from the page. As you can see, creating a print-media style sheet is easy by simply adapting your style sheet for screen-media.

Removing unneeded styles

Even with the changes you made in the previous exercises, many rules in the two style sheets are identical. Keeping two sets of styles that do the same job doesn't make sense. Whenever you can, remove unneeded code from your pages to reduce file size and allow the pages to download and respond more quickly. Let's remove from the print-media sheet any rules that haven't changed or that don't pertain anymore. You can delete unneeded styles using the CSS Designer. But be careful—even though a rule hasn't changed doesn't mean it's not needed for print rendering.

1 In the CSS Designer, select all rules that style the hyperlinks in the vertical and horizontal menus in **print_styles.css**; this includes rules that style a, a:link, a:visited, a:hover, and a:active properties. Click the Remove Selector icon.

Since the menus are no longer being displayed, you don't need rules styling hyperlinks contained within them. In fact, you can remove all the rules that format hyperlink behavior. But stay away from `.top-nav` and `.sidebar1`. Remember, these rules are being used to hide the two sections that contain the menus.

2   Save all files. Choose File > Preview in Browser and select your preferred browser.

3   Preview or print the page one last time.

You have adapted a screen-media style sheet and optimized it for fast and efficient download. You have completed the basic design of the page that will be used as the project template, and you have adapted it for print media. In the next lesson, you will learn how to convert this layout into a Dreamweaver template.

CSS Designer Redux

The CSS Designer is such an essential part of the new Dreamweaver workflow that it's important to know the proper way to use it to create new rules.

1   Insert the cursor in the element you wish to style (optional).

If you do not select an element intentionally, Dreamweaver will use the current position of the cursor on which to base the name of the new rule. The names may be used as is, or edited as desired.

2   Select the style sheet in which you wish to create the rule.

If no style sheet is selected, Dreamweaver will not allow you to create a new selector.

3   Select the media query, if applicable.

If no media query is selected, Dreamweaver will add the new rule to the default style sheet.

4   Select an existing rule to establish the desired cascade (optional).

By choosing a rule at this point, Dreamweaver will insert the new rule immediately after the selection. If no rule is chosen, the new selector is added at the end of the style sheet selected in step 2.

5   Create the selector.

Dreamweaver will create a specific selector based on the position of the cursor. You may use this selector as is, or edit it as desired. While open, the field will provide hinting with HTML elements, class, and ID names to help you create the selector name. Press ESC at any time to close the hinting pop-up menu.

6   Press Enter/Return to close the selector. To cancel the creation of the new selector altogether, press ESC a second time. No rule will be created.

Review questions

1 How do you attach an existing external style sheet to a webpage?

2 How can you target a specific type of formatting to content in a webpage?

3 What method can you use to hide specific content on a webpage?

4 How do you apply an existing CSS class to a page element?

5 What is the purpose of creating style sheets for different media?

Review answers

1 In the CSS Designer, choose Attach Existing CSS File from the Add Source pop-up menu. In the Attach Existing CSS File dialog box, choose the desired CSS file and select the media type by selecting the Conditional Usage area.

2 You can create a custom class or ID using descendant selectors to target formatting to specific elements or element configurations on a page.

3 In the style sheet, set the display property of the element, class, or ID to none to hide any content you don't want to display.

4 One method is to select the element and then choose the desired style from the Class menu in the Property inspector.

5 Creating and attaching style sheets for different types of media enables the page to adapt to devices or workflows other than web browsers, such as print applications.

6 WORKING WITH TEMPLATES

Lesson Overview

In this lesson, you'll learn how to work faster, make updating easier, and be more productive. You'll use Dreamweaver templates, library items, and server-side includes to do the following:

- Create a Dreamweaver template

- Insert editable regions

- Produce child pages

- Update templates and child pages

- Create, insert, and update library items

- Create, insert, and update server-side includes

 This lesson will take about 1 hour and 30 minutes to complete. If you have not already done so, download the project files for this lesson from the Lesson & Update Files tab on your Account page at www.peachpit.com, and store them on your computer in a convenient location, as described in the Getting Started section of this book. Your Accounts page is also where you'll find any updates to the lessons or to the lesson files. Look on the Lesson & Update Files tab to access the most current content. If you are starting from scratch in this lesson, use the method described in the "Jumpstart" section of "Getting Started."

Dreamweaver's productivity tools and site management capabilities are among its most useful features for a busy designer.

● **Note:** If you have not already downloaded the project files for this lesson to your computer from your Account page, make sure to do so now. See "Getting Started" at the beginning of the book.

● **Note:** If you are completing this lesson separately from the rest of the lessons in book, see the detailed "Jumpstart" instructions in the "Getting Started" section at the beginning of the book. Then, follow the steps in this exercise.

Previewing completed files

To better understand the topics in this lesson, let's preview in a browser the page you will complete.

1 Launch Adobe Dreamweaver CC.

2 If necessary, press Ctrl-Shift-F/Cmd-Shift-F to open the Files panel, and select DW-CC from the site list.

3 Expand the Lesson06 folder. Double-click **template_ finished.html** to open it. Observe the design and structure of this page.

This page was created from a template; Dreamweaver displays the name of the parent file in the upper-right corner of the document window. The layout is identical to the page completed in Lesson 5, "Working with Cascading Style Sheets," with some notable exceptions. Two areas on the page display blue tabs and borders. These areas, or *editable regions*, represent the most significant differences between your own layout and the finished template-based one.

4 Move the cursor over the GreenStart banner in the header in Design view. Note the mouse icon Dreamweaver displays.

The Locked (🚫) icon signifies that the area is locked and uneditable.

5 Select the placeholder *Add main head*ing *here* in `<article.content>`. Type **Get a fresh start with GreenStart** to replace the text. Save the file.

The `<article.content>` element is contained in one of the blue editable areas labeled *MainContent*, which allows you to select and change content within it.

6 Choose File > Preview in a Browser. Select your default browser.

The browser display won't give you any clues as to how this page differs from the one you created earlier—that's the beauty of a template-based page. For all intents and purposes, a template-based page is just a normal HTML file. The extra code elements that enable its special features are basically comments added and read only by Dreamweaver and other web-aware applications and should never affect the performance or display in a browser.

7 Close your browser and return to Dreamweaver. Close **template_finished.html**.

Creating a template from an existing layout

A template is a type of master page from which related child pages are produced. Templates are useful for setting up and maintaining the overall look and feel of a website, while providing a means for quickly and easily producing site content. A template is different from your completed pages; it contains areas that are editable and other areas that are not. Templates enable a workgroup environment where page content is created and edited by several team members, while the web designer controls the page design and specific elements that must remain unchanged.

Although you can create a template from a blank page, converting an existing page into a template is far more practical, and common. In this exercise, you'll create a template from your existing layout.

1 Launch Dreamweaver CC.

2 If necessary, open the **mylayout.html** file (which was complete at the end of Lesson 5) by double-clicking its filename in the root folder of the DW-CC website in the Files panel. Or, if you are starting from scratch in this exercise, see the "Jumpstart" instructions in the "Getting Started" section at the beginning of the book.

The first step for converting an existing page to a template is to save the page as a template.

3 Choose File > Save as Template.

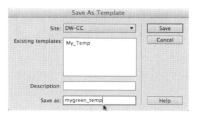

● **Note:** If you don't feel confident working with your own layout, use the method described in the "Jumpstart" section of "Getting Started" at the beginning of the book and open *mylayout.html,* from the Lesson06 folder.

▶ **Tip:** Adding the suffix *temp* to the filename, like adding styles to the name of the CSS file earlier, helps to visually distinguish files from one another in the site folder display, but it's not a requirement.

● **Note:** A dialog box may appear, asking about saving the file without defining editable regions; just click Yes to save anyway. You'll create editable regions in the next exercise.

Because of their special nature, templates are stored in their own folder, Templates, which Dreamweaver automatically creates at the site root level.

4   When the Save As Template dialog box appears, choose DW-CC from the Site pop-up menu. Leave the Description field empty. (If you have more than one template in a site, a description may be useful.) Type **mygreen_temp** in the Save As field. Click Save.

An untitled dialog box appears, asking whether you want to update links.

5   Click Yes to update the links.

Since the template is saved in a subfolder, updating the links in the code is necessary so that they will continue to work properly when you create child pages later.

Although the page still looks exactly the same, you can identify that it's a template by the file extension .dwt displayed in the document tab, which stands for Dreamweaver template.

A template is dynamic, meaning that Dreamweaver maintains a connection to all pages within the site that are derived from the template. Whenever you add or change content within the dynamic regions of the page and save it, Dreamweaver passes those changes to all the child pages automatically, keeping them up to date. But a template shouldn't be completely dynamic. Some sections of the page should contain areas where you can insert unique content. Dreamweaver allows you to designate these areas of the page as editable.

Inserting editable regions

When you first create a template, Dreamweaver treats all the existing content as part of the master design. Child pages created from the template would be exact duplicates, except that the content would be locked and uneditable. This setup is great for repetitive features of a page, such as the navigation components, logos, copyright and contact information, and so on, but the downside is that it stops you from adding unique content to each child page. You get around this barrier by defining editable regions in the template. Dreamweaver creates one editable region automatically for the `<title>` element in the `<head>` section of the page; you have to create the rest.

First, give some thought to which areas of the page should be part of the template and which should be open for editing. At the moment, two sections of your current layout need to be editable: `<article.content>` and a part of `<div.sidebar1>`. Although editable regions don't have to be limited to such elements, they are easier to manage.

1 Insert the cursor in the heading *insert main heading here.* Click the `<article.content>` tag selector.

2 Choose Insert > Template > Editable Region.

3 In the New Editable Region dialog box, type **MainContent** in the Name field. Click OK.

Each editable region must have a unique name, but no other special conventions apply. However, keeping them short and descriptive is a good practice. The name is used solely within Dreamweaver and has no other bearing on the HTML code. In Design view, you will see the name in a blue tab above the designated area, identifying it as an editable region.

You also need to add an editable region to `<div.sidebar1>`. It contains an image placeholder and caption that you can customize on each page. But it also includes the vertical menu, which will hold the main navigation links for the site. In most cases, you'll want to leave such components in the locked regions of the page, where the template can update them as needed. Luckily, the sidebar is divided between two distinct elements: `<nav>` and `<aside>`. In this case, you'll add the editable region to the `<aside>` element.

4 Insert the cursor in `<aside>`. Click the `<aside>` tag selector.

5 Choose Insert > Template > Editable Region.

6 In the New Editable Region dialog box, type **SideContent** in the Name field. Click OK.

Adding a title to each page is a good practice. Each title should reflect the specific content or purpose of the page. But many designers also append the name of the company or organization to help build more corporate or organizational awareness. Adding the name in the template will save time typing it in each child page later.

7 In the Title field of the document toolbar, select the placeholder text *Untitled Document.* Type **Meridien GreenStart Association – Add Title Here** to replace the text.

Note: If you are building this template using an alternative HTML 4 layout suggested in Lesson 4, "Creating a Page Layout," it is suggested that you apply these steps to `<div.aside>` instead.

● **Note:** The Update
Template Pages dialog
box may appear when
you save the file. Since
no template pages exist
yet, click Don't Update.

◆ **Warning:** If you
open a template in a
text editor, all the code
is editable, including
the code for the non-
editable regions of
the page.

8   Press Enter/Return to complete the title. Choose File > Save.

9   Choose File > Close.

You now have two editable regions, plus an editable title you can change as needed when you create new child pages using this template. The template is linked to your style sheet files, so any changes in those files will also be reflected in all child pages made from this template.

Producing child pages

Child pages are the *raison d'être* for Dreamweaver templates. Once a child page has been created from a template, only the content within the editable regions can be modified in the child page. The rest of the page remains locked. This behavior is supported only within Dreamweaver and other web-aware HTML editors. Be aware: If you open the page in a text editor, like Notepad or TextEdit, the code is fully editable.

The decision to use Dreamweaver templates for a site should be made at the beginning of the design process so that all the pages in the site can be made as child pages of the template. That's the purpose of the layout you've built up to this point: to create the basic structure of your site template.

1   Choose File > New, or press Ctrl-N/Cmd-N.

    The New Document dialog box appears.

2   In the New Document dialog box, select the Site Templates option. Select DW-CC in the Site list, if necessary. Select **mygreen_temp** in the Template For Site "DW-CC" list.

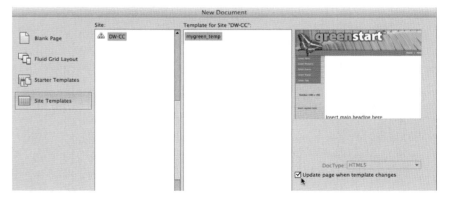

3 Select the Update Page When Template Changes option, if necessary. Click Create.

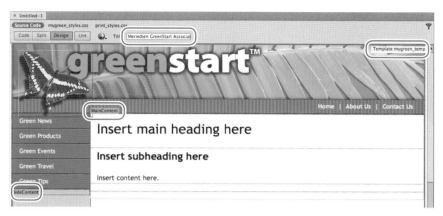

Dreamweaver creates a new page based on the template. Note the name of the template file displayed in the upper-right corner of the document window. Before modifying the page, you should save it.

4 Choose File > Save. In the Save As dialog box, navigate to the root folder for your project site. Type **about_us.html** in the File Name field. Click Save.

5 Move the cursor over the different page areas.

Certain areas, such as the header, horizontal and vertical menus, and footer, are locked and cannot be modified. Whereas, the content in the editable regions can be changed.

6 In the Title field, select the placeholder text *Add Title Here*. Type **About Us** and press Enter/Return.

7 In the MainContent editable region, select the placeholder text *Insert main heading here*. Type **About Meridien GreenStart** to replace the text.

8 In the MainContent editable region, select the placeholder text *Insert subheading here*. Type **GreenStart – green awareness in action!** to replace the text.

9 In the Files panel, double-click **content-aboutus.rtf** in the Lesson06 folder to open the file.

> **Tip:** To add a little editorial flair, use the command Insert > Character > Em Dash to insert a long dash in the heading.

Dreamweaver opens only simple, text-based file formats, like .html, .css, .txt, .xml, .xslt, and some others. When Dreamweaver can't open the file, it will pass the file to a compatible program, such as Word, Excel, WordPad, TextEdit, and so on.

10 Press Ctrl-A/Cmd-A to select all the text. Press Ctrl-C/Cmd-C to copy the text.

11 Switch back to Dreamweaver. In the MainContent region, select the placeholder text *Insert content here.* Press Ctrl-V/Cmd-V to paste the text.

The pasted text replaces the placeholder copy.

12 In the SideContent region, double-click the image placeholder. In the Select Image Source dialog box, select **shopping.jpg** from the default images folder. Click OK.

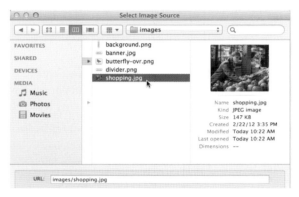

13 Select the placeholder text *Insert caption here* and replace the text with **When shopping for groceries, buy fruits and vegetables at farmers markets to support local agriculture.**

14 Save the file.

15 Click the Live view button to preview the page.

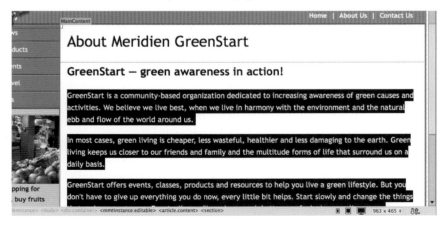

As you can see, there is no indication that this template child page is any different from any other standard webpage. Editable regions don't limit the content you can insert into them; the regions can include text, images, tables, video, and so on.

16 Click the Live view button to return to standard document display. Choose File > Close.

Updating a template

Templates can automatically update any child pages made from that template. But only areas outside the editable regions will be updated. Let's make some changes in the template to learn how a template is updated.

1 Choose Window > Assets.

The Assets panel appears. Typically, it is grouped with the Files panel. The Assets panel gives you immediate access to a variety of components and content available to your website.

2 In the Assets panel, click the Template category (🖹) icon. If no templates appear in the list, click the refresh (🔁) icon.

The panel changes to display list and preview windows for site templates. The name of your template appears in the list.

3 Right-click **mygreen_temp**, and choose Edit from the context menu.

The template opens.

4 In the horizontal menu, select the text *Home*. Type **GreenStart Home** to replace the text.

5 In the vertical menu, select the text *News*. Type **Headlines** to replace the text.

6 Select and replace the text *Insert* with the word **Add** wherever it appears in the MainContent or SideContent editable regions.

7 Save the file.

The Update Template Files dialog box appears. The filename **about_us.html** appears in the update list.

8 Click Update.

The Update Pages dialog box appears. Select the Show Log option to display a report detailing which pages were successfully updated and which ones were not.

9 Close the Update Pages dialog box.

10 Choose File > Open Recent > **about_us.html**. Observe the page and note any changes.

The changes made to the horizontal and vertical menus are reflected in this file, but the changes to the sidebar and main content areas were ignored, and the content you added to both areas remain unaltered. That way, you can safely make changes and add content to the editable regions without worrying that the template will delete all your hard work. At the same time, the boilerplate elements of the header, footer, and horizontal menu all remain consistently formatted and up to date based on the status of the template.

11 Click the document tab for **mygreen_temp.dwt** to switch to the template file.

12 Delete the word *GreenStart* from the *Home* link in the horizontal menu. Change the word *Headlines* in the vertical menu back to **News**.

13 Save the template and update related files.

14 Click the tab for **about_us.html** to switch back. Observe the page and note any changes.

The horizontal menu has been updated. Dreamweaver even updates linked documents that are open at the time. The only concern is that the changes have not been saved; the document tab shows an asterisk, which means the file has been changed and unsaved. If Dreamweaver or your computer were to crash at this moment, the changes would be lost; you would have to update the page manually or wait until the next time you make changes to the template to take advantage of the automatic update feature.

▶ **Tip:** Always use the Save All command whenever you have multiple files open that have been updated by a template.

15 Choose File > Save All.

Using library items

Library items are reusable bits of HTML—paragraphs, links, copyright notices, tables, images, navigation bars, and so on. You use them frequently, but not on every page within a website, and therefore would not necessarily include them in the site template. You can use existing page elements or create original library items from scratch and add copies of them where needed. A library item is like a template, only on a small scale. As with templates, when you make and save changes to a library item, Dreamweaver automatically updates every page that uses that item. In fact, they are so similar in behavior that some workflows may favor library items over templates altogether.

Creating a library item

In this exercise, you'll experiment by creating an alternative workflow model using library items in place of a site template.

1   Open **about_us.html**, if necessary. Choose File > Save As.

2   Save the file as **library_test.html**.

     A new tab appears at the top of the document window for the new file. It's an exact copy of the existing About Us page, down to its link to the site template. To implement the new workflow properly, you'll need to detach it from the template first.

3   Choose Modify > Templates > Detach from Template.

     The new file is no longer connected to the template. The editable regions have been removed, and you can modify them freely. Without a link to a site template, you won't be able to update changes to the common features of the page quickly and easily. Instead, they'll have to be made page by page, manually. Or, you could implement common page elements using library items.

4   Insert the cursor in the vertical menu. Click the <nav> tag selector.

5   Choose Window > Assets to display the Assets panel, if necessary.

6   Click the Library category (📖) icon.

     No items appear in the library for this lesson.

● **Note:** The Library folder doesn't need to be uploaded to the server.

7   Click the New Library Item (➕) icon at the bottom of the panel.

     A dialog box appears, explaining that the library item may not look the same when placed in other documents because style sheet information is not included.

8   Click OK.

     When you click OK, Dreamweaver does three things simultaneously: It creates a library item from the selected menu code and inserts an *Untitled* reference to it in the Library list, allowing you to give it a name; it replaces the existing menu with the library item code; and it creates a folder named Library at the site root level to store this and other library items. In Lesson 13, "Publishing to the Web," you will learn more about what files need to be uploaded, or published, to the Internet.

9 In the Library item Name field, type **vertical-nav**. Press Enter/Return to complete the name. Save the file. If the Update Files dialog box appears, close the dialog box without updating any files.

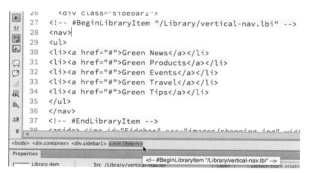

Working with library items is similar to using a template. You insert the library item on each page as desired and then update the items as needed. To test this functionality, you'll make a copy of the current page.

10 Choose File > Save As. Name the file **library_copy.html**.

11 Close **library_copy.html**.

The original file, **library_test.html**, is still open.

12 Click the vertical menu. Position the cursor over the vertical menu. Observe the menu display.

The link text is obscured, indicating that the menu is basically uneditable. The <nav> element has been replaced by <mm.libitem>. This is how Dreamweaver displays a library item.

13 Click the <mm.libitem> tag selector. Switch to Code view. Insert your cursor in the selected code.

● **Note:** A dialog box may appear at any time in this or the next two steps, warning you that the changes you made will be discarded the next time you update the page from the template. For the purpose of this exercise, click OK/Yes to preserve the manual changes.

```
26    <div class="sidebar1">
27    <!-- #BeginLibraryItem "/Library/vertical-nav.lbi" -->
28    <nav>
29    <ul>
30    <li><a href="#">Green News</a></li>
31    <li><a href="#">Green Products</a></li>
32    <li><a href="#">Green Events</a></li>
33    <li><a href="#">Green Travel</a></li>
34    <li><a href="#">Green Tips</a></li>
35    </ul>
36    </nav>
37    <!-- #EndLibraryItem -->
38    <aside> <img id="Sidebar" src="images/shopping.jpg" wid
```

<body> <div.container> <div.sidebar1> <mm.libitem>

Properties

Library item   Src /Library/vertical-nav.lbi   <!-- #BeginLibraryItem "/Library/vertical-nav.lbi" -->   Open   Detach from origin.

Note that the library item still contains the same code for the menu, although it's highlighted in a different color and enclosed in some special markup. The opening tag is

```
<!-- #BeginLibraryItem "/Library/vertical-nav.lbi" -->
```

The closing tag is

```
<!-- #EndLibraryItem -->
```

But be careful. Although the library item is locked in Design view, Dreamweaver doesn't prevent you from editing the code in Code view.

14 In the code, select the text *News*. Type **Headlines** to replace the text.

15 Activate Live view.

Dreamweaver displays the page showing the edited menu. You may be wondering why no warning dialogs appeared and why you weren't prevented from making the change in the first place. But the news isn't entirely bad. Dreamweaver is keeping track of the library item and your edits, intentional or otherwise. As you will see shortly, the change you made will be short-lived.

● **Note:** The manual change to the library item will remain in the menu for the time being.

16 Choose File > Close All.

Finally, a dialog box appears, warning that you have made changes to locked code. It further explains that the original code will be restored the next time you update the template or library item.

17 Click OK to preserve your manual edits. Save all changes.

18 Right-click `vertical-nav` in the Library list, and choose Update Site from the context menu.

The Update Pages dialog box appears.

19 Click Start.

Dreamweaver updates any pages in the site using the library item and reports the results of the process. At least one page should be updated. The **library_copy.html** file contains the unedited menu, so it should not have to be updated.

20 Click Close to exit the dialog box.

21 In the Welcome Screen, click **library_test.html** to reopen the file.

22 Click the Live view button to preview the page.

The menu has been restored to the original code. Library items allow you to insert repeatable content throughout the site and update it without having to open the files individually.

Updating library items

Templates, library items, and server-side includes exist for one reason: to make updating webpage content simple. Let's update the menu library item.

1 In the Library category list in the Assets panel, double-click to open the `vertical-nav` item, or right-click the item in the list and choose Edit from the context menu.

   The vertical menu opens without formatting as a bulleted list. Formatting is applied via CSS in the actual page layout. The library item is not a stand-alone webpage; it merely contains the `<nav>` element itself and no other code.

2 Switch to Code view. Select the text *News* and type **Gossip** to replace it.

3 Choose File > Save.

   The Update Library Items dialog box appears.

4 Click Update.

   The Update Pages dialog box appears and reports which pages were successfully updated and which ones were not.

5 Click to close the Update Pages dialog box.

6 Click the Live view button. Observe the vertical menu.

   The vertical menu has been updated successfully. Let's check **library_copy.html**.

7 Select the Files panel and double-click **library_copy.html** to open it. Observe the vertical menu in Live view.

The menu in the copy was updated, too.

8 Save all files.

You've successfully used a library item to add repetitive content to your webpages. As you can see, using library items and templates can save you a lot of time when you want to change and update more than one page. But, when the site starts to grow larger, say 100 pages or more, templates and library items may not be the most efficient method for creating repetitive and reusable content. For larger sites, many web designers turn to an option that's similar in concept, but one that relies on your web server instead: server-side includes.

Using server-side includes

Server-side includes (SSIs) are like templates and library items in some ways. They are reusable bits of HTML—paragraphs, links, copyright notices, navigation bars, tables, images, and so on—that you use almost anywhere in your site. The main differences between these Dreamweaver features and SSIs are in the way they are handled in the page code and then managed within the site.

Dreamweaver library item   Server-side include

In Dreamweaver there is a slight visual difference between library items and server-side includes. Both are uneditable directly.

For example, to use a library item, a complete copy of it must be inserted in the page's code *before* it's uploaded to the web. (That's why the library items themselves don't have to be stored on the server.) Then, each affected page must be updated and then uploaded before the change takes effect on the Internet—every one of them.

Dreamweaver library item   Server-side include

The difference in implementation couldn't be more striking. Library items insert a complete copy of the code into the targeted file, whereas server-side includes simply point to a resource on the server itself.

Unlike library items, SSIs must be stored on the web, preferably in your site folder. In fact, the SSI code doesn't appear anywhere in the page itself, only a reference to its filename and path location. The SSI appears only when the page is accessed by a visitor and rendered by the browser. This technique has advantages and disadvantages.

On the upside, server-side includes are the most efficient and timesaving way to add reusable HTML code elements to a large number of pages. They are faster and easier to work with than either templates or library items. The reason is simple: You need only a single file containing a menu or piece of important content—once edited and uploaded—to update the entire site.

On the downside, dozens or even hundreds of pages on your site could depend on one file to operate correctly. Any error in the code or path name, even a minor one, could cause your entire site to fail. For small sites, library items can be a perfectly workable solution. For large sites, living without SSIs would be hard.

In this exercise, you will create an SSI and add it to a page in your site.

Creating server-side includes

An SSI is almost identical to a library item—it's an HTML file stripped clean of any superfluous code. In this exercise, you will create an SSI from the code that creates the vertical menu. First, you'll have to make the menu editable again.

1   Open the file **library_test.html**, if necessary. In Design view, right-click the vertical menu. Choose Detach From Original from the context menu.

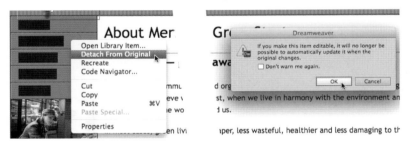

A dialog box appears, explaining that if you make this item editable, it will no longer automatically update when the original changes.

2   Click OK.

The markup for the library item is removed, making the menu editable.

3   Select the <nav> tag selector. Switch to Code view. Choose Edit > Copy or press Ctrl-C/Cmd-C to copy the code for the vertical menu.

The <nav> element should still be selected when you switch to Code view, so that you are copying the HTML markup completely.

4   Choose File > New. Select Blank Page from the Category section. In the Page Type list, select HTML. In the Layout list, select <none>. Click Create.

5   Switch to Code view, if necessary.

Note that the Untitled document is a completely formed webpage, with root, head, and body tags. However, none of the existing HTML code is needed for the SSI and could actually cause trouble if inserted into another page.

6   Press Ctrl-A/Cmd-A to select all the code in the new file. Press Delete.

All the code is deleted, leaving an empty window. The menu code is still in memory.

● **Note:** If you copy elements in Code view, you must be in Code view to paste them.

7   Choose Edit > Paste.

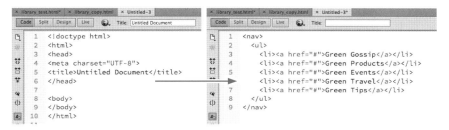

8   Choose File > Save. Navigate to the site root folder. In the Save As dialog box, click the Create New Folder button. Name the folder **includes**. Select the newly created includes folder, if necessary. Name the file **vertical-nav.html**. Click Save.

9   Close **vertical-nav.html**.

You have completed the SSI for the vertical menu. In the next exercise, you will learn how to insert it into a webpage.

Inserting server-side includes

On a live website, you must upload the includes files or folder to the server along with the normal pages of your site. A command inserted in the code of any page on your site would make a *call* to the server to add the HTML include in the indicated location. The include command will look something like this:

```
<!--#include virtual="includes/vertical-nav.html" -->
```

You can see that it consists of an includes command and the path location to the SSI file. Depending on the type of server you are using, the exact markup may vary. It may also affect the file extension you use for both the SSI and the webpage file itself. The include behavior is considered a dynamic function and typically requires a file extension that supports these capabilities. If you save the file with the default .htm or .html extension, you will probably find that the browser won't load the SSI at all. In the following example, you'll have to use the extension .shtml to support SSI functionality. Other types of file extensions—like .asp, .cfm, and .php intended for dynamic, data-driven websites—support SSIs natively. Each server type may require you to save the SSI itself with different extensions.

In this exercise, you will replace the existing menu with the one stored in the SSI.

1 If necessary, open **library_test.html**.

The file still contains the original vertical menu; to insert the SSI you'll need to delete the menu.

2 Insert the cursor in the vertical menu. Click the <nav> tag selector. Press Delete.

The entire <nav> element disappears, but don't move your cursor—it's in the perfect position to insert the SSI. Dreamweaver only directly supports server-side includes for ASP and PHP server models, but you can always write the code manually for any other file types.

3 Switch to Code view. Press Enter/Return to insert a new line.

4 Type `<!--#include virtual="includes/vertical-nav.html" -->`.

5 Press Enter/Return to insert a new line.

The line breaks have no effect on the server-side include or how it functions, they just makes the code easier to read.

6 Switch to Design view.

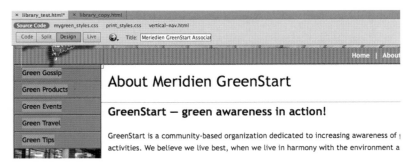

The vertical menu is visible again, but with two significant differences: The menu is not editable and, more importantly, the code for the menu is not even resident in this file.

Invisible includes?

SSIs can be seen in Dreamweaver in Design view and in Live view. However, an SSI may not render in a browser while it is still located on your local hard drive unless you're using a testing server or local web server, like Apache or Internet Information Services (IIS). To test SSIs properly, you may have to upload the page to a server configured to work with dynamic content.

If you don't see the SSI in Dreamweaver, however, you may have to flip a switch in your program preferences.

1 Press Ctrl-U/Cmd-U to edit Dreamweaver preferences. Or, choose Edit > Preferences (Windows) or Dreamweaver > Preferences (Mac) to display the Preferences dialog box.

2 From the Category list, select Invisible Elements. Select the Show Contents Of Included File option, if necessary. Click OK.

7 Click the Live view button to preview the page. Test the functionality of the vertical menu.

The menu appears and behaves as before.

8 Choose File > Save As. Name the file **library_test.shtml**.

As long as you didn't miss the additional *s* in the extension, you just created a new version of **library_test.html** and left the original file unchanged. Without the new extension, the SSI may not appear at all when it's uploaded to a web server. As it is, you'll also discover that the SSI probably can't even be tested in your local browser. That's because SSIs need specific server functionality to manage and load them into a browser. Testing them on your local hard drive requires that you install and run a *local web server*.

So far, you've created a server-side include and inserted it on a page in the site. In the next exercise, you'll learn how easy it is to update a file that uses an SSI.

> ▶ **Tip:** The name of the server-side include may need to change depending on the server model you are using. Dynamic server models (ASP, CF, or PHP) require different extension names and include commands.

Updating server-side includes

Although working with templates and library items offers vast improvements in productivity, it can also be a tedious chore. Changes made must be saved and updated to all the appropriate pages, and then each newly updated page must be uploaded to the server. When the change involves hundreds of pages, the problem is compounded. When you use SSIs, on the other hand, the only file that must be changed, saved, and uploaded is the include file itself. To see this method in action, insert the SSI into more than one page.

1 Open the file **library_copy.html**. Replace the library item holding the vertical menu with the SSI, **vertical-nav.html**, as you did in **library_test.shtml**.

2 Save the file as **library_copy.shtml**.

Let's change the include file and see how Dreamweaver handles the change.

3 Choose File > Open Recent > **vertical-nav.html**. You can also open the SSI by double-clicking its name in the Files panel.

4 In Design view, insert the cursor at the end of the last bullet, *Green Tips*. Press Enter/Return to insert a new list item. Type **Green Club** on the new line.

You created a new bulleted item, but it won't be formatted the same way as the other menu items if you don't add a hyperlink placeholder.

5 Select the text *Green Club* and type # in the Link field of the Property inspector to create a hyperlink placeholder.

You have added a new menu item, complete with hyperlink placeholder.

6 Click the tab for **library_test.shtml** and then the tab for **library_copy.shtml** to bring each file to the front. Observe the vertical menu in each file.

The menu has not changed.

7 Click the tab for **vertical-nav.html** to bring this page to the front. Save the file.

8 Examine the vertical menu in **library_test.shtml** and **library_copy.shtml**.

The menus have changed in both files. You should also notice one more thing: The file tabs at the top of the document window don't show an asterisk indicating a changed file that needs to be saved. Why? Because the SSI is not really part of the file. So when the code was changed in **vertical-nav.html**, it had no impact on the file one way or another.

9 Close all files.

You've learned how to create a server-side include, add it to a page, and update it. Many other webpage elements—such as logos, menus, privacy notices, and banners—can be added to your site using these easily maintained server-side includes. For small sites, templates and library items are fine; but for large sites, using SSIs instead can garner huge productivity gains. There's no need to upload dozens or even hundreds of updated pages at a time—you need to upload only one.

Dreamweaver's productivity tools—templates, library items, and server-side includes—help you build and automatically update pages quickly and easily. In the upcoming lessons, you will use the newly completed template to create files for the project site. Although choosing to use templates and the other productivity tools is a decision you should make when first creating a new site, it's never too late to use them to speed up your workflow and make site maintenance easier.

▶ **Tip:** In most cases, Dreamweaver will update the SSI instantly. If it doesn't, simply press F5 to refresh the display, or check to make sure you actually saved the SSI, as needed.

Sorry, no SSIs for now

A server-side include is a logical and important element for any web designer. So you may be wondering why we're not adding the SSI to the project template you just completed. The reason is simple: You won't be able to see the SSI in a browser if it's stored on your local hard drive without a testing server. So for convenience, we'll stick to the template-based components in the current workflow. However, once you have a full-fledged testing server installed and operating, feel free to permanently replace any appropriate template and library items with equivalent SSIs.

SSI in Dreamweaver   SSI without local web server

Review questions

1 How do you create a template from an existing page?

2 Why is a template dynamic?

3 What must you add to a template to make it useful in a workflow?

4 How do you create a child page from a template?

5 What are the differences and similarities between library items and server-side includes?

6 How do you create a library item?

7 How do you create a server-side include file?

Review answers

1 Choose File > Save as Template and enter the name of the template in the dialog box to create a .dwt file.

2 A template is dynamic because Dreamweaver maintains a connection to all pages derived from it within a site. When the template is updated, it can pass the changes to the dynamic areas of the child pages.

3 You must add editable regions to the template; otherwise, unique content can't be added to the child pages.

4 Choose File > New, and in the New Document dialog box select Pages From Templates. Locate the desired template and click Create. Or, right-click the template name in the Assets > Template category and choose New From Template.

5 Library items and server-side includes are used to store and present reusable code elements and page components. But whereas the code for library items is inserted fully in the targeted page, the code for server-side includes is inserted in the page by the server, dynamically.

6 Select the content on the page you want to add to the library. Click the New Library Item button at the bottom of the Library category of the Assets panel, and then name the library item.

7 Open a new, blank HTML document. Enter the desired content. In Code view, remove any page elements from the code except the content you want included. Save the file in the proper format for your workflow.

7 WORKING WITH TEXT, LISTS, AND TABLES

Lesson Overview

In this lesson, you'll create several webpages from your new template and work with headings, paragraphs, and other text elements to do the following:

- Enter heading and paragraph text
- Insert text from another source
- Create bulleted lists
- Create indented text
- Insert and modify tables
- Spell check your website
- Search and replace text

 This lesson will take about 2 hours and 15 minutes to complete. If you have not already done so, download the project files for this lesson from the Lesson & Update Files tab on your Account page at www.peachpit.com, and store them on your computer in a convenient location, as described in the Getting Started section of this book. Your Accounts page is also where you'll find any updates to the lessons or to the lesson files. Look on the Lesson & Update Files tab to access the most current content. If you are starting from scratch in this lesson, use the method described in the "Jumpstart" section of "Getting Started."

Contact Meridien GreenStart

For general questions and information email: info@green-start.org

When you contact our offices in Meridien, our friendly and knowledgeable staff is ready to serve you and answer your questions:

Association Management

Elaine is the President and CEO of GreenStart Association. She has 20-years experience in the environmental sciences and has worked at several grassroots organizations developing programs and services for co...

You may find her answering...
order.

Email Elaine at: elaine@gre...

Green Events and Classes

2013-14 Event Schedule

Date	Event	Location	Cost
Apr 14, 2013	Nature Preserve Hike	Burkeline Nature Preserve	$10.00
May 12, 2013	Mothers Day Walk	Meridien Park	Free
Jun 02, 2013	Day Hike	East Side Park	$10.00
Jun 23, 2013	Glaciel Park Tour	Meridien Park	$10.00
Jul 06, 2013	Beginners Backpacking - 3 days	Burkeline Mountains Resort	$125.00
Jul 14, 2013	East Trail Hike	East Side Park	$10.00
Sep 13, 2013	3-Day Backpack	Burkeline Mountains Resort	$125.00
Sep 14, 2013	Book Club	East Side Community Center	Free

Dw

× Untitled-1

Source Code   mygreen_styles.css   print_styles.css

Code   Split   Design   Live   Title: Meridien GreenStart -- Add t

greenstart™

Home | About Us | Contact Us

MainContent

Green News
Green Products
Green Events
Green Travel
Green Tips

Add main heading here

Add subheading here

Add content here.

SideContent

Sidebar (180 x 150)

Insert caption here.

Green Tips

At Home

- Wash clothes in cold water
- Hang clothes to dry
- Turn off lights in empty rooms
- Use motion sensors to turn lights on
- Plan driving errands to combine trips
- Walk more, drive less
- Install Compact Fluorescent lighting (CFL)
- Turn the thermostat down
- Unplug AC/DC adapters when batteries are charged
- Don't use the dry cycle in the dishwasher
- Install proper installation
- Use reusable containers
- Pick up canned and dry goods once a week or a month
- Use glass and aluminium
- Take your shoes off to save the carpet
- Unplug unused appliances
- Make cold dinners

Green News

Green Buildings earn more Green

There is a growing trend in commercial real estate to earn the EPA's Energy Star label. The award goes to the buildings that qualify in the top 25 percent in energy performance. Tinted windows, heat recovery systems, good insulation, high-efficiency lighting are all taken into consideration to lower a building's energy signature.

The reason is simple: tenants are attracted to the green label achieving higher occupancy rates, increased rents and higher profit margins for buildings that are sold. Energy Star buildings usually cost far less to operate, reducing overhead. Qualified buildings could realize increases in revenues of up to $120,000 for buildings with 50,000 sq ft.

Soon, it may not be an option. Many municipalities and government agencies are reviewing the need to mandate or regulate the process of labeling energy performance in homes and commercial buildings. Who wants to be an owner or tenant of a building that's labeled as an "Energy Waster"?

Dreamweaver provides numerous tools for creating, editing, and formatting web content, whether it's created within the program or imported from other applications.

Note: If you have not already downloaded the project files for this lesson to your computer from your Account page, make sure to do so now. See "Getting Started" at the beginning of the book.

Note: If you are completing this lesson separately from the rest of the lessons in book, see the detailed "Jumpstart" instructions in the "Getting Started" section at the beginning of the book. Then, follow the steps in this exercise.

Previewing the completed file

To get a sense of the files you will work on in the first part of this lesson, let's preview the completed pages in a browser.

1   Launch Adobe Dreamweaver CC, if necessary. Close any files currently open if Dreamweaver is running.

2   If necessary, press F8/Cmd-Shift-F to open the Files panel, and select DW-CC from the site list. Or, if you are starting from scratch in this lesson, follow the "Jumpstart" instructions in the "Getting Started" section at the beginning of the book.

3   In the Files panel, expand the Lesson07 folder. If you are using the Jumpstart method, all lesson files will appear in the site root folder.

Dreamweaver allows you to open one or more files at the same time.

4   Select **contactus_finished.html**. Press Ctrl/Cmd and select **events_ finished.html**, **news_finished.html**, and **tips_finished.html**.

By pressing Ctrl/Cmd before you click, you can select multiple nonconsecutive files.

5   Right-click any of the selected files. Choose Open from the context menu.

All four files open. Tabs at the top of the document window identify each file.

6   Click the **news_finished.html** tab to bring that file to the top.

Note the headings and text elements used.

7 Click the **tips_finished.html** tab to bring that file to the top.

Note the bulleted list elements used.

8 Click the **contactus_finished.html** tab to bring that file to the top.

Note that text elements are indented and formatted.

9 Click the **events_finished.html** tab to bring that file to the top.

Note the two table elements used.

Each of the pages uses a variety of elements, including headings, paragraphs, lists, bullets, indented text, and tables. In the following exercises, you will create these pages and learn how to format each of these elements.

10 Choose File > Close All.

Creating and styling text

Most websites are composed of large blocks of text with a few images sprinkled in for visual interest. Dreamweaver provides a variety of means of creating, importing, and styling text to meet any need. In the following exercises, you will learn a variety of techniques for how to work with and format text.

Importing text

In this exercise, you'll create a new page from the site template and then insert heading and paragraph text from a text document.

1 Choose Window > Assets to display the Assets panel. In the Templates category, right-click **mygreen_temp** and choose New From Template from the context menu.

A new page is created based on the site template.

2 Save the file as **news.html** in the site root folder.

3 In the Files panel, double-click **green_news.rtf** in the Lesson07 > resources folder.

The file opens in a compatible program. The text is unformatted and features extra lines between each paragraph. These extra lines are intentional. For some reason, Dreamweaver strips out single paragraph returns from text when you copy and paste it from another program. Adding a second return forces Dreamweaver to honor the paragraph breaks.

This file contains four news stories. When you move the stories to the webpage, you're going to create your first semantic structures. As explained earlier, semantic web design attempts to provide a context for your web content so that users and web applications can easily find information and reuse it, as necessary. To aid in this goal, you'll move each story over to the webpage one at a time and insert them into their own individual content structures.

4   In the text editor or word processing program, insert the cursor at the beginning of the text *Green Buildings earn more Green* and select all the text up to and including *"Energy Waster"?* (the first four paragraphs). Press Ctrl-X/ Cmd-X to cut the text.

Tip: When moving stories individually, cutting the text helps you keep track of which paragraphs have already been moved.

Tip: When you use the clipboard to bring text into Dreamweaver from other programs, you must be in Design view if you want to honor the paragraph returns and other formatting.

5   Switch back to Dreamweaver. In Design view, select the placeholder heading *Add main heading here* in `<article.content>` and type **Green News** to replace it.

6   Insert the cursor in the placeholder heading *Add subheading here* and note the tag selectors at the bottom of the document window.

The heading and the paragraph text are contained in one of the new HTML5 semantic elements: `<section>`. By inserting each news story into its own `<section>` element, you'll identify them as separate stand-alone content that can be viewed independently of each other.

7   Click the `<h2>` tag selector to select the element. Holding the Shift key, click at the end of the placeholder text *Add content here*.

The heading and paragraph placeholders are selected.

Tip: Use the `<h2>` tag selector to select the placeholder text and the HTML tags, too.

8   Choose Edit > Paste or press Ctrl-V/Cmd-V to paste the text from the clipboard and swap out the placeholder text.

The clipboard text appears in the layout. Now you're ready to move the next story.

9   Save the file.

Using a technique you learned earlier, you will create three new `<section>` elements and then populate them with the remaining news stories.

Alternative HTML 4 workflow

The upcoming sections describe and build an HTML5 workflow using semantic elements and structures. If you are unable to use this type of workflow and must still rely on HTML 4–compatible elements and structures, never fear. You can build your pages using an equivalent HTML 4–compatible CSS layout and simply insert your content entirely in the `<div.content>` element that appears therein, or you can substitute generic `<div>` elements in place of the semantic elements described next. You can even create a semantic structure by adding an attribute such as `class="section"` to the containing `<div>` element.

Creating semantic structures

In this exercise, you will insert three HTML5 `<section>` elements to hold the remaining news stories. If you need to work in HTML 4, an alternative method would be to insert the stories into individual `<div>` elements and then assign them a `class` attribute of `section`. But such a technique doesn't convey the same semantic weight as the HTML5 `<section>` element.

1   Switch to the text editor or word processor. Select the next four paragraphs, beginning at *Shopping green saves energy* and ending at *…in your own community*. Press Ctrl-X/Cmd-X to cut the text.

2 Switch to Dreamweaver. In Design view, insert the cursor anywhere in the existing news story and click the `<section>` tag selector.

The entire `<section>` element and its contents are selected.

3 Press the Right Arrow key once to move the cursor after the closing `</section>` tag in the code.

4 Choose Insert > Structure > Section. Click OK to insert a new `<section>` element.

▶ **Tip:** You may have to press Enter/Return twice to create the new element.

5 Press Ctrl-V/Cmd-V to paste the text from the clipboard and insert it into the new `<section>` element.

The second news story appears in the new `<section>` element.

6 Repeat steps 1 through 5 to create new `<section>` elements for the remaining two news stories.

When you're finished, you will have four `<section>` elements, one for each news story.

7 Close **green_news.rtf**. Do not save any changes.

8 Save **news.html**.

Creating headings

In HTML, the tags `<h1>`, `<h2>`, `<h3>`, `<h4>`, `<h5>`, and `<h6>` create headings. Any browsing device, whether it is a computer, a Braille reader, or a cell phone, interprets text formatted with any of these tags as a heading. Headings are used to introduce distinct sections with helpful titles, just as they do in books, magazine articles, and term papers.

Following the semantic meaning of HTML tags, the news content begins with a heading *Green News* formatted as an `<h1>`. Since `<h1>` is the most important heading, to be semantically correct in HTML 4 only one such heading should be used per page. However, in HTML5 best practices have not been formalized yet. Some believe that we should continue the practice used in HTML 4. Others think that using an `<h1>` in each semantic element or structure on a page should be permissible; in other words, each `<section>`, `<article>`, `<header>`, or `<footer>` could have its own `<h1>` heading.

Until the practice is codified, let's continue to use only one <h1> element per page (as the page title). All other headings should therefore descend in order from the <h1>. Since each news story has equal importance, they all can begin with a second-level heading, or <h2>. At the moment, all the pasted text is formatted as <p> elements. Let's format the news headings as <h2> elements.

▶ **Tip:** If the Format menu is not visible, select the HTML mode of the Property inspector.

1 Select the text *Green Buildings earn more Green*, and choose Heading 2 from the Format menu in the Property inspector or press Ctrl-2/Cmd-2.

The text is formatted as an <h2> element.

2 Repeat step 1 with the text *Shopping green saves energy*, *Recycling isn't always Green*, and *Fireplace: Fun or Folly?*

All the selected text is now formatted as <h2> elements. Let's create a custom rule for this element to set it off from the other headings.

▶ **Tip:** A good designer carefully manages the naming and order of CSS rules. By selecting a rule in the panel before clicking the Add Selector icon, Dreamweaver inserts the new rule immediately after the selection. If the new rule doesn't appear in the proper location, just drag it to the desired position.

3 Insert the cursor in any of the newly formatted <h2> elements. Choose Window > CSS Designer to open the CSS Designer, if necessary.

4 In the CSS Designer, select **mygreen_styles.css** in the Sources pane. In the Selectors pane, select the h1 rule. Click the Add Selector (➕) icon.

A new .container .content section h2 selector appears below the h1 rule. Dreamweaver created the name automatically based on your selection in the layout. This selector is a descendant selector, as described in Lesson 3, "CSS Basics," and will target its formatting only to <h2> elements that appear in a <section> element within <article.content>. Since all the content appears in <div.container>, there's no need to keep that element in the name, too.

▶ **Tip:** To close the selector field without adding other tag names, you may need to press the Esc key and then press Enter/Return.

5 Delete the .container class from the selector and press Enter/Return to complete the name.

6   In the Properties pane, deselect the Show Set option. Select the Layout category and enter **15px** in the Top margin field and **5px** in the Bottom margin field.

7   Click the Text category icon, and enter **#090** in the Color field and **170%** in the Font-size field.

8   In the document Title field, select the placeholder text *Add Title Here*. Type **Green News** to replace the text. Press Enter/Return to complete the title.

9   Save all files.

Creating lists

Formatting should add meaning, organization, and clarity to your content. One method of doing this is to use the HTML list elements. Lists are the workhorses of the web because they are easier to read than blocks of dense text and also help users find information quickly. In this exercise, you will learn how to make an HTML list.

1   Choose Window > Assets to bring the Assets panel to the front. In the Template category, right-click **mygreen_temp** and choose New From Template from the context menu.

    A new page is created based on the template.

2   Save the file as **tips.html** in the site root folder.

3   In the document Title field, select the placeholder text *Add Title Here*. Type **Green Tips** to replace the text. Press Enter/Return to complete the title.

4   In the Files panel, double-click **green_tips.rtf** in the Lesson07 > resources folder.

    The text consists of three individual lists of tips on how to save energy and money at home, at work, and in the community. As with the news file, you will insert each list into its own `<section>` element.

5   In the text editor or word processing program, select the text beginning with *At Home* and ending with *Buy fruits and vegetables locally*. Press Ctrl-X/Cmd-X to cut the text.

6   Switch back to Dreamweaver. In Design view, select the placeholder heading *Add main heading here* in `<article.content>` and type **Green Tips** to replace it.

Note: By default, each heading tag—`<h1>`, `<h2>`, `<h3>`, and so on—is formatted smaller than the preceding tag. This formatting reinforces the semantic importance of each tag. Although size is an obvious method of indicating hierarchy, it's not a requirement; feel free to experiment with other styling techniques, such as color, indenting, borders, and background shading, to create your own hierarchical structure.

7 Select the placeholder heading *Add subheading here* and the paragraph text *Add content here.* Press Ctrl-V/Cmd-V to paste the text from the clipboard.

The text appears, creating the first list section.

8 Switch to the text editor or word processing program; select the text beginning with *At Work* and ending with *Buy natural cleaning products.* Press Ctrl-X/ Cmd-X to cut the text.

9 Switch to Dreamweaver. In Design view, insert the cursor anywhere in the existing list of tips and click the `<section>` tag selector.

The entire `<section>` element and its contents are selected.

10 Press the Right Arrow key once to move the cursor after the closing `</section>` tag in the code.

11 Choose Insert > Structure > Section. In the Insert Section dialog box, click OK to create a new `<section>` element.

The `<section>` element appears with the placeholder text *Content for New Section Tag Goes Here* already selected.

12 Press Ctrl-V/Cmd-V to paste the text from the clipboard and replace the placeholder text in the new `<section>` element.

The second list appears in the new element. To create the last section, you will use the Insert panel.

13 Switch to the RTF file and copy the list items for *In the community.*

14 Switch to Dreamweaver. Click the tag selector to select the current `<section>` element. Press the Right Arrow key to move the cursor outside the element.

15 Choose Window > Insert to open the Insert panel, if necessary. Select the Structure category from the pop-up menu. Click the Section item to insert a new element. In the Insert Section dialog box, click OK.

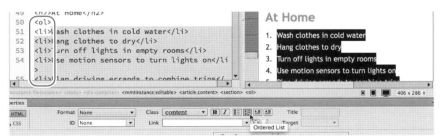

A new section appears with placeholder text.

16 Paste the list for *In the community*.

All three lists now appear in their own `<section>` elements.

As you did with the titles of the news stories, you'll format the headings that identify the tip categories.

17 Select the text *At Home* and format it as a Heading 2.

18 Repeat step 17 with the text *At Work* and *In the Community*.

The remaining text is currently formatted entirely as <p> elements. Dreamweaver makes converting this text into an HTML list easy. Lists come in two flavors: ordered and unordered.

19 Select all the <p> formatted text under the heading *At Home*. In the Property inspector, click the Ordered List (⊞) icon.

An ordered list adds numbers automatically to the entire selection. Semantically, it prioritizes each item, giving them an intrinsic value relative to one another. This list doesn't seem to be in any particular order; each item is more or less equal to the next one. An unordered list is used for formatting a list when the items are in no particular order. Before you change the formatting, let's take a look at the markup.

20 Switch to Split view. Observe the list markup in the Code section of the document window.

▶ **Tip:** The easiest way to select the entire list is to use the <ol> tag selector.

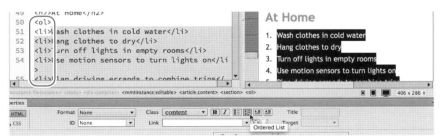

The markup consists of two elements: <ol> and <li>. Note that each line is formatted as an <li> (list item). The <ol> parent element begins and ends the list and designates it as an ordered list. Changing the formatting from numbers to bullets is simple and can be done in Code or Design view.

Before changing the format, ensure that the formatted list is still entirely selected. You can use the tag selector, if necessary.

▶ **Tip:** You could also change the formatting by editing the markup manually in the Code view window. But don't forget to change both the opening and the closing parent elements.

21 In the Property inspector, click the Unordered List (▤) icon.

All the items are now formatted as bullets. Observe the list markup. The only thing that has changed is the parent element. It now says <ul>, for *un*ordered list.

22 Select all the <p> formatted text under the heading *At Work*. In the Property inspector, click the Unordered List (▤) icon.

23 Repeat step 22 with all the text following the heading *In the Community*.

All three lists are now formatted with bullets.

24 Choose File > Save.

Creating text indents

Some designers still use the <blockquote> element as an easy way to indent headings and paragraph text. Semantically, the <blockquote> element is intended to identify whole sections of text quoted from other sources. Visually, text formatted this way will appear indented and set off from the regular paragraph text and headings. But if you want to comply with web standards, leave this element for its intended purpose and instead use custom CSS classes to indent text, as you will in this exercise.

1 Select Design view. Create a new page from the template **mygreen_temp**. Save the file as **contact_us.html** in the site root folder.

2 In the document Title field, select the placeholder text *Add Title Here*. Type **Contact Meridien GreenStart** to replace the text. Press Enter/Return to complete the title.

3 Switch to the Files panel and double-click **contact_us.rtf** in the Lesson07 folder.

The text consists of five department sections, including headings, descriptions, and email addresses for the managing staff of GreenStart. You will insert each department into its own `<section>` element.

4 In the text editor or word processing program, select the first two introductory paragraphs. Press Ctrl-X/Cmd-X to cut the text.

5 Switch back to Dreamweaver. Select the placeholder heading *Add main heading here* in `<article.content>` and type **Contact Meridien GreenStart** to replace it.

6 Press Enter/Return to insert a new paragraph. Press Ctrl-V/Cmd-V to paste the text.

The introductory text is inserted directly below the `<h1>` element. The text is not in the `<section>` element.

7 Switch to the text editor or word processing program and select the next four paragraphs that make up the *Association Management* section. Press Ctrl-X/Cmd-X to cut the text.

8 Switch to Dreamweaver. In Design view, select the placeholder heading *Add subheading here* and the paragraph text *Add content here.* Paste the text from the clipboard.

9 Format the text *Association Management* as a Heading 2.

The first section is completed.

10 Switch to the text editor or word processing program and select the next four paragraphs that make up the *Education and Events* section. Press Ctrl-X/Cmd-X to cut the text.

11 Switch to Dreamweaver. Insert the cursor anywhere in the *Association Management* text and click the `<section>` tag selector. Move the cursor after the `<section>` element.

Some Dreamweaver users prefer to make elements manually with the Quick Tag Editor.

12 Press Ctrl-T/Cmd-T to access the Quick Tag Editor. Type `<section>`, or double-click `section` in the Quick Tag Editor hinting menu and press Enter/Return to create the element.

You may need to press Enter/Return a second time to close the Quick Tag Editor and create the element. Once created, you won't see any evidence of the new `<section>` element other than the tag in the tag selector. Using this method, Dreamweaver creates the code, but it doesn't insert any placeholder text as before. Just start typing or paste the desired content.

13 Paste the text from the clipboard.

14 Select the text *Education and Events* and format it as a Heading 2.

15 Using any of the methods just described, create `<section>` elements for the remaining departments: *Transportation Analysis*, *Research and Development*, and *Information Systems.*

With all the text in place, you're ready to create the indent styling. If you wanted to indent a single paragraph, you would probably create and apply a custom class to the individual `<p>` element. In this instance, you'll use the existing `<section>` elements to produce the desired graphical effect. First, let's assign a `class` attribute to the element. Since the class has not been created yet, you'll have to create it manually, either in Code view or in Design view using the Quick Tag Editor.

16 Insert the cursor anywhere in the *Association Management* `<section>` element. Click the `<section>` tag selector. Press Ctrl-T/Cmd-T.

The Quick Tag Editor appears, displaying the `<section>` tag. The cursor appears at the end of the tag name.

17 Press the spacebar to insert a space.

The code hinting window appears, displaying the appropriate attributes for the `<section>` element.

18 Type **class** and press Enter/Return, or double-click the `class` attribute in the code hinting window.

Dreamweaver automatically creates the attribute markup and provides a list of any existing `class` or `id` attributes. Since the class doesn't exist yet, you'll type the name yourself.

19 Type **profile** as the class name. Press Enter/Return as necessary to complete the attribute and close the Quick Tag Editor.

20 Select the `<section.profile>` tag selector. In the CSS Designer Sources pane, select **mygreen_styles.css**. In the Selectors pane, select the `.content section h2` rule. Click the Add Selector (⊞) icon.

The `.container .content .profile` selector appears in the Selectors pane.

21 Delete `.container` from the selector name. Press Enter/Return to complete the name.

The name now displays as `.content .profile`.

22 In the Properties pane, click the Layout category icon.

23 In the Right and Left margin fields, enter **25px**. In the Bottom margin field, enter **15px**.

Border specifications can be entered individually or all at once.

24 Click the Border category icon.

25 Enter the following specifications for the Left border:

```
border-left-color: #CADAAF
border-left-width: 2px
border-left-style: solid
```

Entering the specifications all at once can often be faster and more efficient.

26 In the Properties pane, select the Show Set option.

The pane displays only properties that are set for the rule. It displays the specifications for the margins and the left border.

27 Click the Add CSS Property icon. Type **border-bottom** and press Enter/Return to create the property.

28 In the value field, type **10px solid #CADAAF** and press Enter/Return.

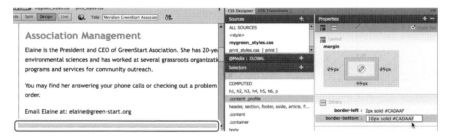

The borders help to visually group the indented text under its heading.

29 Select each of the remaining `<section>` elements and apply `profile` from the Class field menu in the Property inspector.

Each section is indented and displays the custom border.

30 Save all files.

Creating and styling tables

Before the advent of CSS, HTML offered few tools to execute effective page designs. Instead, web designers resorted to using images and tables to create page layouts. Today, tables are eschewed for page design and layout purposes for several reasons. Tables are hard to create, format, and modify. They can't adapt easily to different screen sizes or types. And, certain browsing devices and screen readers don't see the comprehensive page layouts, they only see tables for what they actually are—rows and columns of data.

When CSS debuted and was promoted as the preferred method for page design, some designers came to believe that tables were bad altogether. That was a bit of an overreaction. Although tables are not good for page layout, they are very good, and necessary, for displaying many types of data, such as product lists, personnel directories, and time schedules. In the following exercises, you will learn how to create and format HTML tables.

1 Create a new page from the template **mygreen_temp**. In the site root folder, save the file as **events.html**.

2 In the document Title field, select the placeholder text *Add Title Here*. Type **Green Events and Classes** to replace the text. Press Enter/Return to complete the title.

Dreamweaver enables you to create tables from scratch, to copy and paste them from other applications, or to create them instantly from data supplied by database or spreadsheet programs.

Creating tables from scratch

Dreamweaver makes it easy to create tables from scratch.

1 In Design view, select the placeholder heading *Add main heading here* in `<article.content>` and type **Green Events and Classes** to replace it.

2 Select the placeholder heading *Add subheading here* and the paragraph text *Add content here*. Press Delete.

3 Choose Insert > Table.

> **Tip:** When you select complete elements, using the tag selectors is a good practice.

The Table dialog box appears. Some aspects of the table must be controlled by HTML attributes, but others can be controlled either by HTML attributes or by CSS. You should avoid using HTML to format tables since many of these specifications have been deprecated, but certain HTML table attributes continue to be used and are supported by all popular browsers. Although best practices lean heavily toward using CSS for its power and flexibility, nothing beats the down-and-dirty convenience of HTML. For example, when you enter values in the Table dialog box, Dreamweaver still applies them via HTML attributes.

4 Enter the following specification for the table:

Rows: **2**

Columns: **4**

Width: **95 percent**

Border thickness: **0**

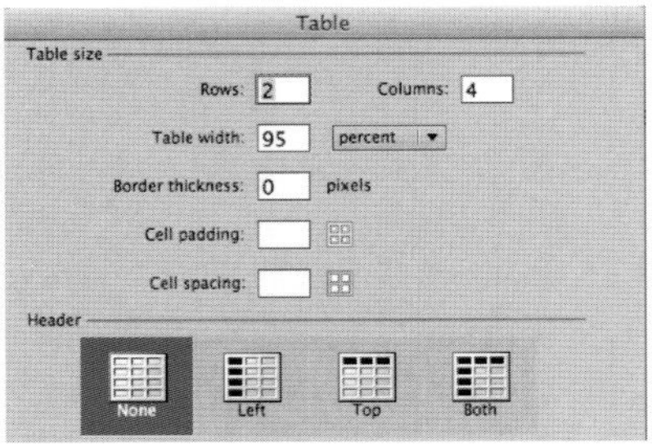

▶ **Tip:** Pressing Tab moves the cursor to the next cell on the right. Holding Shift when pressing Tab moves the cursor to the left, or backward, through the table.

5 Click OK to create the table.

A four-column, two-row table appears below the heading. Note that it is flush to the left edge of `<article.content>`. The table is ready to accept input.

6 Insert the cursor in the first cell of the table. Type **Date** and press Tab to move into the next cell in the first row.

7 In the second cell, type **Event** and press Tab. Type **Location** and press Tab. Type **Cost** and press Tab to move the cursor to the first cell of the second row.

8 In the second row, type **May 1** (in cell 1), **May Day Parade** (in cell 2), **City Hall** (in cell 3), and **Free** (in cell 4).

Inserting additional rows in the table is easy.

9 Press Tab.

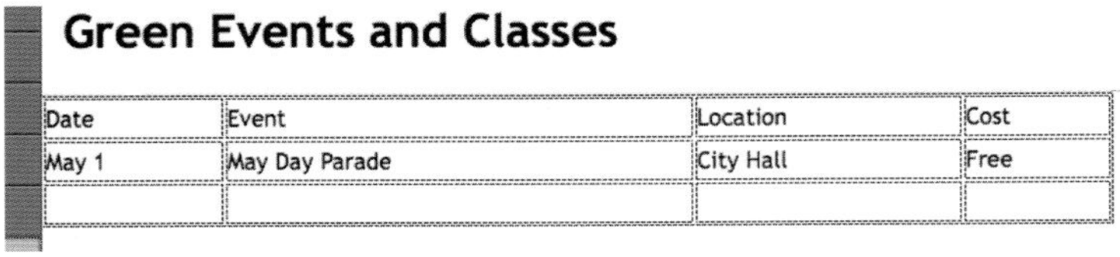

Green Events and Classes

Date	Event	Location	Cost
May 1	May Day Parade	City Hall	Free

A new blank row appears at the bottom of the table. Dreamweaver also allows you to insert multiple new rows at once.

10 Select the `<table>` tag selector at the bottom of the document window.

The Property inspector displays the properties of the current table, including the total number of rows and columns.

11 Select the number 3 in the Rows field. Type **5** and press Enter/Return to complete the change.

Dreamweaver adds two new rows to the table. The fields in the Property inspector create HTML attributes to control various aspects of the table, including table width, the width and height of cells, text alignment, and so on.

You can also add rows and columns to the table interactively using the mouse.

12 Right-click the last row of the table. Choose Table > Insert Row from the context menu.

Another row is added to the table. The context menu can also insert multiple rows and/or columns at once.

13 Right-click the last row of the table. Choose Table > Insert Rows Or Columns from the context menu.

The Insert Rows Or Columns dialog box appears.

14 Insert 4 rows below the selection and click OK.

15 Save all files.

Copying and pasting tables

Although Dreamweaver allows you to create tables manually inside the program, you can also move tables from other HTML files or even other programs by using copy and paste.

1 Open the Files panel, and double-click **calendar.html** in the Lesson07 > resources folder to open it.

This HTML file will open in its own tab in Dreamweaver. Note the table structure—it has four columns and numerous rows.

● **Note:** Dreamweaver allows you to copy and paste tables from some other programs, such as Microsoft Word. Unfortunately, it doesn't work with every program.

2 Insert the cursor in the table. Click the `<table>` tag selector. Press Ctrl-C/ Cmd-C to copy the text.

3 Click the **events.html** tab to bring that file to the front.

4 Insert the cursor in the table. Select the `<table>` tag selector. Press Ctrl-V/ Cmd-V to paste the table.

The new table element completely replaces the existing table.

5 Save the file.

Styling tables with CSS

Right now, your table aligns to the left, touching the edge of `<article.content>`, and stretches most of the way across the element. Tables can be formatted by HTML attributes or by CSS rules. HTML attributes must be applied to and edited for each table individually. As you've already learned, CSS gives you the power to control table formatting site-wide using only a handful of rules.

1 Select the `<table>` tag selector. Select **mygreen_styles.css** in the Sources pane with the CSS Designer. Select the `.content .profile` rule in the Selectors pane, and then click the Add Selector icon.

A new descendant selector named `.content section table` appears, targeting the `<table>` element.

2 Delete `.container` from the Selector Name field and press Enter/Return.

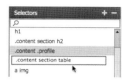

Before you apply formatting to the table, you should know what other settings are already affecting the element and what ramifications new settings could have on your overall design and structure. For example, the `.content` rule sets the width of the element to 770 pixels. Other elements, such as `<h1>` and `<p>`, feature left padding of 15 pixels. If you apply widths, margins, and padding totaling a number larger than 770 pixels, you could inadvertently break the careful structure of your page design.

3 In the Properties pane, select the Show Set option, if necessary.

4 Enter the following specifications for the `.content section table` rule:

```
font-size: 90%
width: 740px
margin-left: 15px
border-bottom: 3px solid #060
```

● **Note:** By adding the width to the margin, you'll get a total of 755 pixels, 15 pixels less than the current width of `<article.content>`. Keep this in mind going forward in case other settings conflict with the table specifications.

▶ **Tip:** Properties like border-bottom can be entered directly and written all at once as shown to save time.

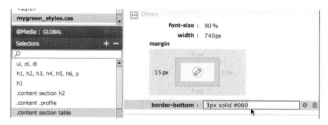

The table resizes, moves away from the left edge of `<article.content>`, and displays a dark green border at the bottom. You have applied the desired styling to specific table properties, but you can't stop there. The default formatting of the tags that comprise table markup is a hodgepodge of different settings that are honored haphazardly in various browsers. You'll find that the same table can be displayed differently in every browser.

One setting that may cause trouble is the HTML-based `cellspacing` attribute, which produces a margin-like effect between individual cells. If you leave this attribute blank, some browsers will insert a small space between cells and may split any cell borders in two. In CSS, this attribute is handled by the `border-collapse` property. If you don't want the table borders to be split inadvertently, you need to include this setting in the styling.

5   In the CSS Designer, select the `.content section table` rule. In the Properties pane, disable the Show Set option. Select the Border category and click the border-collapse: collapse option icon.

In Design view, you will not see any difference in how the tables are displayed, but don't let that dissuade you from the need for this attribute.

6   Save all files.

The `.content section table` rule you just created will format the overall structure of every table inserted into `<article.content>` on any page using this style sheet throughout the site. But the formatting isn't complete yet. The widths of the individual columns are not controlled by the `<table>` element. To control the column widths, you need to look elsewhere.

Styling table cells

Just as for tables, specifications for columns can be applied by HTML attributes or CSS, with similar advantages and disadvantages. Formatting for columns is applied through two elements that create the individual cells: `<th>` for table header and `<td>` for table data. The table header is a handy element you can use to differentiate titles and header content from regular data.

Creating a generic rule to reset the default formats of the `<th>` and `<td>` elements is a good idea. Later, you will create custom rules to apply to specific columns and cells.

1   Insert the cursor into any cell of the table. Select the `.content section table` rule before you click the Add Selector icon.

2   Create a new selector named `.content section td, .content section th` and press Enter/Return to complete the name.

This simplified selector will work fine.

3   In the Properties pane, select the Show Set option.

4   Create the following properties for the `.content section td, .content section th` rule:

```
text-align: left
padding: 5px
border-top: 1px solid #090
```

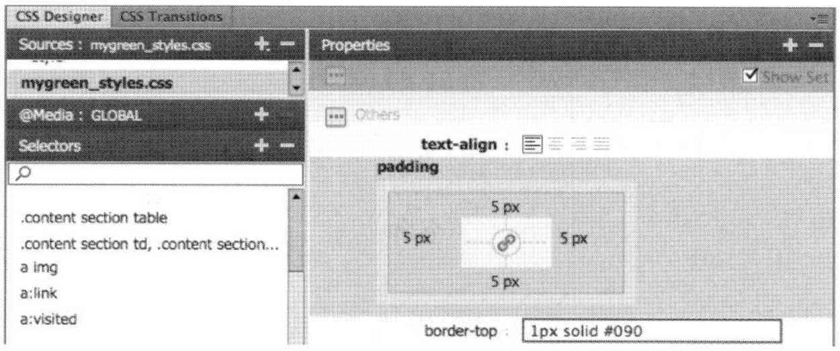

A thin green border appears above each row of the table, making the data easier to read. To see the border properly, you may need to preview the page in Live view first. Headers are usually formatted in bold to help them stand out from the normal cells. You can make them stand out even more by giving them a touch of color.

● **Note:** Remember that the order of the rules can affect the style cascade, as well as how and what styling is inherited.

5 In the Selectors pane, select `.content section td, .content section th`. Create a new `.content section th` selector.

6 Create the following properties in the `.content section th`: rule

```
color: #FFC
background-color: #090
border-bottom: 6px solid #060
```

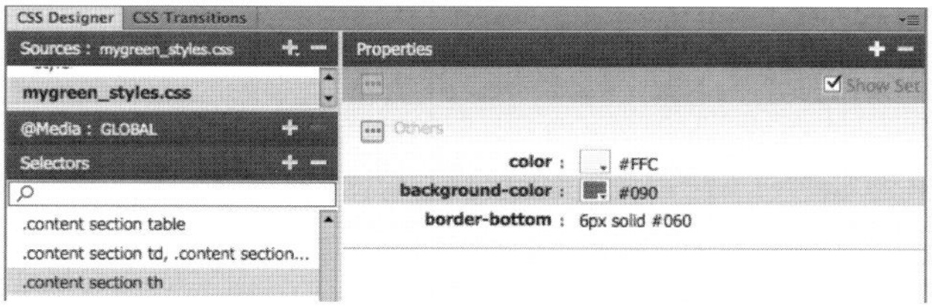

● **Note:** The order of these rules is important. The formatting from the stand-alone rule for the `<th>` element will be reset if it appears out of order.

The rule is created, but it still needs to be applied. Dreamweaver makes it easy to convert the existing `<td>` elements into `<th>` elements.

7 Insert the cursor into the first cell of the first row of the table. In the Property inspector, select the Header option. Note the tag selector.

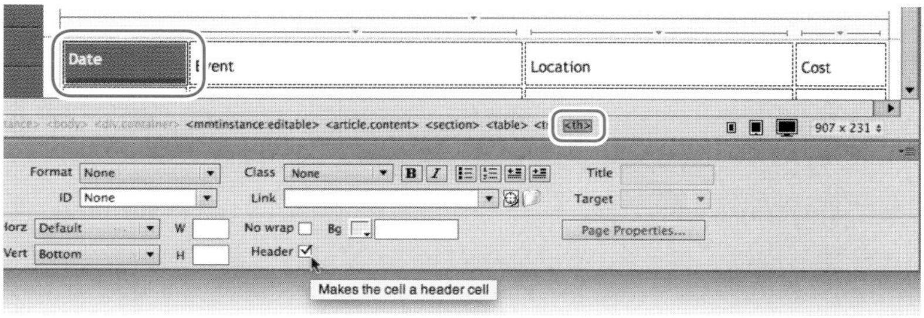

The cell is filled with green. When you click the Header check box, Dreamweaver automatically rewrites the markup, converting the existing `<td>` to `<th>` and thereby applying the CSS formatting. This functionality will save you lots of time over editing the code manually. You can also convert multiple cells at one time.

8 Insert the cursor into the second cell of the first row. Drag to select the remaining cells in the first row. Or, you can select an entire row at once by positioning the cursor at the left edge of the table row and clicking when you see the black selection arrow appear.

9 In the Property inspector, select the Header option to convert the table cells to header cells.

The whole first row is filled with green as the table cells are converted to header cells.

10 Save all files.

Controlling column width

Unless you specify otherwise, empty table columns will divide the available space between them equally. But once you start adding content to the cells, all bets are off—the table seems to get a mind of its own and divvies up the space in a different way. It usually awards more space to columns containing more data.

Allowing the table to decide for itself probably won't achieve an acceptable balance, so many designers resort to HTML attributes or custom CSS classes to control the width of table columns. When you create custom styles to format column widths, one idea is to base the rule names either on the width value itself or on the content, or subject, of the column.

● **Note:** Rule names can't start with numerals or punctuation characters, except for a period (which indicates a class) or a hash mark (#) (which indicates an ID).

1 In the CSS Designer, select the `.content section th` rule, and then click the Add Selector icon. Enter `.content section .w100` as the selector name.

In the new value for the selector name, the *w* stands for *width* and *100* signifies the value 100 pixels.

2 In the Properties pane, create a `width: 100px` entry.

Controlling the width of a column is quite simple. Since the entire column must be the same width, you only have to apply a width specification to one cell. If cells in a column have conflicting specifications, typically the largest width wins. Let's apply a class to control the width of the Date column.

3 Insert the cursor into the first cell of the first row of the table. Select the `<th>` tag selector. In the Property inspector, choose w100 from the Class menu.

> **Tip:** Be sure to click the tag selector; otherwise, Dreamweaver may apply the class to the cell content instead of to the `<th>` element itself.

> **Note:** Remember that the cell can't be any smaller than the largest word or graphic element contained within it.

The first column resizes to 100 pixels wide. The remaining columns automatically divvy up the available space. Column styling can also specify text alignment as well as width. Let's create a rule for the content in the Cost column.

4 In the Selectors pane, select the `.content` section `.w100` rule, and then click Add Selector. Create a `.content section .cost` selector.

Obviously, this rule is intended for the Cost column. But don't add the width value to the name as you did before; that way, you can change the value in the future without worrying about changing the name (and the markup) as well.

5 Create the following properties:

```
text-align: center
width: 75px
```

Unlike with the previous example, to apply text alignment to the contents of a column, you must apply the class to every cell in the column.

6   Click in the first cell of the Cost column and drag down to the last cell of the column to select all the cells. Or, position the cursor over the top of the column and click using the black arrow to select the entire column at once. In the Property inspector, choose `.cost` from the Class menu.

The Cost column resizes to a width of 75 pixels, and the text aligns to the center. Now if you want to change only the Cost column, you have the ability to do so. Note that the header now shows `<th.cost>`, and the cells show `<td.cost>` tag selectors.

7   Save all files.

Inserting tables from other sources

In addition to creating tables by hand, you can also create them from data exported from databases and spreadsheets. In this exercise, you will create a table from data that was exported from Microsoft Excel to a comma-separated values (CSV) file. As with the other content models, you will first create a `<section>` element in which to insert the new table.

1   Insert the cursor anywhere in the existing table. Select the `<section>` tag selector. Press the Right Arrow key to move the cursor after the closing `</section>` tag in the code.

2   Using any of the methods described earlier, create a new `<section>` element.

    A new `<section>` element is added to the page.

3   Without moving the cursor, choose File > Import > Tabular Data.

    The Import Tabular Data dialog box appears.

4   Click the Browse button and select **classes.csv** from the Lesson07 > resources folder. Click Open.

    Comma is automatically selected in the Delimiter menu.

5 Select the following options in the Import Tabular Data dialog box:

Table width: **95%**

Border: **0**

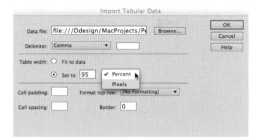

6 Click OK.

A new table—containing a class schedule—appears below the first. The new table consists of five columns with multiple rows. The first row contains header information but is still formatted as normal table cells.

7 Select the first row of the Class schedule. In the Property inspector, select the Header option.

The first row instantly fills with green background and white text. You'll notice that the text is wrapping awkwardly in the last three columns. You will use the .cost class for the Cost column in the new table, but the other two will need custom classes of their own.

8 Select the Cost column. In the Property inspector, choose .cost from the Class menu.

9 In the CSS Designer, right-click the .content section .cost rule and choose Duplicate from the context menu.

10 Change the new Selector Name field to `.content section .day` and press Enter/Return.

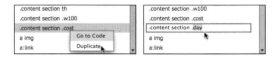

11 Apply `.content section .day` to the Day column in the Classes table, as in step 8.

12 Duplicate `.content section .day`, name the new `.content section .length` rule and apply it to the Length column in the Classes table.

By creating custom classes for each column, you have the means to modify each column individually. One more rule is needed to format the Class column. This column requires only a generic rule to apply a more appealing width.

13 Right-click the `.content section .w100` rule and duplicate it. Name the new rule `.content section .w150`.

▶ **Tip:** When applying a width value, only one cell needs to be formatted.

14 Edit the properties of the new rule. Change the Width to **150px** and apply the new rule only to the header cell for the Class column.

Class	Description	Length
Choices for Sustainable Living	This course explores the meaning of sustainable living and how our choices have an impact on ecological systems.	4 weeks
Exploring Deep Ecology	An eight-session course examining our core values and how they affect the way we view and treat the earth.	4 weeks

15 Save all files.

Adjusting vertical alignment

If you study the content of the Classes table, you will notice that many of the cells contain paragraphs that wrap to multiple lines. When cells in a row have differing amounts of text in them, the shorter content is aligned vertically to the middle of the cell, by default. Many designers find this behavior unattractive and prefer to have the text align to the tops of the cells. As with most of the other attributes, vertical alignment can be applied by HTML attributes or CSS. To control the vertical alignment with CSS, you can add the specification to an existing rule.

1 In the Sources pane, select **mygreen_style.css**.
Select the `.content section th, .content section td` rule.

The `<th>` and `<td>` elements style the text stored in the table cells.

2 In the Properties pane, create the `vertical-align: top` property.

▶ **Tip:** Some designers like to leave the text in `<th>` cells aligned to the middle or even the bottom. If you wanted to do this, you'd need to create separate rules for each element.

All the text in both tables now aligns to the top of the cells.

3 Save all files.

Adding and formatting <caption> elements

The two tables you inserted on the page contain different information but don't feature any differentiating labels or titles. To help users distinguish between the two sets of data, let's add a title to each and a bit of extra spacing. The `<caption>` element was designed to identify the content of HTML tables. This element is inserted as a child of the `<table>` element.

1 Insert the cursor in the first table. Select the `<table>` tag selector. Switch to Code view.

By selecting the table in Design view, Dreamweaver automatically highlights the code in Code view, making it easier to find.

2 Locate the opening `<table>` tag. Insert the cursor directly after this tag. Type `<caption>` or select it from the code hinting window when it appears.

3 Type **2013-14 Event Schedule** and then type `</`, which prompts Dreamweaver to close the element.

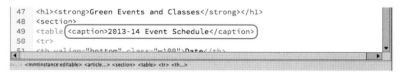

4 Switch to Design view.

The caption is complete and inserted as a child element of the table.

5   Repeat steps 1 and 2 for the second table. Type **2013-14 Class Schedule** and then type </ to close the element as in step 3.

6   Switch to Design view.

The captions are relatively small, and they're lost against the color and formatting of the table. Let's beef them up a bit with a custom CSS rule.

7   Select the `.content section table` rule.
Create a new `.content section caption` selector.

8   Create the following properties for the `.content section caption` rule:

```
font-size: 160%
line-height: 1.2em
font-weight: bold
color: #090
margin-top: 20px
padding-bottom: 20px
```

9   Save all files.

10 Examine your work using Live view or a browser.

Formatting the tables and the captions with CSS has made them much easier to read and understand. Feel free to experiment with the size and placement of the caption and specification settings that affect the tables.

Spell checking webpages

Ensuring that you post error-free content to the web is important. Dreamweaver includes a robust spell checker capable of identifying commonly misspelled words and creating a custom dictionary for nonstandard terms.

1 Click the **contact_us.html** tab to bring that document to the front, or open it from the site root folder.

2 Insert the cursor at the beginning of the main heading Contact Meridien GreenStart in `<article.content>`. Choose Commands > Check Spelling.

  Spell checking starts at the cursor location. If the cursor is located lower on the page, you will have to restart the spell check at least once to examine the entire page. It will not check content locked in non-editable template regions.

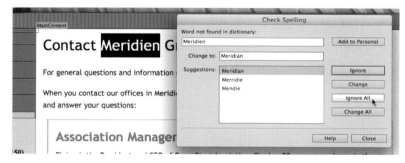

The Check Spelling dialog box highlights the word *Meridien*, which is the name of the fictional city where the association is located. You could click Add To Personal to insert the word into your custom dictionary, but for now you'll skip over other occurrences of the name during this check.

3 Click Ignore All.

  Dreamweaver highlights the word *GreenStart*, which is the name of the association. If GreenStart was the name of your own company you would also add it to your custom dictionary. However you don't want to add a fictional company name to your dictionary.

4 Click Ignore All again.

  Dreamweaver highlights the domain for the email address *info@greenstart.org*.

5 Click Ignore All.

  Dreamweaver highlights the word *Asociation*, which is missing an *s*.

6 To correct the spelling, locate the correctly spelled word (Association) in the Suggestions list and double-click it.

7 Continue the spell check to the end. Correct any misspelled words and ignore proper names, as necessary. If a dialog box prompts you to start the check from the beginning, click Yes.

Dreamweaver will start spell checking from the top of the file to catch any words it may have missed.

8 Click OK when the spell check is complete. Save the file.

Finding and replacing text

Find and replace is one of Dreamweaver's most powerful features. Unlike other programs, Dreamweaver can find almost anything, anywhere in your site, including text, code, and any type of white space that can be created in the program. You can search the entire markup, or you can limit the search to just the rendered text in Design view or to just the underlying tags. Advanced users can enlist powerful pattern-matching algorithms called regular expressions to perform the most sophisticated search operations. And then you can replace the targeted text or code with similar amounts of text, code, and white space.

In this exercise, you'll learn some important techniques for using the Find And Replace feature.

1 Click the **events.html** tab to bring that file to the front, or open the file from the site root folder.

There are several ways to identify the text or code you want to find. One way is simply to type it in the field manually. In the Events table, the name *Meridien* was spelled incorrectly as *Meridian*. Since *Meridian* is an actual word, the spell checker won't flag it as an error and give you the opportunity to correct it. So, you'll use find and replace to make the change instead.

2 Switch to Design view, if necessary. Insert the cursor in the heading *Green Events and Classes*. Choose Edit > Find And Replace.

The Find And Replace dialog box appears. The Find field is empty.

3 Type **Meridian** in the Find field. Type **Meridien** in the Replace field. Choose Current Document from the Find In menu, and choose Text from the Search menu.

4 Click Find Next.

Dreamweaver finds the first occurrence of *Meridian*.

5 Click Replace.

Dreamweaver replaces the first instance of *Meridian* and immediately searches for the next instance. You can continue to replace the words one at a time, or you can choose to replace all occurrences.

6 Click Replace All.

If you replace the words one at a time, Dreamweaver tells you at the bottom of the dialog box how many items were found and how many were replaced. When you click Replace All, Dreamweaver closes the Find And Replace dialog box and opens the Search report panel, which lists all the changes made.

7 Right-click the Search report tab and choose Close Tab Group from the context menu.

Another method for targeting text and code is to select it *before* activating the command. You can use this method in either Design or Code view.

8 In Design view, locate and select the first occurrence of the text *Burkeline Mountains Resort* in the Location column of the Events table. Choose Edit > Find And Replace.

The Find And Replace dialog box appears. The selected text is automatically entered into the Find field by Dreamweaver. This technique is even more powerful when used in Code view.

9 Close the Find And Replace dialog box. Switch to Code view.

10 With the cursor still inserted in the text *Burkeline Mountains Resort*, click the `<tr>` tag selector at the bottom of the document window.

11 Choose Edit > Find And Replace. The Find And Replace dialog box appears.

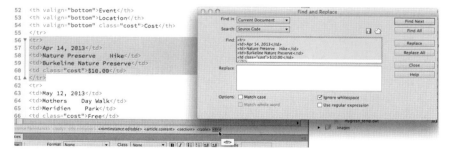

Observe the Find field. The selected code is automatically entered into the Find field by Dreamweaver, including the line breaks and white space. The reason this is so amazing is that there's no way to enter this type of markup in the dialog box manually.

12 In the Find field, select the code. Press Delete to remove it. Type `<tr>` and press Enter/Return to insert the line break. Observe what happens.

Pressing Enter/Return did not insert a line break; instead, it activated the Find command, which finds the first occurrence of the `<tr>` element. In fact, you can't manually insert any type of line break within the dialog.

You probably don't think this is much of a problem, since you've already seen that Dreamweaver inserts text or code when it's selected first. Unfortunately, the method used in step 8 doesn't work with large amounts of text or code.

13 Close the Find And Replace dialog box. Click the `<table>` tag selector.

The entire markup for the table is selected.

14 Choose Edit > Find And Replace. Observe the Find field.

This time Dreamweaver did not transfer the selected code into the Find field. To get larger amounts of text or code into the Find field, and to enter large amounts of replacement text and code, you need to use copy and paste.

15 Close the Find And Replace dialog box. Select the table, if necessary. Press Ctrl-C/Cmd-C to copy the markup.

16 Press Ctrl-F/Cmd-F to activate the Find And Replace command. Insert the cursor in the Find field, and press Ctrl-V/Cmd-V to paste the markup.

The entire `<table>` selection is pasted into the Find field.

17 Insert the cursor into the Replace field, and press Ctrl-V/Cmd-V.

The entire selection is pasted into the Replace field. Obviously, the two fields contain identical markup, but you can see how easy changing or replacing large amounts of code can be.

18 Close the Find And Replace dialog box. Save all files.

In this lesson you created four new pages and learned how to import text from multiple sources. You formatted text as headings and lists, and then styled it using CSS. You inserted and formatted tables, and added captions to each one. And you reviewed and corrected text using Dreamweaver's spell check and find and replace tools.

Superpowerfindelicious!

Note the options in the Find In and Search menus. The power and flexibility of Dreamweaver shines brightest here. The Find And Replace command can search in selected text, the current document, all open documents, in a specific folder, in selected files of the site, or the entire current local site. But as if those options weren't enough, Dreamweaver also allows you to target the search to the source code, text, advanced text, or even a specific tag.

Review questions

1 How do you format text to be an HTML heading 2?

2 Explain how to turn paragraph text into an ordered list and then an unordered list.

3 Describe two methods for inserting HTML tables into a webpage.

4 What element controls the width of a table column?

5 Describe three ways to insert content in the Find field.

Review answers

1 Use the Format field menu in the Property inspector to apply HTML heading formatting or use the shortcut keys Ctrl/Cmd-2.

2 Highlight the text with the cursor, and click the Ordered List button in the Property inspector. Then click the Unordered List button to change the numbered formatting to bullets.

3 You can copy and paste a table from another HTML file or a compatible program. Or, you can insert a table by importing the data from a delimited file.

4 The width of a table column is controlled by the widest `<th>` or `<td>` element within the column.

5 You can type text into the field; you can select text before you open the dialog box and then allow Dreamweaver to insert the selected text; or you can copy the text or code and then paste it into the field.

8
WORKING WITH IMAGES

Lesson Overview

In this lesson, you'll learn how to work with images to include them in your webpages in the following ways:

- Inserting an image
- Using Bridge to import Photoshop or Fireworks files
- Using Photoshop Smart Objects
- Copying and pasting an image from Photoshop and Fireworks

This lesson will take about 55 minutes to complete. If you have not already done so, download the project files for this lesson from the Lesson & Update Files tab on your Account page at www.peachpit.com, and store them on your computer in a convenient location, as described in the Getting Started section of this book. Your Accounts page is also where you'll find any updates to the lessons or to the lesson files. Look on the Lesson & Update Files tab to access the most current content. If you are starting from scratch in this lesson, use the method described in the "Jumpstart" section of "Getting Started."

Dreamweaver provides many ways to insert and
adjust graphics, both within the program and in
tandem with other Creative Suite tools such as Adobe
Bridge, Adobe Fireworks, and Adobe Photoshop.

Reviewing web image basics

● **Note:** If you have not already downloaded the project files for this lesson to your computer from your Account page, make sure to do so now. See "Getting Started" at the beginning of the book.

Vector graphics excel in line art, drawings, and logo art. Raster technology works better for storing photographic images.

The web is not as much a place as it is an experience. And essential to that experience are images and graphics—both still and animated—that populate most websites. In the computer world, graphics fall into two main categories: *vector* and *raster*.

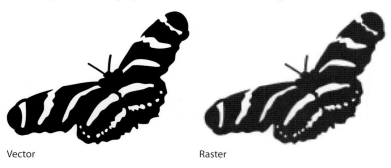

Vector   Raster

Vector graphics

Vector graphics are created by math. They act like discrete objects, allowing you to reposition and resize them as many times as you want without affecting or diminishing their output quality. The best application of vector art is wherever geometric shapes and text are used to create artistic effects. For example, most company logos are built from vector shapes.

Vector graphics are typically stored in the AI, EPS, PICT, or WMF file formats. Unfortunately, most web browsers don't support these formats. The format that is supported is SVG (scalable vector graphic). The simplest way to get started with SVG is to create a graphic in your favorite vector-drawing program—like Adobe Illustrator or CorelDRAW—and then export it to this format. If you are a good programmer, you may want to try creating SVG graphics using XML (Extensible Markup Language). To find out more about creating SVG graphics, check out www.w3schools.com/svg.

Raster graphics

Although SVG has definite advantages, web designers primarily use raster-based images in their web designs. Raster images are built from pixels, which stands for picture elements. Pixels have three basic characteristics:

*   They are perfectly square in shape.
*   They are all the same size.
*   They display only one color at a time.

Raster-based images are composed of thousands, even millions, of different pixels arranged in rows and columns, in patterns that create the illusion of an actual photo, painting, or drawing. It's an illusion, because there is no real photo on the screen, just a bunch of pixels that fool your eyes into seeing an image. And as the quality of the image increases, the more realistic the illusion becomes. Raster-image quality is based on three factors: resolution, size, and color.

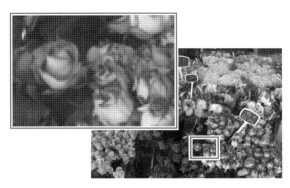

Raster images are built of thousands or even millions of pixels that produce the illusion of a photograph.

Resolution

Resolution is the most well known of the factors affecting raster image quality. It is the expression of image quality measured in the number of pixels that fit in one inch (ppi). The more pixels you can fit in one inch, the more detail you can depict in the image. But better quality comes at a price. An unfortunate byproduct of higher resolution is larger file size. That's because each pixel must be stored as bytes of information within the image file—information that has real overhead in computer terms. More pixels mean more information, which means larger files.

● **Note:** Printers and printing presses use round "dots" to create photographic images. Quality on a printer is measured in dots per inch, or dpi. The process of converting the square pixels used in your computer into the round dots used on the printer is called screening.

Resolution has a dramatic effect on image output. The web image on the left looks fine in the browser but doesn't have enough quality for printing.

72 ppi   300 ppi

Luckily, web images only have to be optimized to look best on computer screens, which are based mostly on a resolution of 72 ppi. This is low compared to other applications—like printing, where 300 dpi is considered the lowest acceptable quality. The lower resolution of the computer screen is an important factor in keeping most web image files down to a reasonable size for downloading from the Internet. Because webpages are intended for viewing and not printing, the pictures don't need to have a resolution higher than 72 ppi.

Size

Size refers to the vertical and horizontal dimensions of the image. As image size increases, more pixels are required to create it, and therefore the file becomes larger. Since graphics take more time to download than HTML code, many designers in recent years have replaced graphical components with CSS formatting to speed up the web experience for their visitors. But if you need or want to use images, a method to ensure snappy downloads is to keep image size small. Even today, with the proliferation of high-speed Internet service, you won't find too many websites that depend on full-page graphics.

Although these two images share the identical resolution and color depth, you can see how image dimensions can affect file size.

500KB

1.6MB

Color

Color refers to the color space, or *palette*, that describes each image. Most computer screens display only a fraction of the colors that the human eye can see. And different computers and applications display varying levels of color, expressed by the term *bit depth*. Monochrome, or 1-bit color, is the smallest color space, displaying only black and white, with no shades of gray. Monochrome is used mostly for line-art illustrations, for blueprints, and to reproduce handwriting.

The 4-bit color space describes up to 16 colors. Additional colors can be simulated by a process called *dithering*, where the available colors are interspersed and juxtaposed to create an illusion of more color. This color space was created for the first color computer systems and game consoles. Because of its limitations, this palette is seldom used today.

The 8-bit palette offers up to 256 colors or 256 shades of gray. This is the basic color system of all computers, mobile phones, game systems, and handheld devices. This color space also includes what is called the *web-safe* color palette. Web-safe refers to a subset of 8-bit colors that are supported on both Mac and Windows computers. Most computers, game consoles, and handheld devices now support higher color palettes, but 8-bit is the fallback for all web-compatible devices.

Today, some cell phones and handheld games support the 16-bit color space. This palette is called *high color* and sports a grand total of 65,000 colors. Although this sounds like a lot, 16-bit color is not considered good enough for most graphic design purposes or professional printing.

The highest color space is 24-bit color, which is called *true color*. This system generates up to 16.7 million colors. It is the gold standard for graphic design and professional printing. Several years ago a new color space was added to the mix: 32-bit color. It doesn't offer any additional colors, but it provides an additional eight bits of data for an attribute called *alpha transparency*.

Alpha transparency enables you to designate parts of an image or graphic as fully or even partially transparent. This trick allows you to create graphics that seem to have rounded corners or curves and can eliminate the white bounding box typical of raster graphics.

24-bit color   8-bit color   4-bit color

Here you can see a dramatic comparison of three color spaces and what the total number of available colors means to image quality.

As with size and resolution, color depth can dramatically affect image file size. With all other aspects being equal, an 8-bit image is over seven times larger than a monochrome image. And the 24-bit version is over three times larger than the 8-bit image. The key to effective use of images on a website is finding the balance of resolution, size, and color to achieve the desired optimal quality.

Raster image file formats

Raster images can be stored in a multitude of file formats, but web designers have to be concerned with only three: GIF, JPEG, and PNG. These three formats are optimized for the Internet and compatible with most browsers. However, they are not equal in capability.

GIF

GIF (graphic interchange format) was one of the first raster image file formats designed specifically for the web. It has changed only a little in the last 20 years. GIF supports a maximum of 256 colors (8-bit palette) and 72 ppi, so it's used mainly for web interfaces—buttons and graphical borders and such. But it does have several interesting features that keep it pertinent for today's web designers: index transparency and support for simple animation.

JPEG

JPEG, also written JPG, is named for the Joint Photographic Experts Group that created the image standard back in 1992 as a direct reaction to the limitations of the GIF file format. JPEG is a powerful format that supports unlimited resolution, image dimensions, and color depth. Because of this, most digital cameras use JPEG as their default file type for image storage. It's also the reason most designers use JPEG on their websites for images that must be displayed in high quality.

This may sound odd to you since high quality—as described earlier—usually means large file size. Large files take longer to download to your browser. So, why is the format so popular on the web? JPEG's claim to fame comes from its patented user-selectable image compression algorithm that can reduce file size as much as 95 percent. JPEG images are compressed each time they are saved and then decompressed before they are opened and displayed.

Unfortunately, all this compression has a downside. Too much compression damages image quality. This type of compression is called *lossy*, because it loses quality each time. In fact, the loss in quality can potentially render the image useless. Each time designers save a JPEG image, they face a trade-off between image quality and file size.

Here you see the effects of different amounts of compression on the file size and quality of an image.

Low quality
High compression
130K

Medium quality
Medium compression
150K

High quality
Low compression
260K

PNG

PNG (portable network graphic) was developed in 1995 because of a looming patent dispute involving the GIF format. At the time, it looked as if designers and developers would have to pay a royalty for using the .gif file extension. Although that issue blew over, PNG has found many adherents and a home on the Internet because of its capabilities.

PNG combines many of the features of GIF and JPEG and then adds a few of its own. For example, it offers support for unlimited resolution, 32-bit color, and full alpha and index transparency. It also provides lossless compression, which means you can save an image in PNG format and not worry about losing any quality each time you open and save the file.

The only downside to PNG is that its most important feature—alpha transparency—was not fully supported in older browsers. As these browsers are retired year after year, this issue is not much of a concern to most web designers.

But, as with everything on the web, your own needs may vary from the general trend. Before using any specific technology, checking your site analytics and confirming which browsers your visitors are actually using is always a good idea.

Previewing the completed file

To get a sense of the files you will work on in this lesson, let's preview the completed pages in the browser.

1 Launch Adobe Dreamweaver CC.

2 If necessary, press F8 to open the Files panel, and select DW-CC from the site list.

3 In the Files panel, expand the Lesson08 folder.

4 Open the **contactus_finished.html** and **news_finished.html** files from the Lesson08 folder, and preview the pages in your browser.

● **Note:** If you are completing this lesson separately from the rest of the lessons in book, see the detailed "Jumpstart" instructions in the "Getting Started" section at the beginning of the book. Then, follow the steps in this exercise.

● **Note:** If you have not already downloaded the project files for this lesson to your computer from your Account page, make sure to do so now. See "Getting Started" at the beginning of the book.

The pages include several images, as well as a Photoshop Smart Object image.

5 Close your browser and return to Dreamweaver.

Inserting an image

● **Note:** If you are starting from scratch in this chapter, use the Jumpstart instructions in the "Getting Started" section at the beginning of the book.

Images are key components of any webpage, both for developing visual interest and for telling stories. Dreamweaver provides numerous ways to populate your pages with images, using built-in commands and even using copy and paste. One method is to insert the image using Dreamweaver's built-in tools.

1 In the Files panel, open the **contact_us.html** file from the site root folder (this is the file you completed in Lesson 7, "Working with Text, Lists, and Tables").

   An image placeholder appears in `<div.sidebar1>` to indicate where an image should be inserted.

2 Double-click the image placeholder labeled *Sidebar (180 x 150)*.

   The Select Image Source dialog box appears.

3 Select **biking.jpg** from the site images folder. Click OK/Open.

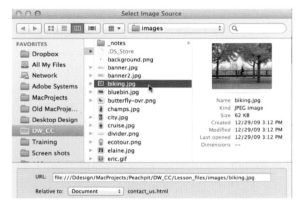

The image appears in the sidebar.

In the best of all worlds, your images will always appear at the place and size you specified on your pages. But frequently, images will not display as desired. This can be caused by numerous situations, such as incompatible devices or file types, as well as server and browser errors. Some users may have disabilities that prevent them from "seeing" the images altogether. What can you do when your images won't display or can't be seen? HTML provides an alternate text (`alt`) attribute just for those situations. When the images do not appear or can't be seen, the alternate text will be displayed instead or can be accessed by assistive devices.

Dreamweaver no longer prompts you for the alternate text each time you insert a new image from scratch. You'll have to remember to do it yourself each time.

4 Insert the cursor in the Alt field in the Property inspector, select the placeholder text, and type **Bike to work to save gas** to replace the text.

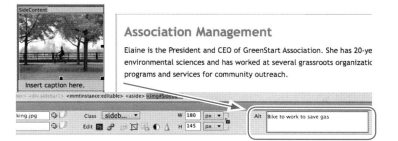

5 To give your image a caption, select the placeholder text *Add caption here* and replace it with **We practice what we preach, here's Lin biking to work through Lakefront Park.**

You've successfully inserted an image using one technique, but Dreamweaver offers other techniques, too. You'll now add an image to the page using the Assets panel.

6 Insert the cursor at the beginning of the first paragraph under the heading *Association Management* in `<section.profile>`, before the name *Elaine*.

7 Choose Window > Assets to display the Assets panel, if necessary. Click the Images category (icon) icon to display a list of all images stored within the site.

8 Locate and select **elaine.jpg** in the list.

A preview of **elaine.jpg** appears in the Assets panel. The panel lists the image's name, dimensions in pixels, and file type, as well as its directory path.

9 Note the dimensions of the image: 150 pixels by 150 pixels.

10 At the bottom of the panel, click the Insert button.

● **Note:** The Images window shows all images stored anywhere in the defined site—even ones outside the site's default images folder—so you may see listings for images stored in the lesson subfolders, too.

◆ **Warning:** If more than one file with the same name appears in the Assets panel, make sure you select the image stored in the default images folder.

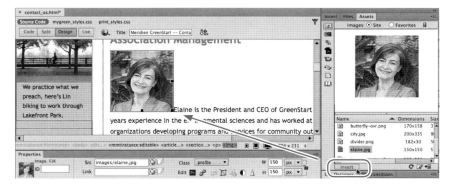

The image appears at the current cursor location.

11 In the Alternate text field in the Property inspector, type **Elaine, Meridien GreenStart President and CEO**.

12 Choose File > Save.

You inserted Elaine's picture in the text, but it doesn't look very nice at its current position. In the next exercise, you will adjust the image position using a CSS class.

Adjusting image positions with CSS classes

The `<img>` element is an inline element by default. That's why you can insert images inline into paragraphs and other elements. When the image is taller than the font size, the image will increase the vertical space for the line in which it appears. In the past you could adjust its position using either HTML attributes or CSS, but the HTML-based attributes have been deprecated from the language as well as from Dreamweaver CC. Now you must rely completely on CSS-based techniques.

If you want all the images to align in a certain fashion, you can create a custom rule for the `<img>` tag to apply specific styling. In this instance, you want the employee photos to alternate from right to left going down the page, so you'll create a custom class to provide options for left and right alignment.

1 If necessary, open **contact_us.html**.

2 In the Sources pane of the CSS Designer, select **mygreen_styles.css**. In the Selectors pane, click the Add Selector icon.

3 Type `.flt_rgt` and press Enter/Return to create the name.

The name is short for "float right," hinting at what command you're going to use to style the images.

4 If necessary, select the Show Set option. Create the following properties:

```
float: right
margin-left: 10px
```

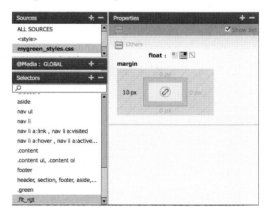

You can apply the class from the Property inspector.

5 In the layout, select the image **elaine.jpg**. From the Class menu in the Property inspector, choose `flt_rgt`.

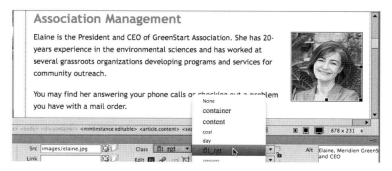

The image moves to the right side of the section element, and the text wraps around on the left. The margin setting keeps the text from touching the edge of the image itself. You will create a similar rule to align images to the left in the next exercise.

Working with the Insert panel

The Insert panel duplicates key menu commands and has a number of options that make inserting images and other code elements both quick and easy.

1 Insert the cursor at the beginning of the first paragraph under the heading *Education and Events*, before the name *Sarah*.

2 Choose Window > Insert to display the Insert panel, if necessary.

3 In the Insert panel, choose the Common category. Click the Images drop-down menu.

The menu offers three options: Image, Rollover Image, and Fireworks HTML.

4 From the pop-up menu, choose Image.

The Select Image Source dialog box appears.

5 Select **sarah.jpg** from the default images. Click OK/Open.

● **Note:** If you don't see the Insert panel docked on the right side of the screen, it may appear as a toolbar at the top of the document window—as it does in the Classic workspace, for example.

6   In the Property inspector, type **Sarah, GreenStart Events Coordinator** in the Alternate text field.

7   In the CSS Designer panel, select **mygreen_styles.css** in the Sources pane. Click the Add Selector icon.

8   Enter `.flt_lft` as the rule name.

    The name is short for "float left."

9   Create the following properties:

    ```
    float: left
    margin-right: 10px
    ```

10 Apply the `flt_left` class to the image **sarah.jpg**.

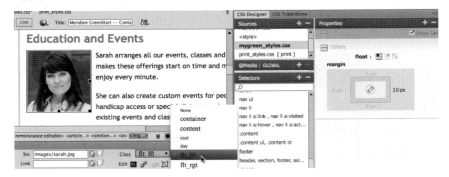

The image drops down into the paragraph on the left side, with the text wrapping to the right.

11 Save the file.

Another way to insert images in your webpage is by using Adobe Bridge.

Using Adobe Bridge to insert images

Adobe Bridge CC—an essential tool for web designers—can quickly browse directories of images and other supported assets, as well as manage and tag files with keywords and labels. Bridge works well with Dreamweaver; you can drag images into your layouts directly from Bridge or use specific commands. Starting in the new Creative Cloud edition, Bridge will not be installed by default with apps other than Photoshop CC. You will have to log in to Creative Cloud and download and install the program separately from Dreamweaver.

1   Insert the cursor at the beginning of the first paragraph under the heading *Transportation Analysis*, before the name *Eric*.

2 Launch Adobe Bridge CC.

● **Note:** Bridge is installed separately from Dreamweaver. If it is not present on your computer, you can access it via the Creative Cloud and install it before performing this exercise.

The interface in Bridge can be set up to your liking and saved as a custom workspace. For most operations, you can use the Essentials workspace, as shown.

3 Click the Folders tab to bring the Folders panel to the top. If necessary, choose Window > Folders Panel. Navigate to the folder designated as your default site images folder on your hard drive. Observe the names and types of files displayed in the folder.

Bridge displays a thumbnail image of each file in the folder. Bridge can display thumbnails for all types of graphic files, including AI, BMP, EPS, GIF, JPG, PDF, PNG, SVG, and TIFF, among others.

4 Click **eric.png**. Observe the Preview and Metadata panels. Note the dimensions, resolution, and color space of the image.

The Preview panel displays a high-quality preview of the selected image.

Bridge also has capabilities for helping you locate and isolate specific types of files.

5 Choose Window > Filter Panel to display the panel if it's not visible.

The Filter panel displays a default set of data criteria—such as file type, ratings, keywords, date created, and so forth—that are then populated automatically by the contents of a particular folder. You can filter the contents to these criteria by clicking one or more of these items.

6 In the Filter panel, expand the File Type criterion. Select the JPEG File criterion.

A check mark appears beside the JPEG File criterion. The PNG file you selected earlier is no longer visible. The Content panel in the center of Adobe Bridge displays only JPEG files.

7 In the File Type criteria, select GIF Image.

A check mark appears beside the GIF Image criterion. The Content panel now displays only GIF and JPEG files. Other file types are hidden by Bridge but still exist in the folder. You can use Bridge to insert one of these files into Dreamweaver or another Creative Suite application.

8 In the Content panel, select **eric.jpg**. Note the dimensions in the Metadata panel: 150 pixels by 150 pixels. Choose File > Place > In Dreamweaver.

Your computer switches back to Dreamweaver automatically. The **eric.jpg** image appears in the Dreamweaver layout at the last position of the cursor.

9 In the Property inspector, type **Eric, Transportation Research Coordinator** in the Alternate text field.

10 Apply the `flt_rgt` class to this image.

11 Save the file.

Dreamweaver is not limited to the file types GIF, JPEG, and PNG; it can work with other file types, too. In the next exercise, you will learn how to insert a Photoshop document (PSD) into a webpage.

Inserting non-web file types

Although most browsers will display only the web-compliant image formats described earlier, Dreamweaver also allows you to use other formats; the program will then automatically convert the file to a compatible format on the fly.

1 Insert the cursor at the beginning of the first paragraph under the heading *Research and Development*, before the name *Lin*.

2 Choose Insert > Image > Image. Navigate to the resources folder in the Lesson08 folder. Select **lin.psd**.

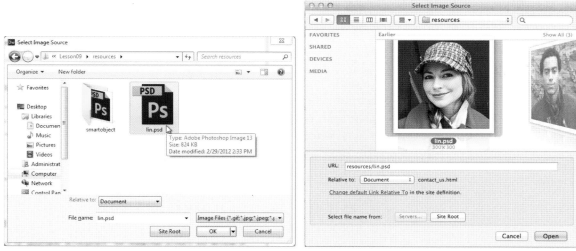

Windows   Mac

3 Click OK/Open to insert the image.

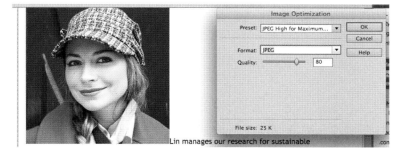

The image appears in the layout, and the Image Optimization dialog box opens; it acts as an intermediary that allows you to specify how and to what format the image will be converted.

4 Observe the options in the Preset and Format menus.

The presets allow you to select predetermined options that have a proven track record for web-based images. The Format menu allows you to specify your own settings from among five options: GIF, JPEG, PNG 8, PNG 24, and PNG 32.

● **Note:** When an image has to be converted this way, Dreamweaver usually saves the converted image into the default site images folder. This is not the case when the images inserted are web-compatible. So before you insert an image, you should be aware of its current location in the site and move it to the proper location first, if necessary.

5 Choose JPEG High For Maximum Compatibility from the Presets menu. Note the Quality setting.

This Quality setting produces a high-quality image with a moderate amount of compression. If you lower the Quality setting, you automatically increase the compression level and reduce the file size; increase the Quality setting for the opposite effect. The secret to effective design is to select a good balance between quality and compression. The default setting for the JPEG High preset is 80, which is sufficient for your purposes.

6 Click OK to convert the image.

The Save Web Image dialog box appears with the name *lin* entered in the Save As field. Dreamweaver will add the .jpg extension to the file automatically and saves the file to the default images folder.

7   Click Save.

The Image Optimization dialog box closes. The image in the layout is now linked to the JPEG file saved in the default images folder.

8   Enter **Lin, Research and Development Coordinator** in the Alternate text field.

The image appears in Dreamweaver at the cursor position. The image has been resampled to 72 ppi but still appears at its original dimensions, which are larger than the other images in the layout. You can resize the image in the Property inspector.

9   In the Property inspector, click the Toggle Size Constrain (🔒) icon and change the Width field to **150px**.

● **Note:** Whenever changing HTML or CSS properties you may need to press Enter/Return to complete the modification.

The change to the image size is only temporary at the moment, as indicated by the Reset (⊘) and Commit (✔) icons. An exclamation mark appears in the upper-left corner of the image indicating that the image has been modified but the changes have not been committed. In other words, the HTML attributes specify the size of the image as 150 pixels by 150 pixels, but the JPEG file still holds an image that's still 300 pixels by 300 pixels, four times as many pixels as it needs to have.

10 Click the Commit (✔) icon.

The image resizes to 150 by 150 pixels. The linked image is now permanently resized. The exclamation mark on the image disappears.

11 Apply the `flt_lft` class to this image. Save the file.

The image now appears likes the other images in the layout, but something is different about it. An icon appears in the upper-left corner that identifies this image as a Photoshop Smart Object.

Working with Photoshop Smart Objects

Unlike other images, Smart Objects maintain a connection to the original Photoshop (PSD) file. If the PSD file is altered in any manner and then saved, Dreamweaver will identify those changes and provide the means to update the web image used in the layout. The following exercise can be completed only if you have Photoshop CC installed on your computer with Dreamweaver.

● **Note:** Dreamweaver and Photoshop can work with the existing quality of an image only. If your initial image quality is unacceptable, you may not be able to fix it in Photoshop. You will have to re-create the image or pick another.

1   If necessary, open **contact_us.html**. Scroll down to the image **lin.jpg** in the Research and Development section. Observe the icon in the upper-left corner of the image.

Research and Development

Lin manages our research for sustainable development. She researches products and services of every local restaurant, store, hotel, spa or other business that we recommend to our visitors. She listens to your

The icon indicates that the image is a Smart Object. The circular green arrows indicate that the original image is unchanged. If you want to edit or optimize the image, you can simply right-click the image and choose the appropriate option from the context menu.

To make substantive changes to the image, you will have to open it in Photoshop. (If you don't have Photoshop installed, copy Lesson08 > resources > smartobject > **lin.psd** into the Lesson08 > resources folder to replace the original image, and then skip to step 6.) In this exercise, you will edit the image background using Photoshop.

2   Right-click **lin.jpg**. Choose Edit Original With > Adobe Photoshop CC from the context menu.

Photoshop launches—if it is installed on your computer—and loads the file.

3 In Photoshop, choose Window > Layers to display the Layers panel, if necessary. Observe the names and states of any existing layers.

The image has two layers: Lin and New Background. New Background is turned off.

4 Click the eye (👁) icon for the New Background layer to display its contents.

The background of the image changes to show a scene from a park.

5 Save the Photoshop file.

6 Switch back to Dreamweaver.

Lin manages our research for sustainable development. She researches products and services of every local restaurant, store, hotel, spa or other business that we recommend to our visitors. She listens to your comments on our recommendations and checks out your complaints

In a moment or two, the Smart Object icon in the upper-left corner changes to indicate that the original image has been changed. The icon appears only within Dreamweaver itself; visitors see the normal image in the browser. You don't have to update the image at this time, and you can leave the out-of-date image in the layout for as long as you want. Dreamweaver will continue to monitor its status as long as it's in the layout. But for this exercise, let's update the image.

7 Right-click the image and choose Update From Original from the context menu.

Lin manages our research for sustainable development. She researches products and services of every local restaurant, store, hotel, spa or other business that we recommend to our visitors. She listens to your comments on our recommendations and checks out your complaints

This Smart Object and any other instances of it change to reflect the new background. Notice how the Smart Object icon shows that the image is up to date. You can also insert the same original PSD image multiple times in the site using different dimensions and image settings under a different file name. All the Smart Objects will stay connected to the PSD and will allow you to update them as the PSD changes.

8 Save the file.

As you can see, Smart Objects have several advantages over a typical image work-flow. For frequently changed or updated images, using a Smart Object can simplify updates to the website in the future.

Copying and pasting images from Photoshop and Fireworks

As you build your website, you will need to edit and optimize many images before you use them in your site. Adobe Fireworks and Adobe Photoshop are both excellent programs for performing these tasks. A common workflow is to manually export the optimized GIF, JPEG, or PNG to the default images folder in your website when you're finished working on it. But sometimes simply copying images and pasting them directly into your layout is faster. Whether you're working with Fireworks or Photoshop, the steps are nearly identical and the result is the same; in this exercise, feel free to use whichever program you are most familiar with.

1 Launch Adobe Fireworks or Adobe Photoshop, if necessary. Open **matthew.tif** from the Lesson08 > resources folder. Observe the Layers panel.

   The image has only one layer. In Fireworks, you can select multiple layers and copy and paste them into Dreamweaver. In Photoshop, either you will have to merge or flatten layers before you copy and paste them or you will have to use the command Edit > Copy Merged to copy images with multiple active layers.

2 Press Ctrl-A/Cmd-A to select the entire image. Press Ctrl-C/Cmd-C to copy the image.

3 Switch to Dreamweaver. Scroll down to the section Information Systems in **contact_us.html**. Insert the cursor at the beginning of the first paragraph in this section, before the name *Matthew*.

4 Press Ctrl-V/Cmd-V to paste the image from the clipboard.

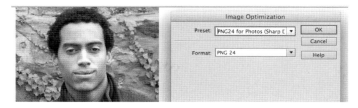

The image appears in the layout, and the Image Optimization dialog box opens.

5 Choose the preset PNG24 for Photos (Sharp Details), and choose PNG 24 from the Format menu. Click OK.

The Save Image dialog box appears.

6 Name the image **matthew.png**, and select the default site images folder, if necessary. Click Save.

7 Enter **Matthew, Information Systems Manager** in the Alt text field in the Property inspector.

The **matthew.png** image appears in the layout. As in the earlier exercise, the PNG image is larger than the other images.

8 In the Property inspector, change the image dimensions to **150px** by **150px**. Click the Commit (✔) icon to apply the change permanently.

9 Apply the class `flt_rgt` to **matthew.png**.

The image appears in the layout at the same size as the other images and aligned to the right. Although this image came from Fireworks or Photoshop, it's not "smart" like a Photoshop Smart Object and can't be updated automatically. It does, however, keep track of the location of the original image if you want to edit it later.

● **Note:** Raster images can be scaled down in size without losing quality, but the opposite is not true. Unless a graphic has a resolution higher than 72 ppi, scaling it larger without noticeable degradation may not be possible.

● **Note:** The Edit Original With option may not be available to users who do not have Photoshop or Fireworks installed.

10 In the layout, right-click the **matthew.png** image and choose Edit Original With > Browse from the context menu.

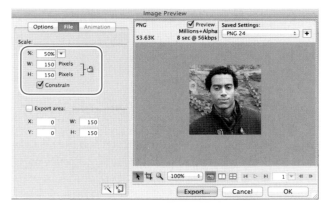

▶ **Tip:** The executable program file is usually stored in the Program Files folder in Windows and in the Applications folder on a Mac.

11 Navigate to and select the Fireworks or Photoshop program on your hard drive. Click Open.

The program launches and displays the original TIFF file. You can make changes to the image and copy and paste it into Dreamweaver by repeating steps 2 through 9. Although there's no way to replace the image automatically, as with Smart Objects, there's a more efficient way than using copy and paste. Photoshop users should skip to step 13.

12 In Fireworks: Choose File > Image Preview. In the Options mode, choose PNG 24 from the Format menu. In the File mode, change the Width and Height fields to **150px**. Click Export.

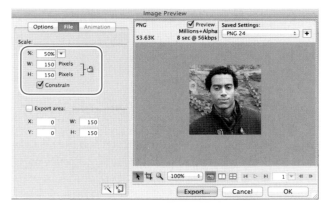

The Image Preview dialog box allows you to specify the export size of the image. Fireworks will remember the specifications you select in this dialog box when you save and close the file. Fireworks users can skip to step 15.

13 In Photoshop, choose File > Save For Web. Choose PNG-24 from the Preset menu. Change the Image Size Width field to **150px**.

► **Tip:** Clicking the name inserts the existing filename in the dialog box field and avoids any spelling or typing errors, which is vital for Unix-based web servers.

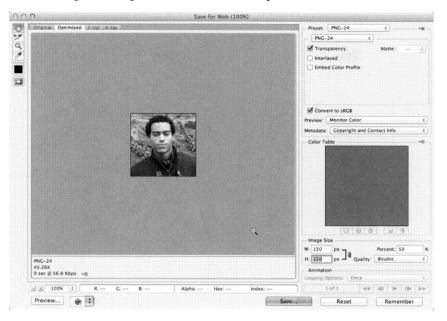

● **Note:** Although Dreamweaver automatically reloads any modified file, most browsers won't. You will have to refresh the browser display before you see any changes.

The Save For Web dialog box appears.

14 Click Save. Navigate to the default site images folder and click to select the existing **matthew.png** file.

The name *matthew.png* appears in the Filename field of the dialog box.

15 Click Export/Save.

16 Switch back to Dreamweaver. Scroll down to view **matthew.png** in the Information Systems section.

No further action is needed to update the image in the layout, because you saved the new image over the original file. As long as the filename hasn't changed, Dreamweaver isn't concerned and no other action is necessary. This method saves you several steps and avoids any potential typing errors.

17 Save the file.

Copy and paste is just one of the handy methods for inserting images. Dreamweaver also allows you to drag images into your layout.

Inserting images by drag and drop

Most of the programs in the Creative Suite offer drag-and-drop capabilities. Dreamweaver is no exception.

1 Open the **news.html** file you created in the last lesson from the site root folder.

2 Choose Window > Assets to display the Assets panel, if necessary. The Assets panel is no longer opened by default in the Dreamweaver workspace. You can leave it as a floating dialog or dock it to keep it out of the way.

3 Drag the Assets panel to dock it beside the Files panel.

4 In the Assets panel, click the Images (🖻) icon.

▶ **Tip:** If you don't see specific image files listed in the Assets panel, click the Refresh (**C**) icon to reload site images. You may also have to select the Site radio button to see all images in the site.

▶ **Tip:** Dreamweaver also allows you to drag the image from Bridge to the page.

5 Drag **city.jpg** from the panel to the beginning of the first paragraph under the heading *Green Buildings earn more Green*.

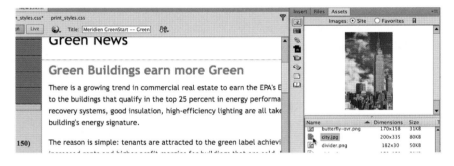

6 In the Alternate text field, enter **Green buildings are top earners** and click OK.

7 Apply the flt_lft class to the image. Save the file.

You need a steady hand and a little practice to perfect your drag-and-drop technique, but it's a good way to get images into your layout quickly.

Optimizing images with the Property inspector

Optimized web images try to balance image dimensions and quality against file size. Sometimes you may need to optimize graphics that have already been placed on the page. Dreamweaver has built-in features that can help you achieve the smallest possible file size while preserving image quality. In this exercise, you'll use tools in Dreamweaver to scale, optimize, and crop an image for the web:

1   Insert the cursor at the beginning of the first paragraph under the heading *Shopping green saves energy*. Choose Insert > Image > Image. Select **farmersmarket.png** from the site images folder, and click OK/Open.

2   In the Alternate text field, enter **Buy local to save energy**.

3   Apply the class `flt_rgt` to the image.

   The image is too large and could use some cropping. To save time, you can use tools in Dreamweaver to fix the image composition.

4   If necessary, choose Window > Properties to display the Property inspector.

   Whenever an image is selected, image-editing options appear in the lower-right corner of the Property inspector. The buttons here allow you to edit the image in Fireworks or Photoshop or to adjust various settings in place. See the sidebar "Dreamweaver's graphic tools" for an explanation of each button.

   There are two ways to reduce the dimensions of an image in Dreamweaver. The first method changes the size of the image temporarily by imposing user-defined dimensions.

5   Select **farmersmarket.png**. In the Property inspector, click the Toggle Size Constrain (🔒) icon and change the image width to **300px** and press Enter/Return.

   The height automatically conforms to the new width. Dreamweaver indicates that the new size is not permanent by displaying the current specifications in bold and the Reset (⊘) and Commit (✔) icons.

6   Click the Reset (⊘) icon.

   The image returns to its original size. The image can also be resized interactively.

Tip: As you scale the image, the Property inspector gives a real-time display of the image dimensions.

7 Drag the lower-right corner to scale the image down to a width of 350 pixels. If you hold down the Shift key as you start scaling, the height will change proportionately; otherwise, click the Toggle Size Constrain (🔒) icon when you're finished to enforce proportionate scaling.

The Reset (⊘) and Commit (✔) icons appear in the Property inspector.

8 Click the Commit (✔) icon.

A dialog box appears that indicates the change will be permanent.

9 Click OK.

Dreamweaver can also crop images within the program.

10 In the Property inspector, click the Crop (⊠) icon.

A dialog box appears, indicating that the action will permanently change the image. Click OK. Crop handles appear on the image.

11 Crop the image to a width and height of 300 pixels.

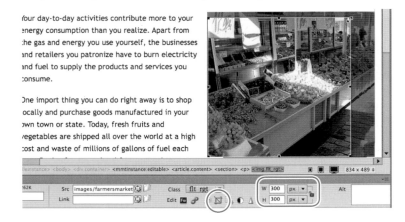

12 Press Enter/Return to finalize the change.

13 Save the file.

Bonus exercise: Completing the news page

The news page still needs a couple of images and a caption for the sidebar. Take a few minutes and apply some of the skills you have learned in this lesson to complete the page.

1 If necessary, open **news.html**. Using any of the techniques you have learned in this lesson, replace the sidebar image placeholder with **sprinkler.jpg**. Enter **Check watering restrictions in your area** as the Alt text.

2 Add the following caption to the sidebar: **The Meridien city council will address summer watering restrictions at the next council meeting.**

3 In the article *Recycling isn't always Green*, insert the **recycling.jpg** image with the Alt text **Learn the pros and cons of recycling**. Apply the `flt_lft` class.

4 Save all files.

In this lesson, you learned how to insert images and Smart Objects into a Dreamweaver page, work with Adobe Bridge, copy and paste from Fireworks and Photoshop, and use the Property inspector to edit images.

There are numerous ways to create and edit images for the web. The methods examined in this lesson show but a few of them and are not meant to recommend or endorse one method over another. Feel free to use whatever methods and workflow you desire based on your own situation and expertise.

Dreamweaver's graphic tools

All of Dreamweaver's graphic tools are accessible from the Property inspector when an image is selected. Here are the seven tools:

 Edit—Opens the selected image in the defined external graphics editor. You can assign a graphics-editing program to any given file type in the File Types/ Editors category of the Preferences dialog box. The button's image changes according to the program chosen. For example, if Fireworks is the designated editor for the image type, a Fireworks () icon is shown; if Photoshop is the editor, you'll see a Photoshop () icon.

 Edit Image Settings—Opens the Image Optimization dialog box, allowing you to apply user-defined optimization specifications to the selected image.

 Update From Original—Updates the placed Smart Object to match any changes to the original source file.

 Crop—Permanently removes unwanted portions of an image. When the Crop tool is enabled, a bounding box with a series of control handles appears within the selected image. You can adjust the bounding box size by dragging the handles. When the box outlines the desired portion of the image, double-click the graphic to apply the cropping.

 Resample—Permanently resizes an image. The Resample tool is active only when an image has been resized.

◑ Brightness And Contrast—Offers user-selectable adjustments to an image's brightness and contrast; a dialog box presents sliders for each that can be adjusted independently. A live preview is available so that you can evaluate adjustments before committing to them.

△ Sharpen—Affects the enhancement of image details by raising or lowering the contrast of pixels on a scale from 0 to 10. As with the Brightness And Contrast tool, Sharpen offers a real-time preview.

You can undo most graphics operations by choosing Edit > Undo until the containing document is closed or you quit Dreamweaver.

Review questions

1 What are the three factors that determine raster image quality?

2 What file formats are specifically designed for use on the web?

3 Describe at least two methods for inserting an image into a webpage using Dreamweaver.

4 True or false: All graphics have to be optimized outside of Dreamweaver.

5 What is the advantage of using a Photoshop Smart Object over copying and pasting an image from Photoshop?

Review answers

1 Raster image quality is determined by resolution, image dimensions, and color depth.

2 The compatible image formats for the web are GIF, JPEG, and PNG.

3 One method to insert an image into a webpage using Dreamweaver is to use the Insert panel. Another method is to drag the graphic file into the layout from the Assets panel. Images can be copied and pasted from Photoshop and Fireworks. Images can also be inserted from Adobe Bridge.

4 False. Images can be optimized even after they are inserted into Dreamweaver by using the Property inspector. Optimization can include rescaling, changing format, or fine-tuning format settings.

5 A Smart Object can be used multiple times in different places on a site, and each instance of the Smart Object can be assigned individual settings. All copies remain connected to the original image. If the original is updated, all the connected images are immediately updated as well. When you copy and paste all or part of a Photoshop file, however, you get a single image that can have only one set of values applied to it.

9 WORKING WITH NAVIGATION

Lesson Overview

In this lesson, you'll apply several kinds of links to page elements by doing the following:

- Creating a text link to a page within the same site

- Creating a link to a page on another website

- Creating an email link

- Creating an image-based link

- Creating a link to a location within a page

 This lesson will take about 1 hour and 30 minutes to complete. If you have not already done so, download the project files for this lesson from the Lesson & Update Files tab on your Account page at www.peachpit.com, and store them on your computer in a convenient location, as described in the Getting Started section of this book. Your Accounts page is also where you'll find any updates to the lessons or to the lesson files. Look on the Lesson & Update Files tab to access the most current content. If you are starting from scratch in this lesson, use the method described in the "Jumpstart" section of "Getting Started."

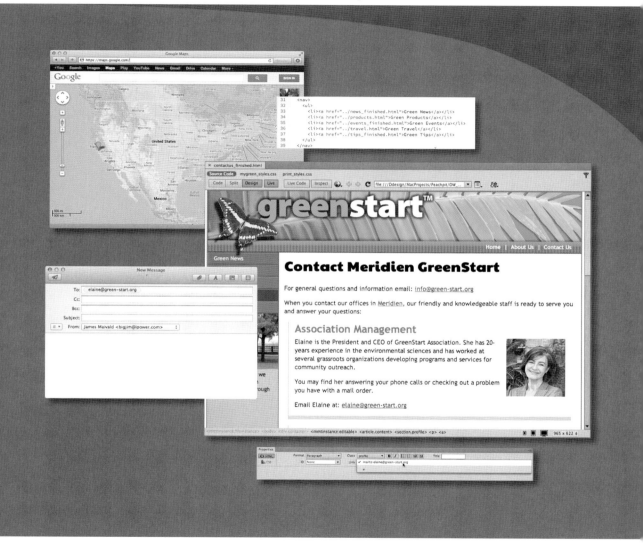

Dreamweaver can create and edit many types of
links—from text-based links to image-based links—
and does so with ease and flexibility.

● **Note:** If you
have not already
downloaded the project
files for this lesson to
your computer from
your Account page,
make sure to do so now.
See "Getting Started"
at the beginning of
the book.

Hyperlink basics

The World Wide Web, and the Internet in general, would be a far different place without the hyperlink. Without hyperlinks, HTML would simply be ML for markup language. The *hypertext* in the name refers to the functionality of the hyperlink. So what is a hyperlink?

A hyperlink, or *link*, is an HTML-based reference to a resource available on the Internet or within your own computer. The resource can be anything that can be stored on and displayed by a computer, such as a webpage, image, movie, sound file, PDF, in fact, almost any type of computer file. A hyperlink creates an interactive behavior specified by HTML and CSS, or the programming language you're using, and is enabled by a browser or other application.

```
<a href="http://www.sitename.com/pagename.html" target="_bank">Link text</a>
```

HTML element | Uniform resource locator (URL) | Value (new browser window) | Closing tag

Attribute (hypertext reference) | Attribute | Link text (visible to visitor)

An HTML hyperlink consists of the anchor <a> element and one or more attributes.

Internal and external hyperlinks

The simplest hyperlink—an internal hyperlink—takes the user to another part of the same document or to another document stored in the same folder or hard drive. An external hyperlink is designed to take the user to a document or resource outside your hard drive, website, or web host.

Internal and external hyperlinks may work differently, but they both have one thing in common: They are enabled in HTML by the <a> anchor element. This element designates the address of the destination, or *target*, of the hyperlink and can then specify how it functions using several attributes. You will learn how to create and modify the <a> element in the exercises that follow.

Relative vs. absolute hyperlinks

The hyperlink address can be written in two ways. When you refer to a target by where it is stored in relation to the current document, it is called a *relative* link. This is like telling someone you live next door to the blue house. If someone were driving down your street and saw the blue house, he would know where you live. But those directions don't really tell them how to get to your house or even to your neighborhood. A relative link frequently will consist of the resource name and perhaps the folder it is stored within, such as logo.jpg or images/logo.jpg.

Sometimes, you need to spell out precisely where a resource is located. In those instances, you need an *absolute* hyperlink. This is like telling someone you live at 123 Main Street in Meridien. This is typically how you refer to resources outside your website. An absolute link includes the entire uniform resource locator, or URL, of the target and may even include a filename—such as http://forums.adobe.com/index.jspa—or just a folder within the site.

Both types of links have advantages and disadvantages. Relative hyperlinks are faster and easier to write, but they may not work if the document containing them is saved in a different folder or location in the website. Absolute links always work no matter where the containing document is saved, but they can fail if the targets are moved or renamed. A simple rule most web designers follow is to use relative links for resources within a site and absolute links for resources outside the site. Then, testing all links before deploying the page or site is important.

Previewing the completed file

To see the final version of the file you will work on in this lesson, let's preview the completed page in the browser.

1 Launch Adobe Dreamweaver CC.

2 If necessary, press F8 to open the Files panel, and select DW-CC from the site list.

3 In the Files panel, expand the Lesson09 folder.

4 In the Files panel, right-click **aboutus_finished.html**. Select Preview In Browser, and then select your preferred browser to preview the file.

Note: If you are completing this lesson separately from the rest of the lessons in book, see the detailed "Jumpstart" instructions in the "Getting Started" section at the beginning of the book. Then, follow the steps in this exercise.

Note: If you have not already downloaded the project files for this lesson to your computer from your Account page, make sure to do so now. See "Getting Started" at the beginning of the book.

The **aboutus_finished.html** file appears in your default browser. This page features only internal links in both the horizontal and vertical menus.

5 Position the cursor over the vertical menu. Hover over each button and examine the behavior of the menu.

The menu is the same one you created in Lesson 4, "Creating a Page Layout," and formatted in Lesson 5, "Working with Cascading Style Sheets."

6 Click the *Green News* link.

The browser loads the *Green News* page.

7 Position the cursor over the *About Us* link in the horizontal menu. Observe the browser to see if it's displaying the link's destination anywhere on the screen.

▶ **Tip:** If you don't see the status bar in Firefox, choose View > Status Bar to turn it on. In Internet Explorer, choose View > Toolbars > Status Bar to turn it on.

Typically, the browser shows the link destination in the status bar.

8 In the horizontal navigation menu, click the *Contact Us* link.

The browser loads the *Contact Us* page, replacing the *Green News* page. The new page includes internal, external, and email links.

9 Position the cursor over the Meridien link in the main content area. Observe the status bar.

The status bar displays the link http://maps.google.com.

10 Click the Meridien link.

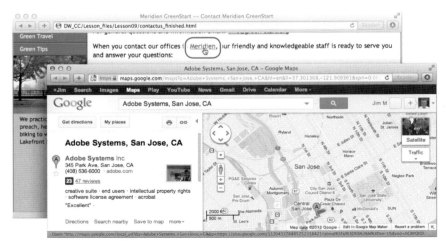

A new browser window appears and loads Google Maps. The link is intended to show the visitor where the Meridien GreenStart Association offices are located. You can even include address details or the company name in this link so that Google can load the exact map and directions, if desired.

Note that the browser opened a separate window or document tab when you clicked the link. This is a good behavior to use when directing visitors to resources outside your site. Since the link opens in a separate window, your own site is still open and ready to use. This practice is especially helpful if your visitors are unfamiliar with your site and may not know how to get back to it once they click away.

Note: Many web visitors don't use email programs installed on their computers. They use web-based services like AOL, Gmail, Hotmail, and so on. For these types of visitors, email links like the one you tested won't work. To learn how to receive information from visitors without relying on client-based email, see Lesson 12, "Working with Forms."

11 Close the Google Maps window.

The *Contact Us* page is still open. Note that each employee has an email link.

12 Click an email link for one of the employees.

The default mail application launches on your computer. If you have not set up this application to send and receive mail, the program will usually start a wizard to help you set up this functionality. If the email program is set up, a new message window appears with the email address of the employee automatically entered in the To field.

13 Close the new message window and exit the email program.

14 Scroll down to the *Education and Events* section. Click the *events* link.

The browser loads the *Green Events and Classes* page. The browser focuses on the table containing the list of upcoming events at the top of the page.

15 In the horizontal menu, click the *Contact Us* link.

The *Contact Us* page loads again.

16 Scroll down to the *Education and Events* section. Click the *classes* link.

The browser loads the *Green Events and Classes* page again. But this time the browser focuses on the table containing the list of upcoming classes at the bottom of the page.

17 Click the *Return to top* link that appears above the class schedule. You may need to scroll up or down the page to see it.

The browser jumps back to the top of the page.

18 Close the browser and switch to Dreamweaver, if necessary.

You have tested a variety of different types of hyperlinks: internal, external, relative, and absolute. In the following exercises, you will learn how to build each type.

Creating internal hyperlinks

Creating hyperlinks of all types is easy with Dreamweaver. In this exercise, you'll create text-based links to pages in the same site using a variety of methods.

1   In the Files panel, double-click the **about_us.html** file in the site root folder to open it. Or, if you are starting from scratch in this lesson, follow the "Jumpstart" instructions in the "Getting Started" section at the beginning of the book.

2   In the horizontal menu, position the cursor over the Home text in the horizontal menu. Observe the type of cursor that appears.

The (⊘) icon indicates that this section of the page is locked. The horizontal menu was not added to an editable region in Lesson 6, "Working with Templates," so it's considered part of the template and is locked. To add a hyperlink to this menu item, you'll have to open the template.

3   Choose Window > Assets. In the Assets panel, click the Template (▤) icon. In the list, right-click **mygreen_temp** and choose Edit from the context menu.

4   In the horizontal menu, select the *Home* text.

The horizontal menu is editable in the template.

5   If necessary, choose Window > Properties to open the Property inspector. Examine the contents of the Link field in the Property inspector.

To create links, the HTML tab must be selected in the Property inspector. The Link field shows a hyperlink placeholder (#). The home page doesn't exist yet, but the link can be created by typing the name of the file or resource into this field.

▶ **Tip:** When editing or removing an existing hyperlink, you don't need to select the entire link; you can just insert the cursor anywhere in the link text. Dreamweaver assumes you want to change the entire link by default.

● **Note:** If you are using the Jumpstart method, your file may be named mygreen_temp_09.

6 In the Link field, select the hash mark (#). Type **../index.html** and press Enter/Return to complete the link.

You've created your first text-based hyperlink. Since the template is saved in a subfolder, you need to add the path element notation (../) to the filename so that the link properly resolves once the template pages are updated. This notation tells the browser or operating system to look in the parent directory of the current folder. Dreamweaver rewrites the link when the template is applied to a page, depending on where the containing page is saved.

If you want to link to a file that already exists, Dreamweaver also offers interactive ways to create links.

7 In the horizontal menu, select the *About Us* text.

8 Click the Browse For File (📁) icon, adjacent to the Link field. In the Select File dialog box, select **about_us.html** from the site root folder. Make sure that the Relative To menu is set to Document. Click OK/Open.

The hyperlink placeholder is replaced by the text *../about_us.html*. Now let's try a more visual approach.

9 In the horizontal menu, select the *Contact Us* text.

10 Click the Files tab to bring the panel to the top, or choose Window > Files.

Note: The link won't have the typical hyperlink appearance because of the special formatting you applied to this menu in Lesson 5.

Note: You can select any range of text to create a link, from one character to an entire paragraph or more; Dreamweaver will add the necessary markup to the selection.

Tip: If a folder in the Files panel contains a page you want to link to but the folder is not open, drag the Point To File icon over the folder and hold it in place to expand that folder so that you can point to the desired file.

11 In the Property inspector, drag the Point To File (⊕) icon—next to the Link field—to **contact_us.html** in the site root folder displayed in the Files panel.

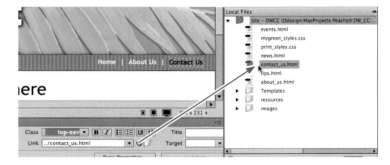

Dreamweaver enters the filename and any necessary path information into the Link field. To apply the links to all the pages formatted by this template, just save the page.

12 Insert the cursor into the *Green News* link in the vertical menu.

You don't have to select all the text for an existing link. Dreamweaver will update the entire link as long as any part of it is selected.

13 Using any of the methods you learned already point the link to the **../news.html** file.

14 Modify the rest of the menu as follows:

Green Products: **../products.html**

Green Events: **../events.html**

Green Travel: **../travel.html**

Green Tips: **../tips.html**

For files that have not been created, you will have to enter the link manually. Remember all the links added to the template must include the notation **../** so that the link resolves properly in the template. Remember, Dreamweaver will modify the link as needed once the template is applied to the child page.

Tip: If you don't see the update report, select the Show Log option.

15 Choose File > Save.

The Update Template Files dialog box appears. You can choose to update pages now or wait until later. You can even update the template files manually, if desired.

16 Click Update.

Dreamweaver updates all pages created from the template. The Update Pages dialog box appears and displays a report listing the updated pages.

17 Close the Update Pages dialog box. Close **mygreen_temp.dwt**.

Note the asterisk in the document tab for **about_us.html**, which indicates that changed page hasn't been saved.

18 Save **about_us.html** and preview it in the default browser. Position the cursor over the *About Us* and *Contact Us* text.

When the template was saved, it updated the locked regions of the page, adding the hyperlinks.

19 Click the *Contact Us* link.

The *Contact Us* page loads to replace the *About Us* page in the browser.

20 Click the *About Us* link.

The *About Us* page loads to replace the *Contact Us* page. The links were added even to pages that weren't open at the time.

21 Close the browser and switch to Dreamweaver.

You learned three methods for creating hyperlinks with the Property inspector: typing the link manually, using the Browse For File function, and using the Point To File tool.

Creating an image-based link

Links can also be applied to images. Image-based links work like any other hyperlink and can direct users to internal or external resources. In this exercise, you will create and format an image-based link directing users to the organization's *About Us* page.

1 If necessary, open the Assets panel and click the Template (▤) category icon. Double-click the site template to open it.

2 Select the butterfly image at the top of the page. In the Property inspector, click the Browse For File icon next to the Link field.

3 In the site root folder, select **about_us.html**. Click OK/Open.

The *../about_us.html* text appears in the Link field.

Note: Normally an image formatted with a hyperlink would display a blue border, similar to the blue underscore that text links get. But the predefined CSS that came with the layout includes an `img` rule, which sets this default border to None.

4   In the Alt field of the Property inspector, replace the existing text with **Click to learn about Meridien GreenStart** and press Enter/Return.

The Alt text will appear whenever the picture doesn't load or if the user is using an assistive device to access the webpage.

5   Save the template. Update all child pages and close the template.

The Update Pages dialog box appears, reporting how many pages were updated.

6   Close the Update Pages dialog box. Open **contact_us.html**, if necessary, and preview it in the default browser. Position the cursor over the butterfly image. Test the image link.

Clicking the image loads **about_us.html** in the browser.

7   Switch back to Dreamweaver. Close the template file.

Creating an external link

The pages you linked to in the previous exercise were stored within the current site. You can also link to any page—or other resource—stored on the web if you know the full web address, or URL. In this exercise, you'll apply an external link to some existing text.

1   Click the document tab for **contact_us.html** to bring it to the top, or open it from the site root folder.

2   In the second <p> element in the MainContent region, select the word *Meridien*.

You'll link this text to the Google Maps site. If you don't know the URL of a particular site, here's a simple trick to obtain it.

Tip: For this trick, you can use any search engine.

3   Launch your favorite browser. In the URL field, type **maps.google.com** and press Enter/Return.

Google Maps appears in the browser window.

4 Type **Adobe Systems, San Jose, CA** into the search field and press Enter/Return.

● **Note:** In some browsers you can type the search phrase directly in the URL field.

Adobe headquarters in San Jose appears on a map in the browser. Click the Link icon to display the code dialog box. You can repeat this procedure at any time to create a custom map for your own needs.

5 Select the link intended for email or IM and copy it.

6 Switch to Dreamweaver. In the Property inspector, insert the cursor in the Link field, press Ctrl-V/Cmd-V to paste the link, and press Enter/Return.

The selected text displays the default formatting for a hyperlink.

7 Save the file and preview it in the default browser. Test the link.

When you click the link, the browser takes you to the opening page of Google Maps, assuming you have a connection to the Internet. But there is a problem: Clicking the link replaced the *Contact Us* page in the browser; it didn't open a new window as in the earlier example. To make the browser open a new window, you need to add a simple HTML attribute to the link.

8 Switch to Dreamweaver. Insert the cursor in the Meridien link text, if necessary.

9 Choose **_blank** from the Target field menu.

10 Save the file and preview the page in the default browser. Test the link.

A new, separate window opens for Google Maps.

11 Close the browser windows and switch back to Dreamweaver.

As you can see, Dreamweaver makes it easy to create links to internal or external resources.

Setting up email links

Another type of link is the email link, but instead of taking the visitor to another page it opens the visitor's email program. It can create an automatic, pre-addressed email message from your visitors for customer feedback, product orders, or other important communications. The code for an email link is slightly different from the normal hyperlink and—as you probably guessed already—Dreamweaver can create the proper code for you automatically.

1   If necessary, open **contact_us.html**.

2   Select the email address in the first paragraph underneath the heading (info@green-start.org) and press Ctrl-C/Cmd-C to copy the text.

3   Choose Insert > Email link.

▶ **Tip:** If you select the text before you access the dialog box, Dreamweaver enters the text in the field for you automatically.

The Email Link dialog box appears. The selected text is automatically entered into the Text field.

4   Insert the cursor in the Email field and press Ctrl-V/Cmd-V to paste the email address.

5   Click OK. Examine the Link field in the Property inspector.

Dreamweaver inserted the email address into the Link field and did one more thing. As you can see, it also entered the `mailto:` notation, which changes the link to an email link that will automatically launch the visitor's default email program.

6   Save the file and preview it in the default browser. Test the email link.

The default email program launches and creates an email message. If there is no default email program, your computer's operating system will launch an available email program or ask you to identify one.

7   Close any open email program, related dialog boxes, or wizards. Switch to Dreamweaver.

8   Create email links for the remaining email addresses displayed on the page.

9   Save the page.

Client-based vs. server-side functions

The email link you just created relies on software installed on the visitor's computer, such as Outlook or Apple Mail. Such applications are referred to as *client-based*, or *client-side*, functionality. The email link won't work, however, if a user sends her mail via an Internet application—such as Hotmail or Gmail—and doesn't have a desktop email application installed and set up to send and receive email.

Another detraction is that open email links like the one in these exercises can be picked up easily by spambots that roam the Internet and can open you up to a deluge of unwanted junk mail. If you want to ensure that you'll get feedback from every user who wants to send it, rely instead on functionality supplied by your server. Web-based applications for capturing and passing data are referred to as *server-side* functionality. Using server-side scripts and proprietary languages—such as ASP, ColdFusion, and PHP—capturing data and returning it by email (or even inserting it directly into a hosted database) is relatively easy. You'll learn some of these techniques in Lesson 12, "Working with Forms."

Targeting page elements

As you add more content on a page, navigation gets longer and more difficult. Typically, when you click a link to a page, the browser window displays the page starting at the very top. Whenever possible, provide convenient methods for users to link to a specific point on a page.

In HTML 4.01, two methods target specific content or page structures: One uses a *named anchor* and the other an ID attribute. However, the named anchor has been deprecated in HTML5 in favor of IDs. Named anchors won't suddenly cease to function the day HTML5 is adopted, but you should start practicing now. In this exercise, you'll work only with ID attributes.

1 Open **events.html**.

2 Scroll down to the table containing the class schedule.

   When users move down this far on the page, the navigation menus are out of sight and unusable. The farther they read down the page, the farther they are from the primary navigation. Before users can navigate to another page, they have to use the browser scroll bars or the mouse scroll wheel to get back to the top of the page. Adding a link to take users back to the top can vastly improve their experience on your site. Let's call this type of link an internal *targeted* link.

   Internal targeted links have two parts: the link itself and the target element. Which one you create first doesn't matter.

3   Insert the cursor in the *Class* table. Select the `<table>` tag selector. Press the Left Arrow key to move the cursor before the opening `<table>` tag.

4   Type **Return to top** and select the text. In the Property inspector, choose Paragraph from the Format menu.

The text is inserted between the two tables and is formatted as a `<p>` element. Let's center the text.

5   In the CSS Designer, select **mygreen_styles.css** in the Sources pane and click the Add Selector icon.

6   In the selector name field, type `.ctr` and press Enter/Return.

7   Create the `text-align: center` property.

8   Insert the cursor in the *Return to top* text, and select the `<p>` tag selector. In the Property inspector Class menu, choose `ctr`.

The *Return to top* text is aligned to the center. The tag selector now says `<p.ctr>`.

▶ **Tip:** In some browsers you need only to type the hash mark (#) to enable this function. The browser will jump to the top of the page whenever an unnamed anchor is referenced. Unfortunately, other browsers will ignore them altogether, so using a target element as well is important.

9   In the Link field, type `#top` and press Enter/Return. Save all files.

By using `#top`, you have created a link to a target within the current page. When users click the *Return to top* link, the browser window jumps to the position of the target. This target doesn't exist yet. For this link to work properly, you need to insert the destination as high on the page as possible.

10 Scroll to the top of **events.html**. Position the cursor over the header element.

The mouse icon indicates that this part of the page (and its related code) is uneditable because the header and horizontal navigation menu are based on the site template. Putting the target at the very top is important, or a portion of the page may be obscured when the browser jumps to it. Since the top of the page is part of an uneditable region, the best solution is to add the target directly to the template.

Creating a link destination using an ID

By adding a unique ID to the template, you will be able to access it automatically throughout the site wherever you want to add a link back to the top of a page.

1 Open the Assets panel. Click the Template category icon. Double-click **mygreen_temp** to open it.

2 Click the tag selector for <header>. In the Property inspector, type **top** in the Header ID field, and press Enter/Return to complete the ID.

The tag selector changes to <header#top>; otherwise, the page shows no visible difference. The big difference is in how the page reacts to the internal hyperlink.

3 Save the file and update all template pages. Close the template.

4 Switch to or open **events.html**, if necessary. Save the file and preview it in the default browser.

5 Scroll down to the *Class* table. Click the *Return to top* link.

The browser jumps back to the top of the page.

Now that the ID has been inserted in every page of the site by the template, you can copy the *Return to top* link and paste it wherever you want to add this functionality.

6 Switch to Dreamweaver. Insert the cursor in the *Return to top* link. Select the <p.ctr> tag selector. Press Ctrl-C/Cmd-C.

7   Scroll down to the bottom of **events.html**. Insert the cursor in the *Class* table, and select the `<table>` tag selector. Press the Right Arrow key to move the cursor after the closing `</table>` tag. Press Ctrl-V/Cmd-V.

The `<p.ctr>` element and link appear at the bottom of the page.

8   Save the file and preview it in the browser. Test both *Return to top* links.

Both links can be used to jump back to the top of the document. In the next exercise, you'll learn how to use element attributes as link targets.

Adding an ID to an HTML table

You don't need to add any extra code to create hyperlink destinations if you can add an ID attribute to a handy element nearby.

1   If necessary, open **events.html**. Insert the cursor anywhere in the Events table and select the `<table>` tag selector.

The Property inspector displays the attributes of the *Events* table.

2   In the Property inspector, open the table ID field menu.

● **Note:** An ID can be applied to any HTML element. They don't have to be referenced in the style sheet at all.

● **Note:** On the Mac the ID menu will not open if no IDs are available.

Dreamweaver will display any ID defined by the CSS but currently unused within the page. No IDs that can be applied to the table are displayed in the menu, but creating a new one is easy.

3   Insert the cursor in the ID field. Type **calendar** and press Enter/Return.

● **Note:** When creating IDs, remember that they have to be unique names. IDs are case-sensitive, so look out for typos.

The tag selector now displays `<table#calendar>`. Since IDs are unique identifiers, they can be used for targeting specific content on a page. Don't forget to create an ID for the *Class* table too.

4   Select the *Class* table, as in step 1. Insert the cursor in the ID field.
    Type `classes` and press Enter/Return.

    The tag selector now displays `<table#classes>`. You'll learn how to link
    to these IDs in the next exercise.

5   Save the file.

Targeting ID-based link destinations

By adding unique IDs to both tables, you have provided an ideal target for internal
hyperlinks to navigate to a specific section of your webpage. In this exercise, you
will create a link to each table.

1   If necessary, open **contact_us.html**. Scroll down to the *Education and Events*
    section.

2   Select the word *events* in the first paragraph of the section.

3   Using any of the methods you learned earlier, create a link to the file **events.html**.

    This link will open the file, but you're not finished. You now have to direct the
    browser to navigate down to the *Events* table.

4   Insert the cursor in the Link field. At the end of the filename events.html, type
    `#calendar` and press Enter/Return to complete the link.

● **Note:** Hyperlinks
cannot contain spaces;
make sure the ID
reference follows the
file name immediately.

    The word *events* now displays default hyperlink formatting.

5   Select the word *classes* and repeat step 4 to create a link to the **events.html** file.
    Insert the cursor at the end of the filename, type `#classes` and press Enter/
    Return to complete the link.

6   Save the file and preview the page in a browser. Test the links to the *Events* and
    Class tables.

    The links open the *Events* page and navigate to the appropriate tables.

Checking your page

Dreamweaver can check your page automatically for valid HTML, accessibility, and broken links. In this exercise, you'll check your links and learn what you can do in case of a browser compatibility problem.

1 If necessary, open **contact_us.html**.

2 Choose Site > Check Links Sitewide.

A Link Checker panel opens. The Link Checker panel reports broken links to the files **index.html**, **products.html**, and **travel.html** you created for nonexistent pages. You'll make these pages later, so you don't need to worry about fixing these broken links now. The Link Checker will also find broken links to external sites, should you have any.

3 Right-click the Link Checker tab and choose Close Tab Group from the context menu.

You've made big changes to the appearance of the pages in this lesson by creating links to specific positions on a page, to email, and to an external site. You also created a link that uses an image as the clickable item. Finally, you checked your page for broken links.

Review questions

1 Describe two ways to insert a link into a page.

2 What information is required to create a link to an external webpage?

3 What's the difference between standard page links and email links?

4 How can you check to see if your links will work properly?

Review answers

1 Select text or a graphic, and then in the Property inspector, click the Browse For File icon next to the Link field and navigate to the desired page. A second method is to drag the Point To File icon to a file within the Files panel.

2 Link to an external page by typing or copying and pasting the full web address (a fully formed URL) in the Link field of the Property inspector.

3 A standard page link opens a new page or moves the view to a position somewhere on the page. An email link opens a blank email message window if the visitor has an email application installed.

4 Run the Link Checker to test links on each page or site-wide.

10

ADDING INTERACTIVITY

Lesson Overview

In this lesson, you'll add Web 2.0 functionality to your webpages by doing the following:

- Using Dreamweaver behaviors to create an image rollover effect
- Inserting a jQuery Accordion widget

 This lesson will take about 1 an hour and 15 minutes to complete. If you have not already done so, download the project files for this lesson from the Lesson & Update Files tab on your Account page at www.peachpit. com, and store them on your computer in a convenient location, as described in the Getting Started section of this book. Your Accounts page is also where you'll find any updates to the lessons or to the lesson files. Look on the Lesson & Update Files tab to access the most current content. If you are starting from scratch in this lesson, use the method described in the "Jumpstart" section of "Getting Started."

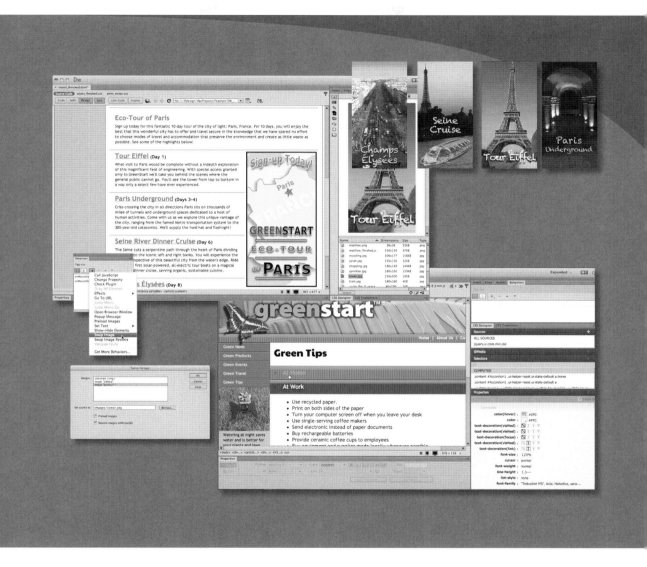

Dreamweaver can create sophisticated interactive
effects with behaviors and accordion panels using
Adobe's jQuery framework.

Learning about Dreamweaver behaviors

Learning about Dreamweaver behaviors

● **Note:** If you have not already downloaded the project files for this lesson to your computer from your Account page, make sure to do so now. See "Getting Started" at the beginning of the book.

The term *Web 2.0* was coined to describe a major change in the user experience on the Internet from mostly static pages, featuring text, graphics, and simple links, to a new paradigm of dynamic webpages filled with video, animation, and interactive content. Dreamweaver has always led the industry in providing a variety of tools to drive this movement, from its tried-and-true collection of JavaScript behaviors and jQuery widgets to the latest support for jQuery Mobile and even PhoneGap. This lesson explores two of these capabilities: Dreamweaver behaviors and jQuery UI widgets.

A Dreamweaver *behavior* is predefined JavaScript code that performs an action—such as opening a browser window or showing or hiding a page element—when it is triggered by an event, such as a mouse click. Applying a behavior is a three-step process:

● **Note:** To access the Behaviors panel and menu, you must have a file open.

1   Create or select the page element that you want to trigger the behavior.

2   Choose the behavior to apply.

3   Specify the settings or parameters of the behavior.

The triggering element often involves a hyperlink applied to a range of text or to an image. In some cases, the behavior is not intended to load a new page, so it will employ a dummy link enabled by the hash (#) sign, similar to ones that you used in Lesson 9, "Working with Navigation." The Swap Image behavior you will use in this lesson does not require a link to function, but keep this in mind when you work with other behaviors.

Dreamweaver offers more than 16 built-in behaviors, all accessed from the Behaviors panel (Window > Behaviors). Hundreds of other useful behaviors can be downloaded from the Internet for free or a small fee. Some are available from the online Adobe Exchange website, or from the new Adobe Exchange panel, which can be added to the program by clicking the Add Behavior (**+**) icon in the Behaviors panel and choosing Get More Behaviors from the pop-up menu. When the Adobe Exchange page loads in the browser, click the link to download the extension. Use Adobe Extension Manager CC to install the extension. You can then launch Adobe Exchange by choosing Window > Extensions and selecting the extension from the menu.

Adobe Exchange offers tons of resources for many of the applications in Creative Cloud, including both free and paid add-ons.

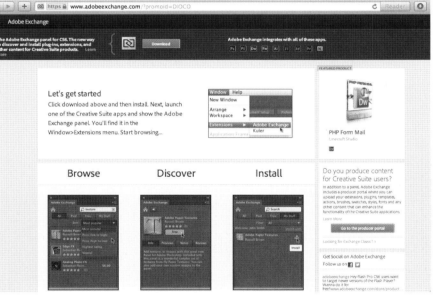

The following are some of the types of functionality available to you using the built-in Dreamweaver behaviors:

- Opening a browser window
- Swapping one image for another to create what is called a *rollover effect*
- Fading images or page areas in and out
- Growing or shrinking graphics
- Displaying pop-up messages
- Changing the text or other HTML content within a given area
- Showing or hiding sections of the page
- Calling a custom-defined JavaScript function

● **Note:** If you have not already downloaded the project files for this lesson to your computer from your Account page, make sure to do so now. See "Getting Started" at the beginning of the book.

Not all behaviors are available all the time. Certain behaviors become available only in the presence and selection of certain page elements, such as images or links. For example, you can't use the Swap Image behavior unless an image is present.

Each behavior invokes a unique dialog box that provides relevant options and specifications. For instance, the dialog box for the Open Browser Window behavior enables you to open a new browser window, set its width, height, and other attributes, and set the URL of the displayed resource. After the behavior is defined, it is listed in the Behaviors panel with its chosen triggering action. As with other behaviors, these specifications can be modified at any time.

Behaviors are extremely flexible, and multiple behaviors can be applied to the same trigger. For example, you could swap one image for another and change the text of the accompanying image caption—and do it all with one click. While some effects may appear to happen simultaneously, behaviors are actually triggered in sequence. When multiple behaviors are applied, you can choose the order in which the behaviors are processed.

Previewing the completed file

● **Note:** If you are starting from scratch in this exercise, see the "Jumpstart" instructions in the "Getting Started" section at the beginning of the book. Then, follow the steps in this exercise.

In the first part of this lesson, you'll create a new page for GreenStart's travel services. Let's preview the completed page in the browser.

1   Launch Adobe Dreamweaver CC.

2   If necessary, press F8 to open the Files panel, and choose DW-CC from the site list.

3   In the Files panel, expand the Lesson10 folder. Right-click **travel_finished.html**, choose Preview In Browser from the context menu, and select your primary browser.

The page includes Dreamweaver behaviors.

4 If Microsoft Internet Explorer is your primary browser, a message may appear at the bottom of the browser window indicating that it has prevented scripts and ActiveX controls from running. If so, click Allow Blocked Content.

This message appears only when the file is previewed from your hard drive. It doesn't appear when the file is actually hosted on the Internet.

5 Position the cursor over the Tour Eiffel heading. Observe the image to the right of the text.

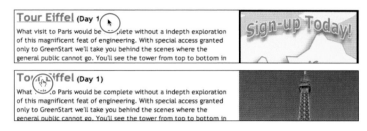

The existing image swaps for one of the Eiffel Tower.

6 Move the pointer to the Paris Underground heading. Observe the image to the right of the text.

As the pointer moves off the Tour Eiffel heading, the image reverts to the Eco-Tour ad. Then, as the pointer moves over the heading Paris Underground, the ad image swaps for one of underground Paris.

7 Pass the pointer over each heading and observe the image behavior.

The image alternates between the Eco-Tour ad and images of each of the cities. This effect is the Swap Image behavior.

8 When you're finished, close the browser window and return to Dreamweaver.

In the next exercise, you will learn how to work with Dreamweaver behaviors.

Working with Dreamweaver behaviors

Adding Dreamweaver behaviors to your layout is a simple point-and-click operation. But before you can add the behaviors, you have to create the travel page.

1 Open the Assets panel and click the Template category icon. Right-click the site template and choose New From Template from the context menu.

A new document window opens based on the template.

2 Save the new document as **travel.html**.

3 In the sidebar, double-click the image placeholder. Navigate to the site images folder. Select **train.jpg** and click OK/Open.

The train image appears in the sidebar.

● **Note:** To add Alt text to this image, use the Alt field in the Property inspector.

4 In the Property inspector Alt field, type **Electric trains provide green transportation** and press Enter/Return.

5 Open the Files panel and expand the Lesson10 > resources folder. Double-click the **travel-caption.txt** file.

The caption text opens in Dreamweaver.

6 Select and copy the entire caption. Close **travel-caption.txt**.

7 In the sidebar, select the caption placeholder. Paste the new caption text to replace the placeholder.

8 In the Files panel in the resources folder, double-click **travel-text.html**.

The **travel-text.html** file contains a table and text for the travel page. Note that the text and table are unformatted.

9 Select and copy all the contents within the page. Close **travel-text.html**.

10 Select the main heading placeholder *Add main heading here* in **travel.html**. Type **Green Travel** to replace the text.

11 Select the heading placeholder *Add subheading here* and type **Eco-Touring** to replace it.

12 Select the <p> tag selector for the *Add content here* text. Press Ctrl-V/Cmd-V to paste the travel text.

The content from **travel-text.html** appears. It assumes the default formatting for text and tables applied by the style sheet you created in Lesson 7, "Working with Text, Lists, and Tables."

Let's insert the Eco-Tour ad, which will be the base image for the Swap Image behavior.

13 Double-click the *SideAd* image placeholder. Navigate to the site images folder and select **ecotour.png**. Click OK/Open.

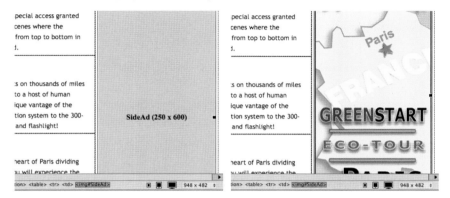

The placeholder is replaced by the Eco-Tour ad. But before you can apply the Swap Image behavior, you have to identify the image you want to swap. You do this by giving the image an ID.

14 If necessary, select **ecotour.png** in the layout. In the Property inspector, select the existing ID SideAd. Type **ecotour** and press Enter/Return. Enter the text **Eco-Tour of Paris** in the Alt field.

▶ **Tip:** Although it takes more time, giving all your images unique IDs is a good practice.

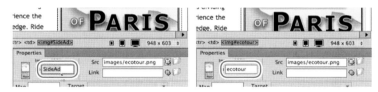

15 Save the file.

Next, you will create a Swap Image behavior for **ecotour.png**.

Applying a behavior

As described earlier, many behaviors are context sensitive, based on the elements or structure present. A Swap Image behavior can be applied to any document text element.

1 Choose Window > Behaviors to open the Behaviors panel.

2 Insert the cursor in the *Tour Eiffel* text and select the <h3> tag selector.

Note: Users of previous versions of Dreamweaver may be looking for the Tag Inspector. It's now called the Behaviors panel.

Note: The Preload Images option forces the browser to download all images necessary for the behavior before the page loads. That way, when the user clicks the trigger, the image swap will occur without any lags or glitches.

3   Click the Add Behavior (**+**) icon. Choose Swap Image from the behavior list.

The Swap Image dialog box lists any images on the page that are available for this behavior. This behavior can replace one or more of these images at a time.

4   Select the `image "ecotour"` item and click Browse.

5   In the Select Image Source dialog box, select **tower.jpg** from the site images folder. Click OK/Open.

6   In the Swap Image dialog box, select the Preload Images option, if necessary, and click OK.

A Swap Image behavior is added to the Behaviors panel with an attribute of `onMouseOver`. Attributes can be changed, if desired, using the Behaviors panel.

7   Click the `onMouseOver` attribute to open the pop-up menu and examine the options.

The menu provides a list of trigger events, most of which are self-explanatory. For now, however, leave the attribute as `onMouseOver`.

8   Save the file and click Live view to test the behavior. Position the cursor over the *Tour Eiffel* text.

When the cursor passes over the text, the Eco-Tour ad is replaced by the image of the Eiffel Tower. But there is a small problem. When the cursor moves away from the text, the original image doesn't return. The reason is simple: You didn't tell it to. To bring back the original image, you have to add another command—Swap Image Restore—to the same element.

Applying a Swap Image Restore behavior

In some instances, a specific action requires more than one behavior. To bring back the Eco-Tour ad once the mouse moves off the trigger, you have to add a restore function.

1   Return to Design view. Insert the cursor in the *Tour Eiffel* heading and examine the Behaviors panel.

    The inspector displays the currently assigned behavior. You don't need to select the element completely; Dreamweaver assumes you want to modify the entire trigger.

2   Click the Add Behavior (➕) icon and choose Swap Image Restore from the pop-up menu. Click OK in the Swap Image Restore dialog box to complete the command.

    The Swap Image Restore behavior appears in the Behaviors panel with an attribute of onMouseOut.

3   Switch to Code view and examine the markup for the *Tour Eiffel* text.

```
<h3 onMouseOver "MM_swapImage('ecotour','','images/tower.jpg',1)" onMouseOut "MM_swapImgRestore()">
```

    The trigger events—onMouseOver and onMouseOut—were added as attributes to the <h3> element. The rest of the JavaScript code was inserted in the document's <head> section.

4   Save the file and switch to Live view to test the behavior. Test the text trigger *Tour Eiffel*.

When the pointer passes over the text, the Eco-Tour image is replaced by the one of the Eiffel Tower and then reappears when the pointer is withdrawn. The behavior functions as desired, but nothing is visibly "different" about the text to indicate that something magical will happen if the user rolls the pointer over the heading. Since most Internet users are familiar with the interactivity provided by hyperlinks, applying a link placeholder on the heading will encourage the visitor to explore the effect.

Removing applied behaviors

Before you can apply a behavior to a hyperlink, you need to remove the current Swap Image and Swap Image Restore behaviors.

1 Turn off Live view. Open the Behaviors panel, if necessary. Insert the cursor in the *Tour Eiffel* text.

The Behaviors panel displays the two applied events. Which one you delete first doesn't matter.

2 Select the Swap Image event. In the Behaviors panel, click the Remove Event (➖) icon. Select the Swap Image Restore event. In the Behaviors panel, click the Remove Event icon.

Both events are removed. Dreamweaver will also remove any unneeded JavaScript code.

3 Save the file and check the text in Live view again.

The text no longer triggers the Swap Image behavior. To reapply the behavior, you need to add a link or link placeholder to the heading.

Adding behaviors to hyperlinks

Behaviors can be added to hyperlinks, even if the link doesn't load a new document. For this exercise, you'll add a link placeholder to the heading to support the desired behavior.

1 Select the *Tour Eiffel* text within the <h3> element. In the Property inspector Link field, type # and press Enter/Return to create the link placeholder.

The text displays with the default hyperlink styling.

2 Insert the cursor in the link. In the Behaviors panel, click the Add Behavior (➕) icon and choose Swap Image from the pop-up menu.

As long as the cursor is still inserted anywhere in the link, the behavior will be applied to the entire link markup.

3   In the Swap Image dialog box, select the item `image "ecotour"`. Browse and select **tower.jpg** from the site images folder. Click OK/Open.

4   In the Swap Image dialog box, select the Preload Images option and Restore Images onMouseOut option, if necessary, and click OK.

The Swap Image event appears in the Behaviors panel along with a Swap Image Restore event. Since the behavior was applied all at once, Dreamweaver provides the restore functionality as a productivity enhancement.

5   Select and apply a link (#) placeholder to the *Paris Underground* text. Apply the Swap Image behavior to the link. Use the image **underground.jpg** from the site images folder.

6   Repeat step 5 for the *Seine River Dinner Cruise* text. Select the image **cruise.jpg**.

7   Repeat step 5 for the *Champs Élysées* text. Select the image **champs.jpg**.

The Swap Image behaviors are now complete, but the text and link appearance don't match the site color scheme. Let's create custom CSS rules to format them accordingly. You will create two rules: one for the heading element and another for the link itself.

8   Insert the cursor in any of the rollover links.

9   In the CSS Designer, select the `.content section h2` rule in the **mygreen_styles.css** style sheet. Click the Add Selector (➕) icon.

10 Create the `.content section h3` selector.

11 Create the following properties and specifications:

    `margin-top: 0px`
    `margin-bottom: 5px`

12 Create the `.content section h3 a` selector.

13 Create the following properties and specifications:

    `font-size: 140%`
    `color: #090`

14 Click OK to complete the rule.

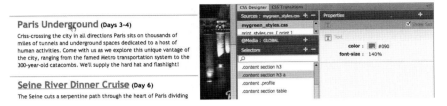

The headings are now more prominent and styled to match the site theme. Note how the underline disappears when the mouse moves over the link based on the styling applied by the CSS hover effect.

15 Save all files and test the behaviors in Live view.

The Swap Image behavior works successfully on all links.

16 Close **travel.html**.

In addition to eye-catching effects, Dreamweaver also provides structural components—such as jQuery widgets—that conserve space and add more interactive flair to your website.

Working with jQuery Accordion widgets

The jQuery Accordion widget allows you to organize a lot of content into a compact space. In the Accordion widget, the tabs are stacked and when opened, they expand vertically rather than side by side. When you click a tab, the panel slides open with a smooth action. The panels are set to a specific height, and if the content is taller or wider than the panel itself, scroll bars appear automatically. Let's preview the completed layout.

1 In the Files panel, select **tips_finished.html** from the Lesson10 folder and preview it in your primary browser.

The page content is divided among three panels using the jQuery Accordion widget.

2 Click each panel in turn to open and close them.

The panels open and close, revealing the bulleted lists of green tips. The Accordion allows you to display more content in a smaller, more efficient footprint.

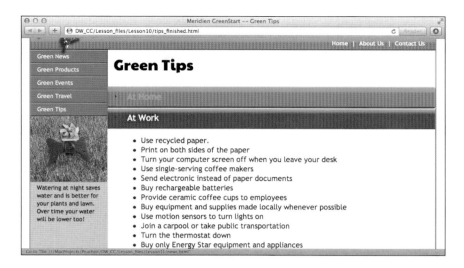

3 Close your browser and return to Dreamweaver.

Inserting a jQuery Accordion widget

In this exercise, you'll incorporate a jQuery Accordion widget into one of your existing layouts.

1 Open **tips.html**.

The page consists of three bulleted lists separated by <h2> headings. Let's start by inserting a jQuery Accordion before the first <h2>.

2 Insert the cursor in the *At Home* heading and select the <h2> tag selector. Press the Left Arrow key once to move the cursor before the opening <h2> tag.

3 In the jQuery UI category of the Insert panel, select Accordion.

Dreamweaver inserts the jQuery Accordion widget element. The initial element is a three-panel Accordion widget that appears with the top panel open. A blue tab appears above the new object with the title *jQuery Accordion: Accordion1*.

4 Select the placeholder text *Section 1* and type **At Home** to replace the text.

5 Scroll down and insert the cursor in the first bullet, *Wash clothes in cold water*, and select the `<ul>` tag selector. Press Ctrl-X/Cmd-X to cut the whole list.

6 Insert the cursor in the `<h2>` heading *At Home* and select the `<section>` tag selector. Press Delete.

The empty `<section>` element is removed.

7 Insert your cursor in the *Content 1* text in the top Accordion widget panel. Select the `<p>` tag selector. Choose Edit > Paste or press Ctrl-V/Cmd-V to paste the bulleted list.

In Design view, the bullet list appears in the first content panel.

8 Select and cut the subsequent `<ul>` element containing the "Work" tips. Delete the empty `<section>` containing the *At Work* heading.

9 Position the cursor over the bar displaying the *Section 2* text. Click the eye (👁) icon to open panel 2, if necessary.

Panel 2 opens; panel 1 closes automatically.

10 Select the *Section 2* text and type **At Work**.

11 Select the `<p>` element containing the *Content 2* text and paste the `<ul>` element.

12 Repeat steps 7 through 10 to create the content section for *In the Community*.

When you're finished, all three lists are now contained within the jQuery Accordion and all the empty `<section>` elements are gone.

13 Save the file.

A dialog box appears reporting that several jQuery asset files will be copied to the site to support the Accordion functionality.

14 Click OK.

You created a jQuery Accordion and added content. Although the content added in this exercise was already on the page, it should be clear that you can enter and edit content directly in the content panels, too. You can also copy material from other sources, such as Microsoft Word, TextEdit, and Notepad, among others. In the next exercise, you'll learn how to customize the styling for the jQuery Accordion.

Customizing a jQuery Accordion

Like other widgets provided by Dreamweaver, the jQuery Accordion is formatted by its own CSS and JavaScript files. If you look at the related file display at the top of the document window, you will see three new style sheets and two new .js files attached to this page that are formatting and controlling the behavior of the widget.

The jQuery style sheets are very complex and should be avoided unless you know what you are doing. Instead, in this exercise, you will learn how to apply the site design theme to the Accordion by using the existing site style sheet and the skills you already know.

1   Insert the cursor into the tab labeled *At Home* and examine the names and order of the tag selectors.

The tabs are comprised of three main elements: `<div#Accordion1>`, `<h3>`, and `<a>`. But that's only on the surface. Behind the scenes, the jQuery functions are manipulating the HTML and CSS to produce the various behaviors controlling the Accordion. As you move your mouse over the tabs and click them, class attributes are being changed on the fly to produce the hover effects and animated panels.

As you learned earlier, hyperlinks exhibit four basic behaviors: link, visited, hover, and active. jQuery is taking advantage of these default states to apply the various effects. Your job will be to create several new rules that will override the jQuery styling and apply the GreenStart theme instead. The first step is to format the default state of the tabs.

2   Switch to Design view, if necessary. Insert the cursor into one of the tabs that appear above a closed content panel.

The tabs above the closed panels are considered the default state, since only one tab can be open at a time.

3   Select the `<h3>` tag selector for the closed tab. In the Sources pane of the CSS Designer, select **mygreen_styles.css**. Click the Add Selector (➕)icon.

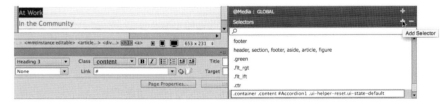

A new selector name field opens automatically filled with a descendant selector targeting the default tab. The selector also includes the classes `.container` and `.content`, indicating that the Accordion appears within the `<article.content>` element of your webpage. You could leave both classes in the name to make the selector more specific than the one contained in the jQuery style sheets, but it's a bit of overkill.

4 Delete the `.container` class from the selector name. Once edited, press Esc and then Enter/Return to close the name.

```
.ctr
.container .content #Accordion1 .ui-helper-reset.ui-state-default
```

```
.ctr
.content #Accordion1 .ui-helper-reset.ui-state-default
```

You may need to open the CSS Designer wider to view the whole selector name.

5 Create the following specifications in the Properties pane:

```
font-size: 120%
background-color: #090
background-image: background.png
background-position: 0% 0%
background-repeat: repeat-x
border-bottom-color: #060
border-bottom-width: 3px
border-bottom-style: solid
margin-bottom: 0px
```

This styling will apply to the default state of the Accordion tabs and then automatically to all others by inheritance. By starting with this state you only have to style the behaviors you want to change through user interaction.

Like all hyperlinks, the text color is controlled by the <a> element.

6 Select the <a> tag selector for the closed tab. In the Sources pane of the CSS Designer, select **mygreen_styles.css**. Click the Add Selector (➕)icon.

A new selector name appears for the <a> element.

7 Delete the `.container` class from the selector name.

8 Create the following specifications in the Properties pane: `color: #FFC`

The text in the tab appears in pale yellow. Next, you'll deal with the `a:hover` state of the hyperlink.

9 In **mygreen_styles.css**, duplicate the `.content #Accordion1 .ui-helper-reset.ui-state-default a` rule.

10 Edit the selector name to add the `:hover` state to it, such as `.content #Accordion1 .ui-helper-reset.ui-state-default a:hover`.

11 Change the color specification to `color: #0F0`

The base design of the Accordion is complete. Now you can add a little flair.

12 Insert the cursor in a tab above an open content panel.

The formatting for both open and closed tabs can be different. By using different background graphics and colors, users can easily find the information they are looking for.

13 Select the <h3> tag selector for the open tab. Select **mygreen_styles.css** in the Sources pane. Click the Add Selector (➕) icon.

A new selector name appears: `.container .content #Accordion1 .ui-helper-reset.ui-state-default.ui-state-active`

14 Delete the `.container` class from the selector name.

15 Create the following specifications:

```
background-image: background2.png
background-position: 0% 0%
background-repeat: repeat-x
```

The last step is to format the text color for the open tab. The color is controlled by the <a> element.

16 Insert the cursor in the open tab for the Accordion. Select the <a> tag selector for the open tab. Select **mygreen_styles.css** in the Sources pane. Click the Add Selector (⊞) icon.

A new selector name appears: `.container .content #Accordion1 .ui-helper-reset.ui-state-default.ui-state-active a`

17 Delete the `.container` class from the selector name.

18 Create the following specifications in the Properties pane:

```
color: #FFF
text-shadow: 0px 0px 15px #000
```

You won't be able to see the background image or the shadow effect in Design view.

19 Save all files and preview the document in Live view. Test and examine the Accordion behavior.

The horizontal tabs display a hover behavior, with the text in the closed panels turning neon green. The text in the open panel appears over a nice drop shadow and doesn't change for the hover effect, which indicates that the panel is already open. The only detraction from the overall effect is that the content windows are all the same size, leaving too much open space in two of the panels. This is a simple fix in the jQuery widget.

20 Switch back to normal Design view and insert the cursor in the Accordion. Select the blue tab that appears above the widget.

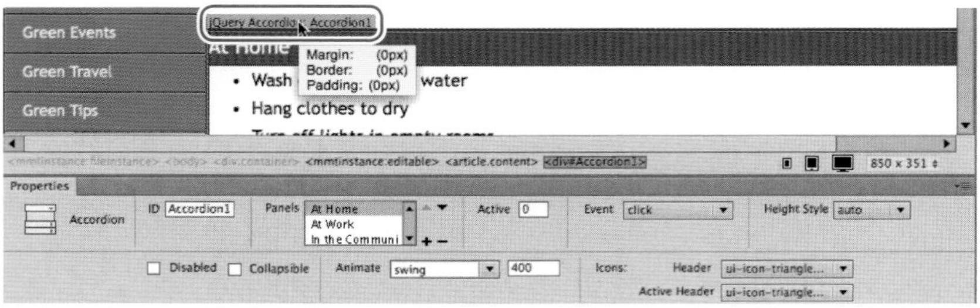

The Property inspector displays various specifications for the jQuery Accordion. In this interface you can easily add new content windows and remove existing ones and control other important properties without having to access the HTML or CSS code. The height style is currently set for auto, which makes each panel the same size.

21 In the Property inspector, open the Height Style pop-up menu and choose the option Content.

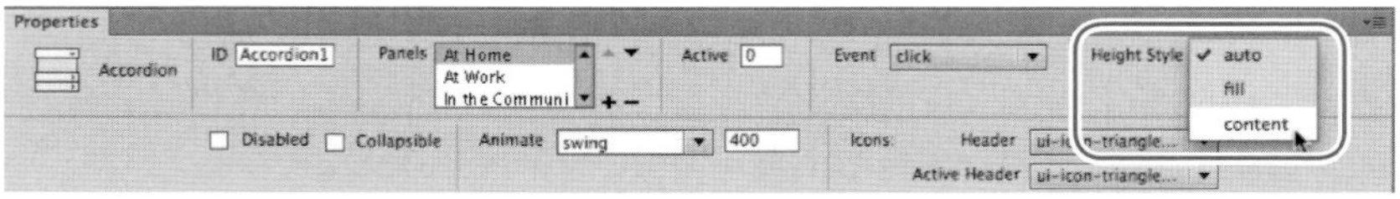

22 Save all files and preview the document in Live view. Test and examine the Accordion behavior.

The panels now scale to the height of their actual content.

You've successfully applied formatting to the Accordion widget so it matches the website color scheme and adjusted the component height to allow the content to display more efficiently. The Accordion is just one of the 33 jQuery widgets and components offered by Dreamweaver that allow you to incorporate advanced functionality into your website, while requiring little or no programming skill. All of these components can be accessed via either the Insert menu or panel. In upcoming lessons, you will learn how to use more of Dreamweaver's built-in jQuery components.

Review questions

1 What is a benefit of using Dreamweaver behaviors?

2 What three steps must be used to create a Dreamweaver behavior?

3 What's the purpose of assigning an ID to an image before applying a behavior?

4 What does a jQuery Accordion widget do?

5 Where can you add or remove panels from a jQuery Accordion widget?

Review answers

1 Dreamweaver behaviors add interactive functionality to a webpage quickly and easily.

2 To create a Dreamweaver behavior, you need to create or select a trigger element, select a desired behavior, and specify the parameters.

3 The ID is essential for selecting the specific image during the process of applying a behavior.

4 A jQuery Accordion includes multiple collapsible panels that hide and reveal content in a compact area of the page.

5 Select the widget in the document window using the blue tab and use the Property inspector jQuery interface.

11 WORKING WITH WEB ANIMATION AND VIDEO

Lesson Overview

In this lesson, you'll learn how to incorporate web-compatible animation and video components into your webpage and do the following:

• Insert web-compatible animation

• Insert web-compatible video

 This lesson will take about 40 minutes to complete. Download the project files for this lesson from the Lesson & Update Files tab on your Account page at www.peachpit.com, and store them on your computer in a convenient location, as described in the Getting Started section of this book. Your Accounts page is also where you'll find any updates to the lessons or to the lesson files. Look on the Lesson & Update Files tab to access the most current content. If you are starting from scratch in this lesson, use the method described in the "Jumpstart" section of "Getting Started."

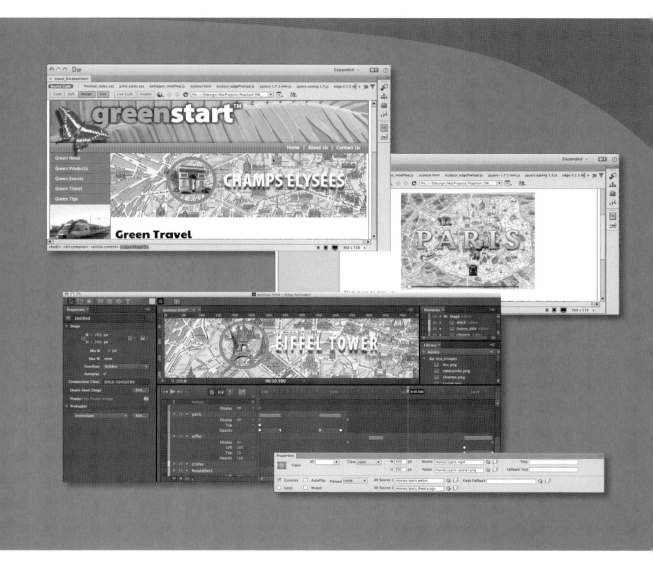

Dreamweaver allows you to integrate
HTML5-compatible animation and video.

● **Note:** If you
have not already
downloaded the project
files for this lesson to
your computer from
your Account page,
make sure to do so now.
See "Getting Started"
at the beginning of
the book.

Understanding web animation and video

The web can provide a variety of experiences to the average user. One second, you are downloading and reading a best-selling novel. Next, you're listening to your favorite radio station or performing artist. Then, you're watching live television coverage or a feature-length movie. Before Adobe Flash, animation and video were hard to incorporate on websites. That's because HTML was invented at a time when even static images were difficult to use on the Internet; video was a dream far off in the future.

Video and animation content was eventually provided in a variety of formats using a hodgepodge of applications, plug-ins, and coder-decoders (codecs) that could transfer data across the Internet to your computer and browser. Often this was accomplished with enormous difficulties and incompatibilities. Frequently, a format that worked in one browser was incompatible with another. Applications that worked in Windows didn't work on the Mac. Most formats required their own proprietary players or plug-ins.

For a time, Adobe Flash brought order to this chaos. It provided a single platform for creating both animation and video. Flash started as an animation program and changed the web for all time. A few years ago, it revolutionized the industry again by making it a simple task to add video to a site. By inserting a video into Flash and saving the file as a SWF or FLV file, web designers and developers were able to take advantage of the almost universal distribution of the Flash Player—installed on over 90 percent of all desktop computers. No more worries over formats and codecs—Flash Player took care of all that.

With the invention and rise in popularity of smartphones and tablet devices over the last few years, Flash has fallen on hard times. For most manufacturers, the power and capability of Flash were too difficult to support on these devices, and it was abandoned. Flash is not dead. It's still unmatched for its multimedia power and functionality. But today, all bets are off when it comes to animation and video. The techniques for creating web-based media are being reinvented. As you may have guessed, this trend away from Flash is ringing in a new era of chaos on the web media front. Half a dozen or more codecs are competing to become the "be-all end-all" format for video distribution and playback for the web.

The only ray of sunshine in this morass is that HTML5 was developed with built-in support for both animation and video. Great strides have already been made to replace much of the capability of Flash-based animation using native HTML5 and CSS3 functionality. The status of video is not as clear. So far, a single standard has not yet emerged, which means that to support all the popular desktop and mobile browsers, you will have to produce several different video files. In this lesson, you will learn how to incorporate different types of web animation and video into your site.

Previewing the completed file

To see what you will work on in this lesson, preview the completed page in the browser. This is the travel page of the travel site you assembled in the previous lesson.

● **Note:** If you are using the Jumpstart method follow the instructions in the "Getting Started" section at the beginning of the book.

1 Launch Adobe Dreamweaver CC.

2 If necessary, press F8 to open the Files panel, and select DW-CC from the site list.

3 In the Files panel, expand the Lesson11 folder.

4 Select the **travel_finished.html** file and preview it in your primary browser.

The page includes two media elements: the banner animation at the top of the MainContent region and the video inserted below. Depending on the browser used to view the page, the video may be generated from one of four different formats: MP4, WebM, Ogg, or Flash Video.

5 Note that the banner ad plays once, when the page loads completely.

6 To view the video, click the Play button. If you do not see a Play button, your browser may be showing a Flash fallback version of the video. Move the cursor over the video to display the control skin, and click the Play button.

Different browsers support different types of video. Depending on the video format your browser supports, you may notice that the controls fade if you move the cursor away from the video, but that they return once you position the cursor over the video again.

7 When you're finished previewing the media, close your browser and return to Dreamweaver.

Adding web animation to a page

After the release of Adobe Edge Animate, Dreamweaver was modified to provide a new built-in and simplified workflow for inserting Edge Animate compositions. The new Dreamweaver workflow makes the process a point-and-click operation.

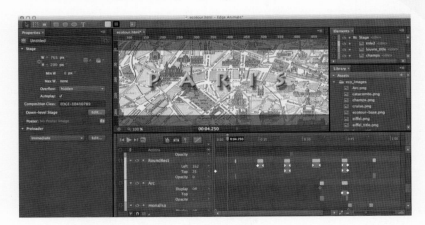

The animation used in this lesson was built in Edge Animate, a new program developed by Adobe—not to replace Flash, but to create web animation and interactive content natively, using HTML5, CSS3, and JavaScript. A new Creative Cloud version of the program is now available to all Creative Cloud subscribers. At the time of this writing, there were plans to offer Edge Animate as an individual product on Creative Cloud. For subsequent versions and upgrades, this model may change. The name "Edge" was coined by Adobe to brand a set of new HTML applications under development to support designers and developers creating webpages and content for the modern web. You can check out all the new offerings at html.adobe.com.

Dreamweaver CC takes advantage of a feature in Edge Animate designed to assist in deploying compositions to other programs and workflows, such as Adobe InDesign, Adobe Dreamweaver, and Apple's iBooks Author. The File > Publish command (shown below) enables you to export your Edge Animate compositions. By defining your Publish settings appropriately, you can create a complete set of files that are compatible with these applications. For the purposes of this exercise, we published an OAM file for you, which is an archive file format that contains all the constituent elements needed to support the animation in Dreamweaver.

1   Open **travel.html** from the site root folder. Or, if you are starting from scratch in this exercise, see the "Jumpstart" instructions in the "Getting Started" section at the beginning of the book.

    The banner needs to be inserted outside any text elements.

2   Insert the cursor in the *Green Travel* heading text and select the <h1> tag selector. Press the Left Arrow key to move the cursor outside the <h1> element.

3   Choose Insert > Media > Edge Animate Composition.

4 Navigate to the folder ecotour > animate_package in the site root folder, and select **ecotour.oam**.

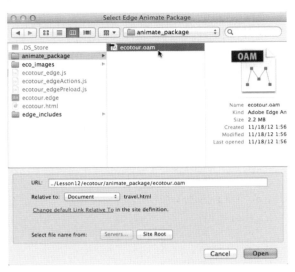

5 Click OK/Open to insert the composition.

◆ **Warning:** Dreamweaver will not automatically upload all the support files needed for the Edge Animate composition. Be sure to upload the entire contents of the edgeanimate_assets folder when publishing the site to the web.

The Edge Animate banner appears at the top of the page, but what you cannot see is that Dreamweaver just created a new folder in the site root directory.

6 Open the Files panel, and observe the list of folders in the site root.

The folder named edgeanimate_assets now appears in the root directory. The folder was generated automatically and contains all the files needed to support the composition. The entire folder must be uploaded to the web host when **travel.html** is posted.

7 Save all files. Select Live view.

The banner animation plays automatically in Live view once the code is processed, but there is an undesirable gap between the animation and the horizontal navigation menu. To identify the cause of the gap, you can use the Code Navigator or the CSS Designer.

8 Position the cursor over the banner animation. Right-click, and choose Code Navigator from the context menu.

The Code Navigator window appears, listing all CSS rules that affect the banner animation.

9 Working up from the bottom, identify the rule creating the gap.

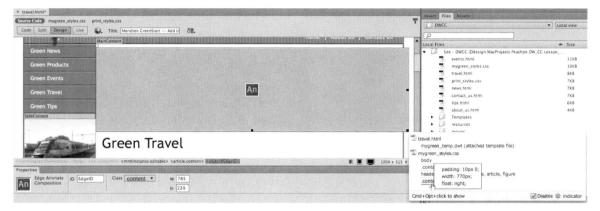

The `.content` rule applies 10 pixels of top padding to `div.content`.

10 In the CSS Designer, select the `.content` rule in **mygreen_styles.css**. In the Properties window, change padding-top from 10px to **0px**.

11 Save all files. Refresh the Live view display.

The banner animation fits flush to the top of the content section of the page. Congratulations, you've successfully incorporated an HTML5- and CSS3-based animation on your page.

Note: Changing this rule will affect all pages using mygreen_styles.css, which may produce undesirable consequences on other pages of the site. Whenever you make global changes to a site-wide rule, reviewing all the affected pages is a good idea.

Poster child

The widespread popularity and support of HTML5 should mean that your animation will run in most browsers and mobile devices. But, there's a very small possibility the animation may be incompatible to older computers and software. Edge Animate can include either a down-level stage or a static, or poster, image that will be viewed in these circumstances.

To add or create a down-level stage or poster within Animate, select the project stage and then add the appropriate content using the Properties panel.

Adding web video to a page

Implementing HTML5-compatible video in your site is a bit more involved than it was when you only had to insert a single Flash-based file. Unfortunately, no single video format is supported by all browsers in use today. To make sure your video content plays everywhere, you'll have to supply several different formats. Dreamweaver CC now provides a built-in technique to add multiple video files so you won't have to do all the coding yourself. In this exercise, you will learn how to insert HTML5-compatible video on a page in your site.

1   If necessary, open **travel.html**.

You will insert the video in the MainContent section of the page.

2   Insert the cursor in the paragraph *Click here to sign up*. Click the <p> tag selector. Press the Left Arrow key to move the insertion point before the opening <p> tag.

3   Choose Insert > HTML5 Video.

This line creates the HTML5-compatible video element. A video placeholder appears on the page, and the Property inspector displays new options for targeting the video resource files. Note that the interface enables you to specify up to three video source files and one Flash fallback file.

4   Click to activate the Browse command for the Source field in the Property inspector. Navigate to the movies folder, and select the **paris.mp4** file. Click OK/Open.

The MP4 file format will be the primary video format loaded. MP4, also known as MPEG-4, is a video format based on Apple's QuickTime standard. It is supported natively by iOS devices and will load the MP4 file, which is compatible with iOS devices and Apple's Safari browser. Many experts advise loading MP4 files first—otherwise, iOS devices may ignore the video element altogether.

5   Enter the following specifications in the Property inspector:

W: **400**

H: **300**

If you did not create the video yourself, you can often obtain the width and height of an MP4 in the File Manager in Windows by selecting properties, or selecting Get Info in the Finder in OS X.

The next format you will load is WebM, which is an open-source, royalty-free video format sponsored by Google. It is compatible with Firefox 4, Chrome 6, Opera 10.6, and Internet Explorer 9 and later.

6   If Dreamweaver has automatically inserted the file for Alt Source 1, go to step 7, otherwise click the Browse icon for the Alt Source 1 field. Navigate to the video folder, select the file **paris.webm**, and click OK/Open.

> **Note:** Dreamweaver may anticipate the use of WebM and insert it automatically as Alt Source 1. If it does so, proceed to step 7.

To round out our HTML5 video selections, the next format you'll load is a lossy, open-source multimedia format: Ogg. It is designed for the distribution of multimedia content that is free of copyright and other media restrictions.

7   Click the Browse icon for the Alt Source 2 field. Navigate to the video folder, select the file **paris.theora.ogv**, and click OK/Open.

These three formats support all the modern desktop and mobile browsers. But to support older software and devices, using a stalwart old friend—Flash video—may be necessary. By adding it last, you ensure that only browsers that don't support the other three formats will load the Flash content. Although many are abandoning Flash, Dreamweaver still provides support for inserting both FLV and SWF files.

8   Click the Browse icon for the Flash Fallback field. Navigate to the movies folder, select the file **paris.flv**, and click OK/Open.

9   Save the file.

10 If necessary, switch to Design view.

    In many browsers, the <video> element won't generate a preview of the video content. You can add a preview by using the Poster specification in the Property inspector.

11 Select the <video> tag selector. In the Property inspector, click the Browse icon for the Poster field. Navigate to the movies folder, select **paris-poster.png**, and click OK/Open.

A preview image has been applied to the <video> element. Nothing is visible in Design view, but you can see the poster in the browser or Live view. The advantage of using a poster is that something will always appear on the page, even in the browsers that do not support HTML5 video formats or Flash video.

● **Note:** The Travel page now contains two notices prompting users to sign up for the Ecotour: one in the animation and one within the text. In Lesson 12, "Working with Forms," you will create a new page with the sign-up form and link this text to it.

12 Save all files. Preview the page in Live view.

The poster appears within the layout; video controls appear below the poster depending on what video format is displayed. Flash video controls will appear within the video itself. In the next exercise, you will learn how to configure these controls and how the video will respond to the user.

Buggy video

At this point, you normally would be finished and ready to test your video configuration in multiple browsers. Unfortunately, the Flash fallback using an FLV source file is missing some essential support files and will not play the FLV correctly as is. As of this writing, the initial version of Dreamweaver CC was being released with a bug affecting the support of both FLV and SWF video using the new HTML5 video workflow described in this section.

The Dreamweaver engineers promised to fix this issue in a subsequent cloud update, but until then you can correct the issue yourself by simply replacing the new code element using the legacy video workflow, like this:

1   Select the <video> tag selector.

2   Switch to Code view. If necessary, select Source Code in the Related Files list at the top of the document window.

3   Select the entire <embed> element containing the reference to **paris.flv** and delete it.

```
        upcoming Eco-Tour and where we're visiting this year. You don't want to miss it!</p>
78   <video width="400" height="300" poster="movies/paris-poster.png" controls >
79   <source src="movies/paris.mp4" type="video/mp4">
80   <source src="movies/paris.webm" type="video/webm">
81   <source src="movies/paris.theora.ogv" type="video/ogg">
82 ▼ <embed src="movies/paris.flv" type="application/x-shockwave-flash" width="400" height="300" />
83   </video>
84   <p>Click here to sign up.</p>
```

4   Choose Insert > Media > Flash Video.

5   In the Insert FLV dialog box, click the Browse icon. Navigate to the movies folder, and select **paris.flv** and click OK/Open.

The filename paris.flv appears in the URL field. Flash video supplies its own controls via a SWF skin interface. You can choose your own skin design in this dialog box.

6   Choose **Corona Skin 2** from the Skin pop-up menu.

Before you can insert the file, you have to specify the dimensions of the video.

7   Click the Detect Size button.

Dreamweaver inserts the dimension 400 by 300 into the width and height fields. You can use the options below these fields to specify whether you want the video to autoplay and autorewind.

8   Click OK to insert the FLV video.

The <embed> element is now replaced by an <object> tag along with all the code necessary to run the Flash video and even detect the presence and version of the needed Flash player. This method is the simplest method to insert FLV-compatible video so it will play properly in all browsers that don't support HTML5 video. But you should only use this method until the feature described within the exercise is fixed.

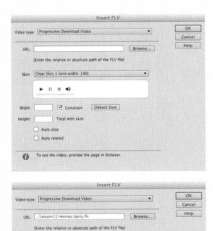

HTML5 Video Options

The final step for configuring the video is to decide what other HTML5-supported options to specify. The options are displayed within the Property inspector whenever the `<video>` element is chosen. The options are not selectable while you are in Live view.

1   Return to Design view. If necessary, select the `<video>` tag selector.

Observe the left side of the Property inspector.

- **Controls**—Displays visible video controls
- **AutoPlay**—Starts the video automatically after the webpage loads
- **Loop**—Causes the video to replay from the beginning automatically once it finishes
- **Muted**—Silences the audio
- **Preload**—Specifies the method in which the video loads

2   If necessary, select the Controls check box and deselect the AutoPlay, Loop, and Muted check boxes. Set Preload to **none**.

The `<video>` element is now complete. The placeholder appears in the layout flush to the left side of `<div.content>`. Let's center it.

3   Click the video placeholder. Select the `<video>` tag selector. In the CSS Designer panel select **mygreen_styles.css** in the Sources pane. Click the Add Selector icon.

By default, the `<video>` tag is an inline element. By assigning it the `block` property, you can control how the video aligns on the page and relates to other elements.

4   In **mygreen_styles.css**, create a new CSS rule named:
    `.content section video, .content section video object`

5 Create the following specifications:

```
display: block
margin-right: auto
margin-left: auto
```

● **Note:** This rule will center all <video> elements inserted in <div.content>. If you need to target a specific video, an alternate method is to create a custom CSS class and apply it as needed.

6 Preview the page in Live view or in a browser. If the video controls are not visible, move your cursor over the still image to display them. Click the Play button to view the movie.

● **Note:** Some versions of Microsoft Internet Explorer may block active content when viewed locally until you give the browser permission to run it. If you don't have Flash Player, or if it's not the current version, you may be asked to download the latest version.

Dreamweaver   Chrome

● **Note:** In Live view you may not see a "play" control, but if you click to the left of the progress bar, the video will play.

Internet Explorer

Depending on where you preview the page, you will see one of the four video formats. For example, in Live view you will see the MP4-based video. The controls will appear differently depending on what format is displayed. This movie has no sound, but the controls will often include a speaker button to adjust the volume or mute the sound.

7 When you're finished, switch back to Design view.

You've embedded three HTML5-compatible videos and an FLV fallback, which gives you support for most browsers and devices that can access the Internet. But you've learned only one possible technique for supporting this evolving standard. To learn more about HTML5 video and how to implement it, check out the following links:

- http://tinyurl.com/video-HTML5-1
- http://tinyurl.com/video-HTML5-2
- http://tinyurl.com/video-HTML5-3

Review questions

1 What advantage does HTML5 have over HTML 4 regarding web-based media?

2 What programming language created the HTML5-compatible animation used in this lesson?

3 True or false: To support all web browsers, you can select a single video format.

4 In browsers or devices that do not support video, what can you do to provide some form of content to these users?

5 What video format is recommended to support older browsers?

Review answers

1 HTML5 has built-in support for web animation and video.

2 The animation used in this lesson was created by Adobe Edge Animate natively using HTML5, CSS3, and JavaScript.

3 False. A single format supported by every browser has not emerged. Developers recommend incorporating four video formats to support the majority of browsers: MP4, WebM, Ogg, and FLV.

4 You can add a static poster image (GIF, JPG, or PNG) via an option in the Property inspector to provide a preview of the video content in nonsupportive browsers and devices.

5 FLV (Flash video) is recommended as the fallback format for older browsers because of the widespread installation of the Flash Player.

12
WORKING WITH FORMS

Lesson Overview

In this lesson, you'll create forms for your webpage and do the following:

- Insert a form
- Include text fields
- Insert radio buttons
- Insert checkboxes
- Insert list menus
- Add form buttons
- Incorporate field sets and legends
- Create an email solution for processing data
- Style your form with CSS

This lesson will take about 2 hours and 15 minutes to complete. Download the project files for this lesson from the Lesson & Update Files tab on your Account page at www.peachpit.com, and store them on your computer in a convenient location, as described in the Getting Started section of this book. Your Accounts page is also where you'll find any updates to the lessons or to the lesson files. Look on the Lesson & Update Files tab to access the most current content. If you are starting from scratch in this lesson, use the method described in the "Jumpstart" section of "Getting Started."

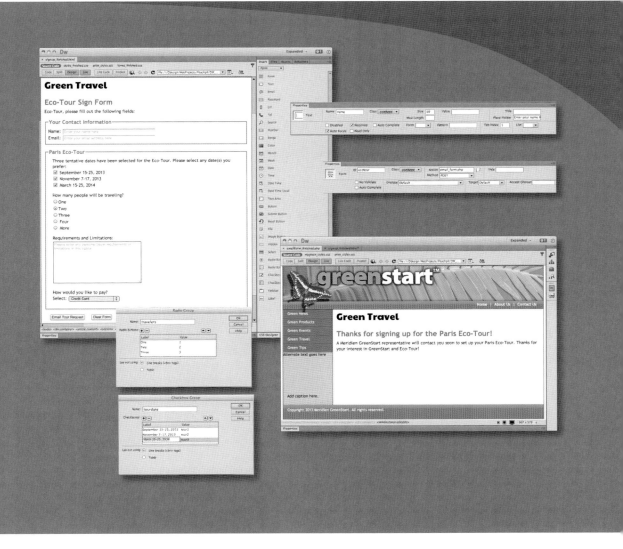

For many people, the first time they encounter inter-activity on the web is when they fill out a form. Forms are an essential tool on the modern Internet, allowing you to capture important information and feedback.

Note: If you have not already downloaded the project files for this lesson to your computer from your Account page, make sure to do so now. See "Getting Started" at the beginning of the book.

Note: If you are starting from scratch in this exercise, see the "Jumpstart" instructions in the "Getting Started" section at the beginning of the book. Then, follow the steps in this exercise.

Previewing the completed file

To understand the project you will work on in this lesson, you can preview the completed Paris Eco-Tour signup page in one of the following browsers: Chrome 10+, Firefox 5+, Internet Explorer 10+, Opera 11+, or Safari 5+. Browsers older than those listed do not support some or all of the advanced features of HTML5 form elements.

1   Launch Dreamweaver CC.

2   Open **signup_finished.html** from the Lesson12 folder and preview it in one of the browsers listed above.

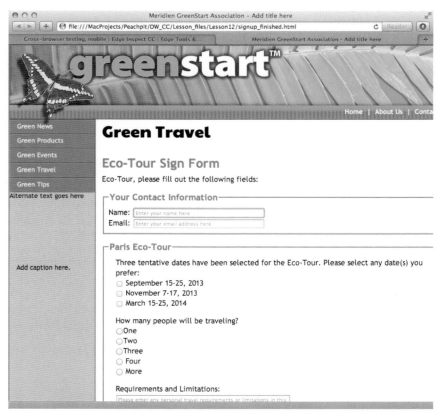

The page includes several form elements. Try them out to observe their behaviors.

3   Click in the Name field and type your name. Press Tab.

Your name appears in the text field.

4   In the Email field, type **jdoe@mycompany.com** and press Tab.

5 Select one or more options to indicate when you plan to travel.

6 Use the radio buttons to choose a number of travelers.

7 Click in the Requirements And Limitations field. Type **I prefer window seats** and press Tab.

> If this form were loaded on your web server, you would normally click the Email Tour Request button to submit the form. A thank-you page like the one pictured below would take the place of the signup page.

8 When you're finished, close all browser windows and return to Dreamweaver.

Before you construct your own form with its various form elements, let's get a perspective on how HTML forms work.

Learning about forms

Forms, on paper or on the web, are tools for gathering information. In both cases, the information is entered into interactive form elements, or *fields*, to make it easier to find and understand. Forms should be clearly delineated to set them apart from the rest of your webpage content.

Paper forms are often provided on a separate page or delineated by graphical borders to distinguish them, while web forms use the `<form>` tag and other specific HTML elements to designate and collect the data.

Online forms have decided advantages over paper forms because the user enters the data in a way that can then be transferred automatically into spreadsheets or databases, reducing the labor costs and error rates associated with paper forms.

Web-based forms are composed of one or more HTML elements, each used for a specific purpose:

- **Text field**—Permits the entry of text and digits. Text fields designated as password fields mask or obscure characters as they are typed.

- **Text area**—Identical to text fields but intended for larger amounts of text, such as multiple sentences or paragraphs.

- **Radio button**—A graphical element that permits users to select one option from a group of choices. Only one item in each group can be chosen at a time. The selection of a new item in the group deselects any currently selected item. Typically, once one item is selected, it can't be deselected unless the form is reset or another item within the same group is chosen.

- **Checkbox**—A graphical element that permits users to indicate a binary selection (yes/no). Checkboxes can be grouped together; however, unlike radio buttons, they allow multiple items to be chosen within the group. Also unlike radio buttons, checkboxes can be deselected if desired.

- **List/menu**—Displays entries in a pop-up menu format. Lists (also called select lists) may enforce the selection of a single element or allow the choice of multiple items.

- **Hidden**—A predefined data field that conveys information to the form-processing mechanism and is unseen by the user. Hidden form elements are used extensively in dynamic page applications. Hidden data may contain information passed from a previous page on your site or default data you do not want the user to see before submitting, such as the actual date or time the form is submitted.

- **Button**—Submits the form or performs some other single-purpose interaction, such as clearing or printing the form.

HTML5 form elements

Dreamweaver CC has added nearly a complete set of new HTML5 form fields to the Insert panel. As with the semantic page elements we've been using, HTML5 also offers over a dozen very interesting new form elements, field types, and attributes. New field types like tel, url, date, time, email, and so on will allow for better data input control and validation capabilities. In other words, the field itself will know what type of data is supposed to be entered as well as provide features to validate and flag incorrect entries.

For example, the new attributes will help you to delineate the difference between a simple text field and a field that contains a phone number or an email address. This opens up a world of programmatic possibilities, both for entering and processing data, but also for validating it.

HTML5 fields and their amazing features are not fully supported by all browsers, cell phones, and mobile devices, yet. Luckily, this should not be an impediment for you to start taking advantage of some of these new fields and attributes, because the fields will act like normal text fields if the browser doesn't support the new functionality. The upcoming exercises use several of the new fields and attributes to give you some hands-on experience.

To learn more about the new HTML fields and attributes, check out www.w3schools.com/html/html5_form_input_types.asp.

Form submission

Paper forms, when completed, are mailed or passed along for processing, usually in a highly manual process. Web forms are usually mailed or processed electronically. The `<form>` tag includes an `action` attribute, and the value of the action attribute is triggered when the form is submitted. Often, the action is the web address for another page or server-side script that processes the form.

Adding a form to a page

For this exercise, you will create a new page for signing up participants for the Paris Eco-Tour described in the travel page completed in Lesson 11, "Working with Web Animation and Video."

1   Open the Assets panel and click the Template category icon. Right-click **mygreen_temp** and choose New From Template from the context menu.

2   Save the file as **signup.html** in the site root folder.

3   In the MainContent region, select the placeholder heading *Add main heading here* and type **Green Travel** to replace the text.

4   In the MainContent region, select the placeholder heading *Add subheading here* and type **Eco-Tour Sign-up Form** to replace the text.

5   Select the placeholder paragraph *Add content here.* Type **To sign up for the Eco-Tour, please fill out the following fields:** and press Enter/Return to create a new paragraph.

In the past, all form fields had to be contained within a `<form>` element. Any field inserted outside the `<form>` element would be ignored when the form is submitted and processed. But one of the advances of HTML5 is a new attribute that allows you to place fields anywhere on the page, as long they include a `form` attribute that targets the form to which the data belongs. For our purposes, we'll add all fields within the form.

6   Open the Insert panel and select Forms from the category list. In the Forms category, click the Form (⬚) icon.

Dreamweaver inserts the `<form>` element at the insertion point, which is indicated visually by a red line. Forms should always feature a unique ID. Dreamweaver will add one automatically; you can customize it, if desired.

● **Note:** If you are using the Jumpstart method, your template may be named mygreen_temp_12.dwt.

7 If necessary, select the `<form>` tag selector. In the Property inspector, select the current form ID. Type **ecotour** and press Enter/Return to replace it.

The tag selector now says `<form#ecotour>`.

8 Open the CSS Designer, if necessary. In the Sources pane, select **mygreen_styles.css**. Select the `.content` rule and click the Add Selector (⊞) icon.

The `.container .content section #ecotour` selector appears in the Selectors pane.

9 Edit the rule name to say `.content section #ecotour`

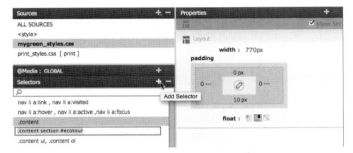

The rule appears in the Selectors pane.

10 Create the following properties:

```
margin-right: 15 px
margin-left: 15 px
```

The red outline of the form indents 15 pixels away from the left and right edges of the MainContent region.

11 Save all files.

You created a form element; next, you'll insert some form fields.

Inserting text form elements

Text fields are the workhorses of all the form elements. Text fields are the basic vehicles for gathering unstructured text and numeric data, and it's hard to imagine a form without them. In fact, many forms are composed exclusively of text-input fields.

In the upcoming exercises, you'll insert basic text fields and text areas. Before you can start, however, confirm that Dreamweaver is configured to add form elements in their most accessible manner.

Creating accessible forms

Accessibility technologies place special requirements on form elements. Assistive technology devices, such as screen readers, require precise code that allows them to correctly read forms and individual form elements. Dreamweaver no longer provides an option to automatically output form code in a format that supports accessibility. You will have to build that structure manually. In the following exercises, you will learn how to add accessibility features to your form elements as they are inserted.

One tag to control them all

Text fields, checkboxes, radio buttons, and many of the new HTML5 form fields have at least one thing in common: They are all created using the HTML `<input>` tag. Just change the `type` attribute, and add one or more other attributes, and you can convert a checkbox into a radio button, a text field, or a list menu. No other HTML element is so flexible and powerful. As you insert form fields in this lesson, feel free to peek in the code to see how this magic is accomplished.

You may see something like the following examples:

```
                  <input type="text" name="color" id="color_0">
☑ <input type="checkbox" name="color"  id="color" value="red">
⊙   <input type="radio" name="color" value="red" id="color_0">
```

Using text fields

Text fields accept any alphanumeric characters—letters, numbers, and punctuation characters. Unless otherwise specified, a text field displays around 12 to 17 characters, by default. This limit doesn't stop you from entering longer text. If you type more characters than will fit, the text will scroll within the field. To show more or fewer characters on the screen, set a specific field size in the Width field in the Property inspector. Although a text field element doesn't have a built-in limit to the amount of text you can enter into it, you're more likely to run into limits imposed by your target data application.

New form workflow

With the addition of new HTML5 form field elements, Dreamweaver overhauled its forms workflow in a dramatic way. Now, the workflow is centered around the Property inspector, which has been revamped to support many HTML5 form field attributes and functions.

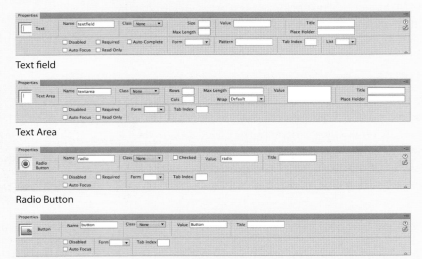

Text field

Text Area

Radio Button

Button

The Property inspector will adapt to each form element as needed and provide many of the available attributes for each. Here are some of the most important attributes you can access via the Property inspector:

Auto Complete—Specifies that the field can be completed automatically by the browser from cached data or other programmatic methods, say via JavaScript.

Auto-Focus—Specifies that a field will be selected automatically upon page load.

Disabled—Specifies that a field is disabled and cannot be modified by the user.

List—Specifies a list of predefined data options that can be selected by the user.

Name—Specifies the name of the element. When you enter the name in the Property inspector, Dreamweaver automatically creates a matching ID attribute.

Pattern—Specifies a regular expression to check user input so that it matches a desired data type.

Place Holder—Specifies hint text displayed within the field to suggest the desired input by the user. Placeholder text will not be passed to the data application when the form is submitted.

Read Only—Specifies that field data can be viewed by the user but cannot be modified.

Required—Specifies that a field must be completed before a form can be submitted.

Size—Specifies the width of an input field in characters.

SRC—Specifies an image source for an input button.

Tab Index—Specifies the order in which the field can be accessed using the Tab key.

Value—Specifies the default value of an input field. This value will be passed to your data application when the form is processed if users don't enter their own data.

Spreadsheet and database fields frequently limit the amount of data that can be entered. If you enter too much data into a field and submit it, the data application usually just ignores, or dumps, whatever exceeds its maximum capacity. To prevent this from happening, you can limit HTML text fields to a specific number of characters by using the Max Chars attribute field in the Property inspector.

1   If necessary, open **signup.html** from the site root folder.

2   Insert the cursor in the red outline defining the form boundary.

    The tag selector displays `<form#ecotour>`.

3   In the Forms category of the Insert panel, click the Text Field (⌷) icon.

A text field appears within the form. If you are working in Design view when you insert a form field, Dreamweaver creates a `<label>` element, some label place-holder text, as well as a `name` attribute. In Dreamweaver, the `name` attribute is tied directly to the element ID attribute. In most cases, Dreamweaver will create the ID to match the `name` attribute. In a form, an ID is a vital attribute because it uniquely identifies the field, which assists in processing the form data later. Dreamweaver creates a generic name/ID combo for you when you add a field, like *textfield*, *textfield2*, *textfield3*, and so on. Generic name/IDs will be difficult to work with, so you need to create descriptive, custom names/IDs.

Setting form field attributes

When you create a new field, the Property inspector focuses on the field allowing you to add or change various property attributes, such as name, size, minimum or maximum characters, and various accessibility features. Let's start with the `name` attribute.

1   In the Property inspector Name field, type **name** and press Enter/Return.

    The Tag selector now displays the text `<input#name>`, which indicates that the field ID attribute has been changed, too.

    Initially, the text field should be about 12 to 17 characters wide. The `size` attribute allows you to control the width of the field within the form. Let's make it a bit wider.

Note: If you insert a field in Code view, Dreamweaver does not add a `<label>` element.

Note: For most form fields, Dreamweaver will make the name and ID the same. For radio button groups, the name will be the same for all buttons in the group but the ID and the value must be unique.

2   In the Property inspector, enter **50** in the Size option field. Press Enter/Return to complete the change.

The `<input#name>` field now displays approximately 50 characters wide. The size field doesn't restrict the maximum number of characters you can enter into the field. To limit the number of characters, you would use the Max Length option.

Another important option is to prevent the form from being submitted with an empty field.

3   In the Property inspector, select the Required option.

When this option is selected, HTML5-compliant browsers will display a message saying that the field must be filled out before the form can be submitted.

HTML5 text fields can include placeholder text to prompt users to enter specific information in the form. The advantage of the placeholder text is that it will not be passed along with the rest of the form data by accident if the user fails to fill in the field.

4   If necessary, select the text field. Insert the cursor into the Place Holder field in the Property inspector and type **Enter Your Name Here** and press Enter/Return.

The placeholder text will appear only in Live view or in an HTML5-compatible browser. If the browser doesn't support this feature, the field will be blank but still function otherwise as a normal text field.

Next, let's add a usability feature. When the webpage loads, the user is presented with the form but in most cases they will have to select the first field of the form before they can enter any text. A new HTML5 option allows you to jumpstart the process.

● **Note:** When you select auto focus for any field, the placeholder text will not display in Live view or in the browser because the cursor will be inserted in the field automatically when the page loads.

5   In the Property inspector, select the Auto Focus option.

Auto Focus automatically selects the field once the page loads and inserts the cursor, which allows users to begin data entry immediately. However, you should select only one field to have auto focus.

6   Save the file.

The first form field is nearly finished. The last step is to make sure that the fields are properly identified to the user.

Working with field labels

Adding labels for each field makes the form easier to use. HTML `<label>` elements can be created using two methods: by wrapping the label around the text field element or by inserting it as a separate element that uses a `for` attribute.

```
11    <label for="textfield">Text Field:</label>
12    <input type="text" name="textfield" id="textfield">
13
14    <label>Text Field: <input type="text" name="textfield" id="textfield"></label>
```

While the `for` attribute is not visible to the average user, it allows you to identify fields for visitors with visual disabilities. This option provides the most flexibility for form design and has the added benefit of complying with Section 508 accessibility mandates.

Dreamweaver created a `<label>` element for you, but Design view doesn't clearly show how it was built. But, it's an easy thing to check.

1   Select the "Text Field:" label and switch to Code view. Examine the `<label>` element and its attributes and how it relates to the `<input#name>` element.

```
52    <label for="name">Text Field:</label>
53    <input name="name" type="text" autofocus required id="name"
54    placeholder="Enter your name here" size="50">
```

A quick check of Code view shows you that the label uses the `for` attribute. All you have to do is change the placeholder label text.

2   Select the placeholder label text and type `Name:` to replace it.

3   Save the file.

This code arrangement allows for maximum flexibility in your form design. For example, you can keep the two elements on the same line, put them on two lines, or format each separately using CSS. In some instances, you may wish to use a table to create the form layout. Using a separate label element allows you to place each item in separate cells and columns of the table.

The first of your form objects is now in place. Inserting other standard fields is a similar operation. In the next exercise, you'll add an email field.

Inserting an HTML5 email field

In this exercise, you'll insert an HTML5 email field to make sure that the user submits an email address.

1   If necessary, open **signup.html**.

2   Insert the cursor at the end of the Name text field inserted in the previous exercise and press Shift-Enter/Shift-Return to insert a forced line break. This moves the cursor to the next line without creating a new paragraph. You may not see the cursor until you create the next field.

Note: If you insert multiple fields of the same type, Dreamweaver will increment their names and IDs, such as email2, email3, and so on automatically.

3 In the Forms category of the Insert panel, click the Email field (**@**) icon.

A new form field appears in the layout. Just as with the previous field Dreamweaver has added a `<label>` and an HTML name attribute automatically (displayed in the Property inspector). In this case, the label and the attribute are fine as is. Let's add some placeholder text.

4 In the Place Holder field of the Property inspector, type **Enter your email address here** and press Enter/Return.

5 In the Property inspector, select the Required option and set Size to **50**.

Another helpful HTML5 feature is the capability to complete field contents automatically using data cached in your browser from previous Internet sessions.

6 In the Property inspector, select the Auto Complete option.

The new field is complete.

7 Save the file.

The first section of the form is complete.

Creating a field set

One way to make forms more user-friendly is to organize fields into logical groupings called field sets. The HTML `<fieldset>` element was designed for this purpose and even provides a helpful description element called *legend*.

1 If necessary, open **signup.html**.

To create a field set, you can work in Code view or Design view. If you work in Design view, selecting the code properly is a vital first step. The best technique takes advantage of the tag selectors.

2 Insert the cursor into the label "Name:" and select the `<label>` tag selector. Hold the Shift key and click at the end of the Email text field to select both fields and their associated markup.

By using the tag selectors, Dreamweaver will select the entire code block.

3 In the Forms category of the Insert panel, click the **Fieldset** (□) icon.

The selected code is inserted into a `<fieldset>` element.

4 In the Legend field, type **Your Contact Information** and click OK.

The field set is not rendered accurately in Design view; however, it does display the legend clearly.

5 Save all files and preview the page in Live view.

The field set neatly encloses the two fields in a labeled container. Note how the Name field is highlighted and the cursor is already inserted in the field.

6 Switch back to Design view.

In the next exercise, you'll learn how to create checkbox form fields.

Inserting checkboxes

Checkboxes provide a series of predefined options that can be chosen in any combination. Like text fields, each checkbox has a unique ID and value attributes. Dreamweaver provides two methods for adding checkboxes to your page. You can either insert each checkbox individually or insert an entire group at once. In this exercise you will insert a checkbox group.

1 If necessary, open **signup.html**.

2 Insert the cursor in the *Your Contact Information* field set, and select the `<fieldset>` tag selector. Press the Right Arrow key to move the cursor outside the element. Press Enter/Return to insert new paragraph.

3 Type **Three tentative dates have been selected for the Eco-Tour. Please select any date(s) you prefer:**

4 Press Shift-Enter/Shift-Return to insert a line break.

5 In the Forms category of the Insert panel, click the Checkbox Group (⊞) icon.

The Checkbox Group dialog box appears, displaying two predefined options.

6 Change the Name field to **tourdate**.

Note how the dialog box offers two columns: Label and Value. Unlike text fields, checkboxes provide predefined options where the label can be different from the value actually submitted. This method offers several advantages over user-fillable fields.

First, the predefined options can deliver specific desired values that may not make any sense to the user. For example, the label can display the name of a product, while the value can pass along the stock-keeping unit, or SKU, number. Secondly, checkboxes and other predefined fields greatly reduce user-entry errors common in many forms.

> **Tip:** Press Tab to move quickly between labels and values to fill out the entire list.

7 Enter the following values in the Checkbox Group dialog box:

Label 1: **September 15-25, 2013**   Value 1: **tour1**

Label 2: **November 7-17, 2013**   Value 2: **tour2**

The dialog box makes it easy to insert additional data values.

8 In the Checkbox Group dialog box, click the Checkboxes Add (+) button to create a third item in the list.

9 Enter the following values in the new row:

Label 3: **March 15-25, 2014**   Value 3: **tour3**

10 For the Lay Out Using option, if necessary, select Line Breaks (
 Tags). Click OK.

● **Note:** Labels for checkboxes and radio buttons appear after the element, by default.

The checkbox group appears in the document below the text typed in step 3. Using the checkbox group eliminates the need to enter any settings in the Property inspector. A quick glance at the code reveals the advantages of using the checkbox group.

11 Insert the cursor in any of the checkbox labels and switch to Split view. Examine the code for the related <input> element.

Each checkbox in the group displays the name="tourdate" attribute. Note how the ID attributes have been incremented automatically as tourdate_0, tourdate_1, and tourdate_2. By using the checkbox group feature, Dreamweaver has saved you time by automating the process of adding multiple checkbox elements.

12 Save all files.

You've created a group of checkboxes. More than one checkbox can be selected in a group. In the next exercise, you will learn how to work with radio buttons.

Creating radio buttons

Sometimes you want users to select only one option from an array of choices. The element of choice in that case is the radio button. Radio buttons differ from checkboxes in two ways. When a radio button is selected, it can't be deselected, except by clicking one of the other buttons in the group. Then, when you click one radio button, any other option in the same group is deselected automatically.

The enabling mechanism behind this behavior is simple but effective. Unlike other form elements, each radio button does not have a unique name and ID; rather, all radio buttons in a group have the same name *and* ID. Radio buttons are differentiated by giving each distinctive *values*, instead.

As with checkboxes, you can add radio buttons to your page using two methods. You can insert each radio button individually or insert an entire group at once. If you choose to insert radio buttons singly, you'll be totally responsible for inserting and naming each manually. If you choose the radio button group, Dreamweaver will take care of all the naming logistics automatically.

1   If necessary, open **signup.html** and switch to Design view.

2   Insert the cursor in the last checkbox label. Select the <p> tag selector and press the Right Arrow key. Press Enter/Return to insert a new paragraph.

3   Type **How many people will be traveling?** Press Shift-Enter/Shift-Return to insert a line break.

4   In the Insert panel, click the Radio Button Group (⌗) icon.

5   Change the Name field to **travelers**.

● **Note:** Checkboxes and radio buttons use identical code markup. To convert a radio button to a checkbox, simply give each item a unique name. To change a checkbox to a radio button, give each item the same name but unique values.

As with checkboxes, you can enter values that are different than the labels.

6   Enter the following values in the Radio Button Group dialog box:

Label 1: **One**   Value 1: **1**

Label 2: **Two**   Value 2: **2**

7   Click the Radio Buttons Add (+) button three times to create a total of five radio buttons.

8   Enter the following values in the new rows:

Label 3: **Three**   Value 3: **3**

Label 4: **Four**   Value 4: **4**

Label 5: **More**   Value 5: **contact**

▶ **Tip:** If you want to reorder the radio buttons in this dialog box, use the up and down arrows.

9   Use the up and down arrows to order the options properly. From the Lay Out Using options, select Line Breaks (
 tags). Click OK.

The radio button group appears below the text entered in step 3. Notice that labels were added automatically by Dreamweaver.

10 Select one of the radio button elements. In the Property inspector, select the Required option.

You have to select only one radio button to apply the required option. Since all the radio buttons use the same name and ID, the attribute applies to the group as a whole.

11 Save all files.

You've created a set of radio buttons. By using a radio button group, you easily made this element a required form.

Incorporating text areas

Every now and then, you may want to give users an opportunity to enter a larger amount of information. Text areas provide this ability. Text areas permit multiple-line entry and word wrapping. If the entered text exceeds the physical space of the text area on the page, scroll bars automatically appear.

1 If necessary, open **signup.html** and switch to Design view.

2 Click within the radio group. Select the <p> tag selector and press the Right Arrow key to move the cursor after the element. Press Enter/Return to create a new paragraph.

3 In the Forms category of the Insert panel, click the Text Area ([|]) icon.

The text area element appears with a generic label.

◆ **Warning:** Design view doesn't render text fields accurately. Always test the widths in Live view or a browser.

4   In the Property inspector, enter the following specifications:

Name: **requirements**

Rows: **10**

Cols: **50**

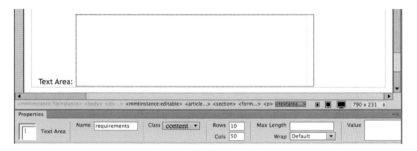

The text area appears 10 rows tall and 50 characters wide. As with the other text fields, you'll have to change the default label manually.

5   Select the text area label and type **Requirements and Limitations:**

The label appears on the same line with the comment text area and aligned to the bottom, which doesn't look very attractive. Let's move the text area to its own line.

6   Insert the cursor in the *Requirements and Limitations* label text. Select the `<label>` tag selector, and press the Right Arrow key. Press Shift-Enter/Shift-Return to create a line break.

The *Requirements and Limitations* text area label is sufficiently vague that it requires a bit more description to generate the desired response. Let's use the new Place Holder attribute to prompt the proper response.

7   Click the `<textarea>` element itself. In the Property inspector Place Holder field, type **Please enter any personal travel requirements or limitations in this space**.

Although the Place Holder field in the Property inspector is too small to display all the text, it will hold as much text as you wish to type. If you need to view or edit the text, you can view it all in Code view. When the website user begins to type in this field, the placeholder text will disappear automatically, but since it's not stored in the field itself, it can't be passed to your data application if the user doesn't enter anything into the field.

8   If necessary, deselect the Required option.

To see the final effect, you'll need to use Live view.

9   Activate Live view.

The final text area appears displaying the placeholder text.

10 Save all files.

The text area you added allows the website user to type comments that aren't limited to a single line or checkbox. Another important form element also allows you to present multiple choices to the visitor, but in a more compact space.

Working with lists

Select elements are a convenient method for providing users a list of predefined choices—such as the names of all 50 states—in a tiny amount of space on the webpage. Using a database connection, the list options can also be populated dynamically and even updated instantly as new entries are made by administrators or other users.

Select form elements can present multiple options in two different formats: menu or list. When displayed as a menu, the element functions like a set of radio buttons. When displayed as a list, the element behaves like a set of checkboxes, allowing a user to select multiple options. In this exercise, you'll insert a select menu with three options.

1   If necessary, open **signup.html** and switch to Design view.

2   Select the text area. Select the <p> tag selector that contains it and press the Right Arrow key. Press Enter/Return.

3   Type **How would you like to pay?** and press Shift-Enter/Shift-Return.

4   In the Forms category of the Insert panel, click the Select (▤) icon.

The Select element appears in the layout. As with the other form fields, give the field a custom name compatible with any data application you may use it in. If the information will be used in a database, write field names and IDs as one word, without spaces or special characters.

5 In the Property inspector, create the following specification:

Name: **paymenttype**

Unlike with the checkbox and radio groups, Dreamweaver didn't open an option dialog box for the `<select>` element automatically. But you can create the values for it by clicking the List Values button in the Property inspector.

6 In the Property inspector, click the List Values button.

The List Values dialog box appears.

Tip: Lists don't have to be in alphabetical order, but alphabetizing the items makes the options easier to search, especially in longer lists.

7 Enter the following labels and values in the List Values dialog box:

Label 1: **Check**   Value 1: **check**

Label 2: **Credit Card**   Value 2: **credit**

Label 3: **Electronic Funds Transfer**   Value 3: **eft**

Click OK.

The options appear in the Selected field of the Property inspector. Once the list menu is complete, you can select one of the items in the list to be displayed by default.

Tip: One strategy favored by some developers is to select your most preferred option to display by default. In other words, if you like the convenience and security offered by credit cards, preselect the credit card option by default.

8 In the Property inspector, from the Selected list, select the **Credit Card** option.

Multiple choice allowed

By default, an HTML5 Select element is formatted as a menu, allowing the user to select only one option from the list. To allow multiple selections, select the Multiple attribute in the Property inspector and specify a Size attribute that will display the desired number of options in the list. If no size is specified, the list will expand to show all the options by default.

Note: In most browsers, to select multiple options you first have to hold the Ctrl/Cmd key. When using a select element as a list, you may need to add instructions for the user that explain how to make multiple selections.

9 Change the label *Select:* to **Payment Type:**

Let's enclose the last four components in their own field set.

10 Select the intro paragraph and the last four form elements you created. In the Insert panel Form category, click the Fieldset button. Name the new field set **Paris Eco-Tour**.

11 Preview the form in Live view.

12 Save all files.

Your form is almost complete—the last step is to add a button to submit the entered information for processing.

Adding a Submit button

Every form needs a control to invoke the dynamic process, or *action*, desired. This job typically falls to the Submit button that, when clicked, sends the entire form for processing. Dreamweaver now offers four button elements. One is simply a generic button that has no specific behavior assigned to it. Then, there's the standard Submit button designed to process the form field data. The third button is designed to reset the form fields to their default, or initial, state. The newest button is the Image button, which allows you to assign button behaviors to any web-compatible graphic.

1 If necessary, open **signup.html** in Design view.

2 Insert the cursor in any form element in the **Paris Eco-Tour** field set and select the `<fieldset>` tag selector.

You'll insert the Submit button outside the last field set but still within the form itself.

3 Press the Right Arrow key to move the cursor after the selected field set. Then press Enter/Return to create a new paragraph for the button.

4 In the Insert panel Forms category, click the Submit Button (☑) icon.

A Submit button appears below the last field set. Although many buttons use the word *Submit*, it is not a requirement, and you can substitute your own text as desired.

5 In the Property inspector, change the Value field to **Email Tour Request**.

Some users may change their minds while filling out a form and want to start over or clear the form. In this case, you also need to add a Reset button in the form.

6 Insert the cursor after the Submit button. Press Ctrl-Shift-Spacebar/ Cmd-Shift-Spacebar to insert a nonbreaking space.

7 In the Insert panel Forms category, click the Reset Button (↩) icon.

A Reset button appears in the layout.

8 In the Property inspector, change the Value field to **Clear Form**.

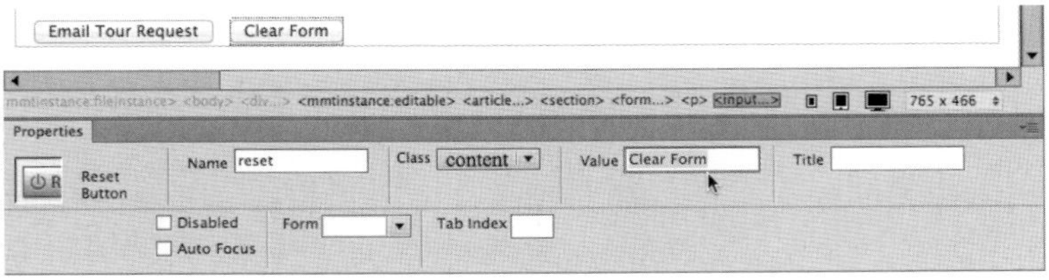

9 Save the file.

The form elements are all in place and ready to be accessed and filled in, but the form itself won't be complete until you add an action to specify how the data will be processed. Typical actions include sending the data by email, passing it to another webpage, or inserting it into a web-hosted database. In the next exercise, you will apply an action and create the supporting code to email the form data.

Tabbing tantrums

When filling out forms online, have you ever pressed the Tab key to move from one form field to the next and nothing happened? Or, worse yet, the focus moved to another field in an unexpected order? The ability to tab through forms is a default process you should support on your website. It may even be required, in some cases, under Section 508 accessibility mandates.

Tabbing to the various form fields you have created should happen automatically, but some browsers may not support every field type automatically or in the order you desire. In the past, you had to set up the tabbing sequence when inserting the elements or resort to Code view and set it up manually afterwards. Luckily, Dreamweaver now provides the Tab Index attribute for all form elements directly within the Property inspector.

Text field

Checkbox

Radio Button

Select element

Add tab index numbers to each field element to establish the order you think the user would select the fields. Typically, you would want to start at the top of the form and work down. For groups of checkboxes, add a tab index to each checkbox, since each one needs to be selected in turn. For groups of radio buttons add a tab index to only the first item, since only one answer will be chosen. Be careful not to use the same number twice.

Specifying a form action

As described in the exercise "Setting up e-mail links" in Lesson 9, "Working with Navigation," sending email is not as simple as inserting the `mailto` command into the Action field and adding your email address. Many of your web visitors don't use email programs installed on their computers; they use web-hosted systems like AOL, Gmail, and iCloud. To guarantee that you receive the form responses, you need to use a server-based application like the one you'll create in this exercise. The first step is to set the form action that passes the data to generate the email.

1   If necessary, open **signup.html**.

2   Insert the cursor in the form. Select the `<form#ecotour>` tag selector.

    The Property inspector displays the settings and specifications for the form.

3   In the Property inspector Action field, type **email_form.php**. If necessary, from the Method pop-up menu, choose **POST**.

4   Save all files.

The signup form is now complete. The next step is to create the script that will send the form data back to you by email.

GET and POST

HTML provides two built-in methods—GET and POST—for processing form data. The GET method transfers data by appending it to the URL. You see this method used most in search engines, like Google and Yahoo. The next time you conduct a web search, examine the URL on the results page and you will see your search term tucked away somewhere after the domain name, usually bracketed by special characters. The GET method has a couple of disadvantages . First, the search term is visible in the URL, which means other people can see what you're searching for and will also be able to retrieve your search from the browser cache/history. Second, URLs have a maximum size of a little over 2,000 characters (including the filename and path information), which limits the total amount of data you can pass.

The POST method doesn't use the URL. Instead it passes the data behind the scenes and places no limits concerning the amount of data. The POST method also doesn't cache the data, so no one can recover sensitive information, like your credit card or driver's license numbers, from the browser history. This is the preferred method used by most high-end data applications and online stores. The only disadvantage to using the POST method is that you can't see how the data is being passed to the next page—as you can using GET—which can help when you are troubleshooting application errors.

Web programming languages

HTML has many capabilities to define pages and page content but it is limited to mostly static displays of information and web graphics. To create movement, animation, or dynamic applications, you must resort to JavaScript or another third-party scripting language. A variety of scripting languages have been developed and used over the history of the web, but today the majority of developers rely on one of the three most popular programming languages: ASP, ColdFusion, or PHP.

Active Server Pages (ASP)—Developed by Microsoft and used mostly in Windows-based web servers. To learn more about ASP, see http://tinyurl.com/asp-defined.

ColdFusion—Developed by Jeremy and JJ Allaire in 1995, it was acquired by Macromedia in 2001 and then by Adobe in 2005. To learn more about ColdFusion, see http://Adobe.com/ColdFusion.

Hypertext Preprocessor (PHP)—Created by Rasmus Lerdorf in 1995, the initials originally stood for Personal Home Page. A free and mostly open-source development environment, it is now one of the most popular web scripting languages being used today. It is owned and developed currently by the PHP Group. To learn more about PHP, see http://tinyurl.com/php-defined.

Emailing form data

The **email_form.php** file targeted by the form action doesn't exist, so you need to create it from scratch. Although the GreenStart template is an HTML file, you can use it to create a PHP-based form mailer.

1   Create a new page from the site template.

2   Save the page as **email_form.php**.

   The file extension .php is used for dynamic pages that use the server-based scripting language PHP. The extension informs the browser that the page needs to be processed differently than a basic HTML page. Some servers may ignore ASP, ColdFusion, and PHP scripting if the files don't use the appropriate extensions.

3   Select the *Add main heading here* text and type **Green Travel** to replace the selected text.

4   Select the *Add subheading here* text and type **Thanks for signing up for the Paris Eco-Tour!** to replace the selected text.

5   Select the *Add content here* text and type **A Meridien GreenStart representative will contact you soon to set up your Paris Eco-Tour. Thanks for your interest in GreenStart and Eco-Tour!** to replace the selected text.

Note: In this exercise, we're using PHP-based code to generate the email form. To set up the action for ASP or ColdFusion coding, you would then add the appropriate code and extension (.asp or .cf) for the target application.

Note: This email address is for the fictitious GreenStart Association. For your own website, insert an email address supported by your server.

6 Switch to Code view.

The page currently is identical to the HTML-based template and has no PHP markup. The scripting that will process the data and generate the server-based email will be inserted before all other code on the page, even before the `<!doctype>` declaration that starts the HTML code.

7 Insert the cursor at the beginning of line 1 in Code view. Type **<?php** and press Enter/Return to create a new paragraph.

Dreamweaver's code hinting window helps you enter the code, but you'll quickly realize that this feature doesn't support PHP as well as it does HTML and JavaScript, so if you like to hand-code PHP, you'll be on your own.

8 Type **$to = "info@green-start.org";** and press Enter/Return to create a new line.

The dollar sign ($) declares a variable in PHP. A variable is a piece of data that will be created within the code or received from another source, such as your form. In this case, the `$to` variable is declaring the email address to which all the form data will be sent. If you want to experiment with PHP, feel free to substitute the sample address with your own personal email.

9 Type **$subject = "Paris Eco-Tour Sign Up Form";** and press Enter/Return to create a new line.

This line creates the variable for the email subject. A `$subject` variable is required in the PHP code, but it can be left blank (`"  "`), although subjects help you organize and filter email quickly.

10 Type **$message** = and press Enter/Return to create a new line.

This variable begins the body of the email. The next code elements you enter will list all the form fields you wish to collect, as well as a bit of structural trickery to make the email easier to read. Note that the code references the ID attribute of each field. Although you can list the fields in any order you want (and more than once), in this exercise you will type them in the same order they are in the form. If you recall, the first field in the signup form was Name.

11 Type "`Customer name: " . $_POST['name'] . "\r\n`".

The first part of this entry is part of the "trickery." The text "`Customer name:`" has nothing to do with the form. You are adding it to the email simply to identify the raw customer data inserted by the `$_POST['name']` variable. The period (`.`) character concatenates, or combines, the text and the data variable into one string. The code element "`\r\n`" inserts a new paragraph after the customer name. Insert this code after each form variable to put each piece of data on its own line.

12 Complete the email body by typing the following code. Insert spaces after the colons (`:`) to indent the variable statements so that they align to the same position. (Some lines will get more spaces than others.)

```
"Email: " . $_POST['email'] . "\r\n" .
"Requested tour: " .  $_POST['tourdate_0'] . "\r\n" .
"Requested tour: " .  $_POST['tourdate_1'] . "\r\n" .
"Requested tour: " .  $_POST['tourdate_2'] . "\r\n" .
"Total travelers: " .  $_POST['travelers'] . "\r\n" . "\r\n" .
"Requirements: " .  $_POST['requirements'] . "\r\n" . "\r\n" .
"Payment type: " .  $_POST['paymenttype'];
```

When finished, the code should look like the following figure.

```
1   <?php
2   $to = "info@green-start.org";
3   $subject = "Paris Eco-Tour Sign Up Form";
4   $message =
5   "Customer name: " . $_POST['name'] . "\r\n" .
6   "Customer name: " . $_POST['name'] . "\r\n" .
7   "Email: " . $_POST['email'] . "\r\n" .
8   "Requested tour: " .  $_POST['tourdate_0'] . "\r\n" .
9   "Requested tour: " .  $_POST['tourdate_1'] . "\r\n" .
10  "Requested tour: " .  $_POST['tourdate_2'] . "\r\n" .
11  "Total travelers: " .  $_POST['travelers'] . "\r\n" . "\r\n" .
12  "Requirements: " .  $_POST['requirements'] . "\r\n" . "\r\n" .
13  "Payment type: " .  $_POST['paymenttype'];
14  <!doctype html>
15  <html><!-- InstanceBegin template="/Templates/mygreen_temp_12.dwt"
```

Adding spaces before the variables aligns the form data when inserted into the message, making the email neater and easier to read. Note that certain lines show code for two paragraph returns ("`\r\n`" . "`\r\n`" .). Putting extra lines between specific data elements can help make the email easier to read.

13 Press Enter/Return, type `$from = $_POST['email'];` and press Enter/Return.

This code creates a variable that will be used to populate the From email address in the message using the information the customer entered in the form.

14 Type `$headers = "From: $from" . "\r\n";` and press Enter/Return.

This line creates the email From header using the variable from step 13.

● **Note:** This email address is for the fictitious GreenStart Association. For your own website, insert an email address supported by your server.

15 Type `$headers = "Bcc: lin@green-start.org" . "\r\n";` and press Enter/Return.

This line is optional. It generates a blind carbon copy of the email to Lin, the transportation expert at GreenStart. Feel free to customize the code by adding your own email here or the email of a coworker.

16 Type `mail($to,$subject,$message,$headers);` and press Enter/Return.

This line creates the email and sends it using a PHP-enabled server.

17 Type `?>` to close and complete the PHP form email function.

Like HTML, PHP requires a closing tag notation.

```
13    "Payment type: " . $_POST['paymenttype'];
14    $from = $_POST['email'];
15    $headers = "From: $from" . "\r\n";
16    $headers =  "Bcc: lin@green-start.org" . "\r\n";
17    mail($to,$subject,$message,$headers);
18    ?>
19    <!doctype html>
```

● **Note:** This code will work only on a PHP-enabled web server. It may not function on a local web server. The specific commands used here may not be supported by your server type. Check with your Internet host provider to obtain a list of the code items supported by your server.

18 Press Enter/Return to insert one last paragraph return. Save all files.

You've completed the PHP-based script that will send an email containing the form data.

Supporting other scripting languages

The server-based functionality you just created is also available in every major scripting language. Although Dreamweaver doesn't provide this functionality out of the box, frequently you can find the exact code structure you need through a quick search of the Internet. Just type the phrase "form data to email" or "web form mail" and you'll get thousands of options. Add your favorite scripting language to the search phrase (like "form data" to "email+ASP") to target or narrow the results.

Here are a few examples:

- **ASP**—tinyurl.com/asp-formmailer
- **ColdFusion**—tinyurl.com/cf-formmailer
- **PHP**—tinyurl.com/php-formmailer

Styling forms

Although the form and the email application you've been working on in this lesson are now functional, it's mostly *un*styled. Good styling can enhance form readability and comprehension and can make forms easier to use. In the following exercise, you'll style the form by creating a new custom style sheet.

1 If necessary, open or switch to **signup.html**.

2 Open the CSS Designer.

You'll create a new style sheet just for forms, so that you can attach it to this and other form pages but not to the entire site. Separating the CSS rules for forms from the master style sheet limits the amount of code that must be downloaded and creates a more efficient site overall. Less code means faster downloads and a better user experience.

3 In the CSS Designer, click the Add CSS Source (**+**) icon. Choose Create A New CSS File from the pop-up menu.

The Create A New CSS File dialog box appears.

4 In the File/URL field, type **forms.css**. Select the Add As: Link option.

5 Open the Conditional Usage menu and choose the Media: Screen option. Click OK.

The name **forms.css** appears in the Related Files interface. The asterisk indicates that the file has not been saved yet.

6 Insert the cursor in the *Your Contact Information* legend text.

7 In the Sources pane, select **forms.css**. Click the Add Selector (**+**) icon.

A selector name appears in the Selectors pane, targeting the legend in the field set for <form#ecotour>.

8 Edit the selector name to `#ecotour fieldset legend`

9 Enter the following properties for the `#ecotour fieldset legend` rule:

```
font-size: 120%
font-weight: bold
color: #090
```

10 Create a new CSS rule in **forms.css** named `#ecotour fieldset`.

11 Enter the following properties for `#ecotour fieldset`:

```
margin-bottom: 15px
padding: 10px
border: solid 2px #090
```

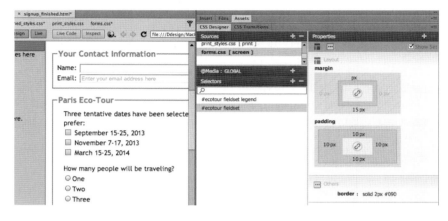

12 Save all files.

13 Preview the page in the primary browser.

Note: Unless all files are uploaded to a PHP-compatible testing server, you will probably receive an error message if you try to submit this page. That's because the code you created is designed to work on the fictitious GreenStart website running a PHP server. For your own website, insert email addresses supported by your server and modify the code as necessary.

In this lesson, you built a user-fillable form with a variety of HTML form elements. You created and attached a custom style sheet to liven up its appearance. In the browser, you will be able to test all the form fields. When you click the Email Tour Request button, the form data will be passed to the **email_form.php** file. If the page is previewed in a PHP-enabled system, an email will be generated and sent to the email address targeted in the PHP code.

At the moment, this form simply collects the data and processes it as a standard, text-based email. The recipient still has to access and process the data manually from that point. To take this process to the next level of automation, you can use Dreamweaver to modify **signup.html** so that it will insert the information directly into a web-hosted database.

More form information

To obtain more information on HTML5 forms, check out these links:

- http://tinyurl.com/html5forms1
- http://tinyurl.com/html5forms2
- http://tinyurl.com/html5forms3

Review questions

1 What is the purpose of the `<form>` tag?

2 What advantage does the `for` attribute have in form design?

3 What advantages do the checkbox and radio button groups have over standard checkbox and radio button elements?

4 What's the difference between a standard text field and a text area?

5 What's the main difference between radio buttons and checkboxes?

6 How do you specify that individual radio buttons belong to a group?

7 What is the purpose of the `<fieldset>` element?

Review answers

1 The `<form>` tag wraps around all the form elements and includes an action attribute that defines the file or script that will process the form and its data.

2 It connects the `<label>` tag to the form field by matching the ID and `for` attributes.

3 Checkbox and radio button groups make creating multiple form elements all at once easier, by completing the element attributes automatically.

4 A standard text field is intended for name or short phrase, whereas a text area can hold much larger amounts of text.

5 Radio buttons allow users to select only one option from several choices, whereas checkboxes permit the user to select as many items as desired.

6 All radio buttons with the same name and ID will be in the same radio button group.

7 A `<fieldset>` element is used to visually group related form fields together with an accompanying `<legend>` element to identify the group. It also helps to organize a form and clarify the purpose of the various form fields.

13

PUBLISHING TO THE WEB

Lesson Overview

In this lesson, you'll publish your website to the Internet and do the following:

- Define a remote site
- Define a testing server
- Put files on the web
- Cloak files and folders
- Update out-of-date links site-wide

This lesson will take about 1 hour and 15 minutes to complete. If you have not already done so, download the project files for this lesson from the Lesson & Update Files tab on your Account page at www.peachpit.com, and store them on your computer in a convenient location, as described in the Getting Started section of this book. Your Accounts page is also where you'll find any updates to the lessons or to the lesson files. Look on the Lesson & Update Files tab to access the most current content. If you are starting from scratch in this lesson, use the method described in the "Jumpstart" section of "Getting Started."

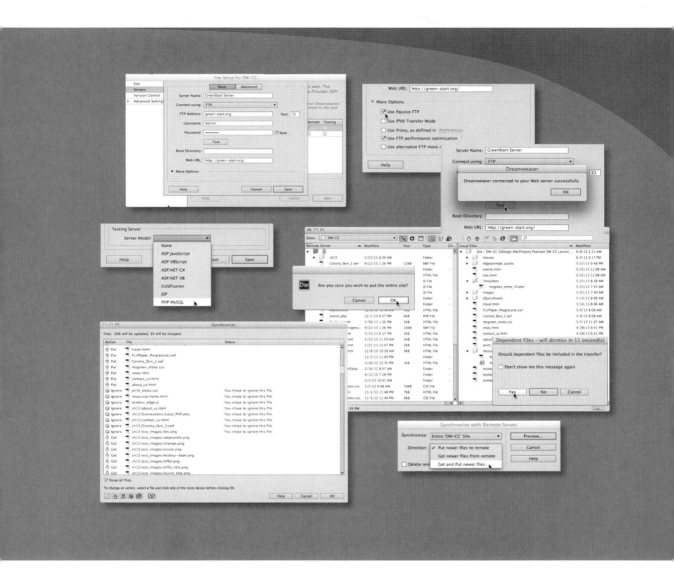

The goal of all the preceding lessons is to design, develop, and build pages for a remote website. But Dreamweaver doesn't abandon you there. It also provides powerful tools to upload and maintain any size website over time.

● **Note:** If you
have not already
downloaded the project
files for this lesson to
your computer from
your Account page,
make sure to do so now.
See "Getting Started"
at the beginning of
the book.

● **Note:** If you are
starting from scratch
in this exercise, see the
"Jumpstart" instructions
in the "Getting Started"
section at the beginning
of the book. Then, follow
the steps in this exercise.

Defining a remote site

Dreamweaver's workflow is based on a two-site system. One site is in a folder on your computer's hard drive and is known as the *local site*. All work in the previous lessons has been performed on your local site. The second site, called the *remote site*, is established in a folder on a web server, typically running on another computer, and is connected to the Internet and publicly available. In large companies, the remote site is often available only to employees via a network-based intranet. Such sites provide information and applications to support corporate programs and products.

Dreamweaver supports several methods for connecting to a remote site:

- **FTP** (File Transfer Protocol)—The standard method for connecting to hosted websites.

- **SFTP** (Secure File Transfer Protocol)—A protocol that provides a method to connect to hosted websites in a more secure manner to preclude unauthorized access or interception of online content.

- **FTP over SSL/TLS** (implicit encryption)—A secure FTP method that requires all clients of the FTPS server be aware that SSL is to be used on the session. It is incompatible with non-FTPS-aware clients.

- **FTP over SSL/TLS** (explicit encryption)— A legacy-compatible, secure FTP method where FTPS-aware clients can invoke security with an FTPS-aware server without breaking overall FTP functionality with non-FTPS-aware clients.

- **Local/network**—A local or network connection is most frequently used with an intermediate web server, called a *staging server*. Staging servers are typically used to test sites before they go live. Files from the staging server are eventually published to an Internet-connected web server.

- **WebDav** (Web Distributed Authoring and Versioning)—A web-based system also known to Windows users as Web Folders and to Mac users as iDisk.

- **RDS** (Remote Development Services)—Developed by Adobe for ColdFusion and primarily used when working with ColdFusion-based sites.

The FTP engine was completely rebuilt in Adobe CC. Dreamweaver now can upload larger files faster and more efficiently, allowing you to return to work more quickly. In the next exercises, you'll set up a remote site using the two most common methods: FTP and **Local/Network***.

Setting up a remote FTP site

The vast majority of web developers rely on FTP to publish and maintain their sites. FTP is a well-established protocol, and many variations of the protocol are used on the web—most of which are supported by Dreamweaver.

1   Launch Adobe Dreamweaver CC.

2   Choose Site > Manage Sites.

3   In the Manage Sites dialog box is a list of all the sites you may have defined. If more than one is displayed, make sure that the current site, DW-CC, is chosen. Click the Edit (✐) icon. If you are using the Jumpstart method, select the name of the site based on Lesson 13.

4   In the Site Setup For DW-CC dialog box, click the Servers category.

    The Site Setup dialog box allows you to set up multiple servers, so you can test several types of installations, if desired.

5   Click the Add New Server (➕) icon. In the Server Name field, enter **GreenStart Server**.

6   From the Connect Using pop-up menu, choose FTP.

◆ **Warning:**
To complete the following exercise, you must have a remote server already established. Remote servers can be hosted by your own company or contracted from a third-party web-hosting service.

7   In the FTP Address field, type the URL or IP (Internet protocol) address of your FTP server.

    If you contract a third-party service as a web host, you will be assigned an FTP address. This address may come in the form of an IP address, such as 192.168.1.000. Enter this number into the field exactly as it was sent to you. Frequently, the FTP address will be the name of your site, such as ftp.green-start.org. Dreamweaver doesn't require you to enter the *ftp* into the field.

8   In the Username field, enter your FTP user name. In the Password field, enter your FTP password.

    Usernames may be case sensitive, but password fields almost always are; be sure you enter them correctly.

Tip: Check with your web hosting service or IS/IT manager to obtain the root directory name, if any.

9 In the Root Directory field, type the name of the folder that contains documents publicly accessible to the web, if any.

Some web hosts provide FTP access to a root-level folder that might contain nonpublic folders—such as cgi-bin, which is used to store common gateway interface (CGI) or binary scripts—as well as a public folder. In these cases, type the public folder name—such as public, public_html, www, or wwwroot—in the Root Directory field. In many web host configurations, the FTP address is the same as the public folder, and the Root Directory field should be left blank.

10 Select the Save option if you don't want to re-enter your user name and password every time Dreamweaver connects to your site.

11 Click Test to verify that your FTP connection works properly.

Dreamweaver displays an alert to notify you that the connection was successful or unsuccessful.

12 Click OK to dismiss the alert.

If you received an error message, your web server may require additional configuration options.

13 Click the More Options triangle to reveal additional server options.

Consult the instructions from your hosting company to select the appropriate options for your specific FTP server. The options are:

- **Use Passive FTP**—Allows your computer to connect to the host computer and bypass a firewall restraint. Many web hosts require this setting.

- **Use IPV6 Transfer Mode**—Enables connection to IPV6-based servers, which use the most recent version of the Internet transfer protocol.

- **Use Proxy**—Identifies a secondary proxy host connection as defined in your Dreamweaver preferences.

- **Use FTP Performance Optimization**—Optimizes the FTP connection. Deselect if Dreamweaver can't connect to your server.

- **Use Alternative FTP Move Method**—Provides an additional method to resolve FTP conflicts, especially when rollbacks are enabled or when moving files.

Troubleshooting your FTP connection

Connecting to your remote site can be frustrating the first time you attempt it. You can experience numerous pitfalls, many of which are out of your control. Here are a few steps to take if you have issues connecting:

- If you can't connect to your FTP server, double-check your user name and password and re-enter them carefully. Remember usernames may be case sensitive, while most passwords frequently are. (This is the most common error.)

- Select Use Passive FTP and test the connection again.

- If you still can't connect to your FTP server, deselect the Use FTP Performance Optimization option, click OK, and click Test again.

- If none of these steps enable you to connect to your remote site, check with your IS/IT manager or your remote site administrator.

Once you establish a working connection, you may need to configure some advanced options.

14 Click the Advanced tab. Select among the following options for working with your remote site:

- **Maintain Synchronization Information**—Automatically notes which files have been changed on the local and remote sites so that they can be easily synchronized. This feature helps you keep track of your changes and can be helpful if you change multiple pages before you upload. You may want to use cloaking with this feature. You'll learn about cloaking in an upcoming exercise. This feature is usually selected by default.

- **Automatically Upload Files To Server On Save**—Transfers files from the local to the remote site when they are saved. This option can become annoying if you save often and aren't yet ready for a page to go public.

- **Enable File Check-Out**—Starts the check-in/check-out system for collaborative website building in a workgroup environment. If you choose this option, you'll need to enter a check-out name for check-out purposes and, optionally, an email address. If you're working by yourself, you do not need to select file check-out.

It is acceptable to leave any or all of these options unselected, but for the purposes of this lesson, enable the Maintain Synchronization Information option.

15 Click Save to finalize the settings in the open dialog boxes.

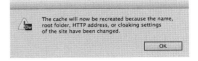

A dialog box appears, informing you that the cache will be re-created because you changed the site settings.

16 Click OK to build the cache. When Dreamweaver finishes updating the cache, click Done to close the Manage Sites dialog box.

You have established a connection to your remote server. If you don't currently have a remote server, you can substitute a local testing server instead as your remote server.

Installing a testing server

When you produce sites with dynamic content you need to test functionality before the pages go live on the Internet. A testing server can fit that need nicely. Depending on the applications you need to test, the testing server can simply be a subfolder on your actual web server or you can use a local web server such as Apache or Internet Information Services (IIS) from Microsoft.

For detailed information about installing and configuring a local web server, check out the following links:

- Apache/ColdFusion—http://tinyurl.com/setup-coldfusion
- Apache/PHP—http://tinyurl.com/setup-apachephp
- IIS/ASP—http://tinyurl.com/setup-asp

Once you set up the local web server, you can use it to upload the completed files and test your remote site. In most cases, your local web server will not be accessible from the Internet or be able to host the actual website.

Establishing a remote site on a local or network web server

◆ **Warning:**
To complete the following exercise, you must have already installed and configured a local or network web server.

If your company or organization uses a staging server as a "middleman" between web designers and the live website, it's likely you'll need to connect to your remote site through a local or network web server. Local/network servers are often used as testing servers to test dynamic functions before pages are uploaded to the Internet.

1 Launch Adobe Dreamweaver CC.

2 Choose Site > Manage Sites.

3 In the Manage Sites dialog box, make sure that the current site, DW-CC, is chosen. Click the Edit (✎) icon.

4 In the Site Setup For DW-CC dialog box, select the Servers category.

5 If you have a testing server already set up in the dialog box, select the Remote option.

● **Note:** If you are starting from scratch in this exercise, see the "Jumpstart" instructions in the "Getting Started" section at the beginning of the book. Then, follow the steps in this exercise.

> Here you'll select the server that will host your pages on the web. The settings for this dialog box come from your Internet Service Provider (ISP) or your web administrator.
>
> *Note: You do not need to complete this step to begin working on your Dreamweaver site. You only need to define a remote server when you want to connect to the web and post your pages.*
>
> | Name | Address | Connection | Remote | Testing |
> |---|---|---|---|---|
> | GreenStart Server | green-start.org | FTP | ☑ | ☐ |

6 Click the Add New Server (✚) icon. In the Server Name field, enter **GreenStart Local**.

7 From the Connect Using pop-up menu, choose Local/Network.

8 In the Server Folder field, click the Browse (📁) icon. Select the local web server's HTML folder, such as C:\wamp\www\DW-CC.

9 In the Web URL field, enter the appropriate URL for your local web server. If you are using WAMP or MAMP local servers, your web URL will be something like http://localhost:8888/DW-CC or http://localhost/DW-CC. You must enter the correct URL or Dreamweaver's FTP and testing features may not function properly.

● **Note:** The paths you enter here are contingent on how you installed your local web server and may not be the same as the ones displayed.

Server Name: GreenStart Local	Server Name: GreenStart Local
Connect using: Local/Network	Connect using: Local/Network
Server Folder: C:\wamp\www\dw-cc	Server Folder: /Applications/MAMP/htdocs/DW-CC/
Web URL: http://localhost/DW-CC/	Web URL: http://localhost:8888/DW-CC/

Windows   OS X

10 Click the Advanced tab, and as with the actual web server, select the appropriate options for working with your remote site: Maintain Synchronization Information, Automatically Upload Files To Server On Save, and/or Enable File Check-Out.

Although leaving all three of these options unselected is acceptable, for the purposes of this lesson select the Maintain Synchronization Information option.

11 If you'd like to use the local web server as the testing server, too, select the server model in the Advanced section of the dialog box. If you are creating a dynamic site using a specific programming language, like ASP, ColdFusion or PHP, select the matching Server Model so you'll be able to test the pages of your site properly.

12 Click Save to complete the remote server setup.

13 In the Site Setup For DW-CC dialog box, select Remote. If you want to use the local server as a testing server, too, select Testing. Click Save.

14 In the Manage Sites dialog box, click Done. If necessary, click OK to rebuild the cache.

Only one remote and one testing server can be active at one time, but you may have multiple servers defined. One server can be used for both roles, if desired. Before you upload files for the remote site, you may need to cloak certain folders and files in the local site.

Cloaking folders and files

Not all the files in your site root folder may need to be transferred to the remote server. For example, there's no point in filling the remote site with files that won't be accessed or that will remain inaccessible to website users. Minimizing files stored on the remote server may also pay financial dividends, since many hosting services base part of their fee on how much disk space your site occupies. If you selected Maintain Synchronization Information for a remote site using FTP or a network server, you may want to cloak some of your local materials to prevent them from being uploaded. Cloaking is a Dreamweaver feature that allows you to designate certain folders and files that will not be uploaded to or synchronized with the remote site.

Folders you don't want to upload include Templates and Library folders. Some other non-web-compatible file types used to create your site, like Photoshop (.psd), Flash (.fla), or Microsoft Word (.doc) files also don't need to be on the remote server. Although cloaked files will not upload or synchronize automatically, you may still upload them manually, if desired.

The cloaking process begins in the Site Setup dialog box.

1 Choose Site > Manage Sites.

2 Select DW-CC in the site list, and click the Edit (✎) icon.

3 Expand the Advanced Settings category. In the Cloaking category, select the Enable Cloaking and Cloak Files Ending With options.

   The field below the check boxes displays the extensions .fla and .psd.

4 Insert the cursor after *.psd* and insert a space. Type **.doc .txt .rtf**

Be sure to insert a space between each extension. Because these file types don't contain any desired web content, adding their extensions here will prevent Dreamweaver from uploading and synchronizing these file types automatically.

5 Click Save. If Dreamweaver prompts you to update the cache, click OK. Then, click Done to close the Manage Sites dialog box.

   You can also cloak specific files or folders manually.

6 Open the Files panel and click the Expand (⊡) button to fill the workspace. If you are using the Jumpstart method, skip steps 7 and 8. You should not have any lesson folders in your workflow.

   Note all the lesson folders. These folders contain a great deal of duplicative content that is unnecessary on the remote site.

7 Right-click the Lesson01 folder. From the context menu, choose Cloaking > Cloak.

8 Repeat step 7 for each of the remaining lesson folders.

   Templates and Library folders are not needed on the remote site because your webpages do not reference these assets in any way. But if you work in a team environment, it may be handy to upload and synchronize these folders so that each team member has up-to-date versions of each on their own computers. For this exercise, let's assume you work alone.

● **Note:** If you are using the jumpstart method, skip steps 7 and 8.

● **Note:** Server-side includes (SSIs) must be uploaded to the server for them to function.

9   Apply cloaking to the Templates folder.

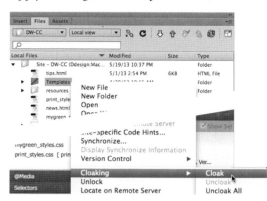

10 In the warning dialog box that appears, click OK.

11 Repeat steps 9 and 10 to cloak the Library folder.

Using the Site Setup dialog box and the Cloaking context menu, you cloaked file types, folders, and files. The synchronization process will ignore cloaked items and not upload or download them automatically.

Wrapping things up

Over the last 12 lessons, you have built an entire website from scratch, including text, images, movies, and interactive content, but a few loose strings remain for you to tie up. Before you publish your site, you'll need to create one important file and make some crucial updates to your site navigation.

Creating a home page

The file you need to create is one that is essential to every site: a home page. The home page is usually the first page most users will see on your site. It is the page that loads automatically when a user enters your site's domain name into the browser window. Since the page loads automatically, there are a few restrictions on the name and extension you can use.

Basically, the name and extension depend on the hosting server and the type of applications running on the home page, if any. In most cases, the home page will simply be named *index*. But *default*, *start*, and *iisstart* are also used.

As you learned earlier, extensions identify the specific types of programming languages used within a page. A normal HTML home page will use an extension of .htm or .html. Extensions like .asp, .cfm, and .php, among others, are required if the home page contains any dynamic applications specific to that server model. You may still use one of these extensions—if they are compatible with your server model—even if the page contains no dynamic applications or content. Be careful—in some instances, using the wrong extension may prevent the page from loading altogether. Whenever you're in doubt, use .html, because it's supported in all environments.

The specific home page name or names honored by the server are normally configured by the server administrator and can be changed, if desired. Most servers are configured to honor several names and a variety of extensions. Check with your IS/IT manager or web server support team to ascertain the recommended name and extension for your home page.

1 Create a new page from the site template. Save the file as **index.html**. Or, use a filename and extension compatible with your server model.

2 Open Lesson13 > resources > **home.html**.

3 Insert the cursor anywhere in the content. Select the `<article>` tag selector. Copy all the content.

4 Switch to **index.html**. Insert the cursor anywhere in the *Add main heading here* text. Select the `<article.content>` tag selector, and paste the content.

The new content appears in the center of the page, but it's unformatted and not conforming to the layout. That's because the content isn't styled yet with the proper class.

5 Select the `<article>` tag selector. Apply the `.content` class to the new element.

The main content is now formatted properly.

6 In the sidebar, replace the image placeholder with **bike2work.jpg** from the site images folder.

7 Replace the caption placeholder with **GreenStart has launched a new program to encourage Meridien residents to leave their cars at home and bike to work. Sign up and tell a friend.**

8 Edit the page title to read **Meridien GreenStart Association – Welcome to Meridien GreenStart**.

Note the hyperlink placeholders in the MainContent region.

9 Insert the cursor in the *News* link. In the Property inspector, browse and connect the link to **news.html**.

10 Repeat step 9 with each link. Connect the links to the appropriate pages in your site root folder.

11 Save and close all files.

The home page is complete. Let's assume you want to upload the site at its current state of completion even though some pages have yet to be created. This happens in the course of any site development. Pages are added and deleted over time; missing pages will be completed and uploaded at a later date.

In this scenario, you have created pages for all but one link in your current navigation system: *Green Products*. If this page cannot be completed by the time the site goes live, you can always remove it from the vertical menu temporarily and then add it back later, when needed. Before you can upload the site to a live server, you should always update any out-of-date links and remove dead ones.

Updating links

All the out-of-date links are contained in the vertical menu, which is currently part of the site template. You can update the entire site by editing the template and saving the changes.

1 Open the default site template from the Assets panel.

This template controls all your current site pages.

2 Insert the cursor in the *Green Products* link. The page is linked to products.html, which doesn't exist. Click the <li> tag selector for this link and delete it.

You can re-create these links at a later date, if and when these pages are developed.

Prelaunch checklist

Take this opportunity to review all your site pages before publishing them to see if they are ready for prime time. In an actual workflow, you should perform most or all of the following actions, which you learned in previous lessons, before uploading a single page:

- Code validation (Lesson 4, "Creating a Page Layout")
- Spell check (Lesson 7, "Working with Text, Lists, and Tables")
- Site-wide link check (Lesson 9, "Working with Navigation")

Fix any problems you find, and then proceed to the next exercise.

---

3 Save the template. Dreamweaver will prompt you to update the site. Click Update.

   The Update Pages dialog box appears, reporting what pages were and were not updated. If you do not see the report, click the Show Log option.

4 Click the Close button. Close the template.

The vertical navigation menu has been updated throughout the site, and your pages are now ready to upload—almost.

Putting your site online

For the most part, the local site and the remote site are mirror images, containing the same HTML files, images, and assets in identical folder structures. When you transfer a webpage from your local site to your remote site, you are publishing, or *putting,* that page. If you *put* a file stored in a folder on your local site, Dreamweaver transfers the file to the equivalent folder on the remote site. It will even automatically create the remote folder or folders, if necessary. The same is true when you download files.

Using Dreamweaver, you can publish anything—from one file to a complete site—in a single operation. When you publish a webpage, by default Dreamweaver asks if you would also like to put the dependent files, too. Dependent files are the images, CSS, HTML5 movies, JavaScript files, server-side includes, and all other files necessary to complete the page.

You can upload one file at a time or the entire site at once.

1 Open the Files panel and click the Expand (⊞) icon, if necessary.

◆ **Warning:**
Dreamweaver does a good job trying to identify all the dependent files in a particular workflow. In some cases, it may miss files crucial to a dynamic or extended process. It is imperative that you do your homework to identify these files and make sure they are uploaded.

Sidebar sideline

As you've built the pages for your site, you've concentrated mostly on the main content and applications and ignored the sidebar content on some pages. These pages were never finished. Since these exercises were intended for training purposes only, there's no need to complete these pages. However, if your design sensibilities prevent you from leaving these pages in their current state of incompleteness, take a few minutes to finish them now. Some suggestions are offered below, but feel free to take any creative license you desire to complete the sidebar content. The images pictured are available in the default site images folder.

events.html   tips.html

2 Click the Connect To Remote Server (🖧) icon to connect to the remote site.

If your remote site is properly configured, the Files panel will connect to the site and display its contents on the left half of the Files panel. When you first upload files, the remote site may be empty or mostly empty. If you are connecting to your Internet host, specific files and folders created by the hosting company may appear. Do not delete these items unless you check to see whether they are essential to the operation of the server or your own applications.

3 In the local file list, select **index.html**. In the Document toolbar, click the Put (⬆) icon.

By default, Dreamweaver will prompt you to upload dependent files. If a dependent file already exists on the server and your changes did not affect it, you can click No. Otherwise, for new files or files that have had any changes, click Yes. Dreamweaver will then upload images, CSS, JavaScript, server-side includes (SSIs), and other dependent files needed to properly render the selected HTML file.

You can also upload multiple files or the entire site.

4 Select the site root folder for the local site, and then click the Put icon in the Files panel.

● **Note:**
If Dreamweaver doesn't prompt you to upload dependent files, this option may be turned off. To turn this feature on, access the option in the Site category of the Dreamweaver Preferences panel.

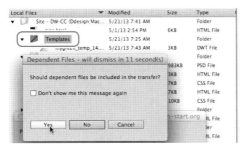

A dialog box appears, asking you to confirm that you want to upload the entire site.

5 Click OK.

Dreamweaver begins to upload the site. It will re-create your local site structure on the remote server. When it's complete, note that none of the cloaked lesson folders were uploaded. Dreamweaver will automatically ignore all cloaked items when putting a folder or an entire site. If desired, you can manually select and upload individually cloaked items.

6 Right-click the Templates folder and choose Put from the context menu.

◆ **Warning:** Among the pages you are uploading are several that may incorporate dynamic content using JavaScript and jQuery resources. Dreamweaver will identify many of these resources, but it won't find them all. You will probably have to locate and upload these files and folders manually. In any case, be aware that additional configuration on the remote server and database may be required before some of this dynamic content will function properly.

Dreamweaver prompts you to upload dependent files for the Templates folder.

● **Note:** A file that is uploaded or downloaded will automatically overwrite any version of the file at the destination.

● **Note:** When accessing Put and Get, it doesn't matter whether you use the Local or Remote pane of the Files panel. Put always uploads to Remote; Get always downloads to Local.

7   Click Yes to upload dependent files.

The Templates folder is uploaded to the remote server. Note that the remote Templates folder displays a red slash indicating that it is cloaked, too. At times, you will want to cloak local and remote files and folders to prevent these items from being replaced or accidentally overwritten. A cloaked file will not be uploaded or downloaded automatically. You will have to select any specific files and perform the action manually.

The opposite of the Put command is Get, which downloads any selected file or folder to the local site. You can get any file from the remote site by selecting it in the Remote or Local pane and clicking the Get (⬇) icon. Alternatively, you can drag the file from the Remote pane to the Local pane.

8   Use a browser to connect to the remote site on your network server or the Internet. Type the appropriate address in the URL field—depending on whether you are connecting to the local web server or the actual Internet site—such as http://localhost/*domain_name* or http://www.*your_domain.com*.

The GreenStart site appears in the browser. Click to test the hyperlinks to view each of the completed pages for the site. Once the site is uploaded, keeping it up to date is an easy task. As files change, you can upload them one at a time or synchronize the whole site with the remote server. Synchronization is especially important in workgroup environments where files are changed and uploaded by several individuals. You can easily download or upload files that are older, overwriting files that are newer. Synchronization can ensure that you are working with only the latest versions of each file.

Synchronizing local and remote sites

Synchronization in Dreamweaver is used to keep the files on your server and your local computer up to date. It's an essential tool when you work from multiple locations or with one or more coworkers. Used properly, it can prevent you from accidentally uploading or working on out-of-date files.

At the moment, the local and remote sites are identical. To better illustrate the capabilities of synchronization, let's make a change to one of the site pages.

1   Open **about_us.html**.

2   In the main heading, select the text *Green* in the name *GreenStart*. Apply the CSS .green class to this text.

3   Apply the CSS .green class to each occurrence of the word *green* anywhere on the page.

4   Save and close the page.

5   Open and expand the Files panel. In the Document toolbar, click the Synchronize (🔁) icon.

The Synchronize Files dialog box appears.

6   From the Synchronize pop-up menu, choose the option Entire 'DW-CC' Site. From the Direction menu, choose the Get And Put Newer Files option.

● **Note:** Jumpstart users will see the name of the current site folder in the Synchronize pop-up menu.

Choose specific options in this dialog box that meet your needs and workflow.

Synchronization options

During synchronization, you can choose to accept the suggested action or override it by selecting one of the other options in the dialog box. Options can be applied to one or more files at a time.

⬇️ **Get**—Downloads the selected file(s) from the remote site

⬆️ **Put**—Uploads the selected file(s) to the remote site

🗑️ **Delete**—Marks the selected file(s) for deletion

🚫 **Ignore**—Ignores the selected file(s) during synchronization

🔁 **Synchronized**—Identifies the selected file(s) as already synchronized

📑 **Compare**—Uses a third-party utility to compare the local and remote versions of a selected file

7 Click Preview.

The Synchronize dialog box appears, reporting what files have changed and whether you need to get or put them. Since you just uploaded the entire site, only the file **about_us.html** appears in the list, which indicates that Dreamweaver wants to put it to the remote site.

8 Click OK to put the file.

If other people access and update files on your site, remember to run synchronization *before* you work on any files to be certain you are working on the most current versions of each file in your site. Another technique is to set up the Check-out/Check-in functionality in the advanced options of the server's setup dialog box.

In this lesson, you set up your site to connect to a remote server and uploaded files to that remote site. You also cloaked files and folders and then synchronized the local and remote sites.

Congratulations! You've designed, developed, and built an entire website and uploaded it to your remote server. By finishing all the exercises in this book, you have gained experience in all aspects of the design and development of a standard website compatible with desktop computers. Now you are ready to build and publish a site of your own. In the next lesson, you will explore the techniques and technology surrounding the latest movement on the Internet: responsive web design, or designing for smart phones and mobile devices.

Review questions

1 What is a remote site?

2 Name two types of file transfer protocols supported in Dreamweaver.

3 How can you configure Dreamweaver so that it does not synchronize certain files in your local site with the remote site?

4 True or false: You have to manually publish every file and associated image, JavaScript file, and server-side include that are linked to pages in your site.

5 What service does synchronization perform?

Review answers

1 A remote site is typically the live version of the local site stored on a web server connected to the Internet.

2 FTP (file transfer protocol) and local/network are the two most commonly used file transfer methods. Other file transfer methods supported in Dreamweaver include Secure FTP, WebDav, and RDS.

3 Cloaking the files or folders prevents them from synchronizing.

4 False. Dreamweaver can automatically transfer dependent files, if desired, including embedded or referenced images, CSS style sheets, and other linked content, although some files may be missed.

5 Synchronization automatically scans local and remote sites, comparing files on both to identify the most current version of each. It creates a report window to suggest which files to get or put to bring both sites up to date, and then it will perform the update.

14 DESIGNING FOR MOBILE DEVICES

In this lesson, you'll adapt and build cascading style sheets (CSS) in Dreamweaver for mobile devices and do the following:

- Create media queries for mobile and handheld devices, such as tablets and cell phones

- Configure page components to work with mobile devices

- Preview these pages onscreen and on mobile devices

 This lesson will take about 2 hours to complete. If you have not already done so, download the project files for this lesson from the Lesson & Update Files tab on your Account page at www.peachpit.com, and store them on your computer in a convenient location, as described in the Getting Started section of this book. Your Accounts page is also where you'll find any updates to the lessons or to the lesson files. Look on the Lesson & Update Files tab to access the most current content. If you are starting from scratch in this lesson, use the method described in the "Jumpstart" section of "Getting Started."

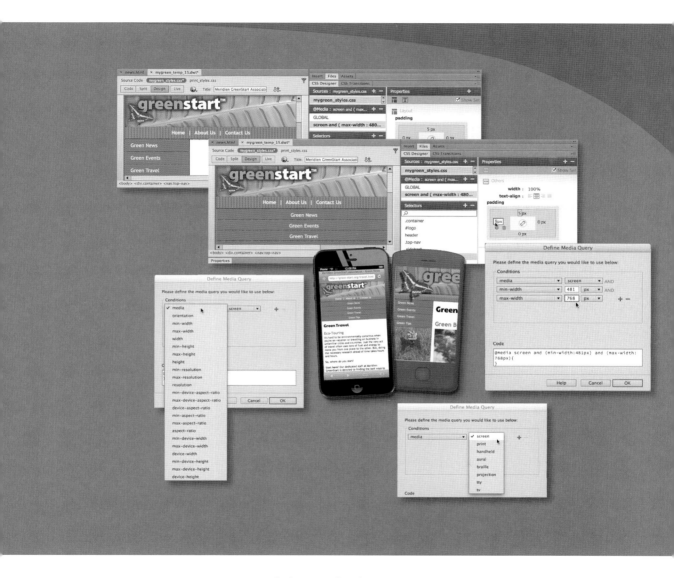

The latest trend on the web is designing your website to respond automatically to smart phones and mobile devices. Dreamweaver has powerful tools to make your site mobile-ready.

● **Note:** If you
have not already
downloaded the project
files for this lesson to
your computer from
your Account page,
make sure to do so now.
See "Getting Started"
at the beginning of
the book.

● **Note:** If you are
completing this lesson
separately from the
rest of the lessons in
book, see the detailed
"Jumpstart" instructions
in the "Getting Started"
section at the beginning
of the book. Then, follow
the steps in this exercise.

Previewing your completed file

To view the completed version of the file you will create in this lesson, let's preview
the page in Dreamweaver.

1   Open **news_finished.html** in Design view. Select Live view.

2   Choose 768 x 1024 Tablet from the Screen Size pop-up menu at the bottom of
the document window.

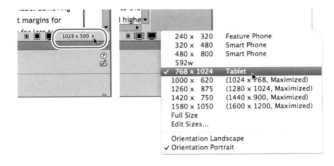

Note how the Tablet Size Resolution Switcher appears selected at the bottom
of the document window. The document window resizes to 768 pixels by 1024
pixels. The content changes and adapts to the new dimensions. A new header
image is visible, and the text and headings resize to fit the available space.

3   Click the Tablet Size (■) Resolution Switcher to return to the original screen
dimensions.

4   Drag the divider at the right edge of the document window to the left.

Note how the display in the Screen Size pop-up menu changes to show you the
current height and width of the Design view window.

5   Resize the document window from full size down to approximately 300 pixels
in width. Observe how the page reformats interactively as it resizes to desktop,
tablet, and phone dimensions.

Note how the design and appearance of page components change based on the
size of the window.

6   Preview the page in a browser.

7 Resize the browser window from full size down to approximately 300 pixels in width. Observe how the browser window mimics the display in Dreamweaver.

● **Note:** Some browsers will not scale down below a minimum size.

The browser display mimics the same behaviors you witnessed in Dreamweaver.

8 Close the browser. Close **news_finished.html**.

This exercise has demonstrated some of the ways you can adapt your web design to the environment of smart phones and other mobile devices.

Designing for mobile devices

The Internet was never conceived for smart phones and tablets. For the first decade, the worst a programmer or developer had to worry about was the difference between a 13- and 15-inch monitor. For years, resolutions and screens sizes only increased over time. In fact, by 2007 over 80 percent of all computers using the Internet were recorded using screen resolutions greater than 1024 pixels by 768 pixels. But, all that is ancient history.

Today, the chances that some or all your visitors are using a smart phone or tablet to access your site are increasing exponentially day by day. Two basic tools—*media type* and *media query*—help you adapt your site and content to this changing landscape; they enable browsers to sense what type of device is accessing the webpage and then load the appropriate style sheet, if one exists.

Media type property

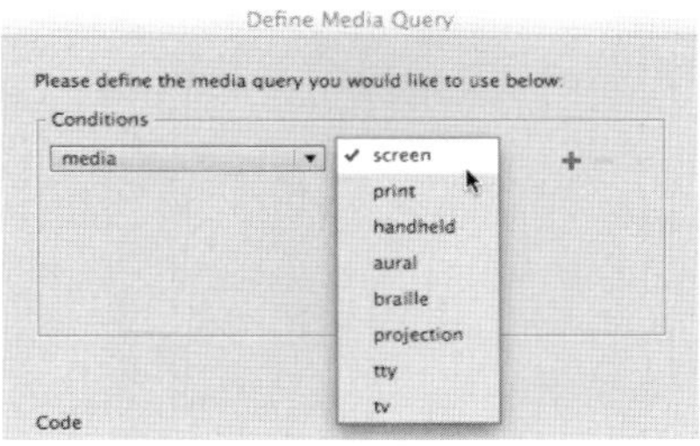

The media type property was added to the CSS2 specifications and adopted in 1998. It was intended to address the proliferation of noncomputer devices that were able to access the web and web-based resources at that time. As you saw with the print-based style sheet, customized formatting is useful to reformat or optimize web content for different media or output.

In all, CSS2 included ten individually defined media types.

Table 15.1 Media type properties

PROPERTY	INTENDED USE
all	Compatible with all devices
aural	Speech synthesizers
braille	Braille tactile feedback devices
embossed	Braille printers
handheld	Handheld devices (small screen, monochrome, limited bandwidth)
print	Documents viewed onscreen in print preview mode and for printing applications
projection	Projected presentations
screen	Primarily for color computer screens
tty	Media using a fixed-pitch character grid, such as teletypes, terminals, or portable
tv	Television-type devices (low resolution, color, limited-scrollability screens, sound available)

In Lesson 5, you created the overall design of the website as it should appear on a standard desktop computer display based on the *screen* media type. Then, you learned how to adapt the existing screen styles to build an alternate style sheet for use with print applications using the print media type property.

While the media type property works fine for screen and print, it never really caught on with browsers used on cell phones and other mobile devices. Part of the problem is the sheer variety of devices in all shapes and sizes. Add to this smorgasbord equally diverse hardware and software capabilities and you've produced a nightmare environment for the modern web designer. But all is not lost.

Media queries

A media query is a newer CSS function that allows code in the webpage to interactively determine not only what kind of device is displaying the page but also what dimensions and orientation it's using. Once the media query knows what type or size of device it has encountered, it will then instruct the browser to load the specified resources to format the webpage and content. This process is as fluid and continuous as a precision dance routine, allowing the user to switch orientations during a session and have the page and content adapt seamlessly without other intervention. The key to this ballet is the development of style sheets optimized for specific browsers, specific devices, or both.

How your site deals with smart phones and mobile devices will depend on whether you're adapting an existing site or developing a new one from scratch. For an existing site, you will first have to create a basic method of treating the underlying design of the site's main components. Then, you'll have to work through each page one at a time to assess existing components individually—like images and tables—that do not inherently adapt to the specific environment.

For new websites, the typical approach is to build *in* the adaptability as you create the overall design, and then build each page to achieve maximum flexibility. In either case, to truly support a mobile design some site components may need to be replaced, left out of the final design altogether, or swapped out live by JavaScript or by the media query itself.

Since the GreenStart site has already been completed, we'll opt for the first method. In Dreamweaver CC, you can proceed in a few ways. You can create the style sheets first and then attach them through a media query; you can create the media query first, then create style sheets later; or you can build the design as you go, live within Dreamweaver. To help demonstrate how media queries work, in this exercise, we'll build the styles interactively.

1   Open **news.html** in Design view.

This page is typical of most of the content in the GreenStart site. You should start working with a page that represents the majority of your website content. When you complete the basic design, you'll then have to adapt content that doesn't work well in a mobile environment, such as tables, web video, and animation.

To see how the page reacts (or doesn't) to a mobile environment, you can simply adjust the width of the Dreamweaver document window. The program is configured to respond using media queries to changes in the document window dimensions. In other words, what you see happening in Design view should be what happens on an actual device using the same dimensions.

2   Drag the edge of the document window to the left to make it narrower.

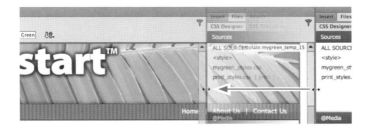

Dreamweaver also offers a built-in feature that can adapt the document window to precise dimensions.

3 Click the Tablet Size (768 x 1024) (▣) Resolution Switcher.

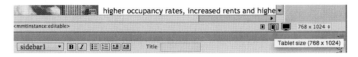

The window is resized to 768 pixels by 1024 pixels. The window dimensions are displayed interactively by the Screen Size pop-up menu. Watch as the dimensions change based on your selections.

4 Click the Mobile Size (468 x 800) (▣) Resolution Switcher.

The window is resized to 468 pixels by 800 pixels. As the window gets smaller, the only thing changing on the screen are the dimensions displayed at the bottom.

Since the GreenStart page is designed to use a fixed width, the changes to the document window have no effect on the design. Instead of adapting to the smaller window, the document merely displays a scroll bar you can use to view the obscured content.

Smart phones and mobile devices may display webpages that are not mobile-ready in different ways.

The display within Dreamweaver may not give you an accurate depiction of what will happen on a mobile device. On an actual cell phone or tablet, the resulting display depends on the manufacturer of the device or the software you are using. Sometimes the device will scale a page down to fit, displaying a miniature version of it, or you may see it as shown in Dreamweaver: full size with a scroll bar. In either case, the experience is suboptimal. A better option would be to develop a style sheet that could adapt the content more equitably to the new environment, making it easier to read and access. Luckily, this is easy to do in Dreamweaver CC.

Creating a media query for smart phones

The first step is to target the screen dimensions of a specific device. If you don't know the size of the device you want to support, you can typically obtain the information on the web, directly from the manufacturer, or from a variety of public forums or from sites that support the web developer community.

Once you know the size, you then adjust the display within Dreamweaver to match it. Besides the three media preset options, Dreamweaver also offers several other optional dimensions and the ability to set your own sizes.

1 From the Screen Sizes pop-up menu, choose 320 x 480 Smart Phone.

The document is now displayed in a window 320 pixels by 480 pixels. This is the standard dimension of an iPhone oriented vertically. To create a custom media query, you need to access the @Media pane in the CSS Designer. You can add a media query to an existing style sheet or create a whole new style sheet for each device or category, such as phone, tablet, and desktop. For our purposes, we'll just add the media query to our existing screen-based style sheet.

Note: Although new iPhones feature a higher-resolution Retina display, the phone should scale the smaller screen size up to fit.

2 In the Sources pane, select **mygreen_styles.css**.

3 In the @Media pane, click the Add Media Query (➕) icon.

The Define Media Query dialog box enables you to build the query interactively. The first query you're going to build will style smart phones 480 pixels wide and smaller.

4 Click to open the first pop-up Conditions menu.

This menu provides a list of conditions—such as media-type or minimum or maximum width—that need to be met before the query can be applied.

5 Open the second pop-up menu.

This menu provides a list of options for each condition. For example, if *media* is selected in the first menu, the second menu supplies the valid media-types that can be used, such as screen, handheld, print, and so on. When you choose an option from either menu, it is added to the query statement, which is displayed at the bottom of the dialog box in the Code window. After you click OK, the media query notation will then be added to one of two places. If you choose to create separate linked style sheets, the media query will be added to the <head> section of the webpage. If you choose to add the media-queries to an existing style sheet, the media query will be inserted within the style sheet itself.

As you can see, Dreamweaver has already created the first condition: *media screen*, which means the style sheet will apply only to devices and browsers that conform to "screen" media types. Next, you specify the width of the device.

6 Move the cursor to the right of the second condition menu.

A plus sign icon appears enabling you to add a new condition.

7 Click the Add Condition (➕) icon.

A new set of condition pop-up menus appears. Note the word AND is added after the first condition. This indicates that both the first and second condition must be met before the query will be applied.

8 Select max-width from the first menu.

A text field appears where you can enter the maximum width supported by this query.

9 Enter **480px**.

If you intend to create a separate media query for smaller devices, you could also enter the minimum width for this query. Instead, we'll just use this query to format all devices 480 pixels wide and smaller.

10 Click OK.

The query statement `screen and (max-width:480px)` now appears in the @Media pane, which reflects the markup added to the actual style sheet.

11 In the Referenced Files list at the top of the document, select **mygreen_styles.css**.

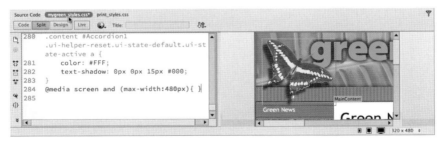

The document window splits, showing the contents of the style sheet on the left side.

12 Scroll to the bottom of the style sheet and examine the media query statement.

The text `@media screen and (max-width:480px){ }` appears at the bottom of the style sheet. For each media query, the applicable rules must be added within the braces { } at the end of the query. When creating CSS rules to style smart phones, be sure to select the appropriate media query first; otherwise the rule will apply to the page in general. In the next exercise, you'll learn how to add CSS rules to your media query.

Media queries: in or out?

A media query tells the browser or device what CSS asset to use to style your webpage. The media query can appear in the <head> section of your page where it can load separate, externally linked (or embedded) style sheets. Or, the query can be added within your existing style sheet itself. So, which method is better/preferred? As with most things on the web, the answer is: It depends.

Adding a query to the <head> section is used normally for linked CSS files. Since the query is in the <head> and not in the style sheet, you can add it to some pages but not to others, as needed. It allows you to more easily customize the design and keep style sheets separate for easier maintenance. But it also means that the browser must wait for multiple files to download before it can render the webpage. If all your style sheets use media queries, there will be no inheritance between the sheets. Each style sheet will have to include all the styles needed to format every part of the page.

Adding the media queries internally in a single CSS file simplifies the workflow and download time (only one file). It can also end up with a smaller CSS footprint overall; since the page can inherit styles from rules that are not controlled by a media query, you only need to create rules that will reset aspects of the page that need to change.

Neither method is perfect; both have advantages and disadvantages. At least for the near future, how you use media queries may come down to personal preference.

Adding rules to a media query

Now that you've added the media query notation in mygreen_styles.css, you're ready to start creating your first mobile CSS rules. As you can see from the resized document window, there's just not much room for the page components using the existing styling. Users are accustomed to scrolling up and down, but not left to right. We need to resize the page components to fit the narrower space and take a different spin on the design.

Before we can make the needed changes, the first step is to identify the rules controlling the basic structure of the page, such as the header, footer, sidebar, and main content areas. In some cases, you will have to create new rules, but more frequently you'll need to reset rules applied by the main style sheet. You can identify these rules with the CSS Designer and techniques you've used throughout the book.

1   In **news.html**, insert the cursor in the *Green News* heading. Examine the rules displayed in the CSS Designer Selectors pane and the tag selectors along the bottom of the document.

The CSS Designer displays the rules responsible for formatting the heading. The tag selectors reveal the underlying HTML structure. The <h1> element is contained within <article.content>, which appears within an editable region controlled by the default site template. The remaining tag selectors for the main components of the page are actually dimmed, indicating that they are locked and uneditable. You can confirm that the top of the pages is undeditable by simply positioning the cursor over the header, or the horizontal or vertical menus, where you will see the locked (⊘) icon.

Although Dreamweaver restricts you from editing the HTML, you can still create and edit any CSS rules using any of the template-based site pages by just using Code view. But, working initially in the site template to build and troubleshoot your mobile styling will be faster and easier.

2   Open **mygreen_temp.dwt** from the Template folder in Split view. Select 320 x 480 Smart Phone from the Sizes pop-up.

● **Note:** If you're using the Jumpstart method, the template may be named mygreen_temp_14.dwt.

The template appears in the document window resized to 320 pixels by 480 pixels. In the template all the boilerplate content is unlocked; you'll be able to insert the cursor in the document <header> and select any element within the layout.

3   Insert the cursor in the <header#top> element. Examine the list of selectors displayed in the CSS Designer. Note the specifications displayed for each rule, especially any that apply width, height, and positioning commands.

▶ **Tip:** You may need to use Code view to properly select certain elements.

4   Repeat this process with the horizontal menu, vertical menu, main content, and footer sections of the page.

As you build a site and add pages, you should be growing more familiar with the basic structure and the CSS rules contributing to the overall design, and especially the main components. Using the CSS Designer or the Code Navigator, identifying the rules that format these components is a simple matter, which include but are not limited to:

- .container
- header
- #logo
- .top-nav
- .sidebar1

- `nav li a:link, nav li a:visited`

- `.content`

- `footer`

Part of the trick to creating style sheets that work for multiple environments is deciding how you want to display text and graphics on screens of different sizes, as well as deciding which elements you want to display and which you want to hide. For example, the current page features a multicolumn design that would be hard to view and use on the small screen of a cell phone. One option is to simply linearize the layout by removing the `float` properties from the main elements and adjusting the width to fit, to make one single long column instead of two.

Let's start with the width of the entire page and then work down to the subcomponents that make up the page. By now you should know that the width of the page overall is set by the `.container` rule.

▶ **Tip:** You may not be able to add a selector for the media query if you don't first select the style sheet name and then the media query in the CSS Designer.

5 In the Sources pane, select **mygreen_styles.css**.
   In the @Media pane, select `screen and (max-width:480px)`.
   In the Selectors pane, click the Add Selector (⊞) icon.

   The `.container` selector appears in the CSS Designer. It's also added to the style sheet within the media query notation.

6 Press Enter/Return to complete the selector name. In the Properties pane, create the following specification: `width: 100%`

   By using a percentage-based measurement, the page will scale automatically to fit devices 480 pixels and smaller, allowing it to adapt to multiple devices with a single media query.

   The `.container` rule also formats the faux column on the template. Since the phone design will feature only one column, you won't need the background-image, and you can turn it off.

7 Add the following property to the `.container` rule: `background-image: none`

When the new rule is completed, it will apply immediately to the page and its components. You may have noticed that the `.container` rule you just created is a duplicate of one already in the main style sheet. Normally, if you inserted an identical rule into the style sheet you'd have to worry about conflicts with existing styling, or other unintended consequences. But, the media query precludes such conflicts. The new styles will be employed only when the browser or device meets the criteria established by the query. But keeping the rules all in one sheet pays some side benefit: You can still use inheritance when styles remain the same between devices. This means you don't have to provide an entire style sheet each time, only the rules needed for the specific device or browser.

After the width was changed, you may have noticed that the placeholders for the headings and text appearing in `<article.content>` dropped down below the content displayed in `<sidebar1>`. The new rule has reset the size of the page to 100 percent of the screen width. Without a predefined width of 950 pixels, there's no room for the `<article>` element or its content so it moves down the page until it can find space to display.

The next component to deal with is the butterfly logo. It's too big to use on a small screen, so let's hide it.

8 Select the butterfly image. Select the `<div#logo>` tag selector.

9 If necessary, select `screen and (max-width:480px)` in the @Media pane.

10 Create a new `#logo` selector with the following specification: `display: none`

● **Note:** When you select a media query in the @Media pane, the document may resize to the specifications listed therein.

The `<div#logo>` vanishes from the layout. Next, let's load a different background image in the `<header>` element.

11 In the mobile media query, create a new **header** selector. Add the following properties:

```
background-image: banner-phone.jpg
height: 90px
```

The new background image takes up much less space than the normal image.

Adapting CSS navigation to mobile environments

Now, let's reformat the horizontal and vertical menus. The template should still be open and displayed in Design view.

1 Insert the cursor in the *About Us* link.

You can see by the CSS Designer display what rules format the horizontal menu. The most important is: `.top-nav`.

2 Create a new `.top-nav` selector in the mobile media query. Add the following properties:

```
text-align: center
padding-top: 5 px
padding-right: 0 px
padding-bottom: 5 px
padding-left: 0 px
```

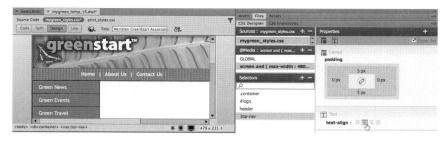

The next major component we have to adapt is the vertical menu. The menu is part of `<div.sidebar1>`. To make the menu work in this environment, you'll have to adjust both the sidebar and the menu itself. When making an element wider, always start with the parent element.

3 In the mobile media query, create a new `.sidebar1` selector.

4 Add the following properties:

```
width: 100%
float: none
```

You may notice that the sidebar expands to fit the screen but the menu has a width specification of its own and has remained at the original size.

5   Insert the cursor into any links within the vertical menu. Examine the CSS Designer display to identify the rule controlling the width of the menu.

The nav li a:link, nav li a:visited rule applies a fixed width of 180 pixels.

6   Add a new nav li a:link, nav li a:visited rule with the following properties:

```
width: 100%
text-align: center
padding-top: 5 px
padding-right: 0 px
padding-bottom: 5 px
padding-left: 0 px
```

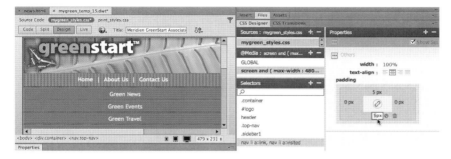

The text is centered and the menu now adapts nicely to the smaller screen size. The remainder of the sidebar holds a picture and caption that aren't essential and can be hidden. This content is contained in an <aside> element.

7   Add a new aside rule with a display: none property.

The image placeholder and the caption disappear. Don't be confused by this CSS-based sleight of hand; although the element doesn't appear on the screen, the code is still downloaded to the phone. Substituting background graphics and hiding content are only two methods of dealing with the smaller screens of smart phones and tablets. Some developers don't agree with these methods.

They believe downloading pages and content built for desktop computers unfairly burdens the bandwidth and storage capabilities of these devices. Many think that a better way is to build a companion or duplicate website optimized for these devices. Such mobile-optimized sites contain only content designed specifically for smaller screens. See the sidebar "Mobile-ready vs. mobile-optimized" for more information on these two concepts.

● **Note:** When you hide the <aside> element, the Editable Region tab may still be visible in Design view, but there will be no trace of this content in Live view or the browser.

Mobile-ready vs. mobile-optimized

Hiding elements is not an ideal solution in all situations. The elements and the associated code are still downloaded even if they're not displayed. If you find yourself hiding an inordinate amount of content or see that you have a large number of visitors via phones and tablets, you may want to consider creating a separate mobile-optimized site.

A mobile-optimized site is often hosted on a subdomain, like *mobile.yourdomain.com*, and contains pages designed specifically for mobile devices. These sites not only reduce page size, they may also select, or filter, content appropriate for the specific device. For example, some sites remove all images, tables, and other large elements that don't scale down very well.

Obviously, producing two or more completely different sites can drastically increase design and maintenance costs, especially if the content changes on a regular basis. So, one good option is to create a website based on an online database or content management system (CMS) like Drupal, Joomla, or WordPress.

A CMS can dynamically create pages as needed based on a template and style sheets with no additional effort. You could create pages for your regular site and a mobile-optimized site for multiple screen sizes simply by creating new templates and deciding what content to display on each.

Styling the main content

The last components that need to be formatted are `<article.content>` and `<footer>`. The `<article.content>` element holds the main content of the page and needs some attention. The template should still be open and displayed in Design view.

1   Insert the cursor in `<div.content>` and identify the applicable rules in the style sheet.

2   Add a new `.content` rule with the following properties:

```
width: 100%
float: none
```

The text and headings are designed to be viewed on a full-sized screen. They look too big on the small screen.

3   Add the following rules and properties:

```
.content h1 { font-size: 150%; padding-left:10px; }
.content section h2 { font-size: 130%; padding-left:10px; }
.content section h3 { font-size: 110%; padding-left:10px; }
.content section p { padding-left:10px; }
```

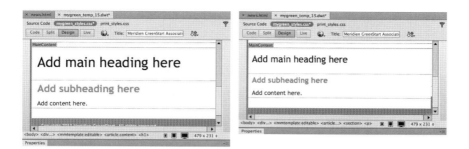

Fonts and colors are still being inherited from the main style sheet, but these rules will maximize the amount of text that can appear in the main content section without wasting space on the cell phone. Also we can adjust the content of the <footer> element.

4 Add the following rule and properties to the media query:

```
footer { font-size: 80%; padding-left:10px; }
```

The basic design of the media query is complete.

5 Save all files. Update child pages, if necessary.

All the changes have been made to the external CSS **mygreen_styles.css** file and not to the template. So, the Update Pages dialog box should not appear when you save the files after creating the media query. But allowing Dreamweaver to update child pages when prompted is a good practice in case you missed some essential change made to the template.

You're ready to test the new media query now.

Testing a media query

Testing a media query can be done easily in Dreamweaver. In fact, most CSS styling can be viewed accurately right in Design view. The template should still be open and displayed in Design view

1 Click the Desktop Size (1000w) (▣) Resolution Switcher.

The document window changes to 1000 pixels wide. The media query is no longer in effect, and the page returns to the original design. No trace of any changes you made should be visible.

2 Click the Tablet Size (768 x 1024) (▣) Resolution Switcher.

The document window changes to 768 pixels by 1024 pixels. Since the page is larger than 480 pixels, the media query has not kicked in.

3 Click the Mobile Size (468 x 800) (■) Resolution Switcher.

The document window changes to 468 pixels by 800 pixels. This display invokes the media query, and the page components resize and reformat as specified. To see how your media query works on smaller screens, you'll have to use some manual intervention.

4 Click the Mobile Size (468 x 800) icon again.

Clicking the icon a second time turns off the Mobile Size screen preview mode. The document window resizes to the full dimensions of the program interface, allowing you to manually resize the window.

5 Drag the divider at the right edge of the document window to the left to make it narrower. Watch the screen size pop-up menu display; it displays the current size of the Design view window. Keep dragging the divider until the width becomes narrower than 480 pixels.

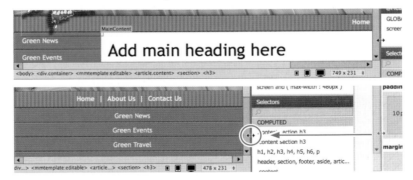

When the screen size reaches 480 pixels, the preview of the page switches to the design applied by the media query, which controls the basic design for all screens 480 pixels wide and smaller.

6 Drag the divider to the right to make the window wider than 480 pixels.

As soon as the screen hits a width of 481 pixels, the display reverts back to the default style sheet specifications.

The basic design and formatting of all main page components are controlled by the media query. But, to see web fonts and other types of dynamic functionality, you'll have to switch to Live view.

7 Click the Live view button, and repeat steps 5 and 6 to test the media query. Test the interactivity of the vertical and horizontal menus while the page is displayed at 480 pixels or less. Look for any inconsistencies in the behaviors or formatting of all components and placeholders.

Background images and web fonts appear and display properly. The page resizes and reformats as before. The menus react as they do at normal size.

Congratulations, you've completed your first media query. Unfortunately, you're not finished. Once the basic layout has been adapted to the new media, you will need to test each page of the site to determine if any page components or content also need to be modified by specific CSS rules.

For example, pictures and tables are especially problematic in adapting websites to mobile environments. Normally, pictures and tables have fixed widths and heights designed to display in a desktop browser. Fixed dimensions don't automatically scale or adapt to changes in the viewport. Obviously, specifying fixed sizes won't work for multiple environments, but what's the alternative?

Responsive design

One trend is to turn to *responsive* web design, a term coined by Ethan Marcotte, a web designer and developer based in Boston. He describes this new technique in his book by the same name: *Responsive Web Design* (A Book Apart, 2011). To obtain a copy of his revolutionary book, go to www.abookapart.com/products/responsive-web-design.

Essentially, he advocates not applying fixed dimensions to images, but setting their width based on the relationship of the image to its containing element. That way if the containing element is set to adapt to different devices, so will the images. The main downside to this method is that it requires some math.

1 Close the template. Save any changes and update child pages.

2 If necessary, switch to or open **news.html**. Switch to Design view and display the page at full size in the document window.

3 In the `article.content` element, select the first image (**city.jpg**) and note its current dimensions: 200 pixels by 335 pixels.

4   In the Property inspector, select the dimensions and delete them.

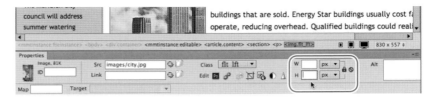

Don't worry, Dreamweaver and all the modern browsers can determine the actual size of the image and display it properly even without the dimensions supplied by the code.

5   Select the image and note the names and order of the tag selectors.

The image was inserted in a `<p>` element, which is part of `<section>` appearing within `<article.content>`. To apply a responsive attribute to the image, you first have to determine which, if any, of these *parent* elements has a formatted width.

6   Examine the CSS rules to determine the width of the nearest parent containing the image. Start with the `<p>` element and then work to the left toward `<body>`.

No width is applied to `<p>` or `<section>`. The element `<article.content>` has a width of 770 pixels. Now for the math part.

7   Divide the width of the image by the width of the parent element:

$$200 \div 770 = .25974026$$

The result is the width of the image as it relates to the width of the parent element at full size. Because you are specifying the width of the image as a percentage, the browser can automatically scale the image properly each time the container adapts to a new media. One way to apply this new dimension is via an inline CSS style.

8   If necessary, select the **city.jpg** image in Design view. Switch to Code view.

The image element is selected in Code view.

9   Locate the opening `<img>` tag for the image, and insert the cursor after the last attribute.

10 Press the spacebar to insert a new space, and type `style="width:25.974026%"`

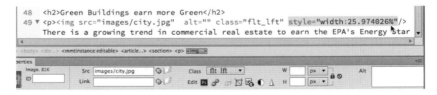

By using the entire fraction, you are enforcing the relationship with the most accuracy. Don't worry, the browser can handle the math.

11 Switch back to Design view. If necessary, click in the Design view window to refresh the display.

The display may appear odd in Design view, but don't worry, it will appear correctly in Live view and, more importantly, in your browser.

12 Select Live view.

The image displays at the correct width now; the height will resolve itself automatically. Since most elements don't have a specific height, there's no easy way to create this dimension—and luckily, there's no need to.

13 Choose 320 x 480 Smart Phone from the Screen Size pop-up menu.

The image scales down to approximately 25 percent of the new window, and the best thing is that the new setting will work at any dimension you support with a media query.

14 Switch off Live view. Select the next image in the layout (**farmersmarket.png**) and observe its dimensions: 300 x 300. Delete both settings.

15 Divide the image width by the container width, as before:

300 ÷ 770 = .38961039

16 Switch to Code view, and insert the following code within the image reference:

```
style="width:38.961039%"
```

The image resizes.

17 Repeat steps 14 through 16 with the **recycling.jpg** image.

18 Save all files.

The *news* page is complete and fully responsive, but this is only the start. You'll have to go through the entire site and adapt all the images using the same method. After addressing the images, you also have to adapt other page components, like tables, videos, animation, and even interactive elements, like the jQuery Accordion.

Adapting page components

Adapting page components is a mixed bag. Some will be easier than others to adapt. In some cases, the easiest method is simply to hide the component altogether.

1   Open **travel.html** in Design view. Display the page at full size.

The page contains an Edge Animate banner ad, a web video, and a table. All the components were designed for a desktop environment.

2   Choose 320 x 480 Smart Phone from the Screen Size pop-up menu.

The document window resizes to the selected dimensions.

3   Select Live view. Observe each of the page elements to see how they appear in the document window.

None of the components adapts to the smaller screen. The animation and video play normally but the visitor would miss most of the content because of the window size.

Although you could create an animation that would scale responsively to fit the screen, you'd have to do it in Edge Animate itself. Nothing can be done inside Dreamweaver to adapt this animation without a lot of unnecessary work. If you can't get a new *responsive* animation to replace, the best thing to do is to hide the animation altogether.

4   Shut off Live view and select the `<object#EdgeID>` tag selector.

The document window remains at the dimensions 320 pixels by 480 pixels.

5   In the Sources pane, select **mygreen_styles.css**. In the @Media pane, select `screen and (max-width:480px)`.

6 Create a `.content #Edge` rule with the property: `display: none`

The animation disappears from the document window.

7 Choose Full Size from the Screen Size pop-up menu.

The animation appears in the full-size layout. The media query will hide the animation on the smaller screen but display it properly on a desktop computer.

The next item to deal with is the HTML5 video component. In most cases, you can deal with a video the same way you adapt images.

8 Select the video placeholder in the layout. Observe the dimensions of the video element.

If you divide the video width (300 pixels) by the width of `<article.content>`, the result is .54948052.

9 Delete the width and height specifications for the `<video>` element, and add the following attribute: `style="width: 51.948052%"`

● **Note:** Since it's not compatible with cell phones and tablets, there's no need to adapt the width and height specifications listed within the embedded Flash fallback code.

10 Save all files.

11 Select Live view and test the video in a full-size window and a window sized at 320 pixels by 480 pixels.

The video scales to fit both windows and plays as normal. Scaling is only one method of dealing with video. Designers are still experimenting and developing new ways of using or hiding video and animation in responsive ways. For some more ideas on how to work with video, check out these links:

▶ **Tip:** You may not see a visible play control on the video in Live view, but if you click to the left side of the progress bar, the video will play.

- http://tinyurl.com/fluid-video-1
- http://tinyurl.com/fluid-video-2
- http://tinyurl.com/fluid-video-3

The last component you need to deal with is the table.

Creating a responsive HTML table

Tables by their very nature are not responsive design. Built with rows and columns of text and images, tables offer a daunting challenge to a would-be responsive designer. Unfortunately, there's no simple, neat, and tidy solution to this problem. You can't always scale tables to fit or hide the content. Each table must be addressed individually. And, the solution may not always be desirable. You can get an idea of what issues you will need to address by tackling the travel page's table.

The table features five rows and two columns. In the second column, four rows are merged into one cell to accommodate an image advertising the GreenStart Eco-Tour of Paris. In Lesson 10, you created nifty interactive rollover effects for each of the links to swap the advertisement for a specific image of the four stops on the tour. The image is 250 pixels wide, and the table has a formatted width of 700 pixels. Scaling the table by itself won't reproduce the same effect on a smartphone that we see on a larger display, and the rollover effects won't work properly on touch screens anyway, since there's no mouse to roll over the link. In cases like this, you need to be ready to ditch a design element to produce a more effective experience for the mobile user.

1 If necessary open **travel.html** in Design view.
   Click the Mobile Size 480 x 800 (▣) Resolution Switcher.

2 Scroll down below the video element and insert the cursor in the table.

   Select the `<table>` tag selector.

   First, you should deal with the overall width of the element. To assist in the job of controlling table styling, assign either an ID or class attribute to each table. An ID allows you to target tables individually, whereas with class attributes you can control several tables at once.

3 Insert the cursor in the ID field of the Property inspector. Enter **travel**, and press Enter/Return.

   The tag selector is now `<table#travel>`.

4 In the `screen and (max-width:480px)` media query, create a `#travel` rule.

5 Add the property: `width: 90%`

   Now we'll deal with the second column containing the image. Since we don't need the rollover effects on a mobile device, just hiding the column completely will be best.

6 In the `screen and (max-width:480px)` media query, create a `.hide` rule.

   Creating a rule with a generic name like this will allow you to use it anytime to hide components within the media query and elsewhere.

7 Add the property `display: none`

8   Select the image in the right column of the table. Select the `<td>` tag selector.

9   In the Property inspector, choose hide from the Class menu.

The tag selector displays `<td.hide>`, but the image still displays in Design view. In this case, to see the final effect you will have to view the page in Live view.

10 Save all files. Select Live view. Observe the content of the entire page.

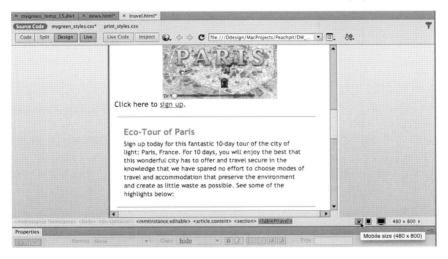

The second column in the table and the image disappear. The table displays now in a single column of text.

You have learned how to adapt or hide various types of HTML content for responsive designs, such as images, video, animation, and tables. The jQuery Accordion is the only component remaining yet to be adapted.

Adapting jQuery Accordions to responsive design

With Dreamweaver's variety of jQuery widgets, you can produce amazing interactivity in your site content. Since the widgets are built with standard HTML code and JavaScript, they should function fine even on smart phones and tablets. The only thing you may have to do is adapt the width and height of specific components or reformat the content itself.

1   Open **tips.html** in Design view. Choose 320 x 480 Smart Phone from the Screen Size pop-up menu.

The jQuery Accordion itself has no problems adapting to the smaller document size, but the size of the text seems a bit large, and the text in the bulleted list is indented too far.

2　Select **mygreen_styles.css** in the Sources pane. Select `screen and` `(max-width:480px)` in the @Media pane. Create a new rule: `.content Accordion1`

3　Add the property: `font-size: 80%`

The text within the tabs and content panes scales to 80 percent of its original size.

▶ **Tip:** The padding property may not appear properly in Design view. Use Live view to preview the effect or preview in a browser.

4　Create a new rule `.content Accordion1 ul` with the following properties:

`padding-left: 15px`
`padding-right: 15px`

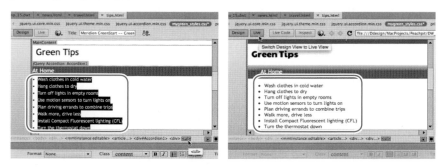

The bulleted list within the Accordion expands to fill the content pane more effectively.

5　Save all files

The basic design and major content elements have been adapted to the new media query. Depending on how much detail you want to delve into, there are other aspects of the design you can address. Some suggestions include removing excessive margins and paddings, reducing the size of text and headings, changing the color of all the text to black (or another legible color), and so on. When you're finished, be sure to save all the related files and use the Screen Size interface to test the new style sheet in all appropriate screen dimensions.

Creating style sheets for tablets

The process for creating a style sheet optimized for a tablet is identical to that of creating a style sheet for smart phones, with a few minor exceptions. The main exception is that the tablet's larger screen size means that you will probably have to do a lot less work to adapt the current page design. In fact, most tablet dimensions are large enough that you may want to just create a smaller version of the existing design.

The first step is to set up the design interface for the tablet design.

1　If necessary, open **news.html**.

2 Click the Tablet Size (768 x 1024) (▣) Resolution Switcher.

The screen resizes to show the default size of the first-generation iPad.

3 In the Sources pane, select **mygreen_styles.css**. In the @Media pane, click the Add Media Query (✚) icon.

The Define Media Query dialog box opens with the *screen* condition already selected.

4 Click the Add Condition (✚) icon.

A new line appears below the media: screen condition.

5 Select min-width from the first condition pop-up menu.

6 Enter **481 px**.

This entry will allow the tablet media query to format devices larger than 480 pixels.

7 Click the Add Condition (✚) icon.

A third condition is added to the media query.

8 Select max-width from the first menu.

A text field appears where you can enter the maximum width supported by this query.

9 Enter **768 px**. Click OK.

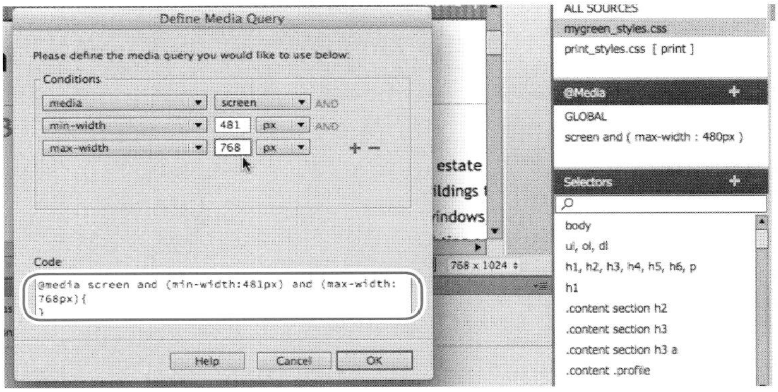

Next, establishing the width of the tablet design is a good idea, because everything else flows from it. As with the base design, let's use a fixed width. It is not an ideal decision to use a fixed width, but few devices fall between these dimensions. This media query is really intended as a catch-all style sheet to format tablet devices held in portrait mode, although it will work for any device supporting resolutions between 481 and 768 pixels.

10 Create a new `.container` rule with the property: `width: 750px`

11 Create a new `.content` rule with the property: `width: 570 px`

12 Create a new **header** rule with the following properties:

```
background-image: banner-tablet.jpg
height: 90 px
```

13 Save all files. Test the new style sheet in Live view and your favorite browsers as described earlier.

That's it. The portrait version of the tablet style sheet is finished. Since we didn't have to modify `<div.sidebar1>`, feel free to tweak the design of the tablet style sheet as much as you want. When you rotate the tablet into landscape mode, the standard desktop style sheet will kick in. Since there is no predefined style sheet for screens wider than 768 pixels, the device should use the default style sheet and merely scale the page down to fit the screen. The landscape screens should be able to support the default styles, but feel free to create and adapt custom media queries for as many resolutions as you think necessary.

Edge Inspect

● **Note:** Edge Inspect works only in Google Chrome (www.google.com/chrome) at the time of this writing.

Another way to test your mobile design is to use a program called Adobe Edge Inspect, which is one of a new family of web-design tools available exclusively through Adobe Creative Cloud. You can learn more about Edge Inspect at http://html.adobe.com/edge/inspect/.

Edge Inspect is designed to mirror the screen display of your laptop or desktop browser via Bluetooth on a variety of mobile devices. Just download Edge Inspect to your computer and install the app. Additionally, a free companion app is available for most smart phones and tablets and must be installed on each device before you begin. Then, check out how your mobile web design responds on an actual phone or tablet without having to upload any files to the Internet.

All you need to do is launch Adobe Edge Inspect and the Google Chrome browser on your desktop or laptop computer. Then launch Edge Inspect on one or more mobile devices, and sync them all to your computer by Bluetooth using the Chrome plug-in. Switch to Dreamweaver and open the file you want to test. Choose File > Preview in Browser, and choose Google Chrome from the list. Activate the Inspect browser (In) plug-in and the next thing you'll see is the sample page mirrored on all your mobile devices.

Once your mobile devices are synced to your computer, they will mirror the browser display and load any pertinent CSS styling. If you rotate the device to change the width, the appropriate media query will kick in and alter the display as specified.

Congratulations, you successfully developed a mobile-enabled website design. Although it's hard to imagine what amazing new features may appear, Dreamweaver clearly continues to be at the forefront of web development. With support for media queries and other responsive techniques, the program continues to innovate.

More information

To learn more about media queries and how to work with them, check out the following links:

* Adobe: http://tinyurl.com/adobe-media-queries
* W3C Consortium: http://tinyurl.com/w3c-media-queries
* Smashing Magazine: http://tinyurl.com/media-queries-smashing

Review questions

1   What are media queries?

2   How do media queries target a specific device or screen size?

3   What can you do with the screen resolution switchers?

4   Do you have to worry about CSS inheritance when using media queries?

5   What happens to the webpage display if you rotate the device?

6   What function does Edge Inspect perform?

Review answers

1   Media queries are a CSS3 specification for loading style sheets interactively, based on the size and other characteristics of the device viewing the webpage.

2   Media queries include a logical expression that instructs the browser what style sheet to load, based on screen and device characteristics.

3   You can instantly switch the Dreamweaver document window to mobile, tablet, and desktop display sizes to test specific media queries.

4   Yes. If all style sheets are not controlled by media queries, styles may be inherited.

5   Media queries are a live function that will load the appropriate styles, based on a constant interrogation of the browser and device.

6   Edge Inspect is a new Creative Cloud app that allows you to instantly test mobile style sheets by linking your desktop computer to various mobile devices via Bluetooth.

15 ONLINE BONUS LESSON: WORKING WITH CODE

In this lesson, you'll learn how to work with code and do the following:

- Select code elements in new ways
- Collapse and expand code entries
- Write code using code hinting
- Use Code Navigator to identify and edit CSS code
- Use Live Code to test and troubleshoot dynamic code
- Use the Inspect mode to identify HTML elements and associated styling
- Access and edit attached files using the Related Files interface

This lesson will take about 60 minutes to complete. Download the project files for this lesson from the Lesson & Update Files tab on your Account page at www.peachpit.com and store them on your computer in a convenient location, as described in the Getting Started section of this book. Your Accounts page is also where you'll find any updates to the lessons or to the lesson files. Look on the Lesson & Update Files tab to access the most current content.

If you're working with the print edition of this book, you'll find this lesson on your Accounts page at www.peachpit.com.

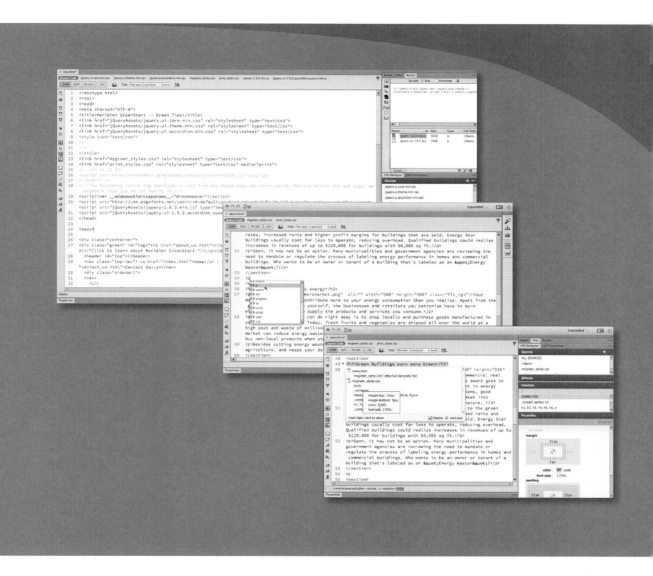

Dreamweaver's claim to fame is as a visually based HTML editor, but its code-editing features don't take a back seat to its graphical interface and offer few compromises to professional coders and developers.

APPENDIX: TINYURLs

Table A.1 TinyURLs

PAGE	TINYURL	FULL URL
Lesson 4		
112	http://tinyurl.com/html-differences	http://www.w3.org/TR/html5-diff/
112	http://tinyurl.com/html-differences-1	http://www.htmlgoodies.com/html5/tutorials/Web-Developer-Basics-Differences-Between-HTML4-And-HTML5-3921271.htm
112	http://tinyurl.com/html-differences-2	http://en.wikipedia.org/wiki/HTML5
Lesson 11		
	http://tinyurl.com/video-HTML5-1	http://www.w3schools.com/html/html5_video.asp
	http://tinyurl.com/video-HTML5-2	http://www.808.dk/?code-html-5-video
	http://tinyurl.com/video-HTML5-3	http://www.htmlgoodies.com/html5/client/how-to-embed-video-using-html5.html
Lesson 12		
	http://tinyurl.com/asp-defined	http://msdn.microsoft.com/en-us/library/aa286483.aspx
	http://tinyurl.com/php-defined	http://php.net/manual/en/intro-whatis.php
	http:// tinyurl.com/asp-formmailer	http://www.devarticles.com/c/a/ASP/Sending-Email-From-a-Form-in-ASP
	http:// tinyurl.com/cf-formmailer	http://www.dreamincode.net/forums/topic/16363-sending-content-in-email-form
	http:// tinyurl.com/php-formmailer	http://www.html-form-guide.com/email-form/php-form-to-email.html
	http://tinyurl.com/html5forms1	http://html5doctor.com/html5-forms-introduction-and-new-attributes
	http://tinyurl.com/html5forms2	http://www.wufoo.com/html5
	http://tinyurl.com/html5forms3	http://www.html5rocks.com/en/tutorials/forms/html5forms

Table A.1 TinyURLs (*continued*)

PAGE	TINYURL	FULL URL
Lesson 13		
376	http://tinyurl.com/setup-coldfusion	http://www.adobe.com/devnet/dreamweaver/articles/setup_cf.html
376	http://tinyurl.com/setup-apachephp	http://www.adobe.com/devnet/dreamweaver/articles/setup_php.html
376	http://tinyurl.com/setup-asp	http://www.adobe.com/devnet/dreamweaver/articles/setup_asp.html
Lesson 14		
413	http://tinyurl.com/fluid-video-1	http://css-tricks.com/NetMag/FluidWidthVideo/Article-FluidWidthVideo.php
413	http://tinyurl.com/fluid-video-2	http://zurb.com/word/responsive-video
413	http://tinyurl.com/fluid-video-3	https://themeid.com/complete-breakdown-of-responsive-videos
413	http://tinyurl.com/adobe-media-queries	http://www.adobe.com/devnet/dreamweaver/articles/introducing-media-queries.html
413	http://tinyurl.com/w3c-media-queries	http://www.w3.org/TR/css3-mediaqueries
413	http://tinyurl.com/media-queries-smashing	http://mobile.smashingmagazine.com/2010/07/19/how-to-use-css3-media-queries-to-create-a-mobile-version-of-your-website

INDEX

SYMBOLS

, (commas), multiple selectors, 169–170
: (colons), generating email forms in PHP, 365
. (period), creating email forms in PHP, 365
/*.*/ (slash and asterisk), comments in CSS, 71
; (semicolon), CSS rule syntax for declarations, 61
$ (dollar sign), PHP variables, 364–365
{} (braces), CSS rule syntax, 60

NUMBERS

1-bit (monochrome) palette, 254
3D visual effect, for menus, 173–174
4-bit color space, 254
8-bit color space, 254–255
16-bit (high-color) palette, 255
24-bit (true color) palette, 255
32-bit color space (alpha transparency), 255–257

A

<a> tag selector
    building menu buttons, 173
    creating descendant selectors, 167–168
    creating dynamic hyperlinks, 168–170
    creating hyperlink text color, 317–319
    creating hyperlinks, 41, 282
    customizing Accordion behavior, 317–318
A:active, 142, 146, 168–172, 183
AATCs (Adobe Authorized Training Centers), 7
Abbreviations, Windows vs. OS X commands, 5
Absolute hyperlinks, 282
Absolute measurements, CSS
    defined, 77
    height, 82–85
    margins and paddings, 85–88
    positioning elements, 88–90
    width, 78–82
ACA (Adobe Certified Associate), 7
Accessibility, adding, 345–348
Accordion. See jQuery Accordion widgets
ACE (Adobe Certified Expert), 7
ACI (Adobe Certified Instructor), 7

Actions, adding to forms, 360–363
Active Server Pages. See ASP (Active Server Pages)
Add Behavior icon, 302, 308–310
Add Condition icon, 399, 417
Add CSS Property icon
    creating text indents, 228
    modifying background color, 125
    modifying existing content, 129–130
    modifying footer, 132
Add Media Query icon, 397, 417
Add New Server icon, 373, 377
Add Selector icon
    adding behaviors to hyperlinks, 311
    adding rules to media query, 402
    creating custom classes, 159
    creating descendant selectors, 167
    creating dynamic hyperlinks, 168
    creating headings, 220
    creating hyperlink rollover effect, 170
    customizing Accordion behavior, 316, 319
    inserting forms on page, 344
    specifying font size, 156
    styling forms, 367–368
    using Edge Web Fonts, 151
Adobe Authorized Training Centers (AATCs), 7
Adobe Bridge, 262–265
Adobe Certified Associate (ACA), 7
Adobe Certified Expert (ACE), 7
Adobe Certified Instructor (ACI), 7
Adobe Edge Animate, 326–330
Adobe Edge Inspect, 418–419
Adobe Edge Web Fonts, 146, 150–153
Adobe Exchange panel, 302–303
Adobe Extension Manager CC, 302
Adobe Flash
    FLV as fallback format for older browsers, 333
    history of and present time, 324
Adobe Muse, 31
A:focus, CSS, 169
Alerts, FTP connection to remote site, 374
Alignment
    adjusting tables for vertical, 240–241
    changing element, 122–123
A:link pseudo-class, hyperlinks, 130, 169

Media queries
  adding in or out, 400
  mobile device design and, 394–397
  mobile device navigation, 404–406
  rules for, 400–404
  smart phone, 397–399
  style sheets for tables, 416–418
Media type property, mobile device design, 393–394
Microsoft Internet Explorer, HTML5 video in, 335
Minimizing, panels, 15–16
Min-width property, relative widths, 79–80
Mobile device design
  adapting jQuery Accordions to responsive, 415–416
  adapting page components, 412–413
  adding CSS navigation, 404–405
  creating responsive HTML table, 414–415
  creating style sheets for tablets, 416–418
  media queries and, 394–397
  media queries for smart phones, 397–399
  media queries in or out, 400
  media query rules, 400–404
  media type property and, 393–394
  mobile-ready vs. mobile-optimized sites, 406
  overview of, 390
  previewing completed file, 392–393
  resources for, 419
  responsive web design, 409–411
  review Q & A, 420
  styling main content, 406–407
  testing media queries, 407–409
  testing with Edge Inspect, 418–419
Mobile Size (468 x 800) Resolution Switcher, 396–397, 408–409, 414
Mobile-optimized sites, vs. mobile-ready, 406
Mockups
  modifying existing CSS layout, 108–113
  page design, 104
Monochrome (1-bit) palette, 254

MP4 file format, web video, 331
Multiple choice, form lists, 359
Muse, Adobe, 31

N

Name attribute, form fields, 347
Named anchors, IDs deprecating, 293–295
Naming conventions
  CSS rules, 236
  editable regions in templates, 191
  form fields, 347
  home page, 380–381
  library item, 198–199
  new site, 105
  radio buttons vs. checkboxes, 353–354
  saving page as template, 189–190
  saving server-side includes, 206
Navigation
  adding CSS to mobile environment, 404–405
  checking page, 298
  creating external link for, 290–291
  creating home page with, 380–382
  creating image-based link for, 289–290
  creating internal hyperlinks for, 286–289
  email link setup for, 292–293
  hyperlinks and, 282–283
  inserting component, 120–121
  modifying existing CSS layout, 111
  overview of, 280
  previewing completed file, 283–285
  review Q & A, 299
  targeting page elements, 293–297
  updating links, 382–383
Network web server, remote site on, 377–378
Nonbreaking space
  adding Submit button to form, 360
  HTML character entity for, 42
  method for inserting HTML, 33
Notepad (Windows), writing HTML code, 32

O

Object formatting, CSS
  borders and backgrounds, 90–91
  height, 82–85
  margins and padding, 85–88
  overview of, 77
  positioning, 88–90
  width, 78–82
<object> tag, HTML5 fix for buggy video, 333
Ogg file format, web video, 331–332
<ol> tag selector, selecting entire list, 223–224
Online resources. See resources, online
OnMouseOut attribute, 309
OnMouseOver attribute, 308–309
Ordered lists, 223–224
OS X instructions, vs. Windows, 5

P

<p> tag selector
  adding form lists, 357
  adding web video, 330–332
  applying inline formatting, 35
  creating external links, 290
  creating headings, 220, 223–224
  creating stand-alone paragraph with, 41
  CSS rule syntax and, 60
  inserting HTML code, 33
  inserting image placeholder and, 131
  inserting jQuery Accordion widget, 314–315
  specifying font size, 155
  targeting page elements, 294
  working with behaviors, 306
Padding
  adding, 86–88
  creating hyperlink rollover effect, 171–172
  CSS rule syntax and, 60
Page layout
  adding background image to header, 113–117
  adding forms to, 343–344
  creating, 102–103
  creating design, 102–103
  creating template from existing, 189–190
  creating thumbnails, 101–102
  creating wireframes, 103–104

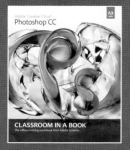

The fastest, easiest, most comprehensive way to learn
Adobe® Creative Cloud™

Classroom in a Book®, the best-selling series of hands-on software training books, helps you learn the features of Adobe software quickly and easily.

The **Classroom in a Book** series offers what no other book or training program does—an official training series from Adobe Systems, developed with the support of Adobe product experts.

To see a complete list of our Adobe Creative Cloud titles go to:
www.adobepress.com/adobecc

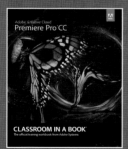

Adobe Photoshop CC Classroom in a Book
ISBN: 9780321928078

Adobe Illustrator CC Classroom in a Book
ISBN: 9780321929495

Adobe InDesign CC Classroom in a Book
ISBN: 9780321926975

Adobe Dreamweaver CC Classroom in a Book
ISBN: 9780321919410

Adobe Flash Professional CC Classroom in a Book
ISBN: 9780321927859

Adobe Premiere Pro CC Classroom in a Book
ISBN: 9780321919380

Adobe After Effects CC Classroom in a Book
ISBN: 9780321929600

Adobe Audition CC Classroom in a Book
ISBN: 9780321929532

Adobe SpeedGrade CC Classroom in a Book
ISBN: 9780321927002

Digital Video with Adobe Creative Cloud Classroom in a Book
ISBN: 9780321934024

Design with the Adobe Creative Cloud Classroom in a Book
ISBN: 9780321940513

AdobePress

WATCH
READ
CREATE

Unlimited online access to all Peachpit, Adobe Press, Apple Training, and New Riders videos and books, as well as content from other leading publishers including: O'Reilly Media, Focal Press, Sams, Que, Total Training, John Wiley & Sons, Course Technology PTR, Class on Demand, VTC, and more.

No time commitment or contract required! Sign up for one month or a year. All for $19.99 a month

SIGN UP TODAY
peachpit.com/creativeedge

creative
edge

Adobe®

Dreamweaver® CC

CLASSROOM IN A BOOK®
The official training workbook from Adobe Systems

Adobe® Dreamweaver® CC Classroom in a Book®

© 2014 Adobe Systems Incorporated and its licensors. All rights reserved.

If this guide is distributed with software that includes an end user license agreement, this guide, as well as the software described in it, is furnished under license and may be used or copied only in accordance with the terms of such license. Except as permitted by any such license, no part of this guide may be reproduced, stored in a retrieval system, or transmitted, in any form or by any means, electronic, mechanical, recording, or otherwise, without the prior written permission of Adobe Systems Incorporated. Please note that the content in this guide is protected under copyright law even if it is not distributed with software that includes an end user license agreement.

The content of this guide is furnished for informational use only, is subject to change without notice, and should not be construed as a commitment by Adobe Systems Incorporated. Adobe Systems Incorporated assumes no responsibility or liability for any errors or inaccuracies that may appear in the informational content contained in this guide.

Please remember that existing artwork or images that you may want to include in your project may be protected under copyright law. The unauthorized incorporation of such material into your new work could be a violation of the rights of the copyright owner. Please be sure to obtain any permission required from the copyright owner.

Any references to company names in sample files are for demonstration purposes only and are not intended to refer to any actual organization.

Adobe, the Adobe logo, Dreamweaver, and Classroom in a Book are either registered trademarks or trademarks of Adobe Systems Incorporated in the United States and/or other countries.

Adobe Systems Incorporated, 345 Park Avenue, San Jose, California 95110-2704, USA

Notice to U.S. Government End Users. The Software and Documentation are "Commercial Items," as that term is defined at 48 C.F.R. §2.101, consisting of "Commercial Computer Software" and "Commercial Computer Software Documentation," as such terms are used in 48 C.F.R. §12.212 or 48 C.F.R. §227.7202, as applicable. Consistent with 48 C.F.R. §12.212 or 48 C.F.R. §§227.7202-1 through 227.7202-4, as applicable, the Commercial Computer Software and Commercial Computer Software Documentation are being licensed to U.S. Government end users (a) only as Commercial Items and (b) with only those rights as are granted to all other end users pursuant to the terms and conditions herein. Unpublished-rights reserved under the copyright laws of the United States. Adobe Systems Incorporated, 345 Park Avenue, San Jose, CA 95110-2704, USA. For U.S. Government End Users, Adobe agrees to comply with all applicable equal opportunity laws including, if appropriate, the provisions of Executive Order 11246, as amended, Section 402 of the Vietnam Era Veterans Readjustment Assistance Act of 1974 (38 USC 4212), and Section 503 of the Rehabilitation Act of 1973, as amended, and the regulations at 41 CFR Parts 60-1 through 60-60, 60-250, and 60-741. The affirmative action clause and regulations contained in the preceding sentence shall be incorporated by reference.

Adobe Press books are published by Peachpit, a division of Pearson Education located in San Francisco, California. For the latest on Adobe Press books, go to www.adobepress.com. To report errors, please send a note to errata@peachpit.com. For information on getting permission for reprints and excerpts, contact permissions@peachpit.com.

Writer: James J. Maivald
Project Editor: Nancy Peterson
Development Editor: Robyn G. Thomas
Copyeditor and Proofreader: Darren Meiss
Production Coordinator and Compositor: Danielle Foster
Technical Reviewers: Candyce Mairs, Clint Funk
Indexer: Jack Lewis
Cover Designer: Eddie Yuen
Interior Designer: Mimi Heft

Printed and bound in the United States of America

ISBN-13: 978-0-321-91941-0
ISBN-10:   0-321-91941-6

9 8 7 6 5 4 3 2 1